OVERVIEW

Introduction 1

Part I: Your Wedding 15

Your Wedding teaches you how to find the best deals on bridal apparel for the bride and the wedding party. Then, you learn how to shop for your ceremony site, wedding flowers, and invitations. Each chapter gives you in depth money-saving tips and shopping strategies.

Part II: Your Reception 221

Your Reception shows you how to save money on everything from catering to entertainment. Our chapter on wedding photography gives you nine creative ways to save money plus eleven important questions to ask any photographer. You'll also learn how to find the best deals on wedding cakes and wedding videos.

Canada 411

Learn about saving money on a Canadian wedding, with tips and advice on web sites, invitation printers and more.

Appendix: Setting a Budget & Phone/Web Directory 422

Advice on how to set up your wedding budget, plus an easy-to-use directory with every phone number and web site address mentioned in this book.

D0107716

CONTENTS

Introduction

Chapter 1

Introduction 1
So, Who Are You Guys? 1
The 4 Truths About Weddings
You Won't Read In Etiquette Books 2
The Goal of this Book 5
Wow! There's No Advertising! 5
How Much Does the Average U.S. Wedding Cost? 5
The Six Fields' Commandments for Bridal Bargains 9
The BRIDAL CLOCK 11
What's New In This Edition? 12

Part I: Your Wedding

Chapter 2

Apparel for the Bride 17
The Olympics of Shopping 17
Hidden Costs Can Add Up 19
Web Sites To Ease Gown Shopping 21
Why Ordering a Gown Takes So Long 24
17 Step-by-Step Shopping Strategies 26
Good vs. Bad Gown Quality 27
Questions to Ask Before You Order the Gown 31
Special Warning: Use Your Credit Card! 32
Destination Wedding Tips: Gowns 35
26 Money-Saving Secrets 36
Real Wedding Tip: eBay Success Stories 38
The Running of the Brides: Filene's Sale 42
Real Wedding Tip: Make you Own Headpiece 48
Games Bridal Shops Play 48
Top Excuses for Why Bridal Shops Rip Tags 51
Designer Trunk Shows: Tips & Traps 54
The Myth of Italian Satin & 4 More Dress Myths 61
"Over-Sizing" and 15 More Pitfalls 64
Bridal 911: What Happens If the Shop Disappears 66
Also Known As: Designer Aliases 76
Chart: Top Bridal Designers Rated & Compared 80

Best Buy: Discount Gown Web Sites 84
Table: Pros & Cons of Buying a Discount Gown 91
Best Buy: China Direct Gowns 91
Best Buy: Bridal Outlets 94
Factory Stores New Twist on Outlets 97
Big Mark-Ups Ahead: Accessories & Extras 100
Not Recommended: David's Bridal 102
Looking for a Large Size 103
Gown Preservation 107

Chapter 3
Apparel for the Wedding Party 111
Bridesmaids' Gowns 111
Our Buying Strategy 112
5 Shopping Strategies 114
Do it Online & 12 More Money-Savers 115
Which Maids Gowns Are Easiest To Alter? 115
Chart: Bridesmaids Options 118
Square Peg, Round Hole and 6 More Pitfalls 122
Real Wedding Tip: Delivery, Sizing Problems 123
Flower Girl Dresses: Our Savings Tips 124
Chart: Top Maids Designers Rated & Compared 130
Tuxedos: The Three Options 132
Grooms in Cyberspace 134
Tux Shopping Tips & Recommendations 135
5 Money-Saving Secrets 136

Chapter 4
Ceremony Sites 139
Religious vs. Civil Ceremonies 140
8 Sources for Ceremony Sites & Officiants 141
Important Questions to Ask the Site Coordinator 143
Real Wedding Tip: Church Fees Can Add Up 143
Most/Least Popular Wedding Months by State 144
Why Civic Sites are Best Bargains 147
Destination Wedding Tips: License 411 & More 148

Chapter 5
Wedding Flowers 149
Average Floral Costs 150
Florists Come in Three Flavors 150
Four Floral Web Sites for Advice, Bargains 151
Florist Shopping: 9 Steps & 11 Questions to Ask 153
26 Money-Savers 156

Table Centerpieces On the Cheap 158
Seven Floral Best Buys 163
Label Flowers and 8 More Helpful Tips 165
The Mercedes Syndrome and 5 More Pitfalls 166
Real Wedding Tip: The Surprise Consulting Fee 167
Trends: Bouquet Bling & More 170
Destination Wedding Tips: Flowers 171
Spotlight on Roses: Types & Colors 171
Best Buy: Buying Flowers at Wholesale on the 'Net 174
Best Buy: Craft Stores 178
Dictionary of Wedding Flowers 180

Chapter 6
Invitations 181
Why Invitations Are Priced a La Carte 181
Where to Buy: Retail vs. Mail-Order 182
8 Cool Invitation Web Sites 185
9 Steps in the Ordering Process 188
5 Questions to Ask A Stationer 190
Real Wedding Tip: How Many Should You Invite? 190
Thermography and 13 More Money-Savers 192
Brazen Bridal Registries & Four More Helpful Hints 197
The "Engraved Invitation" Myth 198
"Pet Postal Peeves" and 7 More Pitfalls 199
11 of the Best Stationary Printers 204
Do It By Mail: 12 Invitation Catalogs 208
Chart: Mail-Order Invites Compared 210
Trends: Belly Bands, Color and More 212
Best Buy: Wedding Invitation Kit 213
Best Buy: Online Invitation Discounters 214
Best Buy: Do-it-yourself Paper Supplies 215
Spotlight: Wedding Favors: 12 Ideas 216

Part II: Your Reception

Chapter 7
Reception Sites 223
The Big Trade-Off 224
Six Surprising Sources 224
Finding Sites on the Web 226
11 Questions to Ask Any Site 228
Best Bargains: Biz Hotels, Civic Sites and More 230
Tent Rental 101 232
The Marriage Mark-Up 234

Destination Wedding Tips & Advice 236
Kickbacks and 6 More Pitfalls to Avoid 237
6 Most Common Site Types: Good, Bad News 241
Real Wedding Tip: Catering Insider Dishes Dirt 242
Hotels: Never Pay the Rack Rate! 243
The Amazing Send-Off: Fireworks 250

Chapter 8
Catering 253
The Big Bucks: Food, Beverages, Labor, Rentals 253
Real Wedding Tip: Open vs. Cash Bars 255
Average Catering Costs 257
The Two Types of Caterers 257
When To Book a Caterer 258
18 Questions to Ask a Caterer 260
The Dessert Reception & 24 More Money-Savers 263
Deals at Wholesale Clubs 268
Real Wedding Tip: Tips on Tipping 270
Plastic Plate Myth 271
How to Feed 100 for $100 271
"Frozen Food" and 5 More Pitfalls 275
Real Wedding Tip: Liquor Slight of Hand 277

Chapter 9
Photography 281
What You're Buying: Candids, Albums, Portraits 281
Digital Albums: The Latest Craze 282
What Are Exposures, Proofs, Prints? 283
Are Wedding Photographers Overpaid? 285
Where NOT to Look For a Good Photographer 286
Digital vs. Medium-Format Cameras 288
Proofless Studios Speed Album Deliveries 290
Why Personality is Just As Important As Skill 293
9 Shopping Strategies 294
16 Questions to Ask Any Wedding Photographer 296
Art Leather Albums: The Inside Story 298
12 Money-Savers on Photography 301
Real Wedding Tip: Mail-Order Albums 304
The Great Before or After Controversy 306
"Bait & Switch" and 8 More Pitfalls 311
Odd Angles & Blurred Shots: Latest Trends 317

Chapter 10
Cakes 319
Average Total Costs 320
8 Wedding Cake Trends 321
The Three Types of Bakeries 322
How Soon To Book the Baker? 324
Taste Tests and More Shopping Strategies 324
Five Questions to Ask 325
Cake Slight-Of-Hand & 11 More Bargains 326
Real Wedding Tip: That's Nuts! 328
The "Mystery White Icing" and 4 More Pitfalls 329
Real Wedding Tip: Small vs. Large Bakeries 331

Chapter 11
Wedding Videos 333
"In-Camera" vs Post-Editing 334
Average Costs 334
How to Find a Good Videographer 335
5 Basics of a Good Wedding Video 337
Videos: Good, Bad, Ugly 340
11 Questions to Ask 342
The Balkans of Bridal 344
Ceremony Only Packages and 12 More Bargains 345
"Director's Disease" and 6 More Video Pitfalls 349
New trends: HDTV, TV Themes, Retrospectives 352

Chapter 12
Entertainment 355
Ceremony Music: Prelude, Processional/Recessional 355
Reception Music: Bands & DJs 356
10 Surprising Sources for Musicians 357
Finding a DJ on the 'Net 359
Step-by-Step Shopping Strategies 360
11 Questions to Ask Musicians 363
iPod Weddings and 9 More Money-Savers 364
Real Wedding Tip: Hiring Student Musicians 366
The "Yucky DJ Myth" 367
Canned vs. Fresh: Hire a Band or DJ? 368
Ashlee Simpson Demo Tapes and 4 More Pitfalls 370
Agents: Helping Hand or Scum of the Earth? 375

Chapter 13
Etcetera 375
Limousines 375

Shopping Strategies, Money-Savers 377
Rent a Caddy and 8 other money-savers 378
Watch out: Sleazy Limo Driver 380
Wedding Rings 381
Best Buy: Get Your Rings at a Discount 383
Royal Prestige Cookware Pitch Exposed 388
Dubious Items: Wedding Insurance, Name Change Kits 390
Bridal Shows: Highway to Bridal Hell? 391
Wedding Consultants 393
Question to Ask a Bridal Planner 394
Pitfalls to Avoid With Planners 395
Gift Registries 398
16 Salt-N-Pepper Shakers and 3 More Pitfalls 401
6 Money-Saving Tips 402
How to turn unwanted gifts into cash 403
Honeymoons 403
15 Honeymoon Bargains 404
Chart: When is the Off Season? 405
Hurricane Proof Your Honeymoon 407
How to Create Your Own Wedding Web Site 410

Chapter 14
Canada 411
Bridal Gowns: Money-Saving Ideas 411
Invitations: Canadian Mail-Order Catalogs 414
A Web Site for Canada Brides 414

Chapter 15
Bridal 911: Last Minute Consumer Tips 417
Meet the Surrogate Bad Cop 417
The Final Checkup 419
Wedding Day Crises: How to Survive Them 419

Chapter 16
Conclusion: What Does it All Mean? 421

Appendix: Setting a Budget 422
Appendix: Phone/Web Directory 429

Index .....
About the Authors ..... Inside Back Cover

Icons

What are You Buying?

Sources

Brides in Cyberspace: What's on the Web?

Getting Started: How Far in Advance?

Step-by-Step Shopping Strategies

Questions to Ask

Top Money-Saving Secrets

Myths

Hints

Pitfalls to Avoid

Destination Wedding Tips

Chapter 1

Intro

Aaaaaaigh!!! So, you're engaged? Well, fasten your seat belts! Soon you will travel through a bizarre and crazy world, where the boundaries of good taste and sane thought are only fuzzy lines. Yes, you've done it now. You have entered the WEDDING ZONE.

See, that's why we are here. We're sort of your tour guides through this wondrous journey of things bridal and ideas nuptial. Of course, right off the bat, you will probably notice a basic difference between this and all those other wedding books and web sites—this book contains actual COMMON SENSE.

Sure, we know we're going out on a limb here but what the heck? Why not write a book you can actually use to plan your wedding? Hey, it's the least we can do. At this point you may have a question: so, who are you guys? Let's put that into bold type.

So Who Are You Guys?

When we got engaged, the first thing we did was trot down to our local bookstore. There has got to be a resource that will help us survive this process, we thought. What we wanted was a consumer guide that would show us how to plan a wonderful wedding without spending an amount equivalent to the Federal Deficit. From recently married friends, we heard all the horror stories—that wasn't going to happen to *us*. We would find out how to shop, what questions to ask and how to avoid scams. A small request, we thought.

Ha! All we found were etiquette books last revised when Eisenhower was President. Plenty of bridal books wanted to tell us what was "proper," what was "socially acceptable" and what was "never to be done except under threat of death." Gee, that's nice, we said, but what we need is help with the money thing, not useless etiquette.

Google weddings (better yet, don't) and you'll find 298 million sites, all trying to pitch you on this bridal trinket or that wedding swag. Yes, there are wedding "portals"—but most are there to pitch you on gowns and registries . . . there is precious little consumer advice or money-saving tips.

So we felt overwhelmed. Now what? Then the idea hit us: hey, why can't we write this book? There must be a few other engaged couples that need practical advice too.

To make a long story somewhat shorter, we were right. To research this book, we have "mystery shopped" over 1000 wedding businesses, from bridal shops to caterers; photographers to bakeries. From these anonymous visits, we learned a lot about planning a wedding. We realized there are tricks to spotting a truly talented wedding photographer or finding a bakery that creates the best wedding cakes. At the same time, we learned the tricks that some merchants use to separate brides and grooms from their money—we'll let you in on the secrets of the wedding biz as we go along!

We first took those experiences and wrote six regional guides to planning a wedding for cities in the Southwest. But we didn't stop there. For this book, we spent over a dozen years interviewing bridal professionals and wedding "experts" across the country. We then spoke to hundreds of engaged couples, carefully documenting problems and challenges they had encountered planning their weddings. When you read this book, you not only get our opinions but the wise advice of many recently married couples who have gone before you.

Full disclosure: we are NOT wedding consultants or planners. Nope, we're just normal folks (well, as normal as two people can be and still live in Boulder, CO). We see our role as consumer activists, working to educate brides on how to be smart shoppers. Believe it or not, this is a full-time job—we write and research about the wedding biz for a living (yes, we also have books on parenting . . . but you might not be ready for *Baby Bargains* yet!).

Many of our best tips and advice come from brides and grooms like you. Feel free to contact us to ask a question or share a story—see the Contact Us page at the back of this book. And join the discussion on our message boards at BridalBargainsBook.com, the web's only commercial-free bridal site.

The Four Truths About Weddings You Won't Read In Etiquette Books

1 So you think your wedding is for you and your fiancé? Ha! Forget it. Unfortunately, weddings often become less a celebration of marriage and more like a huge social torture test for the participants. Parents, and even some brides and grooms, are frequently guilty of turning weddings into spectacles to impress their friends or business associates. Money can become the sticking point since whoever pays for the wedding may feel a divine right to influence the proceedings with their own tastes.

Sometimes, parents or relatives try to make your wedding into the wedding *they* never had (yet always dreamed of). Your friends may be guilty of pressuring you to make your wedding fit some predetermined mold. Put another way, while you may be the stars of the show, you and your fiancé may not be the wedding's directors, producers or choreographers.

Recognize this fact early and learn to negotiate without giving ultimatums. Yes, it is YOUR day, but remembering that others (parents, friends, relatives) are on the stage with you may prevent excessive bloodshed.

2 Weddings always end up twice as large as originally planned. If only we had a dime for every couple we met who said "all we wanted was a small, intimate wedding and what we got was a huge affair for hundreds of guests." A wedding often takes on a life of its own, expanding into a hideous creature several times larger than you ever imagined.

This process usually begins with what we call Guest List Inflation. Here the guest list grows because each family simply *must* invite personal friends, close business associates and people whom they haven't seen in fifteen years. The main problem: adding to the guest list has a direct, *negative* impact on your budget.

Several weddings have nearly unraveled when families have insisted on inflating the guest list without offering to help pay for the additional cost. We suggest you and your families be allowed to invite a certain number of guests each. You may find that someone doesn't want to or can't stick to the limits. The offending party must then finance any invites beyond those targets. Negotiations are often necessary to avoid open warfare on this point. Good luck.

3 Perfect weddings don't exist in the free world. No matter what anyone tells you, understand that the "perfect wedding" is an impossibility on planet Earth. That's because weddings always involve human beings who, on the whole, tend to be less than perfect creatures.

Now, we know everyone tells you that you must have the perfect gown, perfect flowers, perfect cake unless you want to catch the Bridal Plague and die an agonizingly painful death. Don't listen to these demons. Instead, we suggest you aim for a "fantastic" or "wonderful" wedding. Or even just a fun wedding!

Since it's impossible to perfectly script something as complex as a wedding, we say why try? Attendants will miss cues, things will go wrong—if you need any proof of this just watch any of those "outrageous and shocking home video" shows. Ever wonder why so many of those clips are of weddings? Hmmmmm.

Aiming for a wonderful wedding will also give you another benefit—you will probably be able to maintain your sanity.

4 The "wedding industry" isn't as innocent as it looks. You might think the wedding industry is a collection of sweet old ladies whose only desire is to help young couples in love, but the reality is quite the opposite. Instead, think of the bridal biz as a hotly competitive industry (think used cars), populated by merchants who are expert at pushing your emotional buttons. Add to that a field of novice buyers—first-time brides and grooms—and you can see where things go wrong.

Newspaper columnist Dave Barry once wrote that the motto of the wedding industry is, "Money can't buy you happiness, so you might as well give your money to us." Quite true. Weddings are big bucks.

According to the latest research, over $23 billion dollars will be spent this year by couples tying the knot. That's billion with a "b." And that's just the wedding and reception—add in another $19 billion spent on gifts and $8 billion on honeymoons and you've got a $50 billion bridal juggernaut. We like to call it the Wedding Industrial Complex. Scary fact: the wedding industry dwarfs many other businesses, including the breakfast food biz (a paltry $9.4 billion). Yes, Americans spend more on weddings than on Fruit Loops.

And you can bet your bridal veil that the industry knows EXACTLY how lucrative all these "I Do's" can be. To illustrate this, check out what the publisher of *Bride's* magazine told a trade journal about the wedding industry: "Never before in a woman's life, and never again, is she going to be worth this much money to a marketer. There is no price resistance and she is completely open to new brands," Bride's publisher cackled, adding that the internal tag line for *Bride's* is "Where Love Meets Money."

Of course, we're not against folks trying to make a buck. Hey, sell a quality product or service at a fair price and make a profit—that's America. Yet what makes wedding planning so crazy are bridal merchants who view brides and grooms as human ATMs. And price their products and services like they are coming out of a hotel mini bar.

Other wedding vendors seem at war with their customers, as odd as that seems. Take bridal dress retailers—please! As you'll read in the next chapter, these stores are incredibly inventive at separating brides from their money, generating a huge volume of complaints from consumers.

Why do some bridal merchants and vendors think engaged couples are an easy mark? That's because weddings are a one-shot deal. There are no repeat customers (except if you are, say Elizabeth Taylor or Larry King). Unlike other industries that rely on repeat business, wedding merchants know you won't be stopping by next month to buy another bridal gown, cake or ice sculpture. And with a fresh crop of new brides and grooms each year, some sleazy merchants can continue their rip-offs and scams with little fear of getting busted.

So, the mission for this book is to teach you how to separate the good guys from the scamsters out there in wedding land. Yes, there are ethical and honest bridal professionals out there that charge a fair price. Just be aware the wedding business is just that—a business, where folks are trying to make a buck while you tie the knot.

The Goal of This Book: To help you save big money and still have a fantastic wedding!

Here's the take home message of our book: you CAN plan a fantastic wedding at the budget you can afford. And we're going to show you how.

Okay, we realize planning a wedding is a minefield of emotions and consumer pitfalls. And it is easy to get caught up in the bridal whirlwind. That's why we try to keep our perspective about this wedding stuff, and we urge you to do the same. Not maintaining your sense of humor during wedding planning may be hazardous to your health. That's why we've liberally sprinkled what could loosely be described as "humor" throughout this book.

In each chapter we give you Pitfalls to Avoid. As you learn about these bridal scams and wedding frauds, realize that just because you are a bride does not mean you have to be a victim. By using our consumer tips, you can protect yourself from losing hundreds, if not thousands, of dollars and have a good time doing it!

This book is for brides and grooms who want to hire professionals for their wedding. This book does *not* teach you how to sew a bridal gown or give you a recipe for a wedding cake. Instead, we'll show you how to bypass pricey dress shops and order that designer gown online at a big discount. We'll also show you the secrets to finding an affordable baker, photographer and DJ.

There's no advertising in this book?

There are no paid advertisements in this book. Furthermore, no company paid any consideration or was charged any fee to be mentioned in it. The publisher, Windsor Peak Press, derives its sole income from the sale of this book and other consumer guides. As consumer advocates, the authors believe this policy ensures objectivity. The opinions expressed in this book are those of the authors.

So, how much does a wedding cost anyway?

Unless you are a Certified Public Accountant, you may not be inclined to use the words "fun" and "exhilarating" to describe setting the budget for your wedding. As you might expect us to say, however, this is a critical (albeit painful) part of the planning process.

Whether you're spending $100 or $100,000 on your wedding, every bride and groom has a limited amount of money to spend. This means you'll have to make tough choices regarding how you want to allocate your limited resources. For more advice on setting a budget, check out Appendix A at the back of this book.

So, how much does a wedding cost? Following are the average costs for a formal wedding for 175 guests. The table on this page lists the actual costs, while a pie chart on the next page shows you the biggest expense areas. There will be a quiz on this next week.

Average Wedding Costs

Item	$ Amount	% of Total
Apparel		
Bridal gown	$1,025	
Headpiece, veil	167	
Alterations, accessories	340	
Groom's tux rental	145	
Apparel Sub-Total	**1,677**	**7%**
Rings		
Engagement ring	4,086	
Wedding rings	1,980	
Rings Sub-Total	**6,066**	**24%**
Music		
Ceremony music	230	
DJ at reception	600	
Music Sub-total	**830**	**3%**
Miscellaneous		
Marriage License	57	
Gifts (attendants, fiance, parents)	1,182	
Other Stuff	700	
Misc. Sub-Total	**1,939**	**8%**
Ceremony site and officiant	338	1%
Flowers	1,103	4%
Cake	525	1%
Reception/Catering	9,286	37%
Photography	2,000	8%
Videography	1,000	4%
Invitations	426	2%
Limo	259	1%
Total	**$25,449**	**100%**

(Based on industry estimates for 175 guests)
Note: percentages do not add up to 100% due to rounding.

Breakdown of Average Wedding Costs

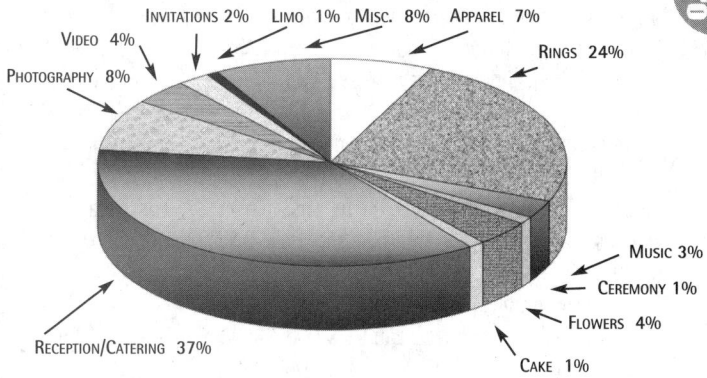

At this point you might want to catch the next flight to Vegas, but we say "Whoa!" Weddings do NOT have to be that expensive. Let's put that into bold caps: YOU DO NOT HAVE TO GO BANKRUPT TO HAVE A BEAUTIFUL WEDDING. Of course, that's the whole point of this book and we'll spend the next 400 pages or so showing you how to cut the cost without compromising on the quality of your wedding.

Of course, where you get married will dramatically impact your wedding costs. Heck, even the cost of a marriage license can vary widely, from a piddling four bucks in Massachusetts to over $80 in California and Florida.

If you are a bride-to-be in the largest metro areas like New York City or Los Angeles, you may be looking at the above numbers and laughing (or crying). That's because many bridal items there cost at least two to three times the average. Keep this in mind throughout the book when we quote "average prices." Here are average wedding costs per region:

Average cost of a wedding

Northeast:	$32.221
NY Metro:	$38,361
South/SE:	$22,662
Midwest:	$23,181
West:	$27,776

(Source: Fairchild Bridal Infobank)

Astute readers will notice those averages are generally greater than the chart on the previous page; that's because the bridal magazines (who came up with those figures) throw in *optional expenses* like wedding favors and other expenses to arrive at their "average" figures.

Wedding favors (a little tchotchke given to each guest) are a regional tradition, common in some areas but not seen in others. Couples spend $284 on average on favors. Another expense we didn't put here: the honeymoon, which runs $3700 on average.

What about bridesmaids' dresses and groomsmen formalwear rentals? Those costs aren't in the above table because each attendant typically pays them out of their own pocket. Of course, if you intend to help out a bridesmaid by paying for her gown, start adding to your budget accordingly. In a similar vein, the rehearsal dinner ($750 on average), ceremony programs ($75), and hair and make-up for the bridal party ($370) are optional items that some couples put in their budgets.

Of course, averages are just that—averages. Walk into any bridal dress shop and you'll notice gowns can be $2000, $3000 or more. The same goes for many other wedding items . . . you can quickly spend many times the average in a flash. For example, that $1000 tab for a wedding video assumes single-camera coverage—that figure can easily double with multi-camera coverage and a more elaborate production.

In each chapter, we'll discuss what "average" means for everything from flowers to invitations.

Are weddings more expensive than they were ten years ago? 25 years ago? Yes, but inflation plays a role in comparing prices. For example, when this book was first published (way back in 1990), the average wedding was $12,675. So, that current average of $25,273 looks rather amazing—wedding costs are up 99%!

But inflation during the past 16 years has been about 55% (total). That is, something that cost $100 back in 1990 runs about $155 today. So if you factor out normal inflation, real wedding costs are "only" up 29% in the past 15 years. Comforting, eh?

And there is some good news: some wedding costs have actually DECLINED. No, that isn't a typo. Take the wedding dress: in 1990, it cost $800 to buy the average wedding dress. Given inflation, we'd expect that dress to run $1250 today. BUT—here's the good news—the average bridal gown today is "only" $1025. So the REAL COST of a bridal gown has actually declined in recent years (thanks to cheaper imported gowns, chain stores and other factors).

Who pays for the wedding?

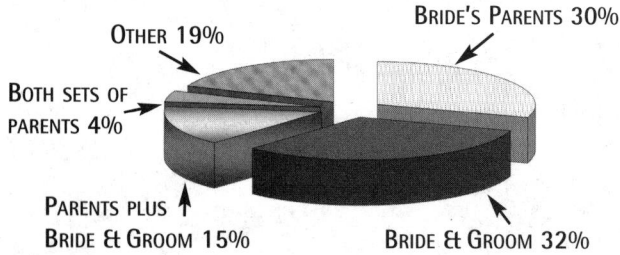

Source: Fairchild Bridal Infobank

Balancing that good news is the reality that some wedding costs have soared—take wedding rings, for example. The average amount spent on wedding rings has DOUBLED in just five years. Why? Are folks buying rings that are twice as big as before? No—but the average wedding ring today is platinum . . . which is much pricier than a good ol' fashioned gold wedding ring, popular prior to 2000.

Another way to look at wedding costs is to consider how big a bite a wedding takes out of the average family income. Before World War I, the average wedding cost was one-fourth of the median income for a family. By the 60's, the number rose to one-third. And today? The average wedding this year is closing in on 40%.

The desire to customize or personalize weddings in recent years has led some couples to spend even more on nuptials, driving the designer-end of the bridal biz. Examples: the number of brides who purchased a gown that cost over $1500 is up 50% from ten years ago. Sales of one-carat or greater diamond engagement rings are up 81% from five years ago. Like everything else, weddings have become super-sized.

Okay, just because many brides and grooms are blowing money faster than a drunken sailor, that doesn't mean YOU have to. You found this book, right? So, how can you save? Let's look at our five commandments for Bridal Bargains:

The Fields' Six Commandments for Bridal Bargains

We went up the mountain and came down with these six commandants for brides on a budget. Please repeat after us:

1 **The Budget is King.** Set a budget and stick to it like a duck on a June bug. Yes, that means making hard choices . . . like whether you really need an flower corsage for the wedding cake knife—but, hey, we'll try to point out where to put your money. And where not to waste it.

2 **Daylight Savings Time.** Timing is everything—and the same goes for weddings. Everyone wants to be married in the peak wedding months of June and August. Do your budget a favor and get hitched in an off-month like October, November, January, February or March. Remember it is also cheaper to get married in the "daylight"—brunch or afternoon weddings are always less than evening bashes.

3 **Plan Ahead.** Do the math—each year 2.3 million couples will tie the knot . . . but there are only 52 Saturdays each year. The best bargain sites and merchants always book up early. Give yourself plenty of time to comparison shop, get competitive bids and ferret out sales.

4 Undress the Dress. If you pay full retail for a bridal gown, please give us your home address so we can come over and whack you on the head with this book. Seriously, we found TWO DOZEN ways to slash that dress bill, from bargains on eBay, special designer sales and outlets to online discounters that can cut your dress bill by 30% to 50% or more.

5 Cut the Cake—and other frills. Brides and grooms pile on the sweets at receptions, but can guests really wolf down a wedding cake, groom's cake AND a dessert table? And do you really need a six-tier confection that looks like a chandelier when a simple cake will do? The same goes for other ridiculous bridal items: wedding favors (guests don't need another dust collector), engraved invitations (other options look just as good at half the cost), or exotic flowers at the ceremony (guests spend much more time looking at your flowers at the *reception*).

6 Be prepared to walk away. Don't let wedding merchants pressure you into buying a package you can't afford. Many salespeople in the bridal biz are experts in pushing your emotional buttons (*isn't that $4000 dress soooo beautiful? Doesn't Daddy want the very best for his little girl?)*. Recognize these ploys and don't be bullied! Another key tip: ASK FOR THE MANAGER when negotiating with any merchant. Go right to the top to get the very best deal.

Getting Set, Getting Organized

Start the process of wedding planning on the right foot by getting organized. To help, we have published a companion planner to this book, called the *Bridal Bargains Wedding Planner*. This spiral-bound planner contains checklists, to-do lists, budgets and more. We designed our wedding planner to be used together with this book—for example, when we show you how to compare three florists or photographers with a certain set of questions in *Bridal Bargains*, we then provide a worksheet in the *Bridal Bargains Wedding Planner* to do just that. See the back of this book for more details.

While the *Bridal Bargains Wedding Planner* is a great place to keep the details organized, you will quickly start collecting quite a bit of paper when planning a wedding. This will easily overwhelm the pockets in any wedding planner. Where should you keep those contracts, proposals and receipts? We suggest going down to a local office supply store and buying a plain accordion file. This costs a mere $5—use the different sections to separate contracts, swatches, receipts and so on.

Another bride organized her wedding using a three-ring binder. She hole punched all the contracts and bought pocket inserts for her receipts, photos and fabric swatches. Total cost: $10. If you bought a similar product specially designed for brides with lacy inserts and full color photos, you'd spend as much as $50.

Regardless of the method you use to organize your wedding, keeping all your receipts and contracts in one place is vitally important. Also, make copies of any written correspondence (emails, faxes, letters) you have with the businesses you hire. Keeping a journal for telephone conversations with vendors is also smart.

Although chances are your wedding planning will be a smooth process, if any problems do crop up, you'll be glad you spent the time and money to be so well organized.

The Bridal Clock

"I'm late! I'm late for a very important date!" said the rabbit in *Alice in Wonderland.*

At times, as you plan your wedding, you might feel a bit harried yourself.

Of course, the first real crisis of any engagement is the realization that you must accomplish 1.6 million things in about 13 seconds in order to get to the church on time. The second crisis is wondering which of those 1.6 million things you should do first.

To solve this problem, we have invented our BRIDAL CLOCK, below. Think of the numbers of the clock as the sequence of events in the wedding planning process. Your wedding is at "midnight."

Start with reserving your ceremony site (two o'clock). Next, find and book a reception site and caterer. From there, shop for your wedding gown . . . and so on.

In each chapter in this book, you'll find specific advice on how much time you need to order everything from invitations to a wedding cake. Of course, the BRIDAL CLOCK gives you a general sense of how far

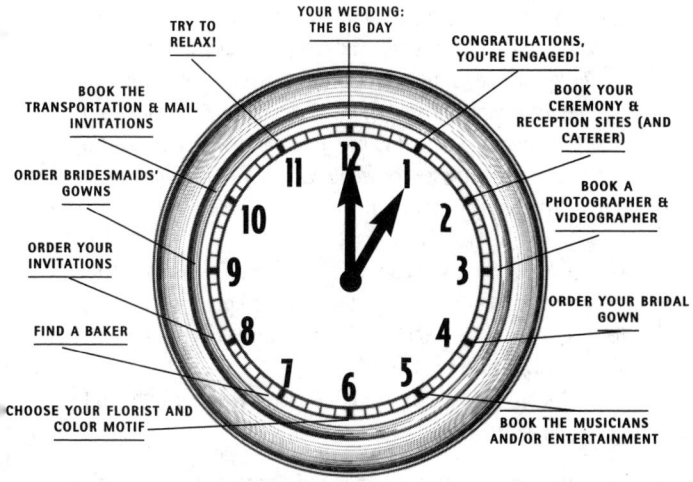

you've gone—and how much further you need to go until the bewitching hour.

As a side note, you'll notice we did not organize this book in the same order as the Bridal Clock. For simplicity's sake, we divided the book into two sections—the wedding and the reception.

To be fair, we should also note that many of the bargain tips and advice in this book may require advance planning—it can take up to six months to order a gown through an online discounter, for example. What if you've just got a few months (or weeks) before your wedding, can you still save money? Of course. Each chapter of this book contains cost-cutting alternatives anyone can use, no matter how much time you have before you walk down the aisle.

What's new in this edition

So, what's changed with the eighth edition of *Bridal Bargains*? As always, we try to make the book better with enhanced reviews and more bargain tips.

As we mentioned on the previous page, our new wedding planner (the *Bridal Bargains Wedding Planner*) has content that is integrated with this book. As you read through *Bridal Bargains*, we'll have a special icon to call out corresponding worksheets and to-do lists in the *Bridal*

Real Wedding Tip

Objects are closer than they appear

What? You want to get married in just three months? If you read most bridal publications or web sites, you'd think it was violating the laws of physics to tie the knot without years of planning. Not true, says one bride who recently emailed us:

"Everyone told us that four months was an impossible length of time for planning a wedding. . . it is not only possible, it's a reality. It's amazing (and disgusting) to me that a store will tell you that shoes or dresses or whatever will take four months to order. Upon learning that your wedding is sooner than that, they make a call and lo and behold that item is in stock and today is your lucky day because it can be here in ONE WEEK! From sixteen weeks to one week in five minutes . . . amazing! I know it's true, because it has happened to us more than once, in more than one store and with different items."

The lesson: don't give up. You CAN plan a wedding with short notice, no matter the lead-time.

Bargains Wedding Planner.

In other news, destination weddings are hot . . . and we've got advice and tips if you're planning a get-away wedding! Look for this special icon (right) in most chapters for destination wedding hints.

As always, we have updated the book with even more bargains—new web sites that discount dresses, sources for affordable invites and even a web resource that lets you create affordable digital photo albums. Read about the latest sources for wholesale flowers, do-it-yourself invites and discount bridesmaids dresses.

All in all, you'll see more bargain tips in each chapter, from cakes to catering. We've added pages of deals and steals on every topic in the book. And for you Canadian brides, you have your own section of *Bridal Bargains*, complete with special ideas on saving money on a wedding in Canada.

Finally, we've added a new section to our web site called *Bridal Bargains Local Talk*, a series of message boards that let you connect with other local readers. Go to BridalBargainsBook.com and click on message boards—from there select local. Now you'll be able to swap tips, advice and stories with other brides in your area. Which bridal shops should you avoid? What photographer in your town has the best prices? And which bakery makes the best cake? As always, our message boards are ad-free and spam-free. No pop-up ads, banner ads, etc. Use this new, free resource to find the best vendors for your wedding from the most credible source out there—other readers of *Bridal Bargains*!

Part 1

Your Wedding

Chapter 2

Bridal Apparel

Wonder how you can save up to 70% off those fancy designer bridal gowns? We'll show you how, with our exclusive list of 26 money-saving tips. Before we go there, however, you'll learn the 17 steps to buying the right dress. Next, we'll expose how some dishonest bridal shops rip-off brides, while we teach you how to outfox them. Last but not least, we'll take a candid look at the country's biggest bridal designers, rating them on price and quality.

The Bridal Gown. Nothing symbolizes a wedding more than the bridal gown. Prospective brides are from birth to fantasize about this ultimate dress, sparkling with beads, sequins and taught pearls delicately sewn onto French lace. Of course, the designers who make those gowns are well aware of this—their ads and web sites are laced with references to "fairy-tale" weddings and "storybook" brides.

Okay, I admit to falling into this fantasy stuff headfirst when I was a bride. But, hey, how often do you get to wear a piece of clothing that costs $1000 or more? Finding the right bridal gown (at a price that doesn't resemble the federal deficit) is the overriding priority for many brides. And why not?

As it turns out, however, bridal gown shopping often morphs into the ultimate battle between women and the evil apparel industry. This is the Olympics of shopping.

Thanks to a host of tricks, scams and outright rip-offs in the bridal apparel business, buying a bridal gown is perhaps the most perilous and tricky task in this journey we call wedding planning. You didn't expect this to be easy, did you?

In this chapter, we explore the reasons why buying a bridal gown generates the biggest number of complaints from engaged couples. We'll teach you how to find the gown that's just right for you and how not to get ripped off doing it.

Where do brides buy bridal gowns? According to our research and consumer surveys, 40% of all brides purchase a gown at a bridal shop, a specialty store that focuses on bridal and formal apparel. Another 30% of brides buy their gowns from David's, the country's biggest bridal chain (more on them later in this chapter). 12% purchase a dress from a department store, while 10% have a gown sewn by a professional or friend. Other brides wear a gown that was a family heirloom (2%), borrow or rent a dress (2%), or buy through a discount online service or mail order (3%).

Since the majority of brides purchase a gown from a bridal retailer or chain store, this chapter will focus on how to get the best deal. Of course, there are several little-known but quite fascinating alternatives to this route. We'll discuss them later in the chapter.

What Are You Buying?

At the simplest level, you are buying a dress. But not just any dress. This is a darn expensive dress. The average bridal gown costs $1025 in most stores, no matter where you live. Many of the premium designer gowns sell for much more, topping $2000 and even $3000.

So what do you think you should get for $1025? Well, before you answer this question, we ask you to shift your mind into BRIDAL MODE. That's because if you think in the REAL WORLD MODE you're going to be in for a shock. For example, if we gave you $1025 and told you to buy a nice party or cocktail dress you'd expect a few things for that amount of money. Fine fabrics like silk? Sure. Quality construction with a lining and finished seams? Why not. How about sewn sequins and detailing? Hey, you'd expect that for $800! Right?

Well, BRIDAL MODE isn't like that. For $1025, you'll see plenty of dresses with synthetic fabric, shoddy construction with unfinished seams and no lining. Want a sophisticated gown made of silk with a splash of delicate embroidery? Sadly, dresses like that are often way over $2000. Or $3000.

Frankly, we can't figure out why this is. Perhaps the entire bridal apparel industry (from the powerful designers to the lowly local bridal shops) thinks that when women get engaged they collectively lose all common sense. Like zombies, brides are supposed to walk into bridal shops and plunk down a cool $1000 for a gown they wouldn't even consider buying for $100 if they saw it at a department store in any color other than white.

As a side note, don't forget that the bridal gown is just the beginning. There are many "hidden costs" when buying a bridal gown–you'll also need undergarments, a slip, shoes and the ubiquitous headpiece and veil. If you think bridal gowns are overpriced, wait until you see what accessories sell for. The "average" headpiece and veil runs $167 (although many top $250), while you can add another $400 for other accessories (see below). Hence, the total ensemble may cost you $1700. Below is a breakdown of extra costs.

And those figures are just averages. Alterations can be much more expensive than $150 (roughly the national average). In major cities, brides report to us that some bridal shops are now charging exorbitant "flat fees" for alterations–$200, $300 or more. While that figure covers any changes to the gown, brides who merely need a minor nip and tuck get socked for the full fare. On the other hand, some shops throw in *free* alterations and a pressing if you spend a certain amount of money in the store. (More on alterations later in this chapter).

What part of the country has the most expensive bridal alterations?

Hidden Gown Costs

(Sample figures for a typical gown—and those necessary extras)

Gown	$1,025
Rush Charge	50
Alterations	150
Pressing	50
Delivery to ceremony	50
Crinoline/Slip	45
Bra	40
Headpiece/Veil	167
Shoes	60
Jewelry	50
Gloves/Stockings	30
Total	**$1,717**

(Note: in the introduction for this book, we say the average cost of the bride's ensemble is $1532. That's because we don't count two of the above items–the rush charge and delivery to the ceremony, since those are charges most brides don't incur. We also didn't count jewelry, assuming you'll receive this as a gift–hint, hint).

Our reader email indicates it must be the Washington DC area. Brides report to us that several shops there now charge $300 to $400 in alteration fees, no matter how little needs to be done to their bridal gowns.

Even if you pay the "average" amounts for a gown and the extras, it's amazing how an $1000 gown can turn into a $1700 total tab in a hurry. Of course, you don't have to pay that much. Order early (at least six months before the wedding) and you won't pay the rush charge. You can save big bucks by borrowing a crinoline/slip, forget the special delivery to the church (carry it yourself), and buy shoes, jewelry, and other accessories at discount stores. More on money-saving strategies later in this chapter.

We should also note that most shops require a 50% deposit on all special orders. (We'll explain later why most gowns are special-ordered instead of bought off-the-rack.) That can be a sizable financial hit several months before the wedding. The balance is due when the dress comes in. The exception to the half-down rule: some discounters (both online and mail order) require payment in full when you order. This certainly requires more of a leap of faith on the consumer's part, but the discount (20% to 30% off retail or more) may make this deal attractive.

Sources to Find a Reputable Bridal Shop

Finding a bridal shop is easy. Finding a good bridal shop is somewhat more challenging. Beyond the basic sources, there are four important ways to locate local shops:

♥ **Friends.** Network, network, network—ask friends, co-workers and others for recommendations. Any shops they recommend? Any shops you should avoid like the plague? Listen carefully to word on the street—if a shop is roundly criticized on message boards, that's your clue to avoid them!

♥ **The 'Net.** Surf the web to find local bridal shops, some of which have established sites that tout their stores. Find them by accessing gown designers' web sites that have store locators or check out the "generic" wedding web sites for links. More on this later. Another idea: surf our message boards at BridalBargainsBook.com (click on message boards). We have a special "local talk" section of the boards where you can query other brides in your area about the best bridal shops. Which stores offer the best service? Which should you avoid? It's all on the boards, which are divided by cities/states.

Another resource: the large wedding web sites the Knot.com and WeddingChannel.com have message boards—each has dress forums and other fashion-related boards.

♥ **Bridal Magazines.** The major bridal magazines are literally plastered with ads from gown makers. On the page next to the dress, you can often find a list of shops that carry the designer (or pop to the designer's web site for a retailer locator). Just look for your city and bingo! There will be at least one candidate for your search. (A few caveats: some ads don't list any local shops. Others have incomplete listings—some local stores may carry the dress, but are not listed in the ad). Before you put much stock in magazines, however, read our article on them later in the chapter.

♥ **The Better Business Bureau.** Check to see if any shops you have heard about have a record of complaints. Any complaint (even if the company resolved it) is a big, red flag. The BBB's web site is BBB.org.

Brides in Cyberspace: What's on the Web?

The sheer volume of gown info on the web is mind-boggling. Here are two of the best places to go, plus some other general ideas on using the web in your gown search.

The Wedding Channel's Gown Search

Web site: www.weddingchannel.com, click on the "fashion & beauty"

FIGURE 1: The Wedding Channel's cool "Sketchbook Search" lets you zero on a gown in your price range. You can search by designer, price or any "gown attribute."

tab, then ""gowns and accessories."
What is it: Gown picture database.
What's cool: The nifty "Gown Search" (see Figure 1 on previous page) lets you zero in on a dress with particular attributes–silhouettes (A-line, ball gown), necklines, price range and so on.
Needs work: A dress that is $1499 is "inexpensive"? Yep, according to the Wedding Channel. Most of the gowns featured on this site are quite pricey (the bulk are over $1500 with some over $5000). FYI: As we went to press, the WeddingChannel.com was being acquired by the Knot.com. It's unclear whether the Knot will keep the WeddingChannel site as a separate brand (most likely) or merge it with the mother ship.

The Knot's Bridal Search

Web site: www.theknot.com
What is it: The Mother of all bridal gown sites.
What's cool: 20,000 gown pictures, in a nut shell. The Knot has an "advanced search" button the lets you sort gowns by silhouette, waist, neckline, sleeves, gown length, train length and "special requests." You can then filter by price range and designer.
Needs work: To view any gowns, you must first register–the Knot asks you to give up your name, email, street address, wedding date and more. (Hint: use a free email account like Hotmail instead of your personal email to protect your privacy . . . and sanity). Another frustration: many of the styles shown online are discontinued (the Knot apparently is a bit lackadaisical about keeping the database up to date). Another major caveat: the Knot doesn't tell you whether you are looking at a major gown designer or a very small dressmaker. Apparently, the Knot will let any gown maker with a sewing machine in the back of their garage advertise their gowns on the site. As a result, it is easy to fall in love with a gown that is sold in just three shops nationwide (or worse, only at the designer's "studio" which turns out to be a double-wide trailer in North Dakota). Finally, be aware of bogus style numbers. Some designers list their gowns on the Knot with fake style numbers in order to frustrate brides who are trying to price shop a dress. We say shame on the Knot for knowingly posting false information about dresses on their site.

Be sure to read the next section on Bridal Web Sites: Friend of Foe for more commentary on the Knot.

Bridal Web Sites: Friend or Foe?

As a newly engaged person, one of the first things you probably did was to start surfing wedding web sites. But what kind of advice are these sites giving? And whose side are they on anyway? The short answers: often bad and not yours.

Let's take a look at TheKnot.com, the 800-pound gorilla of wedding sites. The Knot now includes the WeddingChannel.com, television shows, a site for the newly married and more.

So, if you turn to TheKnot.com for gown shopping advice, here's what you'd read in an article on saving money on wedding dresses:

> **Buyer Beware:** *There are plenty of wedding-related purchases you'll want to make online, but your wedding gown isn't one of them. Trust us, we've heard all the horror stories. Online retailers go out of business regularly and leave brides high and dry. Even the biggest ones disappear (like DBS which went of business in July 2005) leaving brides without gowns close to their wedding date, scrambling for something to wear down the aisle. Additionally, gowns from online retailers are often designer knockoffs (not the real things they claim to be) and once you've bought one, you're stuck with no recourse for exchange or return.*

Wowee, sounds scary? Besides the jaw-dropping irony of a dot-com advising you not to buy something online, let's look at the Knot's claims.

Online retailers go out of business regularly? Not true. Of the 20 discount dress web sites we've tracked since 1996, only two have gone out of business. Sure bridal businesses come and go—but that applies to both brick and mortar AND online companies. As far as bankruptcy odds go, retail bridal shops are just as likely to tank as an online seller. And yes—Discount Bridal Service went out of business in 2005. But that was after a 20-year run as a mail-order discounter. DBS didn't even sell gowns online, so the Knot obviously isn't even doing its homework.

Gowns from online retailers are often designer knock-offs? Please, this is one of the oldest tricks in the book—scare folks into thinking they aren't going to get what they paid for. The reality: ALL of the discount gown sites we recommend in this chapter sell authentic, designer gowns. You'll note that most clearly list their authorized dealer status online. So this claim has no real basis in fact. Trust us—we get 1000's of emails from brides each month. No one has ever complained than an online gown seller sold them a knock-off gown instead of a designer original.

Once you've bought a dress, you're stuck with no recourse for exchange or return? Shocking! But . . . try returning a bridal gown to a retail store! The fact is nearly ALL bridal sellers (on or offline) have no refund or exchange policies. Oddly enough, it is online retailers that are moving in the opposite direction. Several dot-coms actually have return policies that let you return a gown.

So why would the Knot mislead you? Follow the money. Last year, the Knot raked in $25 million in online ad sales—most of that was from the bridal gown biz (both dress designers and retail bridal shops). And trust us, the Knot's sponsors do NOT want you to go online to buy a dress. From the Knot's perspective, it's simple business calculus: you'd much rather have those online advertising dollars from 3000 local bridal shops than 30 web sites.

So take advice from the Knot with a grain of salt . . . when it comes to tips on saving money, it and other, similar sites are mostly interested in having you spend yours, not save it.

Getting Started: How Far in Advance?

Most brides are surprised when they learn how far in advance they must place an order for their gown. In general, most bridal gowns are not bought off-the-rack. You try on sample dresses and then "special order" the gown in your size. It's the special order nature of bridal apparel that takes so long—the *average* dress takes ten to 14 weeks to arrive (yes, that's three to four months). And ordering is just the beginning. When you add in time for shopping, alterations and other necessities, you quickly realize it's best to order your dress five to nine months before the wedding. Let's take a look at the five stages of buying a bridal gown.

1 Shopping. Hey, don't forget that you need time to look for the gown that is just right for you. Sure, you can do this in as little as one day, but most brides we have interviewed said they took two to three weeks. That's because it takes time to visit a handful of the area's best shops and more time to make a final decision.

2 Ordering. Once you place your order, the shop sends it to the manufacturer. Each dress designer has different delivery schedules—some are as quick as six weeks, while others are six months. That's why it's important you know the designer of the gown in order to make sure the gown will arrive in time for your wedding. Some manufacturers offer "rush service," but the extra fee for this may bust your budget. FYI: David's, the country's largest chain of bridal stores, does sell many gowns off the rack—but if your size isn't in stock or the sample is damaged, David's will special order it from their warehouse. This is much like the process for special-ordering a gown from any other bridal shop.

3 Alterations. After the gown comes in, leave another month for alterations. Some shops may be able to do "rush" jobs but the quality may be rushed too. You may have several time-consuming "fittings," appointments with the seamstress where you inch closer and closer to getting the gown to fit just right.

4 Portrait. In some areas, brides have a formal portrait taken before the wedding, which is displayed at the reception. In order to have enough time to view the proofs and get the final print framed, most photographers suggest doing the portrait four to six weeks before the wedding. That means the dress has to be altered and ready to go at that time.

5 Safety Zone for Mistakes. Yes, mistakes can happen, especially with gowns. Bridal apparel is most prone to problems since there are more people involved in this process than any other. Orders can be botched at several points between the manufacturer and final delivery to you. Leaving time (perhaps two weeks) in your schedule to correct problems is prudent.

Whoa! That's a lot of time! The time guideline we recommend is at least six months. If you want an elaborate designer gown, allow for even more time. However, don't panic if your wedding is around the corner. Look for our TOP MONEY SAVING TIPS later in this chapter—many of these strategies can quickly unite you with a gown.

Does the process of special-ordering a gown sound like too much hassle? There is good news: several "off-the-rack" stores have sprung up in recent years that enable you to walk out the same day with a bridal gown in your size. Online options like eBay also can quickly match you with a gown. More on these later.

Just what is 'couture' anyway?

In the world of fashion, "couture" clothing (in French, literally meaning sewing or seam) typically describes a designer's most expensive line of personally designed garments. Unlike less expensive "ready to wear" and "bridge" lines, couture clothes are only sold in a handful of stores to a very moneyed crowd. So, what does couture mean in bridal? Absolutely nothing. Bridal apparel makers have so misused and abused the word "couture" that they slap it on any expensive dress (say, over $1000). To us, a couture bridal gown would be personally designed by a famous designer and then handcrafted by a seamstress in the US or Canada. In bridal, however, "couture" dresses have no special pedigree and are often made in assembly-line fashion. To add insult to injury, some bridal retailers slap extra alteration fees on "couture" dresses (sometimes $400 for a simple nip and tuck). Are these dresses any more difficult to alter than a $500 gown? Nope, some shop owners just think if you spend $2000 or $3000 on a dress, you can be socked with overpriced alterations.

Step-by-step Shopping Strategies

♥ **Step 1:** After you've set the date, sit down with your fiancé to talk about your wedding. The key decision is how formal you want the event to be. Now, the bridal magazines have all kinds of crazy rules to tell you what to wear for each formality degree but just remember this: your gown should reflect your ceremony and reception. The gown that is perfect for an intimate garden ceremony held in the afternoon probably won't work at an evening ceremony for 200 close friends at a big church with a sit-down dinner reception following.

♥ **Step 2:** Now that you have an idea of how formal your wedding is, look through those magazine ads for bridal designers or surf gown sites on the web. Which gowns intrigue you? Which ones make you sick? Key in on the elements of the dresses—the silhouettes, the necklines, waistlines, train length, amount of lace, etc. A caveat: take these ads with a grain of salt. All of them feature anorexic models with Barbie doll figures. What looks good on you (a real bride in the real world) may be vastly different from what you see in the magazines or online. Keep an open mind.

♥ **Step 3:** Before you head out to local bridal shops, ask your ceremony site coordinator if there are any restrictions on the amount of skin you can show in the sanctuary. Some churches frown on off-the-shoulder, strapless or halter-style gowns—unfortunately, the current bridal fashion now popular on runways. Determining what's appropriate before you fall in love with the "wrong" gown is prudent. If you are determined to wear that bare look, consider ordering extra fabric to make a cover-up (shawl or jacket) to wear for the ceremony. Some gown makers now offer "temple-ready" dresses, which show much less skin. Another note of caution: beware of sheath or mermaid-style gowns if you have to kneel during the ceremony. Most of these gowns don't have slits in the back, making kneeling next to impossible. One option is to have your seamstress add a slit in the back (look inside the gown to make sure a back seam is available).

♥ **Step 4:** Listen to the advice of recently married friends and acquaintances about local bridal shops. Their insights on selection, service and prices may be valuable. Using our other sources mentioned above, draw up a list of three to five stores that offer the gowns you want. Don't forget that a store's service (how you're treated when you come through the door) is almost as important as the selection of dresses.

♥ **Step 5:** In addition to the stores on your list, visit a store or two that sells expensive dresses. Why? This is the best way to educate yourself about quality bridal gowns. Expensive gowns (over $1000 or even $2000) typically feature quality construction, luxurious fabrics and exquisite detailing. Then, when you hit the discounters, warehouse stores and outlets, you can tell what's quality—and what's not. You won't be fooled by gowns marked "sale $490, originally $1000," when the fabric and construction indicate the original price should have been much less. Besides, trying on those fancy gowns is fun. But leave your wallet at home.

♥ **Step 6:** Back to reality. It's time to go shopping for real. Try to visit the stores on your list on any day *other* than a Saturday. Weekends at bridal shops are crazy—everyone tries to shop on Saturday. If you can go during the week (some stores are open in the evening), you'll find better service, less-crowded dressing rooms, etc. Call ahead—some shops require an appointment. (A warning: some shops charge brides "try-on fees" to discourage walk-ins). Don't drop into a fancy bridal shop without an appointment and then get upset at the lack of service. Go with

Quality: Good vs. Bad

Walk into any bridal shop and you'll be greeted by a sea of white. This dress is $500; this other one is $900. How about gowns for $1500? What's the difference? The proof is in the details. The more expensive gowns have better fabric, finished seams and built-in crinolines. The following chart summarizes the difference between good and bad quality when it comes to bridal gowns:

	Good	Poor
Beading	Sewn-on	Glued-on
Seams	No visible threads	Threads show through seams
Inside of dress	Completely lined; finished seams	Unlined; unfinished seams
Fabric	Silk or heavy weight satin	Feels like you can tear it
Sewing	Built-in petticoat or slip	Layers sewn together in same seam
Hem	Herringbone-type hem	A simple straight stitch hem
Comfort	Dress is comfortable to wear	Scratchy lace or itchy detailing

just one other person (a friend, a relative or even your fiancé) whose opinion you value. Remember to wear undergarments similar to what you plan to wear under your bridal gown; and have your hair in a similar style as what you plan for the wedding. Skip the makeup and lipstick, since that can damage sample gowns.

♥ **Step 7:** When you visit the shop, be prepared to answer a few questions. The first is probably the most critical: how much do you want to spend? We recommend fibbing here. Most salespeople will try to "upsell" you slightly, so we recommend you under-estimate your price range by 10%. If you really have budgeted about $1000 for a gown (not including alterations, headpiece/veil and any accessories), tell them you want to spend $800 to $900. Undoubtedly, they'll show you a few dresses closer to $1000.

♥ **Step 8:** Next you'll be asked about your wedding date and how formal your wedding will be. We recommend fudging about your wedding date as well—push it forward about three to four weeks. For example, if your real wedding date is June 15, tell the shop the "big day" is May 15 (or the nearest Saturday to that date). This insures that your gown will arrive (and any potential problems will be fixed) in time. The wedding date will also help determine whether you'll want long or short sleeves, for example. Also, they'll ask you what "style" of gown you prefer: Obviously, you won't know all the answers but try to give the salesperson an idea of your preferences. Some shops now put pictures of the gowns they stock in big binders at the front of the store—you're suppose to look through these pictures to pick styles you like before hitting the racks. (A side note: this shouldn't surprise you, but the gowns' manufacturer/designer names are carefully omitted from these pictures).

♥ **Step 9:** Keep an open mind. Try a few different styles, with a friend taking notes on which gowns you like the best. Be careful of "gown overload:" trying on too many gowns in one day can confuse you, blending into a blur of lace and sequins. Our advice: don't try on more than five gowns at each shop. Besides you'll become exhausted.

♥ **Step 10:** Narrow down your choices to two or three gowns. Make an appointment with the same salesperson you talked with on your first visit. Now, it's decision time! Don't be rushed into a snap decision. Compare prices with discounters (see later in this chapter for sources). If you decide to order from a local retailer, be sure to confirm any extra fees for your gown purchase. (Protective gown bag? Pressing? Shipping?) Get a written estimate for alterations BEFORE you commit to the purchase.

♥ **Step 11:** Congratulations! You've selected your bridal gown! Now, before you put down that hefty 50% non-refundable deposit, ask the bridal shop the questions we list later in this chapter. Get measured (bust, waist, hips and from the base of your throat to the hemline) with a vinyl tape measure and ask to see the manufacturer's sizing chart. Given your measurements (and remember your bust measurement is *not* your bra size), select the gown size that corresponds to the largest of your measurements. Remember you can make a gown smaller but you can't easily expand it. It's important that *you* make the decision of what size to order—don't let the bridal shop make it for you. We'll explain why later in our PITFALLS section.

♥ **Step 12:** If you're unsure whether the shop is an authorized dealer for the gown you want, call the manufacturer (a quick Google search can turn up a phone number). Most manufacturers will tell you if the shop is a legitimate re-seller for their gowns. If the shop won't tell you the manufacturer of the gown, we suggest you go elsewhere. If the manufacturer tells you the shop is not an authorized dealer, the shop may be sewing counterfeit gowns or transshipping the gowns from another source. Ask the owner about this and if you don't get a straight answer, go elsewhere. Don't worry: you may be able to get the dress from another, more honest shop even if the first shop claims they have an "exclusive."

An exception to this rule: many discount mail order and warehouse companies are not "official" authorized outlets, according to public statements by bridal manufacturers. While the discounters often purchase gowns through legitimate channels, the designers don't want to admit that they're selling to them.

♥ **Step 13:** When you place an order, get a receipt with the price, color, size, manufacturer, style number, and most importantly, the promised delivery date. Also, listed on the ticket should be any special-order requests (some dresses can be ordered on a rush basis, with changes to the fabric, lace or detailing, etc.). All these requests cost extra. If the store recommends a size for you, write on the ticket "Store recommends size." Then, if the gown comes in needing extensive (and expensive) alterations, you're in a better negotiating position. When you place your order, also get a written estimate on alterations. Be sure you ask about the store's refund policy, as well as any extra charges for pressing and so on. Since these written details are so important, let's sum up what you want on your dress order form:

Dress description. You want the actual manufacturer's name and style number, not the store's bogus internal code. The price, color, and size should be spelled out.

Special requests. Want extra length? A rush delivery? This should all be on the order form.

Promised delivery date. This can be in weeks or a specific day (on or before X).

Alterations estimate.

Deposit, refund and cancellation policies. Payment info (when the balance is due, etc) should be clearly stated.

Your contact info. Give the shop more than just a daytime number–an evening number and cell is important in case they need to get in touch with you after hours. If you order online instead of from a shop, the more contact info you can provide the gown seller, the better. (To protect your privacy, insist the shop not sell this info.)

♥ **Step 14:** One to two weeks after you place the order, call the bridal shop for a "confirmed shipping date." The shop usually receives this date from the manufacturer after it places the order.

♥ **Step 15:** Starting two weeks before your dress is due in, call the bridal shop to confirm the date your dress will actually arrive. Delays at the factory (imported lace arriving late, a larger number of back-orders) can delay the delivery of your gown, as well as the bridesmaids'. Bridal shops are usually aware of such delays. Calling ahead will help avoid surprises.

♥ **Step 16:** Hooray! The dress has arrived! Now, inspect the dress carefully *before* you pay the final balance. Gowns have been known to come in with flaws, stains, tears–you name it. Don't rely on the bridal shop to inspect the dress for you (many let problems slip through the cracks). Also, confirm the size of the dress by actually trying it on (or measuring it). Incorrect sizing is a major problem with some manufacturers. *Remember if you pay for the dress, sign a receipt and walk out the door with the gown, you are accepting the dress as is.* If you don't inspect the dress, take it home and THEN discover a problem, the shop may say "tough luck."

What if you order a gown from the 'net or mail order? Make sure you IMMEDIATELY inspect the dress and try it on. Any problem should be promptly reported to the gown seller. Most 'net and mail order gown sellers refuse to accept a claim for damage after a certain number of days.

♥ **Step 17:** Alterations. Whether you have the shop or an outside seamstress alter the gown, give the alterations person a firm deadline. Get it in writing. Be sure to confirm the experience level of the seamstress–how familiar is she with bridal fabric? How long has she been altering gowns? See our PITFALLS for more advice on alterations.

No matter where you buy your gown (at a store or online), one service you will probably need is pressing or steaming to get out the wrinkles. What's the difference? First, understand that we use the terms interchangeably in this chapter . . . but there is a difference. Most bridal shops use steamers to get out wrinkles from delicate fabrics; other seamstresses may use a press to iron out tough wrinkles.

We'd suggest steaming for most gowns–bridal fabric is delicate and pressing it could damage the finish. Silk gowns should definitely be steamed. While synthetic fabric gowns aren't as delicate as silk, we still worry about the finish on satin gowns if pressed. A good tip: ASK what method your seamstress will use and make sure it is appropriate to your gown's fabric.

Questions to Ask the Shop

1 Who is the manufacturer of this dress? As we previously mentioned, some shops try to hide this from you. Even though they have torn out the tags from the dress (in an illegal effort to keep you from comparison shopping), you can still ask them about who makes the dress. This is important for several reasons. First, you can determine if the store is an authorized dealer for the gown by calling the manufacturer. Second, you know what you are buying–some designers offer better quality than others. If the shop refuses to tell you, or if the salesperson says she just "doesn't know," go elsewhere.

2 How long will it take to get the dress in? A critical question since the delivery times for different manufacturers vary greatly. If you choose to fudge your wedding date (moving it forward a few weeks from the actual date), be careful here. If you move the date up too early, the shop may not be able to order the dress in time for the early date. In general, it takes ten to 14 weeks to special order a typical bridal gown, although some designers take as little as six weeks and others six months.

3 What are your payment policies? Can I put the deposit on a credit card? How about the final balance? This is a very important point, as you'll learn in our next section. Also, confirm the store's refund policy. Nearly all bridal shops have a "no refunds" policy on special-order dresses–even if the wedding is called off or postponed. Read the receipt (or contract) carefully before you sign. Note: some shops are requiring final payment to be made in cash. If this is the case, be sure everything is perfect before leaving the shop with any merchandise.

4 Can I have a written estimate for alterations? Before you order, get this in writing. Remember that you do not have to use the store's in-house alterations department (even though they will strongly encourage you to). Quality alterations are extremely important–we've seen too many unskilled seamstresses (many at bridal shops) botch alterations. Whomever you decide to hire, try to meet the seamstress who will alter your gown. Ask about her experience with bridal gowns. How long have they been doing this work? Have they ever worked with the fabric and lace on your dress before? If you detect any problems here or can't get a written estimate with delivery time, consider hiring another seamstress.

5 What free services are available? Some stores throw in a free "steaming" with all bridal gown orders. Other freebies might include free alterations, delivery to the ceremony site and even wedding coordination (especially when you place a large order with the shop). Some of these services might be offered quietly. Ask and ye shall receive.

6 Are there any extra fees for special orders? As we mentioned earlier in this chapter, some independent bridal retailers are slapping their customers with all kinds of bogus fees and charges. Many such charges aren't disclosed until after you've whipped out the credit card to place an order. So, it would be wise to ask if you will be socked for another $20 for shipping or any other creative "fee." Ask for the TOTAL for your order (gown? Extra size fee? Rush charge? Alterations? Shipping?) to make sure you are getting a good deal.

Bridal Bargains Wedding Planner: Gowns

Our planner, the *Bridal Bargains Wedding Planner*, has 30+ pages to help you stay organized when gown shopping. We have detailed tutorials on bridal fashion lingo (including pictures and photos), comparison charts and tracking worksheets. See the back of this book for details.

CONSUMER WARNING

Use Credit Cards Instead of Cash For All Deposits. Here's a little consumer tip that can protect you from getting ripped off by unscrupulous bridal shops: use your credit card (instead of cash or a check) to pay for a bridal gown. Most consumers do not realize that a special federal consumer protection law protects all deposits and payments made with credit cards. The law, called Federal Regulation C, entitles consumers to receive refunds if the merchandise delivered doesn't live up to what's promised.

Specifically, the law says that if you have a problem with the quality of goods or services that you purchased with a credit card and you have tried in good faith to correct the problem with the merchant, you may not have to pay the bill. (As a side note, this only applies to purchases over $50 and if the purchase was made in your home state or within 100 miles of your mailing address). Note: this protection does *not* apply to debit cards or cash advance checks that some credit card companies send their customers.

So what does that mean for you? Well, let's suppose two brides put $500 deposits on the exact same dress at BRIDAL SHOP XYZ in their town. One bride puts the deposit on her Visa (or any credit card) and the other writes a check. Delivery will take four months.

Let us tell you that four months may not seem like a long time to you but it's an ETERNITY to retailers. Much can happen in four months. In fact, BRIDAL SHOP XYZ has now gone out of business. The owner of the shop has left town without a trace. So what's happened to our two brides? Well, the bride who put the deposit on her credit card will contact the bank that issued her card and, most likely, she will receive a full refund.

And what happens to the other bride who paid with a check (or cash)? Her $500 is probably lost forever. Sure, she can sue the owner in small claims court–if she can find the owner. She can also report the incident (which is technically theft) to the local authorities. But, if the shop owner has left town, the bride may never see her money again.

Does this sound far-fetched? Well, it happens more often than you'd think. In one city we researched, for example, no less than ten bridal shops went out of business in just three years! While four closed "responsibly" (they stopped taking deposits and turned their special orders over to other shops in town), the other six bridal shops did not. Their owners took deposits until the day they closed and then quickly left town. We know dozens of brides who lost hundreds of dollars in deposits because they paid cash (or by check) instead of with a credit card.

In 2004, one of the largest bridal bankruptcies on record hit Pennsylvania. Kaufman's, a 21-store chain with locations in Pennsylvania, Ohio, Maryland and West Virginia, closed its doors suddenly, leaving thousands of brides without dresses. Many of those orders had already been paid for in full.

Kaufman's had left a trail of unhappy brides for months prior to the bankruptcy; consumers complained about late dresses, no dresses and excuse after excuse from the chain. The alleged fraud was so widespread that it prompted a lawsuit from the Pennsylvania Attorney General, who went to court to force the chain to deliver paid-for merchandise. The AG charged Kaufman's owners with numerous violations of consumer protection laws.

So, what can you do in case your shop disappears?

According to several credit card companies we've talked to, deposits paid with credit cards for bridal apparel (or any wedding-related purchase) are protected by Federal Regulation C. Be aware that the rules apparently vary slightly with each issuing bank. One bank we talked to had a requirement that complaints be filed within 60 days of the purchase. The fact that a deposit isn't really a "purchase" clouds the issue somewhat. Another bank told us they would refund money to a bride under a scenario like the one above even if more than 60 days had elapsed from the date the deposit was processed. Why? In clear cases of fraud (where merchants take off with your money, leaving you gownless), there is no time limit for you to dispute a charge.

What if you've already paid the bill? You still may be able to get a refund–contact your card-issuer for more info. What if the shop only takes cash or checks? Go elsewhere. Most bridal shops take credit cards.

Now we are not telling you this to scare you. The odds of you getting ripped off by a dishonest bridal shop are not great, but... BE CAREFUL! This advice applies to other deposits too, not just gowns. If you can, don't pay for any other "wedding" deposits (the cake, flowers, photographer, etc.) with cash or a check. A WORD TO THE WISE: USE YOUR CREDIT CARD.

Tied in Knots: Web site tries to up pressure on brides

In a recent edition of the Knot's wedding magazine, the top-rated wedding web site suggests that brides set aside 10% of their wedding budget for their dress. If you are planning the "average" wedding these days ($25,000), that means shelling out $2500 for a dress.

Please! Don't listen to these rules or guidelines–they are often pushed by the bridal media looking to line its pockets with ad revenue.

Let's look at the dress example. The average wedding dress in this country sells for $1025. And trust us, the Knot knows that–as a major force in bridal media, the Knot churns out all sorts of research and stats on weddings. That makes $1025 about 4% of the typical wedding budget. But the Knot can please its advertisers (many of whom are couture bridal gown makers selling $2000 dresses) by promoting the 10% rule.

Remember this: there are NO rules on what you MUST spend on this or that for your wedding. You plan the wedding YOU can afford, not the one the Knot wants you to go into debt for.

Destination Wedding Tips

What's the perfect wedding bargain for a beach destination wedding? And how do you transport a gown to a tropical locale? We have the low down:

♥ **Looking for an affordable dress for a destination beach wedding?** Check out the chain White House, Black Market (WhiteAndBlack.com). A simple strapless dress in cool, comfortable cotton is just $118 (at right). Dress this up with some bridal jewelry and a headpiece/veil and poof! Instant wedding gown for under $200! The chain also sells simple satin gowns that could easily double as a wedding dress for about $200.

♥ **How do you transport a wedding gown to a destination wedding spot?** Very carefully. But seriously—here are our tips:

♥ **First, consider double bagging the dress.** Usually when you buy a dress from a full-service shop, they give you one of those heavy plastic bags made especially for bridal gowns. Consider buying a second bag (they cost from $15 to $25 each) to protect against any rips, tears or splits in the first bag.

♥ **If you're taking the dress on a plane: never check your dress as luggage!** See if you can hang it in one of the garment compartments. If not, lay it as flat as possible in the overhead compartment (you'll have to have the wrinkles steamed out anyway at the wedding location, so don't be too concerned).

♥ **Consider UPS or Fed Ex.** If you can't take the dress on a plane or don't want to be bothered with the hassle, ship it. Leave yourself at least seven working days (double in December) for shipping time. Insure the gown for full value. Send it to a commercial address (that is, the destination wedding hotel, for example).

♥ **Packing**: Stuff bodice and sleeves with tissue paper; wrap in acid-free tissue paper (available at most craft stores); fill the box with peanuts.

♥ **When it gets there.** Find a competent cleaner or bridal shop in your wedding city that can steam your wedding dress for you (note we didn't say press—don't let *anyone* touch your gown with an iron! The delicate fabric and lace of most gowns rules out ironing. Besides, scorch marks aren't very becoming). Often friends and family can come up with suggestions or look in the Yellow Pages.

♥ **Hanger hazards.** Lay the dress flat on a bed. DON'T hang the dress for longer than a few hours. The weight of the dress and train can cause it to stretch out.

Top Money-saving Secrets

1 Purchase a gown online. Yes, you can buy a gown online—and save a bundle! We found several web sites that sell brand new, name-brand gowns at up to 40% off retail. See the Best Buy section later in this chapter for specifics. Don't want to order your bridal gown through the mail or online? Well, at least consider it for your bridesmaids' gowns. We'll discuss this in-depth in the next chapter.

2 Go for a heavily advertised designer. If you want to order a dress from a gown discounter, pick a gown from a designer that heavily advertises in bridal magazines. Why? It's easier to find a picture of such dresses. Once you know where (and when) a dress was advertised, it's much simpler to get a discount quote. Conversely, pick an obscure designer that rarely advertises and it's darn difficult to price shop. Nope, it doesn't take a rocket scientist to figure out which designers advertise the most—pick up a bridal magazine or surf the Knot!

3 One word: eBay. Yes, you can use eBay to save on bridal gowns—and headpieces, veils, shoes, tuxes and just about anything else bridal you can think of. Pop the words "bridal gown" into eBay's front-page search function and you'll find 1000+ items up for auction on average. And we're talking about designer brands here folks—on our last visit, we noticed a $3000 silk designer gown by Christos up for auction. The top bid? $425. See the Real Wedding Tip on page 38 for reader success stories with eBay. And see the next tip for more on saving with eBay.

4 Buy a gown direct from China via eBay. Why spend $1000 on a bridal gown when you can buy it for just $50? No, that's not a typo. Yes, it is now possible to cut out the middleman and buy your gown direct from China at stunningly low prices. See our Best Buy #2 at the end of this chapter for details.

5 Haggle. How can full-price bridal retailers compete with discounters? It's simple: many quietly match prices quoted by mail order and web discounters . . . if you ask. These "no frills" discount packages typically offer 20% to 30% discounts if you forgo some of the extra perks shops offer (free pressings, gown bags, and more). The rub: most of these discount deals are completely unadvertised. You have to ask. Also: beware of hidden charges that can turn a discount deal into a bum steer. See the earlier box on page 19 for more on this issue.

6 Go "off-the-rack." Chains like David's (reviewed later in this chapter) offer a wide selection of moderately priced gowns with in-stock sizes 2 to 26, as well as women's sizes. Most of David's gowns sell for $500 to $600, about 40% less the national average. So, are the gowns a great value? No, not really. David's just offers more gowns in-stock in the lower price ranges compared to specialty stores. Quality-wise, a David's $500 gown isn't much better (and some critics would say worse) than those you can find in other stores. And other readers give David's decidedly mixed reviews on service and delivery. We'll review the chain in depth later in this chapter. Of course, David's isn't the only player in the off-the-rack bridal store business. Gown maker Alfred Angelo has 30 "company stores" (alfredangelostores.com) that sells gowns off-the-rack.

7 Craigslist. Craigslist.org (the online classified source with editions for most cities) is packed with dress bargains. A search of our local Craigslist site turned up 100+ gowns for sale, including a $50 David's bridal gown (originally $400) and other dresses for half retail. Why do brides sell these gowns? Sometimes weddings are canceled or postponed. In other cases, recent brides who need extra cash are willing to part with their gowns. Most of these gowns are in excellent shape; some have never been worn before. And sometimes you can haggle an even lower price. Of course, you'll need to carefully inspect the gown before buying. Other items available through the classifieds: accessories like crinolines or full slips.

8 Consider "custom-designing." If you want a gown that costs over $1000, consider having a local seamstress create a copy of the original. We've seen several beautiful gowns that were custom-designed by talented seamstresses. Why is this a money-saving tip? Well, first a seamstress can often buy the fabric at wholesale (or at a discount from retail). Second, there are no costly alterations—your gown is made to fit. Through several fittings, you can watch the gown take shape and make suggestions along the way. Certainly the labor costs for an expert seamstress can be substantial, but the results can be striking. Total savings here will vary but we priced one exquisite silk Jim Hjelm gown at $2700 retail, which cost only $1400 to reproduce with a local seamstress. The best deals on custom-designed gowns would be on dresses that would retail for $1000, $2000 or more—seamstresses can usually replicate these dresses for far less than what you'd pay in a store. On the other hand, budget polyester gowns that sell for $500 in stores would be hard to duplicate with a seamstress for less money.

9 Hit Filene's Basement/Macy's bridal sale. Can you buy a $3000 designer bridal gown for just $249? You might if you can brave the Filene's Basement (now Macy's) sale in Boston. Two times a year in Boston (as well as other cities), this sale prompts a stampede of brides who strip the racks of designer gowns in mere seconds. Go to

Real Wedding Tip

eBay Success Stories & Tips

Our readers have been unanimous in their praise of eBay (ebay.com). Here are some of their success stories:

A reader in Florida writes: *"I found my dress on eBay, at a great bargain (I got a $1300 silk dress for only $138!) Granted, many of the dresses on eBay are hideous and should be burned but you can find something nice if you look closely and search well. You can also find veils, shoes, crinoline slips, tuxedo items and other items there."*

A reader in Louisville, KY agrees: *"My biggest bargains, thus far, have been found on eBay. I was able to find an Eden silk dress, brand new (but discontinued) for $87, and it is exactly what I wanted! I found my best friend's headpiece for less than half of the price at a salon. And I found my little dyeable flats for $9 (including shipping)."*

Ditto for this reader: *"One of my co-workers found a $3300 Christian Dior gown for just $99. Another friend snagged a designer silk gown (originally $1600) for just $85."*

If you want to buy a gown in a 'net auction, here are some tips:

1. Learn the lingo. eBay has a language all its own—take a second to surf the site's help section to brush up on how auctions work. Learn jargon like NWT—that's an item for sale that is "new with tags."

2. Avoid the tragedy of a missed auction. eBay has email notification services that clue you in to new auctions. Go to "My eBay" and click on favorites.

3. Use plastic. If possible, never use cash or a check to pay for that winning bid. Instead, whip out the credit card. As we discussed earlier in this chapter, credit cards offer a strong measure of consumer protection against fraud—and that applies to online

Filenesbasement.com (click on Bridal Event) to see the latest schedule and read the box "The Running of the Brides" later in this chapter for more information on this amazing event. Of course, Filene's/Macy's isn't the only company to offer special gown sales. Designer Vera Wang also has frequent sample sales in New York, held twice a year at the Hotel Pennsylvania in February and September. One good site that lists designer sample sales: NewYorkMetro.com (click on shopping) has a good listing of designer sample sales, updated daily.

auctions as well. If you use PayPal, consider items that are covered by "PayPal Buyer Protection," insurance that covers up to $1000 in case an item isn't delivered.

4. Watch out for subtle clues. Worried that "dream bargain" of a bridal gown will really be a trashed sample? Be careful to pour over the descriptions of items with a fine-tooth comb. Often sellers will leave subtle clues that an item may not be brand new. Email the seller with questions and ask about their return policy.

5. Know thy seller. Look at the seller's feedback–eBay tracks feedback on how sellers have conducted themselves on the site. With one click, you can hear what previous customers say about their experiences with the trader. Most sellers try to jealously protect those good ratings–and hence may try to fix any problem you have with the merchandise before you tell the world the seller is a crook.

6. Realize some gown auctioneers are actually bridal shops. eBay isn't just for individual sellers; many bridal retailers have jumped on the bandwagon too. Some stores are desperate to unload their discontinued samples at bargain prices. Yes, these dresses can be steals but be careful–a sample may be trashed from multiple try-ons (try to see detailed pictures of the gown before bidding). And don't think you are safe when buying from an individual–remember that a gown can be altered significantly from its original size. Ask the seller about this issue before bidding.

7. Check with the BBB. A bride in Tennessee emailed this tip. She won an auction for a Maggie Sottero gown from an eBay seller that was a bridal shop. Unfortunately, the shop took her money and never shipped the gown. Turns out the BBB (www.bbb.org) had 500 complaints on file for this scam artist. While online auction fraud is rare (eBay estimates only one-tenth of a percent of all auctions involve fraud), you still should take steps to check out a seller before bidding.

70 Sew it yourself. If you have a flair for sewing (or know a good friend who does), consider making your gown yourself. Patterns for bridal gowns are readily available at local fabric shops. One such store pointed out to us that the exact materials (fabric, lace, pattern) to make a popular designer dress would cost $300. The retail of this dress was $1500—not counting an extra $250 for alterations. One note of caution: sewing with bridal fabric is challenging so be careful if you go this route.

71 Buy a "sample" gown. Bridal shops often sell their samples throughout the year at substantial discounts from retail. Most gowns are marked down at least 50% off, some even more. Since many shops sell most of their gowns by special order, they need these demonstrator samples to entice orders. What happens when a gown is discontinued or they need more room for new styles? It's sale time! Check your local paper since some shops have big sample sales throughout the year. However, most shops have a rack of discounted sample gowns year-round. Before you use this recommendation, read our PITFALLS section for special tips on buying a sample dress.

Fabric Sources

Need a source for bridal fabric or trim? Here are some of the sources our readers have cited:

♥ **Hyman Hendler & Sons** (212) 840-8393 (web: hymanhendler.com) sells fabric and ribbons from both domestic and European sources.
♥ **Dulken & Derrick** (212) 929-3614 (web: www.dulkenandderrick.com) sells silk flower trim for gowns.
♥ **Greenberg & Hammer** (800) 955-5135 (web: www.greenberg-hammer.com) has notions and dressmaking supplies in their mail order catalog.
♥ Our readers have also recommended: David's Textiles (800) 548-1818; The Fabric Mart (800) 242-3695; Fabric Depot (800) 392-3376; McGowen's (908) 965-2298.

For further reading: *Bridal Couture: Fine Sewing Techniques for Wedding Gowns & Evening Wear* by Susan Khalje (Krause Publications, $29.95 US, $37.50 Canada, in bookstores or call 800-258-0929) is an excellent resource for brides who want a custom bridal gown. Even if you don't want to make a dress yourself, the book includes extensive information on fabrics, laces and proper construction techniques.

12 **Wear your mom's dress or borrow a friend's gown.** You'd be surprised how inexpensively a seamstress can restore a vintage gown. Even if you spend $100 to $200 to have the gown altered or jazzed up, this will be much less than buying a gown at retail. Borrowing a gown from a friend is another great money-saving option. Total savings = $800 or even more!

13 **The white bridesmaid dress trick** Most brides don't realize that many bridesmaids' gowns can be ordered in white. For a less formal wedding, you can get a plain bridesmaid's gown for just $90 to $150. Beautiful, less-formal gowns (without trains, sequins, pearls, etc.) are available from ready-to-wear clothing designers like Jessica McClintock. Her stunning line of bridal dresses start at around $200. Jazz up a bridesmaid's gown in white with a detachable train (one bride told us she had a seamstress make one for $25 plus the cost of fabric) and you have a bridal gown at a fraction of the bridal price. One caveat: some designers have tried to stop this trend by charging a penalty fee (an extra $75) for any bridesmaid gown ordered in white. Is white fabric more expensive? Nope, designers just don't want to cannibalize their wedding gown sales. Also: some designers like Vera Wang and Amsale will not sell you a single bridesmaid gown in white or ivory; instead you have to order a minimum of three. Again, that minimum doesn't apply to colored bridesmaids' dresses.

14 **Don't buy a "bridal" gown.** What is a wedding dress anyway but a white gown? You can often save when you shop at places that don't sell "bridal gowns." Many department stores and specialty shops sell white formal dresses—at prices that are half or less than those at so-called bridal stores. Shhhh! Don't tell anyone, but these dresses can easily be used as the perfect dress for your wedding.

15 **Check out vintage clothing shops.** A reader in Berkeley, CA shared with us a great bargain shopping tip: vintage clothing stores. In Berkeley, she found a beautiful 1950's wedding gown in excellent condition for just $200 at a vintage shop. Most large cities have such stores; check your local phone book under "Clothes—Vintage." Want to have a seamstress replicate a vintage gown? We found a great web site on this subject: Sense and Sensibility Patterns (www.sensibility.com), which has vintage wedding dress patterns, sewing tips, links and more. Another idea: go medieval to save on your wedding gown. RomanticThreads.com has medieval, Victorian and other vintage style wedding dresses. Most gowns are under $400—less than half the cost of most wedding dresses.

Continued on page 44

The Running of the Brides: Snagging a Designer Gown for $249 at Filene's

There is probably no bridal event more famous in the U.S. than the sale at Filene's Basement (now part of Macy's). If you happen to be near Boston (or one of a half dozen eastern U.S. cities) when the sale is on and think you can survive the scene, this is definitely one event not to miss. That's because Filene's/Macy's sale features designer gowns that cost $2000, $3000 and even $4000—all marked down to an amazing $249 or $499. Nope, that isn't a typo. As you might expect, bargains like this attract a crowd.

After interviewing several brides who braved the sale and got great deals, we'd like to offer our tips for making the most of Filene's Basement/Macy's Bridal Sale.

1. Plan in advance. Although Filene's Basement store occasionally has a rack of discounted bridal gowns at the downtown Boston store, most Filene's don't regularly carry wedding dresses. For the special sale, Filene's collects discontinued samples (most are size 10's) and other dresses from bankrupt shops and designers. When they've collected enough gowns, it's sale time! A few years ago, the sale was only at the downtown Boston (617) 542-2011 location. In recent years, Filene's has also held bridal sales in Atlanta, Chicago, Washington, DC, Ohio and Pennsylvania. The sale is usually held two times a year—February and July/August. (Call the number above for the latest schedule or surf www.filenesbasement.com). FYI: Filene's owner, Macy's, converted all the Filene's to Macy's as of 2006. As of press time, we were unsure how this would affect the sale.

2. Brace for bargains. No matter what the original retail price, most gowns are marked at $249 or $499 (although a few are priced at $699). Filene's spokesperson told us she's even seen one dress originally priced at $7000, although most would retail in the $1000 to $2000 range. One success story we heard from Chicago last year: one of our readers found a $4400 silk Carolina Herrera gown at the sale for just $249!

3. Arrive early. While the doors open at 8 am, brides start lining up as early as 5:30 am to 6 am. Several hundred brides will be in line by the time the doors open.

4. Bring an entourage. These gowns are heavy—some brides bring an entourage of friends and family to help them hold dresses. Of course, second opinions are nice too. In addition to bridal gowns, Filene's also sells bridesmaids, mothers-of-the-bride and other formal dresses at the sale.

5. Dress appropriately. Sneakers are a must. Forget your purse or let a friend carry it. While dressing rooms are available, most brides just try on the dresses right there in the aisles. "Some women wear leotards or bodysuits," says Filene's spokesperson, "but others are in the underwear they plan to actually wear under the wedding gown—they are not shy." A sports bra and shorts is a good idea.

6. Brace yourself. This is not a sale for the meek—brides can get darn aggressive. Waiting brides have broken down the door at the entrance at least five times over the years. When the doors open, everyone rushes to the racks. All the gowns are gone in 32 to 46 seconds (this has been timed by more than a few amazed reporters, says Filene's.) In the feeding frenzy, fist fight have broken out, although Filene's says security is on-hand to keep the event from becoming a melee. We should note that, fortunately, in recent years the insanity of Filene's sale has toned down a few notches—brides tell us sometimes there are even gowns left on the rack after a few hours! One bride told us at the Chicago sale in the summer, she arrived at 11am and still found plenty of selection. That would probably be the exception to the rule, however.

7. Grab anything. While most gowns are a size 10, remember that bridal sizes don't match the real world. Hence, the best strategy would be to grab just about anything. Then let the bargaining begin.

8. Be prepared to haggle. At many sales, brides will trade with one another to find the style or size they want. That's why you should grab as many gowns as you can—more bargaining power. If you're a size 8 and you've grabbed a size 14, don't put it back on the rack. Instead, trade it with another bride for a dress you like. You might have to barter several times before finding "the" dress.

9. Mix and match. Here's a smart strategy: mix and match different gowns. Some brides have had a seamstress combine pieces of two or more gowns they found at Filene's sale. Take the lace from one dress, combine it with the fabric and train from another and voila! A designer look at a fraction of the designer price. Remember the cost of embroidered lace and silk fabric today is far more than the $249 (or even $499) cost of each dress.

10. Cut it down. You may find the perfect gown at Filene's sale—except it's two sizes too big. Yet at these prices, you may be able to easily afford to have a seamstress cut it down to size. One bride had a size 14 re-made into a size 4.

16 **Shop at bridal outlet stores.** Scattered across the country are outlet stores for bridal designers and retailers that offer substantial savings. See the Best Buy section later in this chapter for more info.

17 **Buy a consignment gown.** These pre-owned gowns are often fantastic bargains. Many apparel consignment shops have popped up in major cities across the nation. Most second-hand gowns sell for at least HALF their original price tags, depending on the condition. How can you find a good consignment bridal shop? One low-tech way is to just look in the phone book under bridal shops or consignment/thrift stores. An online source for consignment shops is the National Association of Resale and Thrift Stores at www.narts.org. Or bypass stores and look for a second-hand gown in the e-classifieds on Nearly New Bridal (www.nearlynewbridal.com), on Craigslist.org or PreownedWeddingDresses.com

One caveat: there is a limit to how many times a gown can be altered without losing its basic design. Consider how much a dress has been previously altered before you buy. The best advice: if you find a second-hand gown you want, place a small deposit ($25) to hold it. Come back to the shop with a seamstress and let her look it over to make sure alterations can be successful and cost effective. If the second-hand shop has a seamstress, get this evaluation in writing—"the gown had these previous alterations, needs the following work and the cost would be $XX." That way if there's a problem, you'll have a paper trail.

18 **Swap the fabric.** Fallen in love with a silk gown but can't afford the silk price? You still might be able to afford that gown—just ask if the manufacturer offers the same style in a less-expensive fabric. Not all designers offer this option, but it might be worth asking. You can save $300 or more with a simple fabric swap.

19 **Check the next state over.** A reader in Los Angeles emailed us this tip. She found the same, brand-new designer gown that cost $2200 to special order in LA . . . for just $1300 in a Portland, Oregon shop. Another bonus: Oregon has no sales tax, saving the bride another 7% ($150). Why the major price difference? It's hard to say, but expensive overhead in big cities like LA or NYC sometimes leads to bigger mark-ups. Hence, it may pay to check out prices in a nearby state (check the designer's web site to find the names of other nearby dealers). Remember that if you order a gown in another state and have it shipped home across state lines, you may not have to pay any sales tax. Yes, you have to arrange for alterations on your own, but that typically isn't that much of a challenge.

20 **Make a run for the border.** If you live near the Mexican border, look for deals in border towns like Juarez (near El Paso, Texas). There are 33 bridal shops on several blocks of Avenida Lerdo in Juarez selling bridal gowns for $150 to $180 and maids' dresses for $75. One tip: a bride suggested NOT telling the shops if you've traveled a long distance–shops tend to charge higher prices to brides who have made major trips to gown shop, figuring you are likely to spend more than brides who live just across the border.

21 **Buy a gown in the "off season."** What's the best time to get the biggest bargains on a wedding dress? Try shopping anytime between Thanksgiving and Christmas. Most bridal shops are absolutely dead in November and December. Hence, many retailers are willing and ready to cut you a deal. Be aware, however, that bargains evaporate after Christmas, as the shops get busy again after all those holiday engagements.

22 **Hire a student.** Got a fashion school nearby? The Academy of Fashion Design in San Francisco (888) 493-3261 refers students and recent graduates who can do custom wedding dresses. One reader told us she got a price quote of $500 (including fabric) for an elaborate gown, which is quite a deal. Check your local phone book for possibilities.

23 **Look for charity sales.** Making Memories, a non-profit foundation based in Portland, Oregon that grants final wishes to women with breast cancer, holds charity bridal gown sales across the country in 14 major cities. All gowns are donated by brides (who get a tax write-off) and all the proceeds go to the foundation's work. Over 3000 gowns are sold each year at these sales. For more information, contact Making Memories at (503) 252-3955 web: www.makingmemories.org. After the wedding, why not donate your gown back to Making Memories, get a tax deduction and help a great cause.

24 **Go for a knock-off.** Like a David's bridal gown style, but scared off by the chain's customer service reputation? Consider a knock-off of David's called DaVinci (web: DaVinciBridal.com). Made by Impression (reviewed later in this chapter), DaVinci's line is a dress-for-dress copy of David's–at prices 20% to 50% below David's. For example, one strapless A-line gown is sold by David's for $900; DaVinci's copy is $550. Sold in specialty stores nationwide, DaVinci also has bridesmaids' gowns for $140 to $160. The quality of DaVinci is similar to David's–that is, most dresses are made of synthetic fabrics and sewn in China. But the value is excellent.

So, is it fair for DaVinci to copy David's? Well, as you'll read in our discussion of David's, that chain is famous for copying the looks of other designers like Maggie Sottero. So, DaVinci is merely copying David's copies!

25 Shop at a place without the word "bridal" in its name. Sometimes the best deals on bridal are from stores that don't have "wedding" on their sign. Case in point: if we said the words "J. Crew," you'd think simple, casual clothes. But what about bridal? Yes, J. Crew now sells bridal—at prices that are very affordable. Crew's "Wedding & Party Shop" is only on their web site (jcrew.com). There we found a simple silk bridal dress for just $285 (see picture at right). Other styles were $300 to $500 (although one dress was $1800). Sure, these are very plain styles (no embroidery or beading), but that might be just the ticket for some brides. J Crew has also moved into the bridesmaid biz, selling a selection of silk and cotton gowns for $150 to $300. Sizes are 0 to 16. So, how's the quality? Very good, our readers report. "The dress is fully lined, 100% silk and fits great! The dresses are not that horrible 'bridal cut,' so I actually got a dress in a size that I wear normally! So on my wedding day, I'll feel like a queen and not a cow!" said one bride.

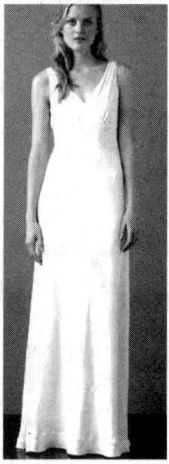

And it's not only J. Crew that is getting into bridal: Lane Bryant has rolled out a plus-size selection of bridal and bridesmaids dresses for $150 (yes, that's the real price). Bryant offers three silhouettes: a floor-length satin gown, a satin gown with chiffon skirt and cocktail-length lace dress. Each is available in sizes 14 to 28. See it on LaneBryant.com.

And if that weren't enough, you can also find bridal now at Ann Taylor. Taylor's "Celebrations" line features a silk strapless bridal gown for $600 (did we mention it is silk?), as well as bridesmaids for $178 to $228. Unlike J Crew and Lane Bryant, Ann Taylor even sells its collection in a limited number of stores (18) as well as online (anntaylor.com).

26 Get your veil at a discount. Veils, headpieces and tiaras are sold at outrageous prices in retail shops . . . it should be a federal crime to sell a comb with a spritz of pearls and a bit tulle for $300. But that's exactly what you'd see at retail for these items.

There are two key ways to save: sew it yourself or buy it online at a discount. Let's look at each.

Sure, few brides attempt to sew their bridal gown, but what about making your own headpiece? The average bridal veil and headpiece is little more than a comb (or headband) with some ribbons, silk flowers and a few fake pearls. Attach a veil and poof! You've got a bridal headpiece. Our advice: make your own. Go to any craft store like Michaels (800-MICHAELS, www.michaels.com) and pick up the forms and supplies to do it yourself. One reader found rhinestone tiaras at Michaels for $15 to $40 and ribbon edged veils for $15. See the box below for stories from our readers about their do-it-yourself headpieces.

Okay, you're not a crafty-type person. In that case, buy that headpiece online. Our readers have had great success buying tiaras, headpieces and veils online, at big discounts. Let's look at the best sites:

We've had several good comments about **VeilShop.com**, whose well-designed site included detailed pictures, great prices (many tiaras under $100) and the option to order headpieces separately from veils (so you can do your own veil if so inclined). **Veils A La Mode** (web: VeilsALaMode. com) sells tiaras for just $40 to $90 and various other headpieces at very affordable prices. If you want, you can buy just the veil for $53 to $188 for cathedral length (the price depends on the edge finish). Together, you can buy a headpiece and veil from this site for $100 or less. Those prices are fantastic savings over retail shops, where headpieces and veils can run $200, $300 or more.

Wedding-veil.com is a Colorado-based operation with a well-designed web site that makes it easy to shop for tiaras, veils, and more. We liked the detailed FAQ and buying tips. One reader we recommended this site gave their service an A+, saying she saved half off on her veil compared to retail prices.

Mary R. of Burbank, CA emailed us a recommendation for **BridalVeilCreations.com**. Her 120" plain edged veil was $41. The site sells handmade veils from $20, or you can customize a veil with a special length, edging and more.

Romantic Headlines (web: romanticheadlines.com) is one of the web's biggest veil and headpiece resources, with a very large selection of rhinestone and crystal tiaras. We found the prices to be excellent (one third to half off retail), but read the return policy carefully before ordering. While the site guarantee's satisfaction, the return procedure has to be followed exactly. That advice would apply to ANY veil web site—be aware of restrictions and restocking fees BEFORE you place an order.

Finally, don't forget about **eBay**—do a search for bridal veils or headpieces and you'll find dozens of small craftsmen who market their wares via the auction site.

See the box on the next page for more headpiece ideas on the cheap!

Games that Bridal Shops Play

Once you identify local bridal shops you want to visit, the fun begins! It's time to hit the streets! But before you get caught up in the whirlwind of Italian satin and imported lace, take a second to learn about some of the games, tricks and scams you might encounter out there. No, not all bridal retailers play these games, but judging by the email complaints we get from brides, this is a problem with many shops. Let's expose some of the tactics you may encounter while searching for a gown:

1 **Mystery Gowns**. Many bridal shops rip the tags out of their sample dresses to keep you from knowing who designed and manufac-

Real Wedding Tip

Make your own headpieces!

Naomi from New York wrote to us about why brides should consider making their own headpieces:

"You mention in your book that most veils and headpieces cannot possibly, in labor or materials, equal the $150-$300 price tag. I tended to agree when I read this, but must admit that I didn't really realize how true this was until I took a visit to a bridal salon. After selecting my gown, I thought it would be a good idea to try on a few headpieces. I did keep an eye on the prices, they ranged from $90 (a comb, a few "silk" flowers, a few ribbon streamers, no veil) to $150 (an elbow tip veil with a slightly embellished comb) to $190 (a "silver" headband wrapped with plastic beads and a few "silk" roses, no veil). How could anyone possibly buy these? Your point, however, was really driven home when I spied a rather simple veil. It was shoulder-length, had no beading, no special finishes, the comb undecorated and as far as I could possibly tell, was made out of plain tulle. You can imagine my reaction when I flipped over the tag. No kidding: $290. I stopped trying on veils at that point.

"A few days later I thought to myself, maybe it's hard to make veils, maybe that's why they're so pricey. Change of mind came quickly after making a trip to my local fabric and crafts store. I bought two patterns (Butterick #4649 and McCalls #7984), some materials and headed home for an afternoon of crafting. All in all, it was a fun day and at the end I had myself a beautiful, fingertip veil (tulle) attached to a crown of organza roses and silk lilies. Was it hard to make? No. And the cost of my unique and elegant headpiece? No word of a lie, $40."

tured the gown. When asked, these shop owners simply refuse to tell brides who made the dresses. Why would they do this? We've interviewed many shop owners who basically admit they do it to prevent brides from price shopping their dresses. Hey, they argue, if we tell you the designer, then you'll go down the street to our competitor and get the dress at a discount.

Hello? What other shops behave like this? Only the bridal biz.

Many bridal shops would prefer brides to remain ignorant, plunk down their money . . . and not ask any questions. Are you getting a designer silk original from Europe–or a cheap polyester copy from China? Keeping the designer info from you is a sneaky way for some shops to pass off an inferior gown as "comparable" to a premium design.

What is most perplexing about this deceptive practice is the fact

Another bride from Los Angeles wrote:

"Brides, I am certainly no Seamstress Extraordinaire, but, for gosh sake, MAKE YOUR OWN VEILS!!!! There are all kinds of guides and patterns at craft stores–costume patterns and historical fashion/costumes books also make excellent sources. Unless you want a rhinestone tiara, please skip the (ahem) "professional" bridal veils. For about $12.50 (that's 3 yards of tulle, some fabric glue, thread, trim, and an extra-large comb from the 99¢¢ store) I will be making a better-quality veil than what I've seen in these so-called "exclusive" salons. . . and it means more to me personally, too. For example, I am also using 24 faux-pearls from an old, broken necklace once belonging to my grandma. The pearls are far better quality than the plastic monstrosities used today, and have the added bonus of being sentimental."

Finally, Anne O. of San Francisco shared this story:

"I have to pass along the greatest bargain. After much searching for a simple hair comb or headpiece for my wedding, the only one I found that I liked was $325 at an expensive bridal boutique in San Francisco. I found that price outrageous since it consisted of two simple twisted strands of freshwater pearls on a four-inch metal comb. After some research, I found The Bead Shop in Palo Alto, CA (beadshop.com). They sell plain combs and every different type, size and color of beads, crystals and pearls you can imagine. They also have step-by-step instructions online on how to make hair combs, which was great because I am NOT a creative or artsy person in any way. But I was able to buy the comb, and one strand of freshwater pearls for about $40 total. I made my own hair comb in about 30 minutes and it looks exactly like the $325 boutique version!

that most brides find out about the shop from a designer's ad online or in a bridal magazine. Designers spend millions trying to get brides to recognize their brand name and for what? To have their retailers tear out the tags is stupid, especially under the guise of stopping "price competition."

Not only is it stupid, it's also illegal. A 40-year-old federal law called the Textile Fiber Products Identification Act of 1963 requires all apparel (yes, even bridal) to be properly labeled. This must include the name of the manufacturer (or their "registered number" assigned by the Federal Trade Commission, www.ftc.gov) as well as the fiber content and country of origin. Both federal and state laws forbid the removal of these tags. Sadly, many bridal shops openly and flagrantly violate this long-standing consumer law. Why? They know they won't get busted, since the FTC doesn't have any bridal police running around to enforce the rules.

There is one big loophole in the label law, however: shops *can* remove manufacturers' tags as long as they substitute their own tags with the store name and the required information (fiber content, country of origin, care instructions). For imported gowns (the vast majority of all gowns sold in the US are made overseas), this store tag must be sewn into the garment. While this sounds like a big loophole, we've noticed many stores don't even bother to replace tags. They just rip out the designer tags and slap on a hangtag that simply lists the price and an internal store code—and omits all the required information.

You can read more about tag requirements at the Federal Trade Commission's web site at ftc.gov. The FTC has a special publication entitled "Wedding Gown Labels: Unveiling the Requirements" at http://www.ftc.gov/bcp/conline/pubs/buspubs/wedgown.htm

What if you encounter a shop that rips tags and won't reveal info on the dress as required by law? First, file a complaint with the FTC. The FTC's web site (ftc.gov) has a quick and easy link to do this at www.ftc.gov/ftc/complaint.htm. The FTC will only take this problem seriously if they receive a good number of complaints from brides. Second, post a message on this to our web site, BridalBargainsBook.com. Click on the message boards and post your story to the bridal gown section. This will warn other readers about such shops.

So, why all the fuss about tags? Without it, you can fall victim to a series of consumer scams we've documented:

♥ **Price Gouging.** By hiding the manufacturer's name, you cannot tell whether you're looking at a designer original . . . or a cheap knock-off made by a copy house. With over 200 manufacturers and importers of bridal apparel sold in North America, there is a WIDE difference in quality of construction, fabric and detailing. We think you have the right to know what you are buying. Tag-ripping bridal shops sometimes try to gouge unsuspecting brides on price—we've seen cases of retailers trying to pawn off affordable tag-less dresses for hundreds *over* the typical retail.

♥ **Fabric fraud.** With the fiber content label torn from dresses, it's hard to say whether the dress you're looking at is silk or polyester. In recent years, many new synthetic fabrics have come on the market that mimic the look and feel of silk. While these fabrics have creative names ("silky satin," for example), they are all polyester or blends. Unscrupulous retailers try to pass off these fabrics as silk.

♥ **Sweatshops and slave labor.** Most bridal gowns sold today are made overseas, typically in Asia. A handful are still sewn in the US, Canada or Europe—these gowns are generally perceived to be of higher quality. When the bridal shop removes a gown's tag that indicates the country of origin, you don't know whether the dress is handcrafted in the USA . . . or mass-produced in a sweatshop in China.

Top 7 Most Outrageous Excuses For Why Bridal Shops Rip Tags

Our email box is always stuffed with brides' gown tales. As a public service, we have been cataloging the most creative excuses used by bridal retailers as to why they rip tags out of their wedding gowns. Yes, these are actual words uttered by retailers to consumers:

1. "The tags are removed to protect the feelings of brides since dress sizes are larger than those in street clothes."
2. "Bridal gown manufacturers forbid us to tell you who makes which dress. So, it's out of our hands."
3. "It's in the computer and that's down, so we don't know."
4. "Designers don't put tags in dresses for copyright purposes (to keep their gowns from being copied) and shops can't do anything about that."
5. "Only the store's buyer knows who makes each dress and she's not telling."
6. "All our dresses are made exclusively for this store in the Orient, so there are no brand names."
7. "We don't know who makes which dress, but if you pay us a 50% non-refundable deposit, we can find out!"

So, what happens when you ask a bridal retailer point blank "Who makes this gown?" Well, some refuse to tell you anything. Others say they'll happily tell you the brand . . . AFTER you place down that hefty 50% deposit (which is non-refundable, of course). You'd be offended if you ran into the same practice in an appliance or electronics store, but for some reason bridal retailers think they can get away with it. (Memo to Gloria Steinem: note that while shops rip out bridal gown tags, the men's tuxedo section has LOTS of tags).

What about style numbers? Well, while federal law prevents the removal of manufacturer, fiber content and country of origin tags, there is NO requirement to reveal a gown's style number (a unique number assigned to each dress). Often, bridal shops will tag their dresses with secret codes, not the actual style numbers.

Are designers upset about retailers that rip out their names from their gowns? Well, yes and no. Some designers (Demetrios/Ilissa, for one) have sent letters to their retailers warning them not to rip tags. Most designers could care less. Why? Most bridal gown makers are just concerned with selling samples into bridal stores; they don't care what the retailers do with the gowns after they get them (as long as they pay their bills, of course).

The bottom line: you're probably going to encounter this problem when you gown shop. We found three out of four bridal shops rip tags and violate federal label laws. This happens in both big and small cities, from some of the country's biggest gown sellers in New York and LA to the smallest town in Alabama. Yes, the FTC did try to crack down on this practice in 1999, sending letters to offending shops warning them to stop. They didn't. And the FTC hasn't done anything about it since.

Solution: Find a few dresses you like in a bridal magazine or online. Then walk into the shops listed in the ads and ask to see those specific dresses. If the salespeople say they don't know who makes which gowns, don't believe them. Before you walk out, you may mention to the salesperson that they just lost a big sale.

Another creative solution: look at wedding message boards on sites like the Knot.com. We've noticed that many brides have posted the key to crack the codes at popular shops. (Most shops aren't terribly creative in how they encode the designer and style number info).

2 Nickel and dime charges. As if bridal gowns weren't expensive enough, some independent bridal retailers have started to add a series of questionable "fees" and "charges" to inflate your final bill. Here are examples:

♥ **Try-on fees.** Hard to believe, but some shops actually charge their customers to try on their dresses! One shop charges their brides $50 for an hour of dress up! Other shops only sock out-of-town brides with such fees (they figure in-town brides are more likely to buy). How do they know you are from out of town? These retailers force all brides to register before browsing the racks—and the registration card asks for your address (as well as other personal information like age, income, blood type, etc). While try-on fees are typically deducted if you make a purchase, we can't think of any better way to drive brides to chain stores than such bogus fees.

♥ **Shipping and handling.** More mom-and-pop shops are slapping brides with shipping and handling fees for any special order. Bridal gown? $10 to $20 in shipping charges. Bridesmaids, $5 to $10 EACH. Veils, headpieces, shoes and anything else is $5 or more. We could understand shipping fees if these items were shipped to your home, but that's not the case in Bridal World. Here, retailers charge you shipping to have an item sent from their supplier to the BRIDAL STORE. Then you have to go pick it up! Even more deceptive: shops that claim these shipping charges also cover "insurance." "What girl doesn't want insurance for her gown against damage?" one retailer told us, bragging that their customers have never questioned this. Why this is bogus: ALL retailers must deliver you a gown free from damage, if you special order brand new merchandise. If UPS damages your gown in route from the maker to the store, the shop has to make it good, whether you paid for "insurance" or not.

♥ **Accounting surcharges.** A Jacksonville, FL bridal shop charges brides a $10 "accounting surcharge" for special orders that are not paid in full at the time of ordering. Never mind that the industry standard for special orders is almost always half down with the balance due when the goods are delivered. (Yes, there are exceptions, but more on this later). Either shops should do the standard half-down deal or require payment up front—surcharges for those who don't pay in full are ridiculous. Another questionable accounting charge: credit card surcharges. Some shops tack on another $2 to $5 for orders paid by credit cards (especially if the order is paid by phone for bridesmaid dresses, for example). Note: credit card companies and some states expressly forbid surcharges on such purchases.

♥ **Penalty fee.** Yes, you can save money by ordering a gown mail order or online, but beware of the penalty box when it comes to alterations. In order to punish brides who buy from discount sources, some bridal retailers add special "penalty fees" and surcharges to do alterations on such gowns. Some shops boost their alterations rates 15% to 50% over regular fees or others add a flat $10 to $100 extra charge to alter any dress *not* bought in their store.

♥ **No show charge.** Want to make an appointment to see gowns at Kleinfeld, one of the largest bridal retailers in the New York area? First, you'll have to whip out your credit card. If you don't show up for your appointment or fail to cancel within 48 hours, Kleinfeld will charge you a $50 "no show" fee. Yes, amazing but true. While we agree you shouldn't miss an appointment, zapping brides for $50 bucks is ridiculous. Noticeably, Kleinfeld doesn't pay brides $50 if *Kleinfeld* is backed up, making a bride wait for her appointment.

♥ **Storage fees.** You're getting married in June, but your gown arrives early in March. Should you let the bridal shop store it for you? Unfortunately, many now charge for this service—one bride in Sacramento said a local shop there quoted her $11 *per month* in storage fees. We say don't do it. First, this is an unnecessary expense, especially if you have room at your home or apartment to keep the gown. Second, bridal shops aren't Fort Knox—they burn down, get robbed or

Designer Trunk Shows: Tips & Traps

Bridal gown designers do have something in common with rock stars—occasionally, both go on tour. For dressmakers, these tours include personal appearances at various bridal shops where they are the stars of "trunk shows." But just what the heck are these trunk shows and are they any benefit to you, the bride?

Trunk shows are "limited time" events where designers will show off their complete collection of gowns at a bridal retail shop (or department store). Brides can meet one-on-one with the designer and discuss the right dress for them.

The advantage for consumers is obvious: for once, you can see a designer's ENTIRE line of dresses. Stores can only stock a limited number of gowns; trunk shows give you the whole enchilada. Another big plus: face time lets you ask designers about possible changes to a dress. The result: a customized dress that's right for you.

Of course, that's the upside. Here are some traps to look out for, plus some general tips for getting the most out of trunk shows:

♥ **Under pressure.** Trunk shows typically last only two to three days (say, Thursday to Saturday). After that, most of the gowns are gone. If you want to go back next weekend and show the dress to your mom, tough luck. As a result, you feel tremendous pressure to make a quick decision. The best advice: shop extensively before you go to a trunk show. That way you know whether a "here-today, gone-tomorrow" dress is the right one . . . or you need to keep looking.

flat out disappear. In 2001, a couple of long-time bridal shops in Tampa, Florida closed suddenly—their inventory (including paid-for gowns) were seized by a landlord for back rent and later auctioned off.

♥ **Bag charge.** You're not going to throw that gown in your trunk, right? Instead, why not protect your gown in our special oversized zippered garment bags? Chains like David's and specialty salons charge brides $10 to $20 for a gown bag. Here's a secret: shops pay just $1 to $2 wholesale for those bags because they buy them in bulk. That's the bridal biz in a nutshell: how to sell a $1 plastic bag for $20 bucks!

♥ **Light bulb fee.** Just kidding—but will it be long before some bridal retailer decides to charge brides $25 to use the light bulbs in their dressing rooms?

♥ **Forget discounts.** Given all the hoopla surrounding trunk shows, you might think the gowns would be on sale. Forget it! The gowns are almost always sold at full retail. The best you can hope for is to negotiate for changes to a dress design without any additional charges.

♥ **Plan in advance.** Designers typically visit a city only once a year. Miss that one weekend and you're out of luck. The best advice: call the designer and get their trunk show schedule. Most designers know by October their travel schedule for the following year. Some net-savvy designers also post trunk show schedules on their web sites (although lists can be out of date; it's best to call and confirm). Another idea: some bridal magazines list upcoming trunk shows in their calendar section or online.

♥ **Make an appointment.** Some designer trunk shows can be mobbed. The best advice is to make an appointment in advance. Typically, you will be given an hour or two time slot to try on gowns.

♥ **Be prepared.** Just in case you decide to order a gown at a trunk show, make sure you're prepared. In order to take correct measurements, you should bring any special undergarments or shoes you plan to wear on your wedding day.6

Why do shops try to zap brides with all these bogus fees? Because they know MOST brides only look at the price of the gown, not the charges for all those little "extras."

We find these nickel and dime charges offensive since they are RARELY disclosed to the bride until the order is written. That way brides will fall in love with a gown before they are hit with the shipping fees, accounting charges and whatever bogus fees a retailer can dream up.

The obvious defense against this is to ask about any extra charges up front, before you start trying on gowns. Yes there are some "legitimate" extra charges—fees for larger sizes, rush delivery, etc. (more on these later). But be careful that your local bridal retailer doesn't try to sneak in some bogus fees on to the final bill.

3 The Big Fuss. No matter what gowns you try on, the salesperson that helps you will invariably gush and say something like "That dress is sooooo beautiful!" Sometimes I wonder if I tried on a gown made out of potato sacks, the salesperson would say something like "Wow! That natural look! It's so you!"

As you might have guessed, most salespeople at bridal shops work on commission. Hence, it's to their advantage to get you to buy any gown, preferably an expensive one. The pressure to buy can get even more intense at designer "trunk shows" (see the box below for more details).

Some salespeople go overboard, taking advantage of brides-to-be by playing on their emotions. For example, at one store we visited, the salespeople couldn't stop complimenting how wonderful one particularly expensive designer gown looked on me. One salesperson came up to me and asked if she could take my picture for "an album of all their brides." After the picture, the salespeople put the camera down and helped me back in the dressing room. That's when Alan looked at the camera and noticed that it didn't have any film! (Yes, this was in the days before digital cameras). Later we visited the same store again and saw no picture album. The whole schtick was a clever ploy to convince me to buy that dress. A word to the wise: don't get caught up in all the false flattery that will be heaped on you by the bridal shop.

In this section, we should also point out a darker side of the "big fuss"—shops that try to pressure brides into thinking their "dream dress" will be GONE if they don't order RIGHT NOW! Listen to what one bridal shop said about this, in a post we intercepted off a retailer-only chat board: "I have been telling my brides when they find their dream dress to buy it now. They won't find anything they like better and will just keep second-guessing themselves. If they wait to order, the dress just might not be available. Create urgency and doubt.... if you wait . . . you may not get your dream gown. Tell them stories of disappointed brides who waited. Ask for the sale . . . and pray!"

Brides have told us they have been pressured to buy their gown TODAY! Or else the gown will be discontinued and gone FOREVER! Or else the special MONSTER sale discount we offer you today will be history! In some cases, shops request a "small deposit" to hold the gown—and retailers promise such deposits are refundable if you change your mind. The sleaziest shops then change *their* minds and try to keep the deposit if brides back out of the deal.

The bottom line: yes, dresses DO get discontinued. But not overnight—no dress deal is so good you can't even sleep on it (or take a day or two to compare prices online). Don't wait forever (several weeks or months is courting disaster), but don't be pressured into making a snap decision either. Any dress deal you can't sleep on is no deal at all.

To avoid pressure from shops, bring ONE trusted friend or relative with you whose opinion you value—this ensures a more objective critique. Another tip: consider leaving your wallet at home. That way you're not tempted to rush into a dress decision (and non-refundable deposit) in the heat of the moment.

Price Comparison

We found wide differences in prices when shopping for bridal accessories in stores and online.

	Shoes	Veil	Purses	Gloves	Slips	Bras
Davids*	$55	89-189	20-45	15-25	37-55	35-50
'Net**	32	60-80	25-35	20	40-55	35
Retail	85	150-250	60	35-55	70	55

Notes:
Shoe prices are for a satin pump with a 1 3/4" inch heel.
Veil price is for a headpiece and veil.
David's also carries tiaras at $180-250

*David's is a chain of bridal superstores reviewed later in this chapter.
**The following Internet sources were used for price selections.
Shoes: DyeableShoesOnline.com
Headpieces: RomanticHeadlines.com
Gloves: BridalGloves.com
Slips: Trousseaux.com
Bras: Barenecessities.com

4 False Discounts. In what is a patently illegal practice, many shops mark their gowns over suggested retail and then offer you a "discount." Gee, thanks! For example, we visited one shop that was offering a 10% discount off all special-order gowns. One gown we saw had a price tag of $1100—we later learned the suggested retail for the gown was just $1000. Their big 10% discount knocked $110 off the gown, bringing the price down to $990. The real discount was just $10 off the real retail price—a puny 1%.

Solution: Find the actual retail price for your dress. Our dress web site (BridalGown.com) includes a free service called BridalQuote—you tell us which gown(s) you are interested in and we email that request to several reputable gown discounters. You can also get a price quote from any of the gown discounters reviewed later in this chapter. Most are happy to tell you the true retail price along with their discount quote.

5 Killer Mark-ups. The profit for bridal shops doesn't stop at the fat mark-up they charge on gowns. Alterations are also a big profit center, averaging $50 to $300 per gown. Euphemistically called "custom fitting," alterations to make the gown fit perfectly add insult to injury when it comes to your gown budget.

Accessories are another big profit area. Shops sell everything from bras, shoes and slips to ring pillows, garter belts, and champagne glasses at steep mark-ups. Veils and headpieces are extraordinarily expensive—some top $200 or $300 for a simple fabric-covered comb and spritz of tulle. Shops regularly take a headpiece/veil that costs $39 wholesale and mark it up to $149—then they might offer a 10% discount if you buy during today's special sale. See the chart on the previous page for comparisons of accessory costs between the full price retailers, discount Internet sources and David's, a national chain of bridal dress superstores.

One ominous trend when it comes to bridal mark-ups: in the past couple of years, more and more bridal retailers are carrying non-advertised or exclusive gowns. These are stealth gowns—you won't see them online (even at the designer's site) or in magazines. Some of these dresses are knock-offs imported directly from China from no-name gown makers; others are part of established designer's "non-advertised" lines.

The problem? These non-advertised and no-name gowns are often sold at three to six times their wholesale cost! That's right, some retailers are taking a $300 no-ad dress and selling it for $1800! Since the dress isn't advertised or online, it is much harder for consumers to price shop . . .and that suits the retailer just fine!

Solution: Just because a dress is un-advertised or part of a store's "exclusive" collection does NOT mean you can't find it elsewhere. You just have to do more detective work.

One key fact to remember: MANY similar dresses are sold by a plethora of designers. Once Maggie Sottero comes out with a hot style, you'll suddenly see it appear as a knock-off from David's. And then DaVinci copies David's knock-off. And if it truly becomes a hot seller, six more designers will come out with their version. Because almost all bridal gowns are made in China, often the very same plant churns out these dresses—they just slap different labels on them! Makes you wonder, eh?

As for accessories and alterations, remember that stores with WEDDING in their name aren't the only places to find these products and services. Those same white dress shoes can be found at an outlet store for 50% less. As we'll discuss later, craft stores carry affordable bridal accessories at prices way below those charged by bridal retailers.

6 Elusive Exclusives. Some bridal designers occasionally give one shop in a city an "exclusive" over certain dresses. These dresses are termed "confined," and you can't find them anywhere else in town. Or can you? Many bridal shops skirt these exclusive rules by a process called "transshipping."

We visited several shops that told us they could order *any* gown we want, even if they don't carry it in their store. How do they do this? Transshipping—a bridal shop that does NOT carry a designer line will turn to another retailer who does to place the order.

Is transshipping illegal? No, there is no law that forbids this practice. However, bridal designers HATE transshipping (which lets retailers skirt their minimum stock requirements) and a few force their dealers to sign agreements saying they will not transship. These agreements are then widely ignored by retailers.

Why does transshipping happen to begin with? Most bridal shops are small in scale and can only stock ten to 12 lines of bridal apparel. But there are over 200 apparel designers out there, and odds are a customer may want a dress they don't carry. Instead of losing the sale, the shop places the order through back-door channels (typically, a friend who owns a bridal shop that does carry the line). By the way, shops often add a small mark-up for the trouble of ordering a dress from another shop.

By limiting the distribution of certain dresses (or entire lines), designers hope to stop the discounting of their gowns. However, designers also need to sell dresses to make a living—and restricting the sale of a dress design to one shop in a huge city doesn't make financial sense.

In fact, that's why we've noticed many designers talk out of both sides of their mouths when it comes to this issue. While they rail against the evils of transshipping and discounting (keeping their retailers happy), the apparel designers then quietly sell to known transshippers. Others turn a blind eye to discounting since, of course, they end up selling more dresses (and making more profit).

The latest twist to this debate involves the Internet. Designers once could control their distribution by just selling to a few small shops, which sold gowns in their local markets. Yet that all has gone out the window with the web—now, shops can market their goods worldwide, if they wish.

To stop this, some designers have issued "no 'net" policies, forbidding their dealers from selling online. Among the biggest designers to do this are Mon Cheri and Alfred Angelo. Of course, manufacturers once again cheat on this—many (including Angelo) quietly sell to dot-coms while officially banning the process. Crazy, eh?

What does this mean for you the consumer? Be careful of bridal shops or web sites that promise they can get in "any dress you want." Call the designer to see if the shop/site is an authorized dealer. Check with past client references and the Better Business Bureau to make sure the shop has fulfilled its previous promises. The bottom line: that "exclusive" dress may not be that exclusive. Don't be fooled into thinking it can't be found from another source.

7 Service? What service? The debate over the web versus Main Street usually breaks down to one central point: do you want the absolute rock-bottom lowest price? Or are you willing to pay a bit more to get service from a locally-owned business?

The usual implication here is the local merchant has a large staff standing at the door, waiting to greet you and lavish attention on you, as they search to find the "perfect gown" in your budget range. Or at least that's the way bridal magazines or the Knot make it sound.

Fast forward to reality: service even at "full service" bridal shops can often be, well, lacking. As one bride wrote in a blog "Are these folks who write for bridal magazines on crack or am I living in the wrong city? I've

Real Wedding Tip

Where's your mother?

A bride in Chicago wrote about the way she was treated at local bridal shops:

"Having been through this quest for a gown over the past month, I am completely amazed and shocked at the bridal industry and some of the tactics I experienced. I am a 34-year-old professional and I was often treated like a child. One shop asked me where my mother was and why she didn't come with me to pick out my dress. Frankly, my mother hasn't picked out my clothes for me since I was 7."

Picture this: Shops Ban Cameras

In the cat and mouse game between discounters and full-price retailers, nothing gets bridal shops' blood boiling more than brides who bring cameras dress shopping. Stores think camera-wielding brides are trying get a snap shot of a gown in order to price-shop it online or have a seamstress copy it. As a result, most shops ban cameras. And yes, shops are on the lookout for consumers wielding cell phone cameras as well. Of course, after you put down a non-refundable deposit, you can snap as many pictures of your dress as you want!

been to SEVERAL bridal salons and literally at each one, some salesperson doesn't even ask my name, takes me to a room, brings in 3-4 winter gowns (for an outdoor July wedding) and leaves me alone to find my way into the big dress by myself (isn't it like crawling head first into a white sleeping bag?) Then the salesperson stops by 40 minutes later to see which one I want to buy. Meanwhile, I'm clipping this damn dress myself to keep it from falling off of me and talking to myself in the fitting room to keep myself from dying of boredom. What's the deal?"

The sad truth: just like many other retail industries today, service at bridal shops has sunk to new lows. We find this especially ironic in light of the ongoing debate about national chains and buying online. Retailers can't expect brides to pay full price when they get far less than full service; no wonder many brides are abandoning independent retailers to order online or even (gasp) shop chains like David's.

Yes, not all retailers have let service slip. Yet, shops that truly service the bride seem to be more the exception these days than the rule.

Biggest Myths about Bridal Gowns

Myth #1 *"Considering how expensive those designer bridal gowns are, I assume they are being hand-crafted by skilled seamstresses."*

Wrong. We spoke to a bridal apparel industry veteran who painted a very unflattering picture of how most bridal gowns are manufactured. Most "designer" gowns advertised in US and Canadian bridal magazines are made overseas in factories in China or other Asian countries, mass-produced in batches and machine stitched or beaded. Here are the details:

First, the bridal manufacturers wait until they receive a certain number of orders for each size (that's why it takes so long to get a gown). Let's say they wait for ten orders of size 8 gowns in a particular style. When the orders come in, they stack 10 layers of fabric on a conveyer belt, which are then cut by a laser. Later, machines sew the seams together. Even the lace added to the dress may have been machine-beaded at another location. Basically, that's why so many gowns have "quality issues," with unfinished seams, no lining and shoddy construction. The manufacturing process has more to do with factory assembly lines than human beings lovingly hand-sewing gowns. As a result, gowns are not custom-made to your measurements but rather are rough approximations that often require additional alterations (read: more money).

And China isn't the only place churning out weddings gowns on the cheap. Many bridal dress manufacturers roam the globe searching for cheap labor. The goal is to produce the dress at the lowest cost, not necessarily the highest quality. Many bridal gowns imported into the U.S. from Central America or Southeast Asia still suffer from quality problems that often have to be fixed by bridal retailers.

Yes, there are a handful of bridal gown makers that still hand-sew gowns here in the US, Canada or Europe, although that number seems to be shrinking every year. Unfortunately, you pay through the nose for such dresses—most are $2000 or more.

Are dresses made in the U.S. or Europe automatically better quality than those imported from China? Ten years ago, we might have said yes. But today, improved technology and Chinese production skills have closed the quality gap. Differences between "domestic" and "imported" gowns may have to do more with materials than craftsmanship. The few remaining "couture" designers in the U.S. or Europe are likely to use fine silk fabrics and fancy embellishments on their $4000 gowns. Imported gowns from China are most likely polyester gowns sold for a price (most are $400 to $800).

Myth #2 *"I saw a dress in a bridal store that was made of Italian satin. Is that a luxury fabric from Europe?"*

Actually, no. More than likely it's a synthetic fabric made in Asia. Of course, Italian satin sounds more romantic than, say, Filipino Polyester. But that's what it is—and that points up a common marketing trick in the bridal industry. In their effort to make bridal gowns at affordable price points (under $500), manufacturers have to use synthetic fabrics instead of silk. But, most makers know that the words "polyester" or "acetate" don't get brides hearts racing. So, instead they come up with bogus names like Italian satin, Regal satin, or (our favorite) Silky Satin. Are they made of silk? Don't bet on it. If the tag doesn't say 100% silk, it isn't.

Myth #3 *"Every bride I see pictured in bridal magazines looks like an overstuffed cream puff. Other dresses look like chandeliers on a bad acid trip. Is this all there is?"*

Getting married does not require you to lose all your fashion sense. Too often, the bridal apparel industry stereotypes all brides to fit certain molds. You must look like Cinderella or, if you're daring, perhaps Snow White. Well, we say, no Virginia, you don't have to look like TRADITIONAL BRIDE on your wedding day if that's not your style. Consider some snazzy alternatives. Designers like Maggie Sottero (call 801-255-3870 for a dealer near you) have high-quality fabrics and sophisticated silhouettes with minimal beading or lace. Most of Sottero's dresses are in the $500 to $1000 range (although a few Sottero couture gowns sell for as much as $2000). J. Crew's new wedding collection features *silk* bridal gowns for as little as $285.\

MYTH #4 *"I am considering ordering my dress from a mail-order discounter or online. Bridal shops warn me if something goes wrong with the dress, the discounters won't fix the problem."*

Here's a common scare tactic full-price retailers use to frighten brides. Retailers say: "If you order online and a problem happens with your order, you are left high and dry." Nothing could be further from the truth. We found many reputable discounters that have excellent customer service reputations and stand behind what they sell. And we've found the best gown web sites will work hard to correct any problem with a dress order. We'll review the best discounters later in this chapter in the "Best Buy" section.

MYTH #5 *"I know brides must always wear white but I've tried on several white gowns and they make me look like death warmed over. My mom says I have no other choice—it's white or nothing."*

Tell your mom you do have a choice. Almost all gowns also come in ivory (although this shade varies from designer to designer). But that's not all the color possibilities. Several gowns now are available in subtle blush colors like platinum (grey), rum pink and "café" (a darker ivory).

Helpful Hints

1 Shopping for a gown is an exhausting process. Take frequent breaks and don't try to squeeze too many shop visits into one day. Limit yourself to two to three stores, leaving time to think about which gown you like most.

2 Sometimes the first dress you try on is the one you buy. The number of brides we've met who buy the first gown they tried on always surprises us. Perhaps the first impression you get from that first gown is the one that most sticks in your mind. Warning: bridal retailers are wise to this phenomenon and, hence, bring out their most expensive gown for you to try on first.

3 Pick your price range carefully. And insist that the bridal shop stay within it. Beware that some bridal retailers will try to "up sell" you—if you tell them you only want to spend $800 or less, they bring out that "extra special" dress that's $1180 . . . hoping you'll fall in love with it anyway. For that reason, if the shop asks your budget, you might want to low-ball the figure somewhat.

4 Practice the bustle. Once the wedding is over, you'd want to have your train bustled for the reception. This is done by hooking the train on to a series of buttons sewn at the back of the gown. A word to the wise: make sure you have someone in your bridal party who knows how to do this, so you aren't carrying around that heavy train all evening!

5 Avoid a strapless disaster. Yes, it is the hip style now—but consider these tips to avoid an, ahem, problem with a strapless bridal gown. Look for a dress with detachable halter "strings" to wear while dancing. Get the best strapless bra you can afford—make sure it is tight! For women with small busts, consider a silicone stick-on bra to help fill out the gown. Pageant adhesive (brand name It Stays, sold on Amazon.com) is also a good idea. And consider how a gown is constructed—the best strapless gowns have stitched-in boning that helps prevent slipping.

Pitfalls to Avoid

PITFALL #1: THE GREAT DISAPPEARING BRIDAL SHOP!

"I ordered my gown from a reputable shop that had been in business for years. Imagine my surprise when I turned on the local news and found the shop has gone bankrupt! And now, I have no gown."

Yes, this DOES happen. We have documented numerous cases of bridal shops that have gone belly-up, taking deposits from brides and delivering nothing but empty promises. A recent example: a large chain of 20 bridal stores in Pennsylvania closed suddenly, sending hundreds of brides scrambling to recover their deposits and dresses.

And it isn't just big cities—we've received emails from readers who report shops that have closed in towns big AND small, in every corner of the US and Canada. Why does this happen? In recent years, bridal retailers have been besieged by new competition, from chains like David's to web sites that discount gowns. This has forced some weak bridal retailers out of business and into bankruptcy court.

Big deal, right? Retailers come and go every day, you say. Yes, they do—but when bridal shops fail, it often leads to near riots. As you know, all bridal retailers take HUGE deposits from consumers for "special order" gowns. If a shop fails, all that money goes POOF! The shop suddenly closes (or, more accurately, their landlord pad-locks its doors), leaving brides without deposits or gowns. Word of this closing usually gets out to local area brides, who storm the store trying to get their merchandise. Police have been called to quell rioting brides in several cities who have actually attacked closed bridal stores (and their employees). It isn't a pretty sight.

So what can you do to protect yourself? Is there a way to pick a shop that won't disappear? As you can guess, it is hard to predict WHICH bridal retailers might fail next, since these small mom-and-pop shops are privately run operations. You can't avoid this problem by picking long-time retailers; we've seen shops tank that have been around for 50 years. And don't expect much help from bridal gown manufacturers—most would prefer NOT to talk about this problem, even if they have put a retailer on credit hold or will only ship them on a COD basis (obvious tell-tale signs a retailer is in trouble).

The best protection: put that deposit for your gown (or any merchandise) on a credit card. As you read earlier, this is your best defense against take-your-money-and-run retailers. If you leave plenty of time before your wedding when ordering a gown (at least six months), you might be able to reorder the dress through another shop.

What if you order from a shop that disappears? Check the box on the next page for advice on what to do if the shop you ordered a gown from suddenly vaporizes.

PITFALL #2 BAIT AND SWITCH WITH ADVERTISED GOWNS.

"I fell in love with this dress in a bridal magazine. I called the local shop listed in the ad—they told me they didn't have that design, but had others 'just like it.' This is so frustrating. . . is this a scam or what?"

Well, it certainly isn't ethical. Believe it or not, dress designers do not always require their dealers to carry the advertised gown—even if the store is listed in the ad! While the shop may have other gowns by the same designer, the dress you fell in love with is sometimes nowhere to be found. Usually the shop comes up with some excuse (our favorite is "the designer decided not to cut that sample yet") and then subtly tries to "switch" you to a "similar design we have in stock."

Why do shops do this? More profit. Shops lure brides into their store with advertised gowns and then try to switch them to unadvertised or private label dresses. These gowns are sold at bigger mark-ups (since, theoretically, they can't be price shopped, right?). In recent years, this trend has accelerated—many bridal shops are now stocking large quantities of "unadvertised" gowns and a small smattering of advertised dresses just to get consumers in the door.

And here's the latest twist: big bridal gown designers have jumped on the "unadvertised" bandwagon. How? Many designers now have *two* lines of bridal gowns—one that they advertise in magazines and feature on their web site. And a second line of "stealth" dresses that doesn't appear online on their own web site, in catalogs or magazines. These dresses are pitched as the perfect way for retailers to boost margins.

Bridal 911: What happens if your bridal shop disappears?

It is the ultimate dress nightmare: you flip on the evening news and the top story is about a bridal shop that has gone bankrupt, leaving an angry mob of jilted brides sans dresses. Then you realize that's your shop.

While no one has exact figures on how many bridal shops go out of business each year, the anecdotal evidence suggests the number is staggering. The simple fact is that the bridal business is brutal and the turnover rate among shops is high.

Among the more egregious examples: one bridal shop owner in Michigan actually drew a jail sentence when a court determined he and his wife bilked customers out of tens of thousands of dollars (this is a rarity—most bankrupt bridal retailers are never prosecuted for stealing their customers' deposits).

So, what can you do? Here are some tips if you've discovered your trusted bridal dress shop has gone Chapter 11:

♥ **Avoid the surprise.** If you can, keep tabs on the shop to make sure it is still in business. Drive by once a month or give them a call to make sure they're still breathing on the other end of the line. While most shops won't announce that they plan to close forever next Tuesday, we have heard of cases where employees have tipped off brides to an impending disaster.

♥ **Time is of the essence.** If there is a problem, you'll need to take immediate steps to protect your deposit and get your dress.

♥ **Beware of confusing press accounts.** Some retailers have put out conflicting statements to the media when they have financial problems. At the outset, they usually promise that everyone is going to get their gowns—despite the fact that their landlord has pad-locked their doors and the electric company has cut off the power for non-payment. Other shops have posted signs on locked doors announcing "vacations" or "remodeling" . . . during their busiest season—yeah, right. Don't get suck-

While we understand why retailers and manufacturers would like to boost their profit margins in a competitive marketplace, resorting to bait and switch tactics to accomplish this is wrong. And we've heard rather blatant stories from brides who allege stores intentionally mislead them when they call regarding an advertised style. "Sure that gown is in stock," says a clerk over the phone. Once you arrive, they announce that the sample "was just sold yesterday. Would you like to see other dresses?"

ered by false hopes—most bridal shops that have financial problems don't rescue themselves. They usually just go bankrupt and close forever.

♥ **Draw up a contingency plan.** If there is time before your wedding (say, at least four months), you may be able to order another gown. If there isn't time, scout out the alternatives: you can buy a consignment gown, have a sample altered to fit, or hit the off-the-rack warehouses mentioned earlier in this book. The best advice is to have a "plan B."

♥ **Contact your credit card company immediately.** You did put that dress deposit on a credit card, right? Well, if you did, it is time to test that federal law that protects credit card purchases. Most banks and credit card issuers will request a written account of what's happened with your dress deposit. Since there may be a time limit on this process, you should do this as soon as possible.

♥ **What about the designer?** Can't you just call up the designer and have them ship your special-order dress to another shop? Fat chance. The sad fact is that most designers turn a deaf ear to brides. That's what's happened over and over again in the past few years when bridal bankruptcies rolled over the industry. Frantic brides who called the designers about their orders were simply referred to other retail stores . . . who were happy to sell the bride another gown. At full retail. While that produces nice profits, it makes for lousy consumer relations. Yes, there are exceptions to this rule, the bridal industry should be ashamed of itself. The designers set up this crazy special-order system to begin with. They buy expensive ads to convince brides to patronize their "authorized dealers." Then when those shops fail, the bridal designers simply shrug their shoulders and say "Whoops! It's not our problem." And then the bridal industry wonders why brides are running for the exits, abandoning the special-order process for bridal gowns? Here's our solution: designers should set up a toll-free hotline or web site when a shop fails. That number should be given out to local media, so brides know where to turn. The designers could verify the orders and then ship the gowns directly to consumers. We're not holding our breath waiting for that to happen though!

PITFALL #3 INFLATING THE ALTERATIONS BILL.

"I wear a size 6 in street clothes and I was rather surprised when the saleswoman at the bridal shop told me I needed to order a size 10. In fact, the sample gown was a 10 and it really didn't fit. What size should I order?"

First, understand that bridal sizes do not correspond to real-world sizes. Clothes sold in department stores generally conform to an industry-wide sizing chart. Hence, a dress that's a size four in Macy's is roughly the same dimensions as a size four at Bloomingdales. Not so in the bridal world. As amazingly stupid as it sounds, EVERY bridal gown manufacturer uses its own size chart, which can greatly vary from designer to designer. Adding to the confusion: bridal gown sizes run small compared to ready-to-wear. If you wear a size 8 dress, you might be a 10 or 12 in bridal apparel. (Brides LOVE to hear that!).

Given the uncertainty surrounding wedding dress sizing, some dishonest bridal shops may recommend sizes that they know are too large for the bride. Then, when the dress comes in, guess what? It needs expensive alterations! Here are our tips to make sure you get the correct size bridal gown:

♥ **Don't pay attention to the sample gown.** Most sample gowns are tried on so many times that they stretch—what once was a 10 may now be a 12 or even a 14! Bridal gown manufacturers even warn their own dealers not to rely on sample gowns when sizing a bride!

♥ **Instead, get measured with a vinyl tape measure.** Needed measurements include bust, waist, hips, and from the base of the throat to the hemline (called "hollow to hem"). Don't let the bridal shop use a cloth measuring tape, since it can stretch over time and give inaccurate measurements.

What if you are measuring yourself for a gown you plan to order online? Keep in mind these measurement guidelines we found at the web site BridesandProm.com:

Bust/Chest: Lift your arms up your sides and measure around your body, crossing over the fullest part of your chest. When measuring your self, wear only a bra, and make sure not to make tight measurements.

Waist: Measure at your waistline. Keep a finger between your body and the measuring tape for an accurate fit.

Hip: Stand with your heels together and measure the fullest part of your hip.

♥ **Ask to personally see the manufacturer's sizing chart.** Each manufacturer has its own sizing chart; a copy is sent to each of their retail dealers. Why is this important?

Let's show you how nutty the sizing process is for bridal gowns. Consider a bride with the measurements of 36, 26, 38 (bust, waist, hips). This woman would wear a size 8 in a European designer, size 10 in a Sweetheart and a size 12 in a Demetrios/Ilissa. In fact, we analyzed the size charts of the top 35 bridal manufacturers and found the above bride would be a size 8 in 3% of the designers' gowns, a size 10 in 34%, a size 12 in 45% and even a size 14 in 18% of the designers. Yes, this very same woman could wear a size 8 OR a size 14, depending on the gown's maker.

The take home message: check that size chart before ordering. Retailers typically have these charts in their stores; web sites like RKBridal.com (click on size charts) have detailed charts for quite a few major gown makers online.

♥ **Given your measurements, pick a size that closely matches your largest measurement.** Why? That's because it's always easier to make a bridal gown smaller; expanding a bridal gown is much more difficult. Make sure the size you pick is clearly marked on the sales receipt.

♥ **Don't get too caught up in the size number.** Some brides we interviewed get personally insulted when the bridal shop tells them they need X size, which is several numbers larger than their street clothes' size. Our advice: don't fixate on that number. Remember, it's the bridal designers who are insane, not you.

To sum up, in our research we discovered that brides encounter problems in this area when they let the shop pick the size for them. Instead of measuring you, some salespeople just guess what your size is. Then the dress comes in and guess what? It needs to be chopped down, say, from a size 14 to a 10. And guess who pays the $200 or $300 alterations bill?

In retailers' defense, however, we should note that some bridal manufacturers are notorious for shipping gowns that are incorrectly sized (that is, too big or small given their own size charts). Mori Lee and Maggie Sottero are two big offenders in this category, but it happens with other designers as well.

So, if your gown doesn't fit, is this intentional fraud to profit on alterations or an "honest" mistake made by unskilled salespeople—or a manufacturer goof? It's hard to say. The bottom line: be careful. If you accept the shop's sizing "advice," write on the receipt that "Shop Recommends Size." If the dress comes in way too big or too small, you have more leverage in negotiating a solution.

PITFALL #4 MANUFACTURER GOOFS ON SIZING.

"I ordered a bridal gown in a size 12. When it came in, it was way too big! Even though it had a size 12 tag in it, the dress was nowhere near those measurements. The shop owner just shrugged her shoulders and told us their seamstress could fix the problem . . . for a hefty charge. What should I do?"

Sizing goofs are a common problem in the bridal biz; we've seen numerous cases of gowns that came in too big or too small even though the tag indicates a "correct" size. In our opinion, the manufacturer is fully responsible for shipping the correct size (that is, a dress whose dimensions match the manufacturer's size chart for the ordered size). If the order is incorrect, the manufacturer should fix it free of charge. If there is not enough time before the wedding to send the dress back, we believe the manufacturer should pay the shop to alter the gown to the correct size. The bride is definitely not at fault and should never be charged.

In order to protect yourself from this pitfall, make sure all ordered bridal merchandise is inspected and measured when it comes in BEFORE you make a final payment. Try on the gown or use a tape measure to confirm that a garment's dimensions match what was ordered. If you leave the bridal shop without trying your dress on first to check size and quality, you may have little or no recourse later if you discover a defect.

Compounding this rip-off are some shops that refuse to fix defective merchandise. Whether it's the wrong size or botched lace detailing, we've encountered some merchants who refuse to make good. Some claim "there's not enough time before the wedding to send the dress back." We say that's tough—bridal retailers have a clear responsibility to deliver the right merchandise in the correct size within the time frame promised. The best bridal shops will go to bat for their customers, insisting manufacturers "rush cut" a new gown to replace defective merchandise.

How many dresses come in flawed? One major retailer who sells 10,000 bridal gowns a year told us that, shockingly, two out of every three dresses comes in with a flaw. In about half of those cases, the problem is minor and can be easily fixed. However, the other half include such serious problems as the wrong size or poor workmanship. These must be sent back to the manufacturer to correct.

PITFALL #5 THE BIG SWITCHEROO.

"My bridal gown came in yesterday and boy was I surprised! The lace and fabric looked nothing like the sample gown I tried on or even the magazine picture. What recourse do I have?"

"The bridal shop told me my gown would take 14 weeks to get in. However, after just three weeks, the shop called to say the dress is here! It looks suspiciously like the used sample I tried on. I ordered a brand new, full price designer gown. I got a stained dress with missing beading that had been dry-cleaned and a size too small!"

This scam often appears in two flavors: the lace/fabric switcheroo and the "sample gown shell game." Here's a look at each.

First, you must realize that many manufacturers reserve the right to change the lace, fabric and trim on any bridal gown. We've seen several cases where a manufacturer substituted a cheaper lace when they ran out of the more expensive kind. A recent example that crossed our desk involved a designer who omitted the beading on a dress—without telling the store or customer first.

If you're unhappy with the substitutions, ask the bridal shop to go to bat for you. Reputable bridal shops may be able to negotiate a solution (free alterations, a partial refund, etc.) with the manufacturer. If time permits, the gown may be sent back to the manufacturer to make it correct. (Note: many manufacturers can ship a correct dress overnight—don't let the shop bully you into thinking you don't have enough time).

We urge all bridal manufacturers to deliver what they promise. If they can't, the bride should be notified and given the opportunity to cancel the order. Substituting lace, fabric or detailing is a deceptive practice and should be stopped.

What about the "sample gown shell game"? This is when a store promises to order a brand new gown, but instead tries to pawn off the used sample dress you originally tried on. The bottom line: you are duped into paying full price for a used gown—clearly an unlawful deceptive trade practice. We've heard reports that this insidious scam is rampant at some shops in Chicago and Detroit, though it can happen anywhere.

Here are some rather ingenious ways to spot this rip-off, as submitted by our readers. First, take a needle and red thread with you to the bridal shop. While you're in the dressing room, sew this thread inside the sample dress in an inconspicuous location. If the shop tries the scam, you can spot the used "sample" by the thread.

Another protection is to take a picture of the gown. But most shops don't allow pictures, you say? Sneak a small camera in your purse or use a cell phone camera and snap a few pictures in the dressing room, after the salesperson leaves. The pictures will help you remember all the details and styling of the sample dress—just in case the shop tries to substitute that used sample or a different gown altogether. One bridal shop employee tipped us off to this scam, saying they often substituted cheaper dresses on brides since they could never remember what they ordered several months ago!

Another tip: once you place a gown order, ask for a catalog picture of your dress. Many (but not all) designers produce catalogs of their gowns and authorized retailers should have these pictures at their fingertips.

A side bar to this issue: sometimes a dress really does come in early. While you might be suspicious that a shop is trying to pull a "sample shell game" on you, there are cases when special order dresses arrive with lightening quickness. Why? Some bridal manufacturers keep "hanging stock" of popular styles in common sizes. These can be quickly shipped to stores, despite stated 12-week order times. Unfortunately, shops don't know what stock a manufacturer has on hand, so it's a crapshoot when you order a dress as to exactly when it will arrive.

PITFALL #6 WHOOPS! WE FORGOT TO PLACE THE ORDER!

"I ordered a gown from a bridal shop five months ago. Now the dress is overdue. I've been calling the shop for the last several weeks to find out when it will be in. Finally, someone at the shop admitted they forgot to place my order! I couldn't believe it! And now they won't give me a refund, instead suggesting I buy a gown out of their stock. What should I do?"

Contact your attorney. When a shop fails to place an order, they are breaking a valid contract and should give you a refund. Instead, some dishonest shops will give you a pitch to buy a sample gown off the rack—that is totally unacceptable. Does this happen every day? Fortunately, no. Yet, we've received enough emails about this problem to warrant this discussion.

Protect yourself by dealing with a reputable shop (find one using the sources we list earlier in this chapter). When you place an order, get a promised delivery date. A few weeks after the purchase, call the bridal shop to confirm the shipping date (they receive this from the manufacturer). The more communication you have with your shop the more likely you will get your gown.

PITFALL #7 BOTCHED ALTERATIONS.

"My bridal gown came in three weeks ago and it was beautiful! However, when I picked it up after alterations, I couldn't believe my eyes! That same gown was a disaster—the seamstress botched the simple hem and bustle! How could I have prevented this?"

Bridal shops love to pitch their "expert alterations" service to brides as the only alternative for their gowns. In reality, their "expert seamstress" is sometimes a person they hired last week for $6 per hour who has only altered her daughter's prom gown. No wonder this is one of the biggest problem areas consumers have with bridal shops.

To be fair, bridal gowns aren't the easiest garments to alter. The fabric is slippery and intricately beaded gowns can make even the most simple alterations challenging. Some bridal shops, however, invite consumer complaints by hiring inexperienced seamstresses who then botch the alterations. This is especially problematic around prom season when overwhelmed bridal shops bring in "stringers" to help complete alterations. (One tip: insist the head seamstress do your dress).

Another troubling trend: bridal retailers that "sub" out alterations to another company and then disavow any responsibility if there is a problem. We estimate one-third to one-half of all bridal retailers sub-contract their alterations. How does this work? When you ask the shop for alterations, they refer you to another company that might be right next door. Or they might have an independent seamstress come visit the shop to do fittings twice a week.

All this works fine when things go right. If a problem happens, however, brides tell us bridal retailers suddenly wave open palms and claim they have no control over or responsibility for the seamstress—despite the fact they referred her and perhaps even let her use their shop for fittings.

In general, you can prevent this problem by asking to meet the seamstress before you do the alterations. (If the shop subs out alterations, ask who is responsible if a problem develops). Ask the seamstress about her experience with bridal gowns. Ask to see the work area. If it looks like a sweatshop or if you sense the seamstress is unqualified, get the gown altered somewhere else. Many communities have "free-lance" seamstresses who do excellent work at much more affordable rates.

Pitfall #8 Sample gowns may not be bargains.

"I don't have enough time to order a gown before my wedding. I was thinking of buying a sample gown. What should I watch out for?"

Sample gowns may be a terrific buy or a terrible nightmare. As we explained earlier in this chapter, sample gowns (just like demonstrator models) are cleared out periodically to make room for new styles. Many are marked 20% to 50% (or more) off the retail price. The big pitfall here: most sample gowns are in less than great shape. That's because most have been tried on dozens (if not hundreds) of times by different shoppers. Sample gowns may be dirty, stained (especially from makeup) and beaten up. We've seen several that have beads missing and lace that is falling off. Furthermore, the gowns are stretched out and often in no way resemble their original size.

Of course, the condition of sample gowns varies greatly from store to store—some simply take better care of their merchandise. And the condition of the sample will determine its price. Nearly new sample gowns with little damage may only be discounted by 20% or less.

If you go this route, pour over the dress with a fine-tooth comb. If the shop agrees to clean the gown, get a written guarantee that the purchase is contingent on your approval of the gown after the cleaning. Cleaning a bridal gown is tricky since some dry-cleaning chemicals can damage a dress. An inexperienced cleaner can destroy a bridal gown.

Another tip: don't forget to factor in repairs to your budget. Extensive cleaning and alterations can make a sample gown bargain no deal at all.

PITFALL #9 SALON-STYLE SHOPS.

"I went to a salon where they kept all the gowns in the back. They told me they'd bring out the gowns they thought I would like. Is this kosher?"

We're not big fans of bridal shops that operate "salon-style." In most cases, these shops keep all their gowns out of sight and then ask you for your likes, dislikes, and price ranges. Unless you know exactly what you want, salons can be trying. First of all, the salesperson brings out what *she* thinks you want to see. We've been to several of these salons and they've yet to figure out what I want. Instead, they tend to bring out what they want to sell (that is, an expensively-priced gown). We suggest you shop at stores that allow you to see the merchandise. While you can't get a complete picture of what a gown looks like hanging on a hanger, you can tell which detailing (necklines, bodices, beading) you like and have a better feel for prices.

PITFALL #10 HOTEL SALES, GOWN COUNTERFEITERS, OBSCURE BRAND NAMES.

"I saw an ad in our paper for a big sale of bridal gowns at a local hotel. They offered large discounts and unbelievable prices. Is this for real?"

Yes, most of these "one day only" sales offer legitimate deals. Where do they get the gowns? Liquidators who are looking to dump merchandise from bankrupt bridal stores run most sales. Of course, these deals are "as is" and "cash and carry"–don't expect any special services like cleaning or alterations. There are typically no refunds in case you get the gown home and decide you don't like it.

The only complaint we hear about hotel bridal gown sales are inflated claims of savings. Some liquidators mark these gowns (mostly samples) with ridiculous "suggested" retail prices–prices that were never charged to begin with. As a result, the huge promised savings is often less than it appears. And, as we mentioned earlier in this chapter, don't forget to factor in repairs, cleaning and alterations into these "deals."

Another issue we hear about: counterfeit gowns. In recent years, a large number of knockoff dresses have flooded the US and Canada. Some bridal retailers market these gowns as "designer originals." Of course, with the tags torn out, who can tell? Prevent being taken in by calling the designer to see if the store is an authorized dealer of the dresses they claim to sell.

Recently, we've noticed another interesting trend in bridal retail: the rise of obscure brand names. In order to compete with discounters and warehouse chains, some bridal retailers have stocked dresses from little-known, unadvertised designers. While this isn't a rip-off per se, we've noticed some stores have taken HUGE mark-ups on these gowns, figuring if you can't comparison shop the dress, how will you ever know if you're paying three times retail?

PITFALL #11 RIP-OFF CHARGES FOR LARGE SIZES, PETITES AND RUSH ORDERS. *"Okay, I'm not one of those anorexic models you see in the magazines. However, when I visited a bridal shop, all they had were size 10 dresses to try on! Then, they told me they charge extra for 'large sizes!' Is this salt in the wound or what?"*

Yes, the bridal industry slaps full-figure brides with a "penalty fee" that can be as much as $50 to $200 or more. But don't feel too singled out, there are also extra charges for petites. The industry claims the extra costs come from "special cuttings" and "increased fabric costs." We're skeptical.

One solution: if you're a petite, order a regular size dress and have it altered. Our sources say it just isn't worth it to shell out the extra money to get a petite.

What's most frustrating about large and petite extra fees: only bridal stores charge them. Walk into any department store or leaf through a clothing catalog and you seldom see extra charges for dresses in sizes 18 or 20. And we've never seen such charges for petites. In the few catalogs that do have up charges for "women's sizes," the extra cost is maybe $10, not the $200 you see in bridal shops.

Another rip-off: rush charges. Even if your wedding is still three months away, some designers insist on "rush fees" to get you the dress on time. However, just because the manufacturers can't figure out how to sew a gown in less than three months, doesn't mean you should pay a premium.

A solution to this pitfall: consider the alternatives (second-hand shops, eBay, off-the-rack warehouse stores) where you can quickly find a gown, without all the penalty fees. Read more about these options later in this chapter.

Finally, we'd reject any bogus fees like those discussed earlier in this chapter. No bride should have to pay extra to have her gown shipped to a bridal shop; penalty fees for not paying in full when an item is ordered should also be avoided. Remember that ALL of these fees are negotiable. Feel free to question any charge and tell the retailer if they want your business, they can remove the junk fees.

PITFALL #12 DECEPTIVE DISCONTINUATIONS.

"I saw a great gown in a bridal shop last week. Yesterday, they called me to tell me my dream dress has been discontinued, BUT if I placed my order by Friday, they could still get my gown. Is this legitimate?"

Probably not. This is a common tactic to pressure brides into quick decisions. Now while it is true that some gowns are discontinued every season, we're suspicious of shops that use this as a tactic to get you to order the gown TODAY. If you doubt a shop's veracity, call another shop that also carries that same manufacturer to confirm the gown's status.

A similar rip-off to this: shops that pressure brides to put down $100 deposits on gowns to hold "special sale prices." Brides have emailed us stories of salespeople who have promised such deposits are fully refundable—only to learn a few days later that isn't true. Remember: no gown deal is so special that you can't sleep on it. And if you want to put a deposit down, get any promises about refunds in writing.

ALSO KNOWN AS

Here's a pocket translator for all the names you'll encounter in the bridal magazines and online. As you'll note, many labels are simply sub-brands of a main designer.

NAME	WHAT IT IS	WHOM TO LOOK UP
AMALIA CARRARA	GOWN COLLECTION	SEE EVE OF MILADY
ANGEL & TRADITION	GOWN COLLECTION	SEE VENUS
AVINE PERRUCI	GOWN COLLECTION	SEE ST. PUCCHI
CHRISTINA	GOWN COLLECTION	SEE JACQUELIN
CLASSIQUE	GOWN COLLECTION	SEE MORI LEE
CRYSTAL	AD NAME	SEE IMPRESSION
DIVA	GOWN COLLECTION	SEE PALOMA BLANCA
EMANUELLE	GOWN COLLECTION	SEE EVE OF MILADY
ENCHANTMENT	GOWN COLLECTION	SEE MORI LEE
EVA FORSYTH	DESIGNER'S NAME	SEE SCAASI BRIDE
FANTASY	GOWN COLLECTION	SEE FOREVER YOURS
GINZA COLLECTION	GOWN COLLECTION	SEE PRIVATE LABEL BY G
ILISSA	COMPANY NAME	SEE DEMETRIOS/ILISSA
INNER CIRCLE	GOWN COLLECTION	SEE JIM HJELM

PITFALL #13 SHOPS THAT HOLD BACK ORDERS.

"I ordered a bridal gown that the shop said would take three months to get in. Four months later, I have no gown and just excuses from the shop. When I ask for a confirmation that they placed the order, I get stonewalled. While my wedding is still two months away, I'm worried."

And you should be! This is another common scam perpetrated by some shops. Instead of immediately placing the order with the manufacturer, they hold on to it. Why? Well, financially-strapped stores may be tempted to use your money to pay other bills—ordering the gown immediately means having to pay their supplier that much faster. How common is this problem? Even Vincent Piccione, president of Alfred Angelo (the second-largest gown maker in the US), recently acknowledged how widespread the tactic is. "A major problem that concerns us is retailers who hold on to orders. This is one practice that should be eliminated, thereby putting an end to the root cause of so many horror stories that

NAME	WHAT IT IS	WHOM TO LOOK UP
INTRIGUE	GOWN COLLECTION	SEE FOREVER YOURS
MADELINE GARDNER	DESIGNER'S NAME	SEE MORI LEE
NOW AND FOREVER	GOWN COLLECTION	SEE FOREVER YOURS
PALLAS ATHENA	GOWN COLLECTION	SEE VENUS
PRINCESS COLLECTION	AD NAME	SEE DEMETRIOS/ILISSA
PRIVATE COLLECTION	GOWN COLLECTION	SEE JIM HJELM
PRIVATE COLLECTION	GOWN COLLECTION	SEE JACQUELIN
ST. PATRICK	GOWN COLLECTION	SEE PRONOVIAS
RICCIO	GOWN COLLECTION	SEE RICHARD GLASGOW
SAISON BLANCHE	GOWN COLLECTION	SEE EDEN
SL SIGNATURE	AD NAME	SEE VICTORIA'S
SPOSABELLA	AD NAME	SEE DEMETRIOS/ILISSA
TANGO	GOWN COLLECTION	SEE MOONLIGHT
TIFFANY	GOWN COLLECTION	SEE JACQUELIN
VISIONS	GOWN COLLECTION	SEE JIM HJELM
YOUNG SOPHISTICATES	AD NAME	SEE DEMETRIOS/ILISSA

plague the industry," Piccione said in an industry trade journal.

A parallel scam is the "involuntary lay-away" rip-off. In this case, the bridal shop claims it will take much longer than reality to get in a special-order dress. Most designers fill orders within three or four months, with six being the maximum. Yet, some of our readers report shops that claim it will take *eight* or *ten* months to get in their dress. What's happening? Perhaps the shop is using your money to pay their electric bill or other expenses—and plans to order your dress a few months down the line. In a sense, this is like an "involuntary lay-away" plan, where the shop holds your money for several months longer than necessary.

How can you avoid this problem? First, put the deposit on a credit card. Second, stay on top of the situation. If your dress is due May 1, don't wait for the shop to call you to say the dress is in. Take the initiative and contact the shop to make sure the dress is on time. And don't wait until mid-June to start complaining about a late dress. Yes, it may take many angry phone calls and emails to get the dress—but don't wait until it's too late.

And what if a shop quotes an eight-month delivery time for a dress? Call around to other dealers or get online quotes to verify delivery time frames. Odds are, you can get the dress much quicker.

PITFALL #14 IT AIN'T OVER IF IT'S OVER.

"My fiancé and I fell on hard financial times and had to postpone our wedding. The problem is I had already ordered a gown. When I contacted the shop, they told me I couldn't cancel the order. Help!"

Most (if not all) bridal shops have "no refund, no cancellation" policies on special-order bridal gowns. Wedding called off? Death in the family? Your fiancé is called to active duty? It doesn't matter—you're still on the hook to buy the dress. That means the shop can also take you to court to force you to pay the balance due on the dress.

If you're merely postponing your wedding, ask the shop if you can get "store credit." At least you might be able to use this in the future, or sell the credit to a friend.

PITFALL #15 LAYAWAY SCAMS.

"I put a bridal gown on layaway at a bridal shop for a few months. After making payments, the shop called to say my dress was now discontinued! My only choice was to take the sample, which was dirty and damaged!"

Layaway sounds like a good idea—in theory. If you don't have the money to buy an item immediately, you reserve it by making monthly payments. While that might work for some items, bridal isn't one of them. Too many things can go wrong when you try to put a bridal gown on layaway—styles get discontinued, items disappear and worse. This is compounded by some unethical retailers, who may try to force you into a deal you don't want because they now have all your money. Our advice: avoid layaway. If you must put a dress on layaway, only do it for a month or so. Payments for six months or a year can open up a can of worms.

PITFALL #16 BUILDING THE TICKET

"I was scammed by a Boston bridal shop. The owner added accessory items to my ticket—even though I made it very clear that I just wanted to buy the dress. She said I had to sign the credit card slip before she would give me the itemized list. Upon reviewing the list, I told her that she had incorrectly added the tiara. To which she said "too bad, it's final sale!"

Some dishonest bridal retailers try to "build the ticket" by adding accessory items to your final tab—sometimes without your permission. Try on a string of pearls with that sample gown? Or a tiara? Some sleazy salespeople will then ADD these items to your order, whether you want them or not.

The obvious defense: do NOT sign any order form or credit card slip BEFORE you see an itemized list of what you're buying. And don't think this just happens to "dumb" brides—that above quote is a true story from a bride . . . who is an attorney!

Ratings of Selected Bridal Manufacturers

The charts on pages 80-83 compares major bridal designers. The rating refers to our opinion of their quality. Our rating system (the key is given below) is based on our extensive research into bridal apparel. We have met many of these designers and evaluated their goods in person, either at trade markets or bridal retail shops.

Want even more info? We have archived reviews of bridal gown designers on our web site, BridalBargainsBook.com (click on "bonus material"). To access this area of our site, use the password "gowns7259."

THE RATINGS

A	EXCELLENT . . . .OUR TOP PICK!
B	GOOD . . . . . .ABOVE AVERAGE QUALITY, PRICES AND CREATIVITY.
C	FAIR . . . . . .COULD STAND SOME IMPROVEMENT.
D	POOR . . . . . .YUCK! COULD STAND MAJOR IMPROVEMENT.

After the charts: let's talk about our best buys for bridal gowns!

The Top Bridal Designers Compared (A-I)

Name	Rating	Cost	Web site	Delivery Standard (weeks)
Alex Hanson	B-	$	alexhansonbridal.com	10 to 12
Alfred Angelo	C+	$	alfredangelo.com	10 to 12
Alfred Sung	B+	$	alfredsungbridals.com	11 to 13
Allure	C	$	allurebridals.com	12 to 16
Alvina Valenta	A-	$$$	alvinavalenta.com	14
Amsale	B-	$$$	amsale.com	13
Amy Michelson	B-	$$$	amymichelson.com	12 to 16
Andaluzia Couture	C	$$	andaluziacouture.com	14
Anjolique	A	$ to $$	anjolique.com	10 to 12
Ann Barge	B+	$$$	annbarge.com	14
Ann Taylor	A	$	anntaylor.com	1
Barbra Allin	B+	$$$	barbraallinbridal.com	10 to 12
Birnbaum & Bullock	B+	$$$	birnbaumandbullock.com	12 to 14
Bonny	A-	$	bonny.com	10 to 12
Carmela Sutera	C	$$$	carmelasutera.com	12 to 16
Casablanca	A-	$	casablancabridal.com	8 to 10
Chris Kole	B+	$$$	chriskole.com	12 to 14
Christos	B-	$$$	christosbridal.com	10 to 14
Couture Bridal	A-	$$$	bridalsbyelma.com	12 to 14
David's Bridal	F	$	davidsbridal.com	off rack
DaVinci	B	$	davincibridal.com	10 to 12
Demetrios/Ilissa	C+	$ to $$$	demetriosbride.com	12 to 14
Eden	A	$ to $$	edenbridals.com	10 to 12
Essense of Australia	A-	$$	essensedesigns.com	11 to 13
Eternity	B-	$ to $$	eternitygowns.com	10 to 12
Eve of Milady	C-	$$$	eveofmiladybridals.com	16
Exclusives by A.C.E.	C	$		10 to 12
Forever Yours	C+	$	foreverbridals.com	12 to 14
Group USA	B-	$	groupusa.com	off rack
Helen Morley	A-	$$$	helenmorley.com	12 to 16
Henry Roth	B+	$$$	henryroth.com	12 to 14
Impression	B	$ to $$	impressionbridal.com	11 to 13

Notes: Rating: *Our opinion of the designer's quality, value and fashion.* **Cost:** *The range in retail prices: $=under $800, $$=$800 to $1200, $$$=over $1200.* **Catalog:** *Does the designer have a consumer catalog?* DELIVERY—**Standard:** *The average number of weeks for delivery* —**Rush Cuts:** *Some designers offer rush service for an extra fee. Some designers don't offer rush cuts, but have certain in-stock styles for quicker delivery.* SIZING—**Petite:** *Designers who offer special petite sizes. Some offer petites for all styles, while others only do petites on a selected number of designs.* **Large:** *Nearly all designers offer gowns in sizes 4-20. We*

Key: ●=YES

	SIZING		OPTIONS		
Rush Cuts?	Petite	Large	Extra Length	Custom Changes	Charge for Color
	●	●	●	●	
	●	●	●		
		●			
		●			
●		●	●	●	
●			●	●	
●				●	
		●	●		
	●	●			
	●				
●		●		●	
●	●	●	●	●	
●		●	●	●	
●			●	●	
●	●	●		●	
			●	●	
			●	●	
●			●		
		●			
		●			
●				●	
●	●	●	●	●	●
●			●		
	●	●			
●					●
		●	●		
		●			
●			●	●	
●			●	●	
●		●			

classify any size larger than a 20 as a "large size." Some designers just offer sizes 22 and 24, while others go up to a 44. As with petites, only selected styles may be available in larger sizes. Most designers charge extra for large sizes. **Extra Length:** *Some designers offer extra skirt length for taller brides for extra fee.* OPTIONS—**Custom Changes:** *Some designers let you customize a dress or offer "custom cuts," dresses that are made to your exact measurements.* **Color Charges:** *Most designers offer dresses in white or ivory for the same price. The few that charge extra for ivory (or for any other color or color combination) are noted here.*

Page 2: The Top Bridal Designers Compared (J-Z)

Name	Rating	Cost	Web site	Delivery Standard (weeks)
J. Crew	A	$ to $$$	jcrew.com	1 to 2
Jacquelin	B+	$	jacquelinbridals.com	10 to 12
James Clifford	B-	$$$	jamescliffordcollection.com	16
Janell Berte	A	$$$	janellberte.com	8 to 10
Jasmine	B+	$ to $$$	jasminebridal.com	12 to 14
Jenny Yoo	B	$ to $$	jennyyoo.com	10 to 12
Jessica McClintock	A-	$	jessicamcclintock.com	2 to 6
Jim Hjelm	A-	$$ to $$$	jlmcouture.com	10 to 12
Judd Waddell	A-	$$$	juddwaddell.com	12 to 14
Justin Alexander	B+	$ to $$$	justinalexanderbridal.com	12 to 16
Justina McCaffrey	A-	$$$	justinamcaffrey.com	12 to 16
Lady Roi	B	$	ladyroibridals.com	14
Lane Bryant	A	$	lanebryant.com	1 to 2
Lazaro	B	$$$	lazarobridal.com	10 to 16
Maggie Sottero	D	$ to $$	maggiesotterobridal.com	20
Marisa	A	$$ to $$$	marisabridals.com	14
Matthew Christopher	A	$$$	matthewchristopher.com	12 to 14
Mary's	C	$	marysbridal.com	10 to 12
Melissa Sweet	B+	$$$	melissasweet.com	10 to 16
Mikaella	B-	$$	mikaellabridal.com	12 to 14
Mon Cheri	B-	$	moncheribridals.com	12
Monique L'Huillier	B	$$$	moniquelhuillier.com	12 to 14
Moonlight	B	$ to $$$	moonlightbridal.com	12 to 14
Mori Lee	B+	$	morilee.com	10 to 12
Oscar De La Renta	C	$$$	oscardelarenta.com	12 to 14
Paloma Blanca	B-	$$ to $$$	palomablanca.com	12
Paula Varsalona	B+	$$$	paulavarsalona.com	12 to 15
Private Label by G	B+	$	privatelabelbyg.com	10 to 12
Pronovias/St. Patrick	A-	$ to $$$	pronovias.com	9 to 10
Ramona Keveza	B	$$$	romonakeveza.com	12 to 14
Raylia	B-	$	rayliadesigns.com	10 to 12
Reem Acra	B	$$$	reemacra.com	10 to 12
Richard Glasgow	B	$$$	glasgowbridal.com	12 to 16
Rivini	B+	$$$	rivini.com	12 to 14
Scaasi/Forsyth	B+	$$$	evahforsyth.com	12
St. Pucchi	B-	$$$	stpucchi.com	16
Sincerity	B-	$$	sinceritybridal.com	10 to 14
Stephen Yearick	B+	$$$	stephenyearick.com	12 to 16
Sweetheart	B	$	thebridalshop.com	10
Tomasina	A-	$$$	tomasina.com	12 to 16
Venus	B+	$ to $$	venusbridal.com	12 to 14
Vera Wang	C	$$$	verawang.com	12
Victoria's	B+	$$	victoriascollection.com	12 to 16
Watters	A	$$	watters.com	10 to 14
Winnie Couture	A	$ to $$	winnecouture.com	10 to 12

Key: ●=YES

	SIZING		OPTIONS		
Rush Cuts?	Petite	Large	Extra Length	Custom Changes	Charge for Color
●	●	●			
		●	●	●	
●		●	●	●	
●			●	●	
●		●	●	●	
●					
	●	●			
●		●	●	●	
●			●	●	
●			●		
●			●	●	●
		●			
●		●			
●		●	●	●	
●		●			
●		●	●	●	
●			●	●	●
●		●	●	●	
			●	●	●
●		●	●	●	
	●	●	●	●	
	●				●
●		●	●	●	
		●			●
●			●	●	●
●		●	●	●	
●			●	●	
●		●	●	●	
●			●		
●				●	
		●			
				●	
●			●	●	
			●	●	
●			●	●	
●			●	●	
●					
●			●	●	
		●	●	●	
●		●	●	●	
●	●	●	●	●	
●			●	●	
●	●	●	●	●	
●		●	●	●	
●		●	●	●	

Spotlight: Best Buy #1

The Best Discount gown web sites

Yes, you can save big bucks on bridal gowns and bridesmaids dresses on the net. In this section, we'll review our picks of the top places on the web to buy gowns. How much can you save? About 20% to 40% off retail. But before you fire up the browser and surf for dress deals, consider these facts:

1. Like many things on the web, selling bridal gowns in cyberspace is evolving. Sites range from those with in-depth pricing information to others that are merely one-page ads with little detail. If you're looking for fancy web sites with on-line pricing guides, you'll be sorely disappointed. Price quotes are given out via the phone or email. And forget about online ordering. When you want to actually buy, most sites direct you to email or call a phone number (sometimes toll-free, sometimes not) to place the order.

2. When shopping a discounter, do your homework first. Gather information on colors and options. After narrowing down your choices to just your top picks, *then* contact a discounter for a price quote. This is only fair, since hogging a discounter's time only reduces the response rate for everyone. We know some brides that have carpet-bombed discounters with email requests for 16 dress quotes . . . or with color questions that could be easily answered on the designer's web site.

3. Our biggest beef with these web sites is that (at this point) they are all run by *local* bridal shops—there is no Amazon of bridal. And it is hard to tell long distance whether the shop is reputable just by the look of their Web graphics. Mail order (which is essentially what bridal shops are doing over the web) is a totally different business than retail—you have to deal with shipping logistics, long-distance customer service and all sorts of other complications. We'd like to see someone have at least three years experience doing this operation (selling dresses online) before we'd give our hard-earned cash as a deposit.

4. Remember that discount deals are typically for mail-order customers only. Most bridal web sites that sell gowns also operate physical stores. So does that mean you can get a discount deal via email and then go to the store and get the same price? No, special web prices are almost always for folks who *don't* come into the store, try on gowns and use the store's alterations services. While most web sites don't explicitly say this, several brides have confirmed these practices to us.

5. Another caveat: many gown designers and manufacturers are livid about web sites that discount their dresses. Some have threatened to cut off accounts who sell through an "unauthorized 800-number or web site." While most of the designers' protests are mere saber rattling (few have actually cut off 'net sellers), there is a risk—albeit it small—that your gown order could be caught in the crossfire.

6. See if the site will do a price match. The Internet is a very competitive world. If you find a site you'd like to work with but you get a lower quote from another source, give them the chance to match it. Most sites have a policy of meeting or beating their competition.

7. Don't order if time is tight. Be aware that many sites say they can ship items like bridal accessories in "7-10 business days." That is the time to *process* your order and typically does NOT include the actual shipping time . . . which can add another week depending on your distance from the shipper. If time is tight, it might be better to buy an item at a retail store than take the chance on a mail order service.

8. You have to arrange for alterations and steaming on your own. That means finding a local seamstress or alteration service. Most dresses are packed rather tightly in their shipping boxes; the resulting gown will probably be wrinkled. Buy a portable steamer at Wal-Mart or Target to get the wrinkles out.

Can a dress be let out?

What if your gown arrives in and it's too tight? Can a bridal gown be let out? As we noted earlier in this book, the general rule of thumb is to order a gown that's slightly larger than your measurements. Why? It's easier to make a gown smaller (that is, take it in) than the opposite direction. Of course, there are exceptions to this rule. Some designers actually leave room in the seams to enable a gown to be taken out. What if there isn't any extra fabric? Well, the only solution then is to make a "gusset," a piece of fabric inserted into the dress to give extra room. If that sounds complex, it is—only skilled seamstresses should attempt this alteration. A gusset may change the way a dress looks, sometimes for the worse.

So, here's our advice: be careful out there. Confirm the web site is an *authorized dealer* for the brand you want. Only a handful of web sites are actually authorized dealers of the manufacturers they claim to sell. A wise move: call the designer or manufacturer *first* before you order. (Remember that some web sites may be authorized under their parent retail shop's name, not their on-line address–ask the site how they would be listed in a designer's records). Finally, use a credit card for all deposits and final payments.

Our round up of discount gown web sites, in alphabetical order:

♥ **Dori Anne Veils** DoriAnneVeils.com (888) 344-6009. Despite the name, this company sells more than just veils–Dori Anne veils discounts bridal gowns, bridesmaids, accessories at 20% to 40% off retail. Owner Debra LaSpina Goldwater started as a veil designer in 1997 with a shop in California's Bay Area; she soon expanded into bridal gowns, maids gowns and other accessories. Dori Anne carries several designers, including Forever Yours and Symphony bridals, as well as maids from Belsoie. The web site is detailed, with an online quote form, sizing advice and more. The only bummer: the online order form must be faxed in. That slight inconvenience mars an otherwise excellent site. **Rating: A-**

♥ **House of Brides.** HouseofBrides.com is probably the oldest retailer to become a player in the dot-com world–the suburban Chicago chain traces its roots to 1929. Now with four locations in the Chicago metro area, House of Brides also has an impressive online outpost.

House of Brides carries basic brands like Alfred Angelo, Impression, Jacquelin, Bonny and DaVinci, but also a fewer better labels such as Marisa and Paula Varsalona. For bridesmaids, the site offers Dessy, Alyce, Bari Jay and Bill Levkoff among others. Yes, House of Brides is an authorized dealer for all the brands listed on their site.

We liked how HouseofBrides.com was organized–once you select a brand name, you get a listing of dresses with pictures, style numbers and prices. Best of all, you can order online, with detailed sizing charts, extra length and other options clearly spelled out.

For one Mon Cheri dress, we noticed House of Brides was offering the gown at a 20% discount. Then an online coupon (listed right on the site) offered another 10% off as well. Overall, House of Brides promises savings of 30% to 40% and carries everything from bridal gowns to shoes, jewelry to veils and more.

Among the site's best features: a "compare to" section for both David's Bridal and Maggie Sottero, filled with knock-offs of these brands at great prices.

So, how's House of Brides reputation for customer service and delivery? Well, that's where we start to get a bit nervous. A quick check of

House of Bride's online Better Business Bureau record (BBB.org) reveals 36 complaints in the last three years (yes, that's one a month). That's about 50% higher than Pearl's Place and significantly more than a site like RK (which had a total of four complaints in three years).

Now, we realize some of this could be attributed to the size of House of Brides' operation—four stores in Chicago will probably generate more complaints than RK or Pearl's, which operate single stores. Given the way the BBB compiles their reports, it's unclear whether the complaints were attributed to House of Brides retail stores or online operation. And to give House of Brides credit, the BBB notes House of Brides addressed or resolved most complaints.

So, we urge caution on this one. We will give House of Brides an average rating and see if their customer service efforts improve. Meanwhile, if you plan to order from this site, leave plenty of time before your wedding. And be sure to read House of Brides' terms and conditions for orders—there are no returns or exchanges. **Rating: C**

♥ **NetBride** NetBride.com; (866) 638-2743. NetBride.com is the online outpost of Minneapolis-based bridal retailer Rush's, which has been in

Be discreet with a discount gown purchase

If you decide to order a gown from a discounter, be smart. Remember that these guys are very controversial among manufacturers and retailers. Don't do what one bride did when her dress (ordered from a discounter) was two days late—she called the dress manufacturer and grilled them about why it was late. And she mentioned what a big discount she was getting. While she got her dress, she also got an obscenity-laden lecture from the designer about supporting those evil discounters. And by loudly boasting about her bargain, the bride jeopardized the discounter's supply lines and perhaps ruined the discount deals for dozens of other future brides. The bottom line: the price you paid for their dress is no business of the designer/manufacturer. Don't call up a bridal designer and rub your bargain in their face.

Another tip: be savvy about alterations. If you take your dress to a full-price shop for alterations, by all means, DO NOT tell them you got it from a discounter. Some bridal shops will sock such brides with HUGE alteration and pressing charges, just to punish them. One bride found this out when she brought her gown to a shop in the discounter's mailing box (not smart). The bridal retailer refused to do the alterations and kicked her out of the shop.

business since 1948 (online since 1995). NetBride carries a wide variety of brands of both bridal and bridesmaids, including such better labels as Marisa and Maggie Sottero. In the past year, NetBride re-designed their web site and it is quite an improvement: we liked the online sizing charts, price quote request, and yes, even an online order form. Feedback on NetBride has been quite positive—brides tell us they like NetBride's speedy response to quote requests and overall good customer service. The only caveat: NetBride will occasionally offer a price quote for a designer they are not authorized to sell. While we think NetBride is reputable, we always urge caution about ordering from a site that is not an authorized dealer for the gown you want (call the designer first to confirm dealer status). Overall, we recommend NetBride. **Rating: A-**

FIGURE 2: A sampling of some of the bargain sites for wedding gowns, maids and more.

♥ **Pearl's Place** PearlsPlace.com; (504) 885-9213. Pearl's Place was one of the first bridal shops to open a cyberspace outpost. The Metairie, Louisiana shop specializes in the "better" couture labels, the ones that are hard to find at a discount anywhere else online. Pearl's has been in business since 1971 and online since 1998. Don't expect much from their web site–it's a one-page affair with lots of text about the lines the store carries, ordering info, etc. Discounts are 20% to 30% off retail, which is impressive considering the couture name brands.

In a past edition of this book , we criticized Pearl's for their customer service. But things have now improved and that is reflected in their rating. Sure, folks still say the store can be a zoo, especially on weekends . . . but if you are ordering online, that isn't a factor. Judging from our reader feedback, brides are now happy overall with the service and price at Pearls. FYI: Pearl's deposit policy is half the *original retail price* of the gown (not half the discounted prices). **Rating: A**

♥ **Priceless Bridals** BargainWeddingGowns.com; (818) 340-6514. The online offshoot of a Southern California bridal shop by the same name, Priceless offers to beat any written price quote by their competitors. A reader who ordered her gown from Priceless said she was happy, even though the gown was a little late (Priceless waived the shipping fee, however). "Priceless is a little harder to get in touch with than Pearl's–that is they don't answer their email as quickly and you have to nag them a bit," said the bride. "But the dress I received was very pretty and for $350, it can't be beat.". Another interesting note: Priceless is one of the few web discounters that also occasionally hosts eBay auctions. **Rating: B**

♥ **RK Bridal** RKBridal.com; (800) 929-9512. This New York City-based retail shop has one of the better-known web sites that sells gowns at a discount. You can get a price quote for dresses from 30 manufacturers. Many of the lines are upper-end, couture dresses that are hard to find at a discount. One plus: RK's price quotes include shipping and delivery charges–and if you find a lower price from another site online, RK offers to beat it by 5%. RK Bridal has a shop in New York's garment district at 318 West 39th Street (between 8th & 9th Ave.), although most of the prices there are not discounted like they are on the web. Our readers generally report positive experiences in dealing with RK, which has been in the bridal retail business since 1985. The company responds quickly to email requests and has been reliable with deliveries. **Rating: A**

♥ **Other sites recommended by our readers. PlusSizeBridals.com** specializes in first-quality gowns in sizes 16-32. The site also sells accessories like shoes, crinolines and veils/headpieces. A reader in Los Angeles praised the site's "great selection." She found a "beautiful gown for

$459—and it was shipped to my house in just two weeks."

ANGERI.COM is an online boutique that sells overstock couture dresses from designers like Givenchy, Nancy Issler (both are defunct labels from Alfred Angelo) and Carmela Sutera. Sample deal: a $2300 silk Sutera dress for $700. The site stocks sizes 2 to 16, but we noticed the selection at either extreme of the size spectrum was limited, as you might expect. All the gowns are new and were either runway samples or designer overstock. One caveat: we were a bit put off by the site's generic size chart—as you know, each designer has a different idea about sizing. Confirm the actual sizing of any gown before buying from this site.

At first glance, you'd think a site like **STUMP'S PROM** wouldn't have anything to offer brides. But a sharp-eyed reader spied tiaras and other headpieces (www.stumpsprom.com, then click on "Royalty") at great prices—she got a $150 tiara for just $30 on that site.

What about other sites on the web that sell gowns? Yes, we realize there are at least a dozen more sites out there, but we didn't review them here. Why? The sites above had the best feedback from our readers and the longest track records. If you are considering ordering from a site we haven't reviewed, first go to the Better Business Bureau's web site (www.bbb.org) to check the site's track record. Then look at the message boards on our site (BridalBargainsBook.com) as well of those of the Knot and Wedding Channel. Do a search of those boards to see what experiences other brides have had with the site.

To sum up the pros and cons of being a gown via a discount web site versus a store, see the chart on the next page.

Designer R.I.P.

If you have a long engagement, you might be tempted to whip out an old magazine to see if you can find a bridal gown. Be careful—bridal designers come and go like pop stars. And most styles are only in production for a short time; some gowns are discontinued just a few months after they debut. Hence, don't go looking for a dream dress from a 2003r bridal magazine. Odds are, it is long gone. Here is a list of designers that have bit the dust in recent years: Bianchi, Carmi Couture, Fink, Galina, Lili, Joelle, Monique, Country Elegance by Susan Lane, San Martin, and Vow & Vogue. (Note: David's, reviewed later in this chapter, purchased the brand names Bianchi, Galina, Monique and Priscilla of Boston to put on their private-label gowns. Hence you might see a Galina gown at David's, but the label is no longer independently manufactured or available elsewhere).

Pros and Cons

Should you buy a dress from local retailer or an online discounter? Here is a summary of the pros and cons of each option.

Option	Pros	Cons
Discount	Great price: 20-40% off retail	Some require upfront payment when ordering
	No sales tax; no pushy salespeople	Must know exact dress you want
	Indie seamstress can be money-saver	Must coordinate alterations yourself (hassle)
	No messy bridal shops	Long-distance relationship via phone or email.
	Get dress shipped directly to you	Must store yourself
Retail	Full service often includes alterations	Full retail price . . . and sometimes more
	Can try on dresses	Limited selection
	Pay half down; half when dress comes in	Service sometimes slips after they have your money
	Extras like pressing, gown storage and payment plans	Did we mention you pay full retail price?

Spotlight: Best Buy #2

Cut out the Middle Man: China Direct Gowns

It's a time-honored strategy to save: cut out the middleman and get a better price.

The bridal version of this today is buying a gown direct from China via eBay or a manufacturer's web site at an unbelievably low price. How low? How about $100 or $150 for a bridal gown like you see in stores? No, we're not making that up.

How is this possible? First, a quick history lesson. Until the 1980's, most bridal gowns sold in the U.S. were made in the U.S. Storied designers like Bianchi and Priscilla (among dozens of others) actually had dress factories in places like Boston, New York or San Francisco.

That ended long ago, as production moved off shore. Today's hot bridal gown makers (just about any name brand you see online or in magazines) don't really make anything at all—they are gown importers. After designing a dress, they farm out production to a gown manufacturer in China (the designer typically doesn't own the Chinese factory). The dress is shipped to the designer's distribution center in the U.S. and then, finally, to a retailer.

Every time the dress changes hands, it gets marked up. According to industry sources, we estimate that a $1,000 bridal gown you see in stores actually costs just $50 to make in China. The importer buys it for $100 and then re-sells it to a retailer for $500. The retailer marks it up to $1,000, the final price you see as a consumer.

But who needs the designer and retailer anyway? What value do they really add to this process? After all, once the gown lands in the U.S., it can be UPS'd direct to you, bypassing the importer and retailer. Chinese gown makers apparently have been pondering that as well—and several have set up eBay accounts and web sites to sell gowns direct to brides.

And given these prices, we can see why this is suddenly the hot bargain trend in bridal. $30 for an A-line dress with a touch of pearls? $50 for an off-the-shoulder dress with a beaded bodice and chiffon overlay skirt? Yes, those are real prices, not typos!

We've interviewed over 70 brides who've bought gowns direct from China. Based on their experiences, here is our advice:

♥ **Where to look.** Many Chinese gown factories have set up eBay stores. The bigger ones include: China-Ekt, blue-catalog, antzinternational, and jeffliu8000. Those are eBay id's (search by seller id to find them). Several Chinese factories have set up English web sites: these include BlueCatalog.com (the same as blue-catalog on eBay), 1koo.com (same as China-Ekt) and JuliusBridal.com. See Figure 3 on the next page.

♥ **How much can you save?** Are you sitting down? Most gowns are under $100 (some as little as $30 or $50). Some sites have a few "pricey" gowns at about $200.

♥ **What about shipping? How much time do I need to leave to order?** Shipping is usually extra, another $50 to $100. It takes about 2-3 months for a gown to arrive at your doorstep. A word to the wise: leave plenty of time for customs delays!

♥ **Is there a language barrier?** All of the above web sites and eBay

FIGURE 3: Some Chinese bridal dress factories have migrated from eBay to selling direct to the public via their own web sites.

stores are in English—but if you want a special request or custom alteration, you may have to deal with a Chinese customer service agent with limited English skills. Set your expectations accordingly.

♥ **How's the quality?** Surprisingly, very good. Remember, these are the same factories that crank out name-brand gowns. Most brides we interviewed have been pleasantly surprised with the quality of fabric, stitching and detailing. Does that mean you won't need alterations? Of course not—you'll still probably have to make an adjustment here or there to the gown. But that's true for a gown you buy anywhere.

♥ **I have my heart set on a $2000 designer gown. But I see a similar design from a Chinese eBay seller for just $150? Should I go for it?** Let's be honest—the Chinese gown will most likely be a copy. A good replica, but a replica nonetheless. That means the fabric and detailing won't be anything like the $2000 designer original. But you could argue: who can really tell? And given the fact that many Chinese eBay gowns sell for as little as $50, what's your risk? We'd say order it in and give it a try. But if you must have the designer label, it is probably better to order a designer original from one of the discount web sites we list above.

♥ **Is there a place to swap info with other brides on which Chinese sellers are best?** Yes. We realize these eBay id's and web sites change, so we have a pinned thread on our message boards on buying a gown direct from China (BridalBargainsBook.com, click on "Message Boards", then "Weddings" and finally the Cyberbride forum; the thread is called eBay China Gowns).

Spotlight: Best Buy #3

Bridal Outlets

Read me first: outlet locations are constantly changing. Be sure to call these locations FIRST before heading out! While these locations were open as of this printing, be sure to check first. If you find an outlet that is no longer around—or a new discovery that you'd like to share—email us at authors@bridalbargainsbook.com.

With an outlet mall in just about every corner of North America, it seems you can find any product at less than retail—sweaters, cookware, stereos, you name it. But what about a bridal gown?

Surprisingly, there ARE bridal outlets out there . . . they just take some effort to find. Most are NOT in those fancy outlet malls on the interstate. Instead, bridal outlets are located in off-the-beaten path locales. Here's our look at the best bets:

♥ **"1385 Broadway"** used to be one of the best places to find a gown deal in New York City. We say "used to be" because the scene there has changed much over the years.

In the heart of Manhattan's garment district, the building at 1385 (and 1375) Broadway used to house the showrooms and offices of the country's top bridal designers. In years past, the designers used to quietly open to the public on Saturday . . . and shhh! The prices were discounted!

In the past few years, however the Bridal Building has changed quite a bit. First, many major gown manufacturers have abandoned the building (and New York's high rents) by moving their showrooms out of the city. In their place, we've seen several smaller designers and seamstresses move into the Bridal Building. In some cases, these smaller salons are selling overstock samples from major gown makers; other times, they are selling their own creations.

So, is it still worth it to trek to the Bridal Building? Well, if you live in or near (or plan to visit) New York City, you might as well go look. It can't hurt. We found some of the deals impressive—one designer bridal gown in excellent condition was originally $1300, marked to $600. Our readers report one major bridesmaid designer sells their $160 gowns for just

Headpieces and Veils

If you think bridal gowns are overpriced, you haven't seen anything yet! Wait until you see the price tags on headpieces and veils! You may have to be revived with smelling salts. That's because hefty mark-ups on these items regularly push the prices of headpieces/veils over $150 and even $300.

Now let's look at what you are actually buying here. Let's see, we have a headpiece frame, which costs about $5 in fabric stores. Or a tiara that wholesales for $20. Then you add some basic lace, fake pearls and plastic beads. Top it off with veiling which costs $2 to $5 per yard at most fabric stores. Sure, the labor involved to assemble these things isn't cheap, but we still don't comprehend how this all adds up to $300.

Bridal retailers tell us one reason headpieces and veils are so expensive is spoilage—these delicate items often get dirty or damaged. Hence shops have to mark up this item to cover the cost of tossing out a certain percentage of their stock. While we see that point, we still think the retail prices on these items are outrageous.

Our best advice on headpieces and veils is to consider going the do-it-yourself route here. A good source for supplies to make headpieces is Michaels Arts & Crafts (800-MICHAELS, michaels.com), a nationwide craft chain. One more tip: when you have your dress altered, ask the seamstress to save any scraps of fabric and lace. You can then use these on your headpiece.

Of course, if you aren't the crafty type, there is the old stand by: buy online. As we noted earlier in this chapter, there are many web sites that sell affordable tiaras and headpieces.

$95 on Saturdays.

But . . . you might find similar deals from other discount sources we list in this chapter (like RK Bridal, the web site and store in the Garment District reviewed earlier). So, educate yourself on designers, prices and selection before you go to the bridal building. And don't forget to factor in the price of parking and tolls for not only the initial visit but also any follow-up fittings.

The Bridal Building isn't the only place to get bridal gown bargains in New York City. If you are looking for a couture gown without the couture price tag, check out the **Bridal Garden**, 54 West 21st St., Suite 907 (web: bridalgarden.org). This non-profit resale bridal boutique sells couture bridal gowns and gives the proceeds to children's charities. You can find overstock and resale gowns here from such labels as Vera Wang, Carolina Herrera and more. Many of these $5000 gowns are on sale for $2000 or so. Don't go here looking for a dress under $1000, however. Brides tell us the pickings are slim unless you want to spend $2000 or more.

Also in New York (Brooklyn, that is): **Kleinfeld**, the massive bridal store in business for over 50 years. Yes, Kleinfeld carries nearly every gown on Earth but we've been turned off by their policies—they rip tags out of sample gowns and refuse to tell you the brand until after you pay. And don't miss an appointment here—the shop has the audacity to charge no-show brides $50. You have to fork over a credit card number on the phone in order to make an appointment.

♥ **Jessica McClintock** (web: www.jessicamcclintock.com) has two California outlets for her popular line of bridal apparel: South San Francisco (415) 553-8390, Mont Clair (909) 985-2770. All outlets carry past-season styles of bridal gowns, bridesmaids' dresses and all kinds of accessories.

We recently visited the San Francisco outlet and were impressed. We saw dozens of bridal gowns (priced from $225 to $500), plus bridesmaids' dresses, flower girls, party dresses and more. Most of the bridal gowns were discounted 10% to 25%, but we understand periodic sales offer even better deals. We've heard of brides who found $5 formal bridal gowns (no, that's not a typo). While the deals weren't that fantastic when we were there, we did notice a large rack of informal gowns on sale for just $80. You can then buy a separate train ($20 each). Top off your bargain ensemble with a pair of white shoes with lace trim, on clearance while we visited for just $5 a pair. Wow.

Most gowns we saw at the McClintock outlet were sizes 8-14, although a few 4-6's and 16-20's were floating around. Surprisingly, the dresses were in pretty good shape—most were in protective bags and had very little damage or wear. Watch for those end-of season clearances for

Factory stores: new twist on outlets

Beset by competition and faltering retail dealers, bridal gown manufacturers have rolled out a new weapon to fight chains like David's: the factory store. Demetrios kicked off this trend in 1999 with the launch of "Brides by Demetrios" in California. The designer then opened a dozen more stores around the US. Call Demetrios at (212-961-5222 or check their website (www.demetriosbride.com) for the latest locations.

So what are these factory stores? In a way, these stores are a hybrid between discount outlets and pure retail locations. The best advantage for consumers is selection. Demetrios loads his stores with his ENTIRE collection (about 800 styles), in sizes 4 to 26. Unlike regular bridal shops that may just carry a few styles in a line, factory stores let a manufacturer showcase their entire line. Of course, if you don't like the Demetrios look, this isn't the place to shop. Brides by Demetrios stores only stock Demetrios bridal gowns (along with bridesmaids dresses, accessories and all the other usual stuff).

Unfortunately, prices are typically at full retail. But we have heard from readers that the Demetrios stores will match quotes brides have received from online discounters, so it may not hurt to ask. Of course, while you might pay full price, you also get full service (on-site alterations are available at most stores). Another tip: look for sale racks at factory stores. Demetrios stores have a large selection of discontinued dresses that are $299 to $699, about 30% to 50% off retail.

Of course, Demetrios isn't the only designer going the "factory store" route. Jessica McClintock has for years operated her own stores. Even industry stalwart Alfred Angelo has opened over 25 company stores in Florida, California, Oklahoma and Texas (go to .alfredangelostores. com for the latest locations). One bride posted to our message boards the bargain she found there—a $650 gown marked down to $199! Angelo recently expanded its company store empire with the purchase of BridesMart in Texas.

Pronovias is also getting into the factory store biz—the Barcelona-based bridal maker is opening a six-floor factory store at 14 East 52nd Street in New York City in fall 2007.

All of this is good for consumers, in our view. Factory stores give brides another option for gown shopping.and piece of mind in knowing the store is manufacturer-owned. Whether these stores will be aggressive with pricing and special sales remains to be seen, but expect to see more in the coming years.

Besides designer-owned factory outlets, we've noticed several new bridal outlets that have popped up in those large outlet malls seen along interstates. Among the more interesting: Bridal Co. Outlet (web: bridalco.com) in Denton, TX is an authorized dealer for Mori Lee, Mary's and Alfred Angelo among others. You can also order gowns at a discount from their web site. (To find a bridal outlet near you, search OutletBound.com's excellent web site.)

the best deals (you can put your name on their mailing list to get notices).

♥ **JCPenney** got out of bridal a couple of years ago, but their outlet stores are still selling bridesmaids gowns. We still get reports from brides about great deals at the outlets (Penney's has seven outlet stores; go to outletbound.com and do a search for "J.C. Penney"). One bride said she found her bridesmaids dresses here for just $39 each.

♥ **Vows Bridal Outlet (AKA Bride Power)** in Newton, MA (866) THE-GOWN specializes in selling overstock and close-outs from top designers like Vera Wang and Helen Morley. You'll see these top names at prices 50% to 70% off retail. We visited the store and found it to be well stocked and the service (as reported by our readers) is excellent. Don't live near Boston? Check out Vows online at BridePower.com. You can browse their collection online and even purchase dresses direct from the site.

♥ **Davids Bridal** has an outlet store in El Paso, TX (915-591-9700) that carries discontinued styles at 50% or more off regular prices. One caveat: last we checked, there were just two aisles of discounted dresses (the store also stocks new gowns, although they are not discounted). So this outlet probably doesn't merit a special trip, unless you find yourself near El Paso in the near future!

• **More outlets:** More outlets: A reader in California praised the **Bridal**

Real Wedding Tip

Newton outlet bargain

A reader in Mass. emailed this bargain on a Romona Keveza dress she got from Vows Bridal Outlet in Newton, MA.

"I had the best experience with Vows Bridal Outlet (Bridepower.com). I ordered a Romona Keveza dress (for $600! 60% off the retail price!) and it arrived in three days. I was unsure about the color, however—it was a true ivory and I thought I wanted something a bit lighter. I emailed them to tell them I was returning the dress and they offered me another in white and they paid the shipping. Vows extended the return deadline so I could choose between the two. They even called me to see how everything was going. The dresses were in perfect shape with the tags still in. I highly recommend Vows."

Mart Factory Outlet (web: bridalmegamall.com) in Rancho Cordova (near Sacramento): "The whole experience was outstanding. Great prices and caring service without any pressure to buy. The place was spotless and the dresses in super clean condition.

The Catalog Chase

As you might guess, major gown designers have catalogs that picture their dresses. So you can just call them up and get a copy, right? Wrong. Most bridal dress designers do not send out catalogs to consumers—and some can be downright hostile on the phone when you ask. Instead, designers dole out glossy full-color catalogs to bridal retailers, hoping they'll use them as sales tools.

Fat chance. Most shops horde the catalogs and reprints of ads from bridal magazines, afraid that if they pass them out, their customers will use them to comparison shop competitors. Interestingly enough, several shops debated this topic in a recent issue of a trade magazine for bridal retailers. "(Catalogs are) just putting a tool in (the bride's) hands to price shop you to death," an Ohio bridal shop owner said. "I think catalogs are wonderful," added a Wisconsin dress shop manager, who uses them as a resource—not for brides, mind you, but for her salespeople. She added: "I don't think they should be finding their way into the hands of consumers."

Some bridal retailers cut up the manufacturers catalogs and put them into binders. That's what we discovered on a recent visit to several bridal shops in Florida—shops asked brides to first flip through the binders to decide on various styles before they hit the racks. Of course, these dress pictures were carefully edited to remove any mention of the gown's manufacturer/designer or style number.

Of course, not everyone has such an anti-consumer attitude. "I don't worry that the bride is going to shop around," said another shop owner who does hand out the catalogs. "We know they are going to shop around. I feel that if they have something with our name on it, they are going to remember us." And even shops that refuse to give out catalogs will relent and give them to customers—that is, after a deposit is placed. Another exception to the catalog chase: bridesmaid dress catalogs. Most shops will hand these out so you can show an out-of-town bridesmaid a picture of the dress.

What about designers' web sites? Can you surf your way around the catalog chase? Yes, most designers have put up web sites in the last couple of years. But don't expect many dress details. Most feature gown pictures, but precious little other information (prices, style numbers, sizes and other details are intentionally omitted).

Big Mark-Ups Ahead: Accessories and Extras

Here's a quick quiz: where do bridal shops make the most profit? If you answered "dresses," think again. Actually, it's those "bridal accessories" that truly keep the cash register humming. Items like crinolines, lingerie, shoes, garters, gloves, stockings and jewelry are a major profit center for bridal retailers.

And, amazingly, the industry makes no bones about the fat profits it fleeces from brides and grooms on these items. According to *Vows* (an industry trade journal), "Accessories are an important, lucrative part of the bridal business." One executive of a hosiery company advises shops to "go ahead and get the garters, the gloves and stockings for the entire bridal party—they're easy add-on sales. The mark-up on them is usually 100 percent and that's quite easy to achieve."

And some shops don't stop at 100%. *Glamour Magazine* interviewed one furious bride who was suckered into buying a $40 bra at a bridal shop. The boutique owner told her she must wear that bra. When she got home, she discovered that the manufacturer's price tag said $32. Hence the bridal shop had taken an $16 bra (at wholesale) and marked it up to $40—a tidy 150% mark-up. Along the same lines, one bridal shop owner in Lincoln, Nebraska confesses: "I buy bridal garters for 85¢¢, put a bow on them and then sell them for $24.95! It's amazing what a fancy little bow will do." At a 2800% mark-up, that IS quite an amazing bow.

According to another recent article in *Vows*, "a three-time mark-up (by bridal retailers) is not unusual" on bras, said a lingerie wholesaler. "I know stores that are getting four times cost," bragged another bra maker. How can they take such huge mark-ups? That's because bras sold to brides have low wholesale prices (thanks to a lack of fancy lace trim). Hence, a bra that sells for to $15 wholesale can be marked up to $45 to $60 retail at a bridal shop, a major rip-off in our opinion.

Of course, the accessories don't stop at the bride. Ring pillows, cake tops, guest books and attendants gifts are items you must have, says the bridal shop. Just listen to what wedding guru Beverly Clark (who, by the way, has her own collection of bridal accessories that she hawks) advises to bridal retailers in *Vows*: "Each time the wedding entourage enters your store, you have an opportunity to increase your overall dollar volume, in excess of $300 per party." And here's the kicker: "In this economy," Clark said, "you [the bridal retailer] have to get every dollar out of the bride." Isn't that nice? And people wonder why the bridal industry gets such a bad rap.

Don't bridal shops have the right to make a profit? Isn't that America? Sure, bridal retailers can price their products like their coming out of a hotel mini-bar. But that doesn't mean consumers have to be suckers. Thanks to the web and discount retailers, you can buy any and all of the items discussed here at much lower prices.

Yet, folks still sometimes pay a premium for bridal accessories. Nearly a third of all brides fall victim to sales hype and buy accessories at bridal shops. While brides try on gowns, owners of bridal shops often sneak out those bras, jewelry, hosiery and other dodads. There may be subtle and not-so-subtle pressure to buy the "whole outfit." We say resist the pressure and shop around. For example, those $100 shoes at bridal shops (which *Glamour Magazine* says are "usually made of poor-quality, dyed-to-match satin") may be much cheaper at chain shoe stores. Those stores also offer a wider selection. One bride told us she found white leather pumps for just $22 at a department store end-of-summer sale. She added some beaded clip-ons ($10 to $15 each) from a shoe store and had a great look for less than half the bridal shop price.

For good deals on shoes, check the web. Shoebuy.com has 40 options for brides and bridesmaids, from basic dyeables for just $38 to designer options like Nina. Dyeableshoesonline.com also has good deals—$35 for a satin pump. Their sister site, DiscountBridalShoes.com, also has a wide selection of bridal shoes that start at $30 or so.

Forget the jewelry at bridal shops. Much of it is fake and grossly over-priced—sometimes two to three times the retail prices of other stores. Other, non-bridal stores are likely to have better prices and quality. The same goes for gloves, lingerie, guest books and more. The best shops will rent slips and petticoats for a fraction of retail prices.

And don't think the bridal industry has forgotten about the groom either. One of the biggest profit areas in formalwear rental has nothing to do with the tuxedo—it's the shoes that are the moneymakers. Yes, we're talking about those cheesy, plastic black shoes that bridal shops and tux places buy for $14 each. Shops turn around and rent them for $10 a pop—since the shoes can be rented out 20 times or more, each pair can reap revenues of $200! According to *Vows*, the magazine conservatively estimated the profit from shoe rental at a fat 55%. "That is over three times the profit that most operators enjoy on a tuxedo rental." And the key word in that sentence is enjoy. Our advice: skip the shoes and buy a nice pair of black shoes. Since you'll wear them again and again, in the long run, you'll probably come out ahead.

David's Bridal: Not Recommended

What a long strange trip it's been.

David's, the country's largest chain of bridal shops (256 and counting, web: DavidsBridal.com), has changed dramatically from their humble beginnings in South Florida in 1990. When we first visited David's in Tampa in 1993, they were known as "David's Bridal Warehouse." And a warehouse was what it was—rack after rack of gowns sold "as is" at deep discount prices. The crammed-together inventory, lack of dressing rooms and harsh fluorescent lighting gave David's all the ambiance of a K-Mart.

How times have changed. We recently visited a brand new David's in Colorado and boy, things *are* different. The airy, 10,000 square foot store featured high ceilings, tapestry carpet, subtle lighting and a HUGE dressing area, all walled in mirrors. It's no wonder David's has dropped "warehouse" from their name—it looks like a regular (albeit big) bridal salon.

What hasn't changed are the gowns—David's still sells most gowns off the rack. Unlike traditional stores that stock only sample gowns and force you to wait months for a "special order," most David brides do cash and carry. You see a gown, find your size (they stock sizes 2 to 24), pay for it and then walk out the door. What a concept.

Over time, David's has strayed from its off-the-rack roots: more and more of David's gowns are special order. Now, nearly a third of the chain's business is special order, including the Oleg Cassini line. Nearly all David's bridesmaids sales are also special order. The chain has also added more premium (read: expensive) merchandise.

So, what exactly is David's selling? Well, these are not designer-brand dresses. In fact, ALL the gowns in David's are their own "private label" or in-house names. David's has plants in Asia that churn out copies of all the hip styles featured in bridal magazines. And the prices are attractive: most synthetic fabric styles are $200 to $1200; the average is $500 to $525.

David's has tried to boost the designer cache in their stores in recent years. Instead of selling their own in-house labels, David's has snapped up the brand names of defunct bridal designers like Galina, Bianchi and, most recently, Monique Luo. In the latter case, the designer herself is now working for David's. At the top end, David's offers the Oleg Cassini collection, which gives David's an entree to the premium gown market with styles running $1000 to $1200.

So, how's the quality? At David's you get what you pay for—a $300 dress is clearly not in the same quality league as one that is $1000. The initial quality of David's gowns is good; it is what happens after they sit in the stores for a while that is the problem (more on this below). All in all, we thought most of David's dresses were comparable in price and quality to other low-end bridal designers like Mori Lee and Alfred Angelo.

Okay, you might be wondering, why is David's "not recommended"? As we just finished discussing, their quality (at least initially) is decent. And the prices give a good value. So, here are our concerns:

♥ **Spam, spam, spam!** The moment you walk into David's, you are implored to "register" your wedding with a cheerful consultant. And once David's has your personal info, expect to receive an avalanche of junk mail, spam and come-ons from just about every wedding vendor in America. You can read it yourself in the fine print of David's privacy policy, posted on their web site. A word to the wise: if you decide to purchase anything at David's, give them only the minimal personal info needed (a cell phone, for example, to notify you of the arrival of a special order). Don't give out your mailing address, especially if you just are buying something cash and carry.

FYI: As we went to press, David's corporate parent (Federated Department Stores) announced it was selling the chain. No buyer was apparent as of this writing, but you can rest assured that no matter who buys David's, their aggressive marketing/spam efforts will continue.

♥ **Trashed gowns.** Among the biggest complaints we get about David's from consumers is the condition of their merchandise. "Deplorable" is often one word we hear; "disgusting" is another.

The bottom line: David's off-the-rack strategy means gowns are tried on multiple times before purchased and that takes a toll on the dresses. So, what is David's answer to brides who complain their dream dress is dirty? They can special order a new, clean version!

Well, that brings us to the next issue with David's: we still get numerous complaints about the chain's "special order" process—orders arriving late, wrong, damaged or worse. This happens with bridal gowns, bridesmaids' dresses and more.

David's is in deep denial on this: a spokesperson for the chain told us there are "no problems" with special ordered merchandise.

Looking for plus sizes?

A reader in Albuquerque, New Mexico called us with this frustrating story—she fell in love with a dress, only to learn the gown's manufacturer doesn't offer large sizes. In fact, less than half of the bridal designers on the market today carry "large" or "women" sizes (that is, sizes larger than 20). Some designers only carry sizes 22 and 24, while others go up to 44. Most charge an extra fee, which ranges from $50 to $200. As we discuss in this section, David's is one of the few bridal chains that sell women sizes.

Our general advice for David's: unless the item is actually in stock at the store, don't buy it.

♥ **Service, or lack thereof.** You don't have to look hard to find complaints about David's service. Wedding message boards are peppered with stories about rude salesclerks, botched alteration jobs and big pressure to buy.

It's that last issue that really bothers us—you might expect the hard sell when shopping for a used car, but some David's salespeople have mastered this for bridal. One Tennessee bride emailed that when she told a David's sales clerk that she wanted to sleep on a gown deal, the salesperson said the dress probably wouldn't be there the next day. After succumbing to the pressure to buy today, the salesperson proceeded to write up the order—and then added shoes, veil, tiara, bra and slip to the sales slip! The bride clearly told the clerk she just wanted to buy the dress. "I can't tell you how upset I was with how I was talked to and treated," said the bride.

A former David's employee echoed that experience—she told us David's salespeople are trained to sell a slip, bra, shoes or headpiece with every gown . . . and they are chastised by a manager if they don't. It's no surprise that brides tell us they get heavy sales pressure to purchase these extras at hefty prices. "I always thought it was pretty disgusting that we had to sell these extras at full price after so many women had tried them on," said the employee. And while David's stresses appointments, they never turn away walk-ins. "Whoever shows up first will get a 'consultant.' A rush of walk-ins will overwhelm consultants, who then have to handle five or six brides at a time."

Even David's seems to acknowledge its service is, uh, underwhelming. In a little-noticed blog, a David's marketing consultant admitted the company's own internal survey found "the service wasn't so good" and complaints were on the increase in recent years.

To be fair to David's, we should note that many comments on David's service are bi-polar—folks either love or hate the place. And Garry Schwartz, David's Vice President of Marketing, told us in a recent interview that the chain has implemented an extensive training process to improve service.

And we wonder, given the general decline of service at many retailers, what can we expect from a chain like David's? Is it likely the chain has an impossible task: hiring clerks at $7 an hour to sell a service-intensive product like a bridal gown? That said, the fish rots from the head first—it is David's corporate office that sets the tone for the chain . . . and the emphasis on high volume sales is driving many of the complaints about the stores.

♥ **Ethics.** Finally, we are most concerned with the behavior of the chain when it comes to advertising and marketing. Take their $99 bridal gown sales. David's spent $38 million on advertising last year and much of it went to plug these promotional events, held three to four times a year. The problem? Brides complain to us that when they arrive at these "sales," all they find is a few trashed sample gowns at $99. True, all other bridal gowns and some bridesmaids are marked down $50 to $300 off during the sale. Yet, if you advertise $99 gowns, you better have a decent selection of, say, dresses at $99.

Alterations are perhaps the biggest flash point for David's customers—while folks run hot or cold on David's merchandise or service, there is almost unanimous loathing for David's alterations services in our research. Just about anything that can go wrong does . . . botched alterations, late alterations, poor-quality alterations. And since most bridal gowns need at least some alterations, this is a major shortcoming of the chain. Of course, just because you buy a dress at David's does NOT mean you have to get it altered there. Our advice: take it elsewhere.

So, what's the bottom line? Frankly, we can't recommend this chain. The volume of complaints is so overwhelming that we can't recommend any of our readers give David's their hard-earned money. We expect a market leader like David's to set an example for other bridal retailers when it comes to customer service and satisfaction . . . instead, the chain sets new lows for the industry.

Yes, David's accounts for nearly 30% of the bridal market—one out of every three brides will get their gown there. And for brides with special needs (say, getting a large size gown in a hurry), David's may be the only choice. We applaud the chain's recent addition of a women's size line (David's sizes now go to 26W).

But, overall, it comes down to this: is David's a bargain? Is this a store we'd recommend to our readers? No, on both counts. You can find similar quality gowns from makers like Mori Lee and DaVinci for less money than David's. And given the feedback we get about the chain's service, special orders and alterations, we simply can't send our readers down that road.

What if you want to ignore this advice and purchase a dress at David's? First, only buy items that are in prefect condition *and* in stock so you can leave with them that very day—don't "special order" anything. If a dress is damaged, don't buy it—David's may promise you they can fix or clean whatever is wrong; don't bet on it. Finally, if you buy a dress at David's, get it altered somewhere else—you'll save both your money and your sanity.

Alterations: $250 for a 'custom' fit?

One of the best euphemisms in the bridal business is what the shops refer to as "custom fitting." Whatever you call them, alterations are a high expense area.

After shelling out big bucks on a gown, many brides are surprised to learn that their gown requires "custom-fitting." That's because few gowns are made to your measurements—most are made on assembly lines to correspond to a standard size. This may be close to your measurements. Close, but not close enough.

Remember the survey we quoted earlier in the chapter, when we revealed the same bride would be a different size in different designers' gowns? Well, the other news from that survey is that 60% of the time, the bride will need additional alterations. Er, "custom-fitting."

So, what's a fair price for a little tuck here and there? The average bridal gown racks up $100 to $200 in alterations. A common fix: the hem, which can run about $50 to $90. To alter the bodice side seams is $35. Other common alterations are train bustles, sleeve adjustments and shoulder alterations. Note those are average prices—couture gowns (dresses that sell for $2000, $3000 and more) can rack up much higher alterations bills, sometimes $250 to $500.

Here's the biggest rip-off: shops that raise the price of alterations for more expensive gowns for no reason at all. According to an article in *Vows: The Bridal Business Journal*, "shops that have a higher price point, charge more for alterations. These more expensive dresses are not more difficult to alter, nor do they fit badly. It's a matter of what the market will bear."

Wow! Can you believe it? Just consider it a little gift from the bridal industry—for those of you who purchase expensive (that is, anything over $1000) dresses, you get the privilege of being overcharged on alterations.

To be fair, we should note that some couture gowns rack up higher alteration fees exactly because they are so well made—shops must spend extra time to de-construct these gowns to do a simple hem. And that extra time is reflected in higher costs.

So, how can you avoid these problems? First, realize that some shops offer alterations for free. Of course, you can also take your gown to an independent seamstress (local fabric stores often have recommendations). This avoids the bridal shop altogether and, in some cases, may be the best route.

Gown Preservation: The Dirty Little Secret of the Bridal Industry?

Bridal gowns in dress shops take an incredible amount of abuse. Make-up stains, filthy hemlines, lace that gets dirty–repeated try-ons can turn the most beautiful white gown into a mess.

So, if a bridal gown gets stained, do dress shops send it out to one of those expensive, national gown cleaners? Or even a local dry cleaner? Nope, here's the surprising secret: most bridal shops just pop that dirty gown into a washing machine in the back of the store.

No, that wasn't a typo–many dress shops simply wash bridal gowns in a regular washing machine to remove dirt, make-up stains and other signs of wear and tear. Now, we find this highly ironic since many of these same shops pitch their customers to use very expensive, nationwide "gown preservation" companies that charge $200, $300 or more to "preserve" the gown after the wedding. In a business where "custom-ordered" gowns require $175 in alterations and accessories like veils are grossly overpriced, this is probably the final insult to brides who have traversed the wedding industry.

Just what do these gown preservation companies do for all this money? Well, just ask recent bride Shelley Brown-Parish of Hampton Falls, NH. On the advice of the bridal shop where she bought her gown, she paid $250 to Nationwide Gown Cleaning Service of Flushing, NY to clean and preserve her $3800 Scaasi wedding gown using their "Zurcion" method. The allegedly clean gown was returned to her in a sealed box, along with a notice saying if the box was opened, the company would not guarantee the dress.

Four years later, Brown decided to sell the gown and took it to a local consignment shop. When the box was opened, she was horrified. "The entire gown had changed color from white to ivory," she said, noting it had "large yellow stains all over the dress, blue ball-point pen marks on the front and on the train, and also had blood stains where the gown had been fastened to the tissue in the preservation box." Nationwide Gown Cleaning (which also goes under the names Continental Gown Cleaning and Prestige Gown Cleaning) said they'd re-clean the gown and have it back to her in two weeks.

One year later, Brown still didn't have her dress.

After complaining to the Better Business Bureau and bringing her story to the *Boston Globe*, the company still refused to return her dress. So, she sued them. After a local TV station picked up the chase, she *finally* got the gown back, which was still dirty and now smelled of cigarette smoke! The dress is now so famous it was featured on a recent talk show on wedding scams as an example of what can go wrong with these gown preservation companies.

Thankfully, the Federal Trade Commission took action in this case. The FTC sued Nationwide (Prestige) Gown Cleaning, charging them with false advertising and deceptive trade practices. Specifically, the FTC charged that Nationwide/Prestige broke the law by claiming its Zurcion method was the only method by which dresses could be cleaned—and for failing to disclose to consumers the conditions of its warranty (which forbids brides from opening their gown boxes). A year later, Nationwide signed a consent order with the FTC and agreed to stop these practices.

So what lessons does this have for other brides?

First, we think this whole "gown preservation box" scheme is a rip-off. According to the National Association of Resale and Thrift Shops, over 80% of bridal gowns brought into re-sale shops to be consigned in their original, unopened, sealed boxes are found to be dirty. These national gown preservation companies are duping brides into thinking their gowns are being preserved when evidence shows they're not even being *cleaned*. Here's our advice for brides who want to preserve their gowns:

1. Don't. If you're saving the dress for your daughter, you're assuming the dress will fit her, not have yellowed or gone out of style. That's a slim shot at best. A better idea: donate your gown to the charity gown sale run by the Making Memories foundation (see earlier in this chapter for details). Donating your gown not only gives you a tax deduction, but also affords another bride a good deal—and all the proceeds go to breast cancer patients. Check their web site at makingmemories.org for details.

2. We recommend consigning your dress at a local re-sale shop as soon as possible after the wedding. Or try selling your gown on Craigslist or eBay. Why? Styles change and dresses start to age quickly. Take the money and put it towards a savings account for your first child.

3. Clean and preserve it yourself. Most bridal gowns are made of synthetic fabrics (polyester satin is common) that can be cleaned in a washing machine. Yes you read right: a regular ol' washing machine. Cold water, a gentle cycle and a pure detergent (no fabric softeners or bleach) is best. Some bridal shop owners first spray the inside and outside of the dress with Shout or Spray 'N Wash. Hang dry on a plastic hanger. Note: before washing, you should test any beading or pearls. Place one bead/pearl in cold water for ten minutes and see if it disintegrates (some designers use very cheap pearls). If it passes the test, you can clean the gown at home.

4. After the dress is clean, wrap it in a clean, dry, white cotton sheet. If you want to stuff it with tissue paper, make sure it's acid free paper (available from local arts supplies or craft stores or call the Container Store at 800-733-3532). Put it in an acid-free box (also available from the sources above) and store it in a cool dry place—no attics or basements.

5. If this sounds too daunting, take/send it to a reputable cleaner. If you decide to use a local cleaner, be sure to check references and the Better Business Bureau. Another tip: if the gown is expensive (over $1000), insist that the shop only release the gown when you show a photo ID.

For a national cleaner, consider Imperial Gown Restoration (gown.com), a Virginia-based cleaner in business since 1947. No, they aren't a bargain, but they do have a 50-year warranty on their work. We've found them to be an excellent source for gown cleaning and preservation. Another great source: Professional Cleaners (professional-cleaners.com; 800-690-2146). Owner David Glausha is a seasoned pro when it comes to gown cleaning and preservation.

One final caveat—even if you do all the above steps and use that acid-free box, there is no guarantee that the dress won't yellow. Whether you pop that dress in the Maytag or send it to an expensive gown preservation company, there is still a good chance it will discolor over time.

Ship it to a business address

If you decide to order a gown from a mail order or Internet discounter, ship your gown to a business/daytime address where someone will be there to accept the delivery. Shipping a gown to a home address is risky—UPS may leave the box on your doorstep even if you're not home. You don't want a $1000 wedding dress sitting in a box on a porch exposed to the weather, squirrels or worse.

Notes

Chapter 3

Maids & Tuxes

Pop quiz: can you name 12 ways to find a bridesmaids dress that won't break the bank? And does not look hideous? We reveal the answers, plus review the hottest maids' designers and the best discount web sites and catalogs. Finally, let's not forget the groom—we'll take a look at tuxedos and several ways to cut that expense.

Bridesmaids' Gowns

What Are You Buying?

Perhaps nothing symbolizes what's wrong with the "wedding industry" more than the bridesmaid's gown. Have you seen any of these abominations to fashion? Cheap polyester fabric, ugly colors, absurd detailing—it seems like a bridesmaid's gown can transform any woman into a shiny satin nightmare. What's most appalling about bridesmaids' gowns is that they are actually designed that way! It's a crime against nature.

Amazingly, these "disposable" dresses (meant to be worn for only one day and then burned) aren't cheap. Most bridesmaid's dresses range from $150 to $240 (the national average is $185), although you can find maids gowns for as little as $79 from discounters. On the upper end, the "couture" bridesmaids' designers expect you to shell out $400+ for their creations. And, of course, those figures don't include expensive alterations—er, "custom fitting."

The most hilarious part of this travesty is the suggestion by bridal shops that (are you ready for this?) most of their bridesmaids' gowns can be worn again! Yea, right. How many New Year's Eve parties have you been to where women wore bridesmaids' gowns? Please, we wish these bridal shop owners would stop saying such drivel. Ninety-nine percent of all bridesmaids' gowns are banished to the back of the closet within hours of the wedding. (The remaining 1% are used as future Halloween costumes.)

Anyway, unless you plan to get married at a nudist camp, your bridesmaids have to wear *something* to your wedding. So here are our suggestions.

Our Recommendations for Bridesmaids' Gowns

♥ **Buy the cheapest bridesmaids' gowns you can stomach.** Some of the basic styles sell for about $100. For example: Penney's Bridal Party collection (jcpenney.com—go to special occasion) features maids dresses starting at $99. And Mori Lee's bridesmaids may not be the best quality, but hey, you can't beat the prices ($105 to $125). The nicest thing you can do for your bridesmaids who are on a tight budget is not burden them with paying for a $300 gown that they can only wear once.

♥ **Consider an alternative to typical bridesmaids' gowns.** Yes, there *are* beautiful gowns your bridesmaids could actually wear again. As you might expect, these gowns are designed not by bridal designers, but by "ready-to-wear" manufacturers. Check out a department store, mail-order catalog or web site for possibilities. One bride told us she found beautiful *silk* dresses at Talbot's (talbots.com, 800-225-8204) for just $138 to $178. And don't forget about J. Crew's new "wedding shop," where you can find a *silk* bridesmaids dress for $195 (online only; jcrew.com). More on these options later in the chapter.

Brides in Cyberspace: What's on the Web?

Chadwicks

Web: chadwicks.com, see Figure 1.

What it is: The online outpost for affordable maids gowns.

What's cool: Chadwick's is perhaps the best alternative to shelling out $200 on a maids' gown at specialty stores. Chadwick's has reorganized their site with a specific location for bridesmaids and mother of the bride dresses. Now you can click and go to the right page without scrolling through social occasion dresses. And the prices! An amazing $79 to $179, with some stunning choices UNDER $100. Chadwicks

FIGURE 1: Whoa! A stylish bridesmaids gown for just $89? Chadwick's makes it possible.

boasts a nice variety of silhouettes and current looks, from strapless dresses to ball gowns.

Needs work. Well, sizing is rather limited (just 4 to 16), although some styles are available in petites and woman's sizes. Brides also complain about styles that go out of stock; so if you see something you like, it's best to order early.

So, can you buy a bridesmaids dress online, direct from a designer at a low price? Well, not yet. Some designers are experimenting with the 'net—Alfred Sung quietly hawks their bridesmaids dresses from a separate site (BestBridesmaid.com), but the prices are no steal (about $30 OVER retail). And readers say BestBridesmaid.com should be named WorstService.com—we've had complaints about delayed deliveries and backordered dresses. Meanwhile, most big bridesmaids designers (Bill Levkoff, Watters & Watters) use the web just as a virtual catalog and direct brides to retailers to place orders. But the day for online bridesmaids dress sales may be just around the corner. Stay tuned.

♥ **Other sites recommended by our readers.** Who's got the lowest prices for bridesmaids' gowns online? We have to give the award to **ShopShop** (aka, CyberGown.com; shopshop.com). Their maids begin at the unbelievably low price of $49! Other dresses run $59 to $159. Another reader recommended **Jessica London** (JessicaLondon.com) as a good source for plus size maids at discounted prices. Check out **BridesAndProm** (bridesandprom.com)—readers compliment their low prices (most gowns are under $135) and the service/delivery is excellent.

Another bargain haunt: **GlamourCloset.com**. This unique site is an online consignment boutique for "previously-worn" and overstock sample maids gowns . . . and the prices are fantastic. Also cool: the site donates a portion of the sales to Parkinson's research.

Getting Started: How Far in Advance?

Most bridesmaids' gowns take two to four months to special order from bridal shops. If you are getting married in popular summer months, give yourself a little more time. In general, once you have selected the bridal gown, begin the search for bridesmaids' apparel. What if you don't have four months? Most of the major bridesmaids makers offer "rush service"—a limited selection of styles available in about six to eight weeks. Mail-order catalogs/web sites take only a week or two to ship most in-stock gowns. And don't forget David's (reviewed in the last chapter). This chain does carry some in-stock maids' gowns in a variety of sizes.

Step-by-step Shopping Strategies

♥ **Step 1:** After buying your bridal gown (and hence deciding on the setting and formality of your wedding), start the search for bridesmaids' gowns. Shopping for bridesmaids' dresses before you find your gown will only distract you.

♥ **Step 2:** Take into account your bridesmaids' ability to pay for the dress. (Traditionally, the bridesmaid pays for her gown plus alterations and accessories.) Are your bridesmaids starving college students or corporate lawyers earning six figures a year? Obviously, this is a big factor in your decision.

♥ **Step 3:** Given the financial condition of your attendants, start the shopping process. Follow much the same steps as for finding a bridal gown. Look at fabrics, finishes, and styles.

♥ **Step 4:** When you decide on a gown, announce your decision to the bridesmaids. Make sure each bridesmaid is individually measured and receives a written receipt that specifies the manufacturer, style number, size and delivery date.

♥ **Step 5:** Be sure to leave two weeks or more for alterations—even longer if the dresses have to be shipped to out-of-town bridesmaids. Get written cost estimates on any alterations before the order is placed.

Top Money-saving Secrets

1 Package discounts. If you order your gown from a bridal shop, they may offer a discount if you order all the bridesmaids' dresses there as well. This discount can range from 10% to 20%. Sometimes this is negotiable, so ask. (Be aware that some bridal shops mark up maids' gowns before they offer you a "discount." See the pitfalls section later in this chapter for more on this. Always check prices with a couple of sources to make sure you are getting a true discount).

2 Check out the discounters. The discount gown web sites reviewed in the last chapter also sell bridesmaids and even flower girl dresses. Typical savings run 20% to 40%, depending on the brand.

3 Sew your own. What's a bridesmaid-style dress, anyway? A basic dress pattern with little detailing or fuss. And can't you just buy typical bridesmaid fabrics like taffeta or crepe at a fabric store? Yes, you can. We've heard from several brides who had their favorite aunt sew their bridesmaids' dresses. While not a solution for everyone, this concept has its merits. One bargain tip: if you go this route, sign up for Joann Fabric's mailing list. Readers say Joann regularly sends out "1/2 price on anything" coupons to their mailing list, making fabric a bargain.

4 Pick a color, any color. Instead of forcing all the bridesmaids to wear the same dress, just give them a color (a swatch is best) and then have them buy separate dresses. Sure, they won't exactly match in style, but who cares? Let the bridesmaids shop their favorite dress shop

Alteration-friendly maids gowns

Not all bridesmaids' gowns are made equal—and some are easier to alter than others. Bridal retailers tell us the GOOD bridesmaids dresses (that is, easy to alter) are made by Alfred Angelo, Bridal Originals and After Six. The worst? Mori Lee, Levkoff (Champagne, New Image), McClintock and Bari Jay are the most difficult, thanks to a lack of seam allowance and other construction shortcuts.

and find a style that they can wear again. (One tip: suggest to the brides a basic style or skirt length). Obviously, you can't be a control freak to follow this tip, but it might be worth a shot.

5 Hit the department stores. Ok, we realize you haven't been in a department store for a while. But don't over look these retail dinosaurs—many offer surprisingly good deals on maids gowns. One big reason: recent bridesmaids fashion looks much like the "dressy" gowns already stocked by departments stores. Even better: department stores offer much lower prices (and higher quality) than bridal shops. One reader emailed us to point out that Bloomingdales has many bridesmaid-looking dresses that are available off-the-rack or orderable in different colors, sizes, lengths, etc. She hit a sale and got her dresses for just $60. Even if you pay full price (about $100 to $200 at most stores), you can at least try on several styles, colors and sizes right in the store. Plus you don't have to wait for an eternity for a "special" order to arrive—most department stores will track down different colors/sizes at nearby locations.

6 Buy the gloves at a discount. Don't pay high retail prices for bridesmaids' gloves—we found an online discounter, Dina's (800-479-4696; bridalgloves.com) that offers a 20% to 30% savings off nationally advertised gloves. Here's how it works: to identify the gloves, give them the page number of a magazine ad or the bridesmaid dress

Made in America maids dresses fast disappearing

The days of the "Made in the USA" bridesmaids dress may be numbered. For years, the production of bridesmaids dresses remained in the U.S. while just about every other clothing article sold in this country was made offshore. Why? Most bridesmaid makers didn't think foreign contractors could ship maids' dresses (which are made in small batches) quickly enough to the U.S. Well, apparently that problem has been solved. In recent years, major maids manufacturers Bill Levkoff and Jordan have moved production offshore, joining such other designers as Mori Lee. What's this mean for consumers? First, we've noticed the quality of gowns has greatly improved for Levkoff and Jordan since they went off shore. That's the good news. The downside? Now, getting a problem fixed takes much longer. When production was in New York, a quick call and UPS shipment could fix it. Now the plant is in China, meaning a longer wait to get a corrected dress.

info (style, color, etc.)—they do the rest. Most gloves (made by the same companies advertised in bridal magazines) are only $16 to $24 a pair. And shipping is only $5 per order (no matter how many gloves you order). The same company also discounts matching handbags and other maids' accessories.

7 Do it online. Who says you have to order a bridesmaids dress from a bridal shop? The best bargains are often from mail order catalogs like Talbot's (which has retail stores and a web site as well, see below), Bloomingdales by Mail (800) 777-0000, Spiegel (800) 345-4500 and Chadwick's of Boston. Heck, even Penney's (800) 527-8345 (web: jcpenney.com—go to special occasion) has a web site that sells bridesmaids gowns for as little as $99. Another key advantage to mail order: returns. Get in a size that doesn't fit? A flaw in the dress? Most catalogs have a "no hassle" return policy that makes exchanges a snap. Contrast that with some bridal retailers whose attitude when something goes wrong is: "Tough! Even if all the sizes are wrong, you ordered those hot fuchsia dresses with butt bows on a NON-RETURNABLE basis, honey!"

Both Talbot's and Chadwicks have been singled out by our readers for great deals. But let's take a second to look at J Crew, which is making a splash in the bridesmaid world:

Click on "the wedding shop" on J Crew's web site and you'll see some amazing good buys on maids gowns. Yes, we realize Crew is better known for their casual clothes, but how about this: a Sophia short silk dress with empire waist for just $195. Did we mention this is a silk gown? Remember that $195 at a bridal shop buys you polyester or polyester when it comes to maids gowns.

As a side note, you can also go mail order to save money on other parts of the bridesmaids' ensemble like hosiery. One Hanes Place catalog and web site (800) 300-2600 (web: onehanesplace.com—click on clearance or sale) sells "slightly imperfect" hosiery for up to 40% off retail. If you want your bridesmaids to wear matching hosiery, we found Silk Reflections line in eight colors for just $11.40 for three pairs. Similar pantyhose in bridal retail shops sells for five times that price!

8 Avoid rush cuts. Bridesmaids' dresses are expensive enough when ordered at full retail. Add in that extra "rush" fee (incurred when you order a dress with less than two to three months before your wedding) and you'll see the price rise another 20%. Don't delay making this decision as you plan the rest of your wedding.

9 For shoes, go surfing. Avoid retail stores and their $100+ price tags. The web has many discount sources for dye-to-match satin shoes. In addition to those sources mentioned in Chapter 2 (see the

Accessories box), DiscountBridalShoes.com (part of DyeableShoesOnilne.com) has shoes that start at an amazing $30. No, this site doesn't do the actual dyeing, but they provide detailed tips and advice on finding a good dyer.

What if you want to have someone else dye the shoes? You don't have to go to a fancy retail shop and pay through the nose for dyeing. Our advice: go to a shoe repair shop instead. They charge $5 to $15 a pair for dyeing—and don't forget to negotiate a discount if you have more than four pairs.

A few notes about dyed-to-match shoes: the dye is NOT waterproof. If you are planning an outdoor wedding, remember wet grass can cause the dye to run and stain. It is also difficult to get every last shoe to match; and the color may look different in outdoor light compared to indoors.

Bridesmaids Options

Why spend $200+ on a bridesmaids gown from a bridal shop when you can get a similar gown from a department store or catalog at HALF the price? Here's how several options compare to the standard issue bridesmaids dress found in bridal stores (we used a Levkoff gown for comparison):

Where	What	Price	Fabric
Levkoff (at a bridal shop)	Strapless A-line dress	$170; others $145-$270	Poly Taffeta
Spiegel spiegel.com	Lace trimmed V-neck, Godet skirt	$99; others $60-$100	Velvet
Chadwicks chadwicks.com	Halter Scarf Gown Georgette Skirt	$99; others $99-$139	Poly Satin Fully Lined
Bloomingdales bloomingdales.com	Strapless A-line Floor Length Dress	$231 others $79-$110	Poly Satin

Notes: As you can see, the biggest advantage to ordering a standard "bridesmaids dress" like a Bill Levkoff design from a bridal shop is the wide availability of sizes and colors. Yes, some mail order sources sell large sizes (above a 16 or 18) . . . but extra length is rarely available. Colors are also limited—if your heart is set on a particular odd hue, a standard bridesmaids dress might be the only solution. Another

10 Don't go to a store with "bridal" in its name. Many specialty stores have great deals on dresses that would work well for bridesmaids—those shops just don't have the word *bridal* in their names! Case in point: Ann Taylor. A bride who posted to our message boards found great deals here—a $118 silk sheath dress marked down to $30. "The store didn't have all the sizes I needed, so the manager gave me the number for their corporate office. Would you believe they not only tracked down the sizes I needed from across the country, but only charged me ten bucks to overnight deliver them! Kudos to Ann Taylor!" Another bride found maids gowns at Ann Taylor for just $55 each (marked down from $175). "You can't beat the quality compared to a typical maids dress either," she said. In the past year, Ann Taylor launched "Celebrations," a line of special occasion gowns that would be

COMPARED

SIZES	COMMENTS	RETURNABLE?
SIZES 4-22 SOME STYLES IN 38-42	AVAILABLE IN 26 COLORS DELIVERY: 12-14 WKS. SHIPPING INCLUDED	ARE YOU KIDDING?
MISSES (4 TO 16) WOMENS (14W-24W)	TWO COLORS; DELIVERY 3-6 DAYS SHIPPING $14	YES, EXCHANGE OR FULL REFUND
MISSES (2-20) WOMENS (14W-26W)	FOUR COLORS; DELIVERY 6-9 DAYS SHIPPING $14-$15	YES, EXCHANGE OR FULL REFUND
MISSES (2-14)	TWO COLORS; DELIVERY 3-9 DAYS SHIPPING: $16-18	YES, EXCHANGE OR FULL REFUND

advantage to standard bridesmaid gowns: they guarantee the dye lots will match if you order several gowns. Of course, you pay for that, almost TWICE the price of mail order options. Plus delivery is much quicker using mail order and department stores, a matter of days versus 12-14 WEEKS for a standard issue bridesmaid gown.

perfect for maids. In sizes 0-16, Taylor maids dresses are available online or in 18 of Taylor's 361 stores. Prices range from $168 to $198 per dress.

11 Hit the outlet stores. Many of the stores we mention in this chapter have outlet stores. Check the web site Outlet Bound (web: outletbound.com) to see if one is near you. Example: Talbot's has 21 outlets around the U.S. While this tip is more hit or miss depending on when you go, it might be worth a trip if you have an outlet within close driving distance.

12 Skip the accessories. Bridesmaids' designers have been turning out all manner of matching accessories like shawls, purses and shoes in recent seasons. The prices, however, are outrageous. One designer now pitches matching purses for $64 and satin dyeable shoes for up to $170! Shawls and wraps add another $30 to $60 to another famous maids designer's dresses. And try to avoid needing a shawl or wrap by selecting a bridesmaids style that isn't so bare to begin with. Finally, just skip some superfluous items altogether. Do your bridesmaids really need a $64 handbag died to match their chartreuse gowns?

13 Try the Rack. If you have a Nordstrom department store near you, odds are you also have a Nordstrom Rack. That's the clear-

FIGURE 2: Why have your maids shell out $75 for dyeable satin shoes when you can find them online for $32?

ance outlet for merchandise that didn't make it in the store. One reader emailed us this incredible story: she found her bridesmaids dresses at Nordstrom Rack for just $14.95. Nope, that isn't a typo. "Every year they put dresses on sale—racks of them! Ours were periwinkle matte satin strapless sheaths. The sizes ran from 0 to 14!" What if you have a tough-to-fit bridesmaid? The same reader said she solved that problem by buying TWO gowns (at $15 each) in different sizes and then had a seamstress piece them together for a tough-to-fit maid. Go to Nordstrom.com to find a store near you.

Helpful Hints

1 Don't go shopping with more than one bridesmaid. If you want to make the process of shopping for bridesmaids' gowns go as smoothly as possible, just take along ONE friend or relative. Too many bridesmaids (each with their own opinions and tastes) will only complicate the decision. Make the decision and announce it to the other bridesmaids. Don't expect everyone to love your choice (and, unfortunately, some bridesmaids may be tacky enough to tell you about it to your face).

2 Take your hardest to fit bridesmaid with you. So, which one bridesmaid should you take along with you? Let's be frank: everything looks great on the bridesmaid who models in her spare time. It's a smarter bet to take another bridesmaid who is, uh, the most challenging to fit.

3 You may be on the hook for deadbeat bridesmaids or groomsmen. Here's an ominous trend: some bridal retailers are forcing brides and grooms to sign contracts that say they are responsible for payment on ANY dress purchase or tux rental by their wedding party. Yes, when your flaky maid of honor passes a hot check to the

Are gown knock-offs legal?

It's a time-honored tradition in fashion: ripping-off your competitor's hot selling design. While we see frequent design-stealing in bridal gowns, it's a virtual epidemic in the world of bridesmaids' designs, where one "hot" style quickly appears in several different versions from different makers. And guess what? It's completely legal. Copyright laws do NOT cover apparel (except for logos and certain patterns of lace). Hence it is completely legal to buy a knock-off gown or to have your aunt (or any seamstress) sew a copy of a hot style.

bridal shop for the balance on her bridesmaid gown, YOU could be on the hook. While we sympathize with any retailer when it comes to dealing with deadbeats, forcing couples to cough up money is a bit much. We would urge couples to refuse to sign such deals.

Pitfalls to Avoid

PITFALL #1 SQUARE PEG, ROUND HOLE.

"Help! I want my bridesmaids to wear this slinky dress I saw in the magazines, but when we went to order, none of the girls fit the size chart! The bridal shop recommended a size 14 for a girl who normally wears a size 6. When the dress comes in, won't she be socked with expensive alterations?"

Do you have the body of a supermodel? Well, we sure don't. But, unfortunately, most bridesmaids dress manufacturers have size charts that are designed for bizarre, alien woman with exaggerated Barbie Doll figures. Giraffes with breasts.

Take, for example, that above story. The bridesmaid in question had measurements of 36" bust, 29" waist, 37" hips. Now, look at the size chart for one of the U.S. and Canada's biggest bridesmaids designers.

	Size								
	4	6	8	10	12	14	16	18	20
Bust	33	34	35	36	37	38.5	40	41.5	43.5
Waist	24	25	26	27	28	29.5	31	32.5	34.5
Hips	36	37	38	39	40	41.5	43	44.5	46.5

So, what size would YOU order? Let's see, the bridesmaids bust (measured at the fullest part of the chest; this is NOT her bra size) would fit into a size 10. BUT, look at that waist—it needs a size 14. And the hips? Try a size 6.

Because it is always easiest to alter IN a dress (instead of letting it out), we recommend ordering the size that corresponds to the bridesmaid's LARGEST measurement. That would indeed be a size 14. As you'll note, however, this will require significant alterations, as the dress will have to be taken in a couple inches at the bust and hips.

This problem has been exasperated in recent years by all the new, body-hugging styles churned out by bridesmaids' designers. Those slinky dresses are definitely a step forward fashion-wise, but all this haute couture has run head long into the reality of women's bodies. The fact is many bridesmaids just don't fit the bizarro size charts. As a result, some are being socked with HUGE alteration bills to remake (or drastically cut down) these gowns.

What makes this problem even more complex is the fact that each bridesmaids' designer has just ONE size chart. This chart covers a wide range of dress styles, from a loosely fitting empire waisted gown to a body-hugging sheath. If you go for an empire-style dress (which is tightly fitted in the bust), the measurement that counts the most is, of course, the bust. But if you plan to have your maids don a sexy strapless number, watch out—those waist and hip measurements will be critical.

One thing you can be sure of: almost all bridesmaids' dresses require alterations. Even if a bridesmaid exactly matches the size chart, she'll still probably need some minor alterations (a skirt hem, a bodice tuck here and there). That's because these dresses are not custom-made to your measurements—heck, sometimes they don't even correspond closely to the size chart itself.

What if your bridesmaids are "off the chart," that is they don't closely correspond to the size charts? Do yourself and them a favor: DON'T order maids dresses from a bridal shop. Instead, consider some of our alternative dress sources. Stores like J Crew and Talbot's carry a wide range of sizes and (here's a shocker) actually let you return a dress that doesn't fit.

Real Wedding Tip

Delivery, sizing problems plague maids' order

This California bride wasn't happy with how her bridesmaids dress order from a local bridal shop turned out.

"I can't begin to tell you how disappointed and sorry we are to have ordered maids gowns from a local shop. We were promised the gowns would takes eight weeks to order. At the end of the 15th week, I called them to see how much longer they would be. The owner said that nobody could have quoted me 8 weeks; they always quote between 10 and 12 weeks for bridesmaid dresses. She had no answer when I told her it was nearing 16 weeks! When the dresses finally arrived, each dress was almost two to three sizes too big. My smallest bridesmaid who wears a size 1 was ordered a size 4 dress. My sister, who wears a size 4, was ordered a size 8 dress. What was the purpose of the 40-minute fitting, if they were all going to be issued dresses that were not ordered to fit them? Oh, I guess it was so that the girls could be charged an additional $100+ dollars for alterations on top of the $300 price tag for the dress. It just makes me sick!"

PITFALL #2 DISINTEGRATING BRIDESMAIDS DRESSES.

"I ordered five bridesmaids dresses from a major designer. When they came in, I was shocked! Every single dress was defective. All of the dresses came out of the boxes with threads hanging from every seam and the seams all pulled and puckered. The buttons and loops on the backs of the dresses fell apart when the girls tried to button them. These had to be sewn on four of the five dresses one half hour before I was to be married! The most appalling defect of all was the detailing on the front of one of the dresses. It was sewn on crooked and had to be taken off and reattached by a professional dressmaker. While my maid of honor was up at the altar next to me, we could actually hear her dress popping apart."

Yes, it is no wonder the bridesmaids dress is the biggest joke in the fashion business. What's most frustrating about this purchase, however, is the "bait and switch" tactics of the largest bridesmaid manufacturers. Here's how it works: the bridesmaid *samples* you first try on at the bridal shop are always pristine and perfect. But what about your special order? Somehow, the quality then slips—and drops through the floor. Consumers we interviewed describe the workmanship on many of these dresses in one word: abysmal. And it's not just on the cheap dresses; the ones described above cost $260 each, according to the bride.

Invisible zippers are an example of the quality problem with brides-

Flower girl dresses: where to get the deals

Sure, those matching flower girl dresses are cute, but do you really want to pay $129 for a dress for a five-year-old girl? No, you don't have to spend a three-figure sum to get a cute flower girl gown. Here are our bargain tips:

♥ **Department store holiday and Easter sales.** After Christmas and Easter, look for deals on dress-up clothes for girls—most of these gowns can double for a flower girl. And you'll save 50% or more by hitting those sales. Hint: also check out the communion dresses for the smallest flower girls—again, much more affordable than the $100+ dresses you see in bridal stores.

♥ **Go online.** Readers found sites like eBay.com have terrific deals on dresses your flower girl can wear. Many dresses are under $35. Another site to check out: Dandylasses.com (dandylasses.com). The discounts aren't huge on this site but the dresses are exceptional and most are priced below $75.

maids' gowns. Yes, these disappearing zippers (seen on such hip lines as After Six and Dessy) are supposed to make gowns look more fashionable. The only problem: they break, don't work well and cause general havoc. Some shops have been so frustrated with invisible zippers (insiders call them "miserable zippers") that they are replacing them during alterations.

Overall, the best advice we can give is to order early. Leaving enough time will enable the shop to fix the problems. Another idea is to by-pass the standard bridesmaid dress entirely. Select dresses at a department store or from a catalog/web site and have the last laugh.

PITFALL #3 SIZING PROBLEMS

"Our $250 bridesmaids gowns arrived yesterday and NONE of them fit the girls! Some were too big, others too small. What happened?"

Yes, you carefully shopped for bridesmaids' gowns and made sure you ordered the correct sizes for all the girls after comparing their measurements to the designer's size charts. But then the gowns came in and whamo! Nothing fit. What happened?

Here's a dirty little secret of the bridesmaids dress biz: sometimes, your "special order" gowns won't fit. That's because the bridesmaid manufacturers goof with the sizing. Among the worst offenders: After Six/Dessy, Mori Lee and Bari Jay.

What makes this more frustrating is there is little rhyme or reason to the miss-sizing—some gowns come in too big; others are too small. Then, adding insult to injury, some dress designers (notably Mori Lee and Bari Jay) take an "it's YOUR problem" attitude toward sizing goofs. Hard to believe, but these manufactures think you are getting such a deal on their gowns that they refuse to fix any problems, leaving shops and brides scrambling to alter miss-sized gowns. (On a positive note, even though After Six/Dessy is guilty of miss-sizing, the designer is at least willing to fix problems).

PITFALL #4 CLASHING COLOR MOTIFS.

"I was a bridesmaid in a wedding recently. The bride picked out lovely peach bridesmaids' gowns. Unfortunately, the church was all decorated in bright red—all her pictures looked like 'Night of the Clashing Circus Clowns!' It wasn't pretty."

Be careful when you select the bridesmaids' gowns to take into account the decor of your ceremony and reception site. Many of your wedding pictures will have the sites as a backdrop. Try to pick a color that not only pleases you but also doesn't clash with the decor. Hint: if you are marrying in a church, ask the officiant what types/colors of hangings and alter cloths they use during your wedding month.

PITFALL #5 DYE LOTS MAY VARY.

"I would like to order bridesmaids gowns from two different stores (in different towns). The shop owners all have told me that they won't guarantee that the colors will match, since the fabric will be from different dye lots. Is that true? Could you really tell the difference?"

If you've got bridesmaids scattered across the country, it may be tempting to have them go to a local bridal shop to order their dress. Our advice: don't. It is true that dye lots can (and do) vary from one batch of dresses to another. The only way to insure they will all match is to order them from the same source at the *same time* (out-of-town bridesmaids will have to get their dresses by mail and have fittings done locally).

Would you really be able to tell a difference in the dye lots? It's hard to say. That depends on the color and fabric—some styles might show more of a color variation than others. It's not worth the risk.

This same advice applies to any extra fabric you order (to make a flower girl's dress or shawls for the ceremony, etc). Order the fabric at the same time you order the gowns.

PITFALL #6 SIGHT UNSEEN COLORS.

"I ordered $300 bridesmaids dresses in 'blue onyx' from a local bridal shop. The only problem? I didn't see the color chart or a swatch before ordering. The shop had samples in green and burgundy, but only a catalog picture of the blue. When the dresses came in, I was shocked. The color looked nothing like the picture and was terrible!"

Since bridal shops carry a limited amount of inventory, you may be tempted to order a bridesmaids dress in a color you can't see. You may want a dress in "cranberry," but the shop only carries the same style in a "hunter green." And even the same color can look different in certain fabrics (velvets versus chiffons, etc.).

The best protection is to insist on seeing a color swatch or color chart to make sure it is what you want. Catalog/web pictures can be notoriously unreliable—funky lighting in the photo or simple variations in printing can make a "deep plum" dress seem more like bright purple.

The best deals on MOB's

What's a Mother of the Bride (MOB) to do? Many bridal stores stock mom's gowns that look like something Grandma Moses might wear. And the prices? Get outta here. Instead, the best deals are in discounters like Marshall's, Filene's Basement, Nordstrom Rack and Loehmann's. There you can find a stylish dress at a price that won't break the bank.

Another related problem: designers who use combo fabrics. To spice up their collections, some designers will combine a velvet bodice with organza sleeves. The only problem? The colors in different fabrics might not match as you think they should.

The quote above is an actual email we received from a New Jersey bride. Unfortunately, she was stuck with dresses she described as "god-awful ugly." (Actually, she used more colorful language than that, but you get the idea.) The bridal shop asked the manufacturer to fix the problem and guess what? The manufacturer refused, saying, "That's what 'blue onyx' is supposed to look like."

We expect to see more complaints like this in the future. Bridesmaids' dress designers are rolling out more "sophisticated" gowns, with fancy fabrics, two-tone colors and other doo-dads. The sheer variety of choices is overwhelming some retail stores, who don't have samples or swatches that show the myriad of options. As a result, brides are gambling on a color or fabric choice, sometimes with less-than-great results. (Another frustration: some designers even charge for small swatches).

The bottom line: make sure you see the color(s) in the fabric(s) you want before committing to a special-order bridesmaids dress.

PITFALL #7 MARK IT UP TO MARK IT DOWN.

"The bridal shop where I bought my gown offered a 10% discount on maids dresses. That sounded great until I did some price shopping. I found the shop was marking up the gowns over retail before they gave me a 'discount.'"

Fake discounts are a problem in the bridal industry. We've talked

The $49 bridesmaids dress

Can you really buy a bridesmaids dress for $49? Yes, you can. **ShopShop.com** (we briefly mentioned them earlier in this chapter) has three dozen bridesmaids dresses that start at just $49. What do they look like? Who cares! They're $49! Just kidding—they look just fine. No, we're not talking the latest couture here, but there are some decent basic dresses. And did we mention the price? Your maids will thank you for not forcing them to pay $200+ for a maids gown that will be thrown away after the wedding. Sizes 8 to 22.

Another reader recommended **CybernetPlaza.com** as a good source for cheap bridesmaids gowns. "They have true sizing, good quality and decent styling. The best thing is that none of us paid over $70 for a dress!"

with retailers who confess to the "mark it up before you mark it down" scam—shops will price dresses OVER retail before they give you a so-called "discount." A word to the wise: do some price shopping before you commit to any package deal.

Another trend: no-name bridesmaids dresses. More and more retailers are now carrying "stealth" bridesmaids gowns by no-name manufacturers. Don't look for those gowns advertised in bridal magazines or all over the web—these makers keep a very low profile. The gowns are typically knock-offs of designer dresses, sewn cheaply and sold to retailers at low wholesale prices. Retailers then can feel free to mark-up no name gowns whatever they want, since it is so hard to price-shop these dresses.

What's worse: some shops do a bait and switch with no-name dresses. We've seen several reports of bridesmaids who ordered a name brand gown and then got a no name knock-off. One bride ordered a Levkoff dress and got an Alexia copy. How can you prevent this? Be sure you get a written order ticket that indicates the manufacturer's name. Some shops only put their bogus in-house codes on order forms, making it hard to prove what was promised. When the bridesmaids dresses come in, check for the designer's label. A telltale sign of the knock-off scam are maids' dresses that come in missing designer labels (legit designers like Levkoff almost always put tags in).

Destination Weddings: Maids

Find a local source for steaming or last minute repairs. When it comes to maids dresses, things go wrong—zippers break, wrinkles happen and worse. Find a local bridal shop or cleaner who can handle last minute repairs or pressing. Be sure to keep this source's contact info handy when you get to the destination!

Ratings of Selected Bridesmaids Designers

With over $800 million worth of bridesmaids dresses sold each year, there is certainly no shortage of options to consider. Besides manufacturers that just make bridesmaids dresses (After Six/Dessy, Jordan), there are many bridal gown designers that make maids' dresses too. But who has the best quality? The best value for the dollar?

To answer those questions, we intensively research all the different brands, designers and manufacturers. We attend industry wholesale markets to view runway shows and inspect garments. We also talk with retailers about which dresses are best ... and worst. Finally, we hear from you, the reader. Our email box is always open to hear your comments.

The chart on the next page compares the top 20 bridesmaid dress

How the bridal designers block rental of bridesmaids dresses

If a guy can rent a tux, why can't a gal rent a bridesmaids dress?

That idea scares the pants off the bridal industry. Several bridal manufacturers have also taken public and not-so-public steps to stop dress rentals. Our investigation into the tactics of Alfred Angelo, one of the largest bridal designers, revealed some surprising information. As one of the top three bridal dressmakers, Angelo's designs are available in hundreds of shops. Angelo recently sent a "marketing statement" to each of its dealers, requiring them to agree in writing that they will "not rent Alfred Angelo Dream Maker dresses to consumers." Stores that rent their dresses face "immediate termination" of their account.

We asked the company about this practice. Bernard Toll, Angelo's public relations liaison, told us that "we do this for obvious reasons. Alfred Angelo dresses are not designed to withstand multiple wearings, countless alterations that leave telltale needle marks and legally required cleanings. Each Alfred Angelo dress is produced to make just one bride's dreams become a lovely reality on her wedding day."

Now, this is a curious argument. Angelo is essentially arguing that their dresses are of such poor quality that they won't "withstand repeated wearings." Considering the average bridesmaids dress costs $170 to $250, we find this to be appalling. Angelo's arguments seem to give credence to the perception that the industry designs "disposable dresses" of such inferior craftsmanship you can't be expected to wear them more than one day.

The bridal industry says that women "don't want to rent dresses. They'd rather buy." However the actions of the magazines and dress designers indicate quite the opposite—they're trying to stifle the consumer demand for a needed service for purely selfish reasons: women buy $800 million worth of bridesmaids dresses each year. Rental of these dresses would cut that business in half—and force the designers to make dresses that don't disintegrate after one wearing. By renting bridesmaids dresses alone, women could save $400 million each year.

designers. The rating refers to our opinion of their quality.

Want even more info? We have archived reviews of bridesmaids designers on our web site, BridalBargainsBook.com (click on "bonus material"). To access this area of our site, use the password "gowns7259."

Bridesmaids designers compared

Name	Rating	Cost	Web	Sizing: Petite	Sizing: Large
After Six	A	$$	aftersix.com		•
Alfred Angelo	C	$$	alfredangelo.com	•	•
Alfred Sung	A	$$	alfredsungdresses.com		•
Alyce Designs	B	$$ to $$$	alycedesigns.com		•
Amsale	B+	$$$	amsale.com		•
Ann Taylor	A-	$$	anntaylor.com	•	
Bari Jay	B	$$	barijay.com		•
Belsoie / B2	A-	$$ to $$$	belsoie.com		•
Bill Levkoff	C+	$$ to $$$	billlevkoff.com		•
Chadwicks	A	$	chadwicks.com	•	•
David's Bridal	D+	$ to $$	davidsbridal.com	•	•
Davinci	B	$	davincibridal.com		•
Dessy	B+	$$$	dessy.com		•
Eden	A	$ to $$	edenbridals.com	•	•
Impression	A-	$ to $$	impressionbridal.com		•
J Crew	A	$$$	jcrew.com	•	
JC Penney	A-	$	jcpenney.com	•	•
Jessica Mclintock	B-	$ to $$	jessicamclintock.com		•
J Hjelm Occasions	B	$$$	jimhjelm.com	•	•
Jordan	B	$$ to $$$	jordanfashions.com		•
Lazaro	B-	$$$	lazarobridal.com	•	
Laundry	B	$$$	laundrybyshellisegal.com		
Mori Lee	B-	$	morilee.com		•
New Image	B-	$$$	billlevkoff.com		•
Raylia	C	$$	rayliadesigns.com	•	•
Siri	B-	$$$	siriinc.com		
Talbot's	B	$$$	talbots.com	•	•
Vera Wang	C-	$$$	verawang.com		
Watters	A-	$$$	watters.com		•

Notes: Rating: *Our opinion of the designer's quality, value and fashion, based on our own hands-on inspections and surveys of bridal retailers.* **Cost:** *The range in retail prices: $=under $140, $$=$140 to $200, $$$=over $200.* **Web:** *The designer's web site.* SIZING—**Petite:** *Designers who offer special petite sizes. Some offer petites for all styles, while others only do petites on a selected number of designs.* **Large:** *Nearly all designers offer gowns in sizes 4-20. We classify any size larger*

Key: •=YES

Easy to Alter?	Comments
•	Good quality; excellent web site with online color swatches
•	Not the cutting edge of fashion, but good value. 46 colors.
•	Big on separates. Made by Dessy/After Six.
	Quality is average; delivery is good. Prices a bit high.
•	Fashion forward, but sizing is limited.
	Generous return policy; matching shoes, accessories.
	Can be difficult to alter; fashion above average.
	B2 is simpler with lower prices, less fancy fabric.
•	Fashionable yes, but quality disappoints. Huge selection.
•	Most under $150; limited colors but good value.
	Complaints and snafus mar rating; do offer maternity styles.
	Knock-off David's maids gowns at lower prices.
•	Quality is above average, but prices are steep.
	Basic traditional styling, good value.
•	Separates a mainstay here; fashion good. Sizing inconsistent.
•	Yes, you can actually wear these again! High price, but all silk.
	Basic styling. Great prices. Only some styles have extended sizes.
	Above-average quality; not-so-great customer service.
	Good quality, great styling. Very expensive.
	Entry-level "Joanie G" line is best value; quality is average.
	A $300 maids dress? Too pricey for only average quality.
	Designed by Liz Claiborne's Shelli Segal, but made by Levkoff.
	Knock-off fashion, low quality but low price. Slow delivery.
	Division of Levkoff has slightly better quality, fashion.
	Mid-price designer, but delivery snafus lower rating.
	Many styles available in different fabrics; difficult to alter.
	Pricey, but mostly silk fabric. Limited colors. Look for sales..
	Overpriced and limited sizes. Did we mention overpriced?
•	Fabrics, styling, color choice above average. A bit pricey.

than a 20 as a "large size." Some designers just offer sizes 22 and 24, while others go up to a 44. As with petites, only selected styles may be available in larger sizes. Most designers charge extra for large sizes. **Easy to Alter?** *Based on our interviews with 150 seamstresses, which bridesmaids dresses are easiest to alter? A lack of seam allowance or other construction shortcuts can be make a dress difficult to alter.*

Tuxedos

Nowhere are the wedding etiquette rules sillier than for men's formal wear. For example, they say you MUST wear a black tux with tails for a formal wedding after six in the evening. If you don't, the vengeful WEDDING GODS will strike you down, ostracize your family and charge obscene amounts of money to your credit cards.

Now if your wedding is before six you can wear a gray or white short coat . . . but not if the moon is full. And, of course, you must follow the omnipotent "formality" rules that dictate proper dress for weddings that are very formal, just plain formal, semi-formal, pseudo-formal and the dreaded para-formal.

Just kidding.

We believe all this is nonsense. Grooms and groomsmen should wear whatever they believe is appropriate. Who cares what time of day the wedding is? If your wedding is an informal ceremony in a local civic rose garden, you don't have to wear a tuxedo. We know we might incur the wrath of Emily Post for saying this, but hey, do what you want to do. If you look good in a double-breasted tux, wear that. If you don't, look for another style. You get the idea.

What Are You Buying?

Actually, most grooms and groomsmen *rent* formal wear for weddings. Imagine what would happen if men had to shell out the same kind of money that bridesmaids spend on those horrendously ugly bridesmaids' gowns. There would be mass revolts and street rioting. Fortunately, for national security's sake, most men's formal wear is rented. Typically, the groomsmen are financially responsible for their tuxedo rentals, so basically you and your fiancé's only expense is the groom's tux. Here are the three basic options for men's formalwear:

1 **Rent.** Good news: you CAN rent a stylish tux for your wedding. Yes, until a few years ago, most tux shops just offered cookie-cutter styles (you could have black or black). Now, the $1.6 billion tux business has received a fashion injection, thanks to Hollywood's influence on formal attire. You can still rent a black tux, but now you can choose from styles with pointed lapels, brocade vests and long satin ties. Yes, you can even rent a white linen tux.

Rentals account for 70% of the tux market (the rest of the guys will purchase a tux). When you rent a tux, you get just about everything: jacket, pants, cummerbund, shirt, tie, cuff links, and, of course, shirt studs (little jewelry that covers your buttons). Notice what's missing?

No, not underwear. If you answered "shoes" give yourself extra points. While most tuxes rent for $100 to $175 (an average is $145), the shoes are often $20 to $30 extra. Of course, it's more expensive in major metropolitan areas (like New York City, where tux rentals can top $200). A small deposit/damage waiver ($10 to $20) is required to reserve a tux. There are three types of places to rent formal wear:

♥ **Chain stores.** Large formalwear chains (such as AfterHours.com and JimsFormalwear.com) are located across the U.S. They basically offer similar styles and brand names. Service can range from helpful to dreadful. Most of these chains don't carry any stock at their stores—a central warehouse is used to dispense the tuxedos. Hence, it's difficult to decide which style is best for you by just looking at the mannequins or a catalog. To try on a particular style, you must ask the shop for a "trial fitting." For no charge, most shops will bring in a style in your size. The only disadvantage is that this requires a second visit to the shop, rather inconvenient for those of you who lead busy lives. David's and Men's Wearhouse have entered the tuxedo rental market with good prices and selection as well. See later in this chapter for more information.

♥ **Bridal Shops.** More and more bridal shops are now getting into the business of renting tuxes. However, instead of stocking tuxes at their store, they use a service, which supplies them with rentals. Hence, the way you pick a tuxedo is to look through a book with pictures of tuxedo-clad soap stars awash in testosterone. Thrilling. Personally, we'd rather look at the mannequins. Anyway, on the up side, the bridal shops may cut you a deal if you buy the bridal and bridesmaids' gowns from them. On the down side, while bridal shop employees may know a lot about bridal gowns, they may know diddly-squat about men's formal wear.

♥ **Independent shops.** Occasionally, we find an independent tuxedo rental shop, one that is not affiliated with a national chain. We often are impressed by the quality of service at these outlets. Furthermore, independent shops may carry a wider selection of styles and designers. You can also find some great deals. For example, Tux-Xpress in Scottsdale, Arizona (480-991-6655; web: tux-xpress.com) rents designer-brand tuxes for $38 to $69, far below the prices of the chains.

2 Buy. If you expect to need a tuxedo again for a fancy party or corporate banquet, it may pay to buy. That's because most tuxedos cost $300 to $500 to purchase (although you can find several at discounters for $200 or less). Considering rental fees of $100 a pop, this might be a good investment. See the money-saving tips in this chapter for places on the web to buy a tux or accessories.

3 **Go with your own suit.** Especially for less formal weddings, it is perfectly acceptable for the groom and groomsmen to wear dark suits.

Grooms in Cyberspace: What's on the Web?

Just like in the magazine world, groom's issues often get short shrift on the 'net. Here are some good links to help:

♥ **AfterHours.com.** If you just want to look at current styles, check out AfterHours.com. Their tux gallery has nearly 60 tux pictures and a detailed question and answer section. We also like Lord West's site (tuxedos.com), Hartz (hartzco.com) and FCGI (fabiancouture.com).

What about accessories? Check out Sanata (SantanaApparel.com) for their large selection of vests and other tux accessories.

♥ **WeddingChannel.com.** Click on "Wedding Dresses" and then "Tuxedos & Suits" to view styles from 15 major designers. Best of all, you can do an "advanced search" for just the tux you want to see—three button jackets? Only cutaways? You can look at these or other choices with just a few mouse clicks. Also cool: don't know a mandarin from a tailcoat? Roll your cursor over these terms and the site will show you a small sketch of what each looks like.

♥ **Local talk.** Click on our message boards to chat with other readers about the best tux shops in your area. It's free—and ad-free.

Bridal Bargains Wedding Planner: Groom's Attire

What are the 7 Things Your Tux Shop won't tell you? We discuss these traps in our new planner, the Bridal Bargains Wedding Planner. You'll also find that dreaded formality matrix and detailed groom's attire worksheet. See the back of this book for details or go to our web site at BridalBargainsBook.com

Getting Started: How Far in Advance?

Boy, this varies greatly from area to area. In small towns, or for less popular months, you can shop one to two months before the wedding. However, you may need to reserve your tuxedos three to four months before the wedding in larger cities or for popular summer wedding months. If you have out-of-town groomsmen, you may want to leave extra time to get their measurements.

Tux Shopping Tips

In the old days, tux shopping was rather simple: if you were planning a formal evening wedding, you wore a single-breasted tux. Daytime or less formal affairs called for cutaways, strollers or morning coats. Now, that's all been thrown out the window—guys are wearing all sorts of tuxes during all times of the day. So, perhaps the best advice is to get a tux that best matches your body. Here are some ideas, given different body types:

♥ **Short, stocky guys.** Jackets with slim shawl collars are a good bet. You don't need any of those broad-shoulder Euro-style tuxes; that would be overkill. Instead jackets with natural shoulder lines are best. For pants, avoid styles that have too much break on the foot (which creates a sloppy look); instead, try reverse double-pleated trousers.

♥ **Short, slender guys.** Skip the double-breasted styles and look at single-breasted jackets with a low button and wide lapels.

♥ **Tall, slender guys.** These folks have it easy—just about everything works. Double-breasted tuxes with those Euro-style broad shoulders are fine, as are those hip three-button styles that close high on the chest. Trousers can have more break at the foot.

♥ **Tall, stocky guys.** Jacket length is a tough one here; try styles with shawl collars. Consider a jacket with a bit of room to allow for movement.

♥ **Other tips.** Vests are a popular alternative to cummerbunds these days. Be sure to ask whether the vest is a full back or half-back (full looks better if you take off your jacket during the reception). Fit is important—look for a tux rental shop that knows how to measure properly (it's more than just jacket size; shops should also take your inseam and waist measurements). And insist on a fitting BEFORE the wedding to avoid any day-of surprises. Finally, pay attention to the fabric. 100% wool tuxes are best, but there are differences among wools. Have a tux retailer show you the difference between a tropical wool fabric and other options.

Money-saving Secrets for Tuxedos

1 Package discounts. Almost all tuxedo shops offer a free tux rental with the rental of four, five or six tuxedos. In some cases, tux shops distribute coupons good for $10 or more off each rental. Our advice: always ask about group discounts.

2 Skip the rental shoes. Why? Those cheap rental shoes can be awfully uncomfortable. Instead, wear your own black dress shoes if you have them and save $10.

3 Surf for discounts. ETuxedo (etuxedo.com; 888-879-7848) is a large discount seller of tuxes, with prices starting at $129 for a wool tux. Or try their tux separates. Even if you don't want to buy a tux online, you can use this site to compare accessory prices like tie & cummerbund sets, cuff links, or shirts. Another site for tux shoppers is CheapTux.com, which offers discounted tuxes as well as accessories at half off retail.

4 Consider new tux alternatives. In years past, if you wanted to buy or rent a tux you had limited choices—typically just a handful of formalwear stores or bridal shops rented tuxes. Now, there is some new competition. Men's Wearhouse (web: menswearhouse.com; see Figure 3 on the previous page) accounts for 20% of the tux market,

FIGURE 3: Men's Warehouse offers tux rentals starting at just $69—their web site also lists several other deals and discounts.

offering rentals in most of their 600 stores in the U.S. (In Canada, Men's Warehouse goes under the name Moore's). Rentals run $69 to $150 (including shoes). Or you can buy a tux at Men's Wearhouse for just $199 for a 100% wool single-breasted style. Since it often costs $100 or more to rent a tux in big cities today, it might be worth buying if you think you'll need a tux more than just once in the next few years. Another new competitor in the tux business: David's Bridal. David's now owns After Hours, the country's biggest tux retailer that operates 242 stores under the names AfterHours, Mitchell, Small's and Sempliner's. Rentals start at $49.

5 Look for coupons. Speaking of Men's Wearhouse, look for a coupon for this chain at local bridal shows or online at menswarehouse.com. Specials vary, but when we lasted looked, there was a 20% discount and a free groom's tux free deal (see figure 3 on the previous page). Other chains offer periodic coupons as well, so check your weekend newspaper and ask any tux chain what coupons/promotions they are currently running.

Helpful Hints

1 Fib. A groom emailed us this tip. Frustrated by his procrastinating groomsmen (who were late for fittings), he suggested other grooms fudge the measurement deadline. For example, tell them they must get measured six weeks before the wedding even though the real deadline is just four weeks. That way you'll have a buffer zone for foot-dragging guys.

2 Ignore the "black tie invited" pressure. Some bridal magazines and retailers are suggesting you put "black tie invited" on your

Are guys easy marks?

Bridal retailers just love the guys. And it's no wonder. Listen to what one bridal retailer in Colorado said in a private online message board about the tux business: "I love tux traffic! Men will drop a wad of cash without thinking twice about it. I also do a significant amount of men's retail . . . which I can hardly keep up with right now. We have been selling cotton shirts and vest sets like nobody's business. I also love the markup on men's retail: 135%-150%." A word to the wise: shop around (and online) for tux shirts and accessories (see earlier in this chapter for ideas) before shelling out big bucks at bridal stores.

invitations. Is this to encourage your guests to dress up? Or to merely line the pockets of tuxedo rental places? Whatever the motivation, we should note that Crane's Wedding Blue Book (the bible of invitation etiquette) says that it is NOT proper to specify the type of dress on an invitation. "The formality of dress is indicated by the time of day (of the wedding). After six o'clock is considered formal." Putting "Black Tie Invited" or "Black Tie Optional" is confusing and not necessary.

3 Consider renting an extra shirt for summer outdoor weddings. A bride called in this excellent tip—if you plan a summer outdoor wedding, consider having the groom and groomsmen rent an extra tuxedo shirt. That way they can change after the wedding into a fresh shirt for the reception.

Chapter 4

The Site

Here's a surprise most folks don't plan for–rental fees for ceremony sites can run hundreds of dollars, even when you belong to a church or temple.. In this chapter, we'll discuss a group of often-overlooked wedding ceremony sites that are extremely affordable–plus we'll give you six important questions to ask your site coordinator.

Selecting a site for your ceremony first requires a decision on the type of ceremony you want. Wedding ceremonies are divided into two categories: religious and civil.

1 Religious ceremonies. Religious ceremonies (75% of all weddings), of course, are most likely held in a house of worship. Requirements for religious ceremonies vary greatly from one denomination to another. Pre-marital counseling is required by some religions; others forbid interfaith marriages. Often the rules are established by the church or temple's local priest, minister, pastor, imam or rabbi. Call your local house of worship for guidelines and requirements.

2 Civil ceremonies. About one-fourth of all weddings are civil ceremonies. Legal requirements vary from state to state, but usually a judge or other officiant presides over the ceremony. Customs and traditions vary greatly from region to region. For example, we spoke to one hotel catering manager who worked in both Boston and Austin, TX. In Boston, she told us nearly 75% of couples had a civil ceremony on site at the hotel. Just the opposite was true in Texas where most weddings are held in a church with only the reception following at the hotel.

Religious vs. Civil: It's All a Matter of State

Interestingly enough, the split between civil and religious ceremonies varies greatly from state to state. According to federal government statistics, the state with the largest number of religious wedding ceremonies is West Virginia. In that state, a whopping 97% of all weddings are religious ceremonies. On the other end of the spectrum, South Carolina leads the nation in civil ceremonies (54% of all weddings), perhaps due to the state's large military population.

So what happened to Nevada, where the large number of Las Vegas weddings probably would rank that state #1 in civil ceremonies? Well, Nevada was omitted from this study for reasons unknown.

Other states with a high number of civil ceremonies include: Florida (45%) New Hampshire (40%), Hawaii (36%), New York (35%), as well as Maine, Georgia and Virginia.

Which states have a large number of religious wedding ceremonies? Besides West Virginia, those states include Missouri (91%), Nebraska (84.2%), Michigan (83.9%), Pennsylvania (83.7%), Idaho (83.5%), California (83.1%).

What Are You Buying?

When you book a ceremony site, you are not only purchasing use of the site for the wedding but also time for set-up and teardown of the decorations. Now we say *purchasing* because many sites charge fees to use the facilities for a wedding. One bride we interviewed was surprised that the church they belonged to charged her over $600 in fees for her ceremony. Of course, these fees often go to reimburse church staff and to pay expenses like utilities, clean up, etc. Unfortunately, some churches use weddings to subsidize other less-profitable operations. Anyway, the fees vary widely from site to site but the charges tend to be more in larger cities.

What if you are not a member of a church but you want a church wedding? Well, some churches allow non-members to use their facilities for weddings . . . but with a few catches. First, the fees are normally higher. Second, members get first shot at dates, so non-members may not be able to book a wedding until, say, three months in advance.

Whether you're planning a civil or religious service, the officiant typically gets paid an honorarium. Sometimes this is in the form of a donation to the house of worship. Other church employees (organist, choir) may require separate payment that covers not only their performance at the wedding but also any prior rehearsals.

Sources to Find a Great Ceremony Site

There are several great sources to find affordable sites.

♥ **Local Visitors/Tourism Bureaus.** Many have a guide to local facilities that are available for weddings and receptions. A local Chamber of Commerce or Historical Society office may also have more leads.

♥ **Local parks departments.** Parks departments administer most city and county parks and historical areas. Ask them which sites are most popular for wedding ceremonies.

♥ **Surf the 'net.** We found an amazing number of web sites (including one reviewed on the next page) with local site information. Another idea: USA CityLink (www.usacitylink.com) links you to the web sites run by local, municipal and other government agencies. Want to find a public rose garden in Austin, Texas for your ceremony? Or a historic home in Walla Walla, WA? This web site opens the door to municipal-owned sites that list great bargains. Don't forget about Bridal Bargains Local Talk, free message boards on our web site (BridalBargainsBook.com). Ask other readers about great sites in your city and swap tips and advice.

Sources to Find an Officiant. If you're planning a civil ceremony, where do you find an officiant? Here are some thoughts:

♥ **Vendor lists.** Many reception sites (including parks departments) have "vendor lists" that list everything from florists to photographers. Often, you can find officiant names on such lists.

♥ **The National Association of Wedding Officiants.** Click on the web site for this group (www.nawoonline.com) to find lists of available officiants by state. Or if you don't see your area listed, fill out an online form and the site will email you with possibilities! "It's free and very helpful," said a reader in Colorado.

♥ **The web** Yes, you can find officiant listings on the Knot.com and WeddingChannel.com—but don't forget about other quirky site like Craigslist.org.

♥ **Check the yellow pages.** Look under "Clergy" and "Wedding."

♥ **Non-denominational churches.** Such houses of worship (example: Unitarian churches) may have officiants who are willing to conduct religious ceremonies for couples who are not members of the church. A side comment: we should note that technically the Unitarian church is NOT non-denominational. The Unitarians do not restrict people from being married in their churches based on previous or current religious affiliation. This is really called "non-creedal." Just an FYI.

Brides in Cyberspace: What's on the Web?

Finding a ceremony site on the web can be a bit tricky—many religious and smaller sites don't have web pages. But many sites that offer both ceremonies and receptions (so-called catering halls and facilities) can be found online. One of the better sites to do this: The Knot (theknot.com) has a local vendor search function that lets you zero in on ceremony and reception sites (and other wedding vendors) by local region. We did a search for sites in the Northern New Jersey area (see Figure 1) and came up with 100+ options.

Getting Started: How Far in Advance?

Especially for popular wedding months, start your search for a ceremony site as soon as you have selected the date. Prime dates can book up to a year in advance—you know, there are only

FIGURE 1: Our search of the Knot for ceremony sites in northern New Jersey returned 100+ options, some of which had web site and map links.

so many Saturdays in June. However, be aware that popular months vary by region. For example, in the South, December is a particularly popular month. In Arizona, and many areas of the desert Southwest, spring months (such as May) are almost as popular as the hot summer months. See the chart later in this chapter for a list of the most and least popular months for weddings by state.

Be aware that religious restrictions may rule out certain times of the year. For example, Catholics and Greek Orthodox avoid marrying during Lent in March. Jews don't have weddings during the High Holy Days (usually in September or October).

Questions to Ask of a Ceremony Site

1 Do you have my wedding date available? Yes, it's an obvious question, but probably the most important one. Many brides forget there are many other brides competing for the same slots on a Saturday afternoon.

2 What are the restrictions, set-up times and clean-up requirements? Many sites have put these items in writing. One local church we know has so many guidelines that they filled a 72-page book! Make sure you are fully aware of these details to avoid any surprises.

Real Wedding Tip

Church ceremony fees can add up

"I would just like to comment on a substantial wedding cost which I did not see addressed in your book. After I got engaged, I called the Episcopal Church I have attended since I was a little girl and booked a date in May. I have always assumed that I would be married there, and so I did not give this aspect of planning the wedding much thought. Recently, I received an information packet from the church that included a price list. Imagine my surprise to learn that getting married at my local church will cost approximately $2,000 ($750 for rental of the church and the rest in fees to various people needed to perform the service). I had not counted on this expense, and frankly, I feel a little angry about it. To make matters worse, when I tried to call other Episcopal churches in the area, the wedding coordinators refused to disclose any prices unless I had the rector of my official church call and give permission for me to be married there."

3 Are there any rules regarding candles or flowers? Some facilities ban candles outright. Others forbid the throwing of rice or birdseed after the ceremony. We've even heard of one church that required the altar flower arrangement be "donated" to the church after the ceremony. One reader emailed us to explain that some congregations, particularly in the Northeast see this type of donation as a sort of "thank you" from the bride for the church community's support.

Most/Least Popular Months

STATE	Most Popular	Least Popular
New England:		
Maine	August, July, June	Jan., Feb., Mar.
New Hampshire	Oct., June, Aug.	Jan. Mar., Feb.
Vermont	July, August, June	Jan., Mar., Feb.
Massachusetts	Oct., Sept., June.	Jan., Mar., Feb.
Rhode Island	Sept., Oct., June	Jan., Feb., Mar.
Connecticut	Oct., Sept., June	Jan., Mar., Feb.
Middle Atlantic:		
New York	Sept., Aug, June	Jan., Feb., Mar.
New Jersey	Oct., Sept., June	Jan., Feb., Mar.
Pennsylvania	Oct., June, Sept.	Jan., Feb., Mar.
East North Central:		
Ohio	June, July, Sept.	Jan., Feb., Mar.
Indiana	June, July, August	Jan., Feb., Mar.
Illinois	June, Sept., Oct.	Jan., Feb., Mar.
Michigan	August, June, Sept.	Jan., Mar., Feb.
Wisconsin	June, Sept., Aug.	Jan., Feb., Mar.
West North Central:		
Minnesota	June, Sept., Aug.	Jan., Mar., Feb.
Iowa	June, August, Sept.	Jan., Feb., Mar.
Missouri	June, May, Oct.	Jan., Feb., Mar.
North Dakota	June, July, August	Jan., Mar., Feb.
South Dakota	August, June, July	Jan., Mar., Feb.
Nebraska	June, July, August.	Jan., Feb., Mar.
Kansas	June, July, May	Jan., Feb., Mar.
East South Central:		
Kentucky	June, July, May	Jan., Feb., Mar.
Tennessee	June, July, Dec.	Jan., Feb., Mar.
Alabama	June, July, August	Jan., Feb., Nov.
Mississippi	June, July, Dec.	Jan., Feb., Nov.
West South Central:		
Arkansas	June, July, August	Jan., Feb., Nov.
Louisiana	July, June, Oct.	Mar., Feb., Jan.

4 Who will be my contact? In order to prevent miscommunications, make sure you find out who is the wedding coordinator. This person will be an invaluable referral source for other wedding services.

5 What kind of equipment must be rented for my wedding? Don't assume that something in the sanctuary or at the site is included in your rental of the facility.

for Weddings by State

STATE	Most Popular	Least Popular
Oklahoma	June, August, May	Jan., Feb., Oct.
Texas	June, July, August	Jan., Nov., Feb.
South Atlantic:		
Delaware	Oct., Sept., June	Jan., Feb., Mar.
Maryland	June, Sept., Oct.	Jan., Feb., Mar.
Wash. D.C.	June, Sept., Oct.	Feb., Jan., Mar.
Virginia	June, July, May	Jan., Mar., Feb.
West Virginia	June, July, Aug.	Jan., Mar., Feb.
North Carolina	June, July, May	Jan., Mar., Feb.
South Carolina	July, June, May	Jan, Feb., Mar.
Georgia	June, July, April	Jan., Feb., Mar.
Florida	Dec., June, April	Jan., Mar., Sept.
Mountain:		
Montana	July, June, August	Jan., Feb., Mar.
Idaho	August, July, June	Jan., Mar., Feb.
Wyoming	July, August, June	Jan., Mar., Feb.
Colorado	June, August, July	Jan., Mar., Nov.
New Mexico	June, August, May	Jan., Sept., Feb.
Arizona	June, May, Apr.	Feb., August, July
Utah	July, August, Sept.	Jan., Feb., Oct.
Nevada	July, August, April	Jan., Mar., Nov.
Pacific:		
Washington	August, Oct., July	Jan., Feb., Dec.
Oregon	August, June, July	Jan., Feb., Mar.
California	June, Sept., July	Jan., April, Feb.
Alaska	August, June, July	Jan., Mar., April
Hawaii	May, July, August	Jan., Mar., Feb.
US (TOTAL)	*June, July, August*	*Jan., Feb., Mar.*

Note: Months are listed in order of popularity. For example, "July, August, June" means that July is the #1 month, followed by August and so on. The least popular month is listed first, followed by the second least popular and so on. Source: US Dept. of Health report.

6 How early will the site be available for decorating? Will the air conditioning or heat be turned on at that time? Your florist may need to access the ceremony site several hours before your wedding. Confirm that heat or A/C will be running to make it easier for vendors to work (and to avoid damage to delicate blooms and other decor).

Questions to Ask an Officiant

1 What is the expected honorarium, donation or fee? When is this normally paid?

2 Are there any travel charges or other costs? If you're planning a wedding at a non-religious site (hotel, home, etc.), you may want to confirm these details.

3 Is any pre-wedding counseling required? Some churches require couples to attend pre-wedding counseling. Others require the couple to promise to raise their children in that religion. Before you are asked to make any commitments, ask the site coordinator about this matter.

4 Do you provide the ceremony/vows or can we write our own? Are you familiar with the wedding site?

5 Are you licensed to perform wedding ceremonies in this county? And will you file all the necessary paperwork (marriage license, etc.) with the county?

6 Will you attend the rehearsal? If so, is there an extra charge for this time? Another issue: ask the officiant when he arrives at the ceremony site and how long he will stay afterward. This is important to coordinate with your photographer. If you are marrying in your or your family's church or synagogue, it is customary to invite the clergy member (and spouse) to the reception.

Bridal Bargains Wedding Planner: Ceremony Sites

Compare three ceremony sites side by side with a special worksheet in our new planner, the Bridal Bargains Wedding Planner. We also have worksheets to help you organize the ceremony music and rentals, plus answers to that age-old question "Where do I stand?" Next, we'll talk about your wedding vows—a special chapter in the Bridal Bargains Wedding Planner tackles the subject of writing your own vows, along with a worksheet to help you compose just the right words. Finally, we have a to-do list for changing your name and a special worksheet for newspaper announcements. Check the back of this book for more details.

Top Money-saving Secrets

1 Consider a civic site. Many sites run by your city (parks, rose gardens, etc.) have lovely facilities available for wedding ceremonies. Best of all: most of these sites are available for a very small fee. For example, we've found rose gardens and historical parks (complete with gazebo or chapel) that cost under $100.

2 Call around to different sites. You wouldn't believe how widely fees vary from facility to facility.

3 Consider becoming a member. Many churches charge less for weddings of members than non-members. Hence, consider joining the church where you'll be married. Of course, you'll be making a commitment to that house of worship, which is something not to take lightly. Don't simply join a church to get married there—that isn't fair to houses of worship that count on members to continue their involvement, both spiritually and financially.

4 Ask about discounts. For example, some churches and temples offer discounts on wedding invitations as a fundraiser.

5 Have a friend officiate. In most states it is fairly easy to become licensed to perform weddings. Have a friend or relative get licensed and perform the ceremony as a gift. A reader in San Diego emailed us about that state's "Deputy Marriage Commissioner for a Day" program. For a modest fee (some counties it's free), you can have anyone perform your ceremony! If you live in California contact your county for specific rules. Essentially, your friend writes a letter to the court requesting this, and then a judge swears your friend in for that specific day. Check with counties in other states to see if a similar program exists for your area.

6 Take a tax deduction. Any fees paid to a church or synagogue for a ceremony may be considered a charitable contribution; check with your tax preparer about deducting this off your taxes. You may have to be a member of the church or temple in order to take the deduction. Also: if the ceremony site requires you leave behind flowers as a "donation," this may also be tax deductible.

Destination Wedding Tips

♥ **Marriage license 411.** Getting a valid marriage license used to be quite a chore if you were being married overseas. But there is good news: more countries are putting their marriage license info online. And some countries (notably in the Caribbean) have relaxed rules and regulations in order to spur more destination wedding biz.

♥ **Lean on that wedding coordinator.** Most folks who marry abroad do so at a resort—and most of those resorts now have full-time wedding coordinators. We've found most of these professionals to be very knowledgeable about local marriage license requirements . . . but it's always smart to double check!

♥ **Be aware that local customs may forbid religious ceremonies for non-residents.** Other countries have convoluted rules for what makes a wedding legal. In Mexico, only civil marriages (in front a judge) are considered legal.

♥ **Consider the secret home ceremony.** If getting a marriage license in a foreign country is too much of a hassle, then consider this tip: get married quietly at home at a courthouse before you go. Then you retake your vows at the destination wedding spot. Of course, the guests don't know this isn't the real wedding—the legal one was back in the U.S.!

Chapter 5

Flowers

A rose is a rose . . . except when you're shopping for flowers for your wedding. Then a "bridal" rose is suddenly eight times more expensive than a regular rose. With the average floral bill for weddings topping $1100, there have to be some creative ways to stretch that budget. We came up with 26 cost-cutters. Plus, in this chapter, we also translate "floral speak" and give you eight floral "best buys."

What Are You Buying?

Flowers are more than petals, stems and leaves. When you contract with a professional florist, you are buying their expertise and creativity. Not only is the florist's knowledge of flowers important but also their understanding of colors and contrasts. Florists must be able to come up with a floral motif to best complement the bride, the bridal gown, the bridesmaids' colors, the ceremony and the reception. To synthesize these elements and the "feel of the wedding" (a formal sit-down dinner versus an informal barbecue) takes talent. Lots of it. Your tastes and desires are key here, and a florist who understands a couple's individuality is the best choice.

There are three basic categories of flowers that you are buying:

♥ **Personal Flowers.** The bride's and bridesmaids' bouquets, corsages for the mothers and house party, and boutonnieres for the men.

♥ **Ceremony Site Flowers.** Altar flowers and/or aisle arrangements (ribbons, candles, pew markers).

♥ **Reception Site Flowers.** Guest book table, table centerpieces and the cake table. Other floral expense areas may include the rehearsal dinner and any other pre-wedding parties.

Average total costs: About $1100 covers the total floral bill at most weddings, according to industry estimates. In the largest cities (such as New York or Chicago) the flower budget can easily zoom past $2500 or even $6000 for lavish affairs. Deposits range from nothing (the exception) to as much as 50% of the estimated bill. Many florists ask for $50 to $100 to reserve the date. The balance is usually due one to two weeks before the wedding (because many florists must order the flowers in advance from their suppliers).

Sources to Find an Affordable Florist

Since there are three general types of florists out there, we thought it might be helpful to explain the differences, and then detail where to find the one that will work best for you:

1 **Cash 'n Carry.** These shops basically specialize in providing an arrangement for Mother's Day, or a friend's birthday. They usually don't do many weddings and may not have as much experience with such a special event.

2 **Full service.** Weddings, wire service arrangements, and special events are within a full-service florist's repertoire. A majority of florists fit in this category, although some are better than others at weddings.

3 **Specialists.** Some florists specialize in one aspect of the floral business, such as corporate affairs. Obviously, those who specialize in weddings are your best bet. Those that don't may have little incentive to do a good job since they don't target that market anyway. Don't assume that your neighborhood florist, who has done great arrangements for you at Christmas and other times, will be best for your wedding.

Where to Find Florists Who are Wedding Specialists

♥ **Ceremony site coordinators.** Ask the person who coordinates (or books) weddings at your church, synagogue, etc. for florist recommendations. This is a great source since they often see florists' work up close and personal. They also know the florists who have been late to set up and those who have not provided the freshest flowers or best service. If your ceremony site coordinator doesn't have any recommendations, call around to a few popular churches in your area. Odds are you'll turn up some valuable referrals.

♥ **Photographers.** Many have opinions as to which florists offer the best service and which don't. However, since a photographer's contact with florists is limited to the final product at the wedding, their opinions could be somewhat biased.

♥ **If you plan to produce your own arrangements** or have a friend do it, look under the Yellow Page heading of "Florists-Wholesale" for supplies. Some wholesalers refuse to sell to the public while others don't have such restrictions. Another source: flower growers. Contact the Association of Specialty Cut Flower Growers (ASCFG) at (440) 774-2887 (web: ascfg.org) to see if there is a grower in your area. Some growers even offer wedding design services.

♥ **Our message boards.** Check out the special local message boards on our web site, BridalBargainsBook.com. Swap leads and ideas with other brides about the best florists in your area. Find out which florists offer the best value.

Brides in Cyberspace: What's on the Web?

Don't know a gladiolus from a glamelia? Does the word "phalaenopsis" make you think of a rare skin condition? (Actually, it's an orchid). Don't fret—you can get a crash course in bridal flowers by surfing the web. Here's the best site we found to answer these and other floral questions:

Flower Council of Holland

Web site: flowercouncil.org
What it is: Web site designed for the industry.
What's Cool: Flower Council of Holland is the bible of flower pics. Click here and you can search for pictures of just about any cut flower. Take alstroemeria, a common bridal flower. A quick search brings up thumbnails of 25 different colors of alstromerias. Bonus: the site has excellent charts that track when blooms are in season.

♥ Looking for ribbons at wholesale? **C.O.D. Wholesale** (codwholesale.com, or cheapribbons.com) sells ribbon at unbelievable prices with no minimum order. For example, we saw wired organza ribbon in 30 colors and three widths starting at $3.95 for 25 yards. Wow. You'll also see satin ribbon, corsage ribbon and more. You can sign up for email only specials too. By the way, the site says all sales are final. They don't accept returns, so make sure to order only what you really want.

♥ **Romantic Flowers** has a great site to view flowers (romanticflowers.com). Here you'll find a gallery of cut roses as well as a bouquet gallery. They also sell ribbon by the yard and by bolt. You'll find a 50 yard bolt of 1.5 inch organza ribbon for about $70. Other ribbons include French wired taffeta, velvet, metallic and other finishes. These are pretty reasonably priced as well (3/4 inch dupioni silk for $45 for a 40 yard. bolt). **Fresh Petals** (freshrosepetals.com) offers wedding packages, assorted rose petal packs for $25 (forget the birdseed), and wedding garlands. Formerly Obies Floral Design, they are reviewed in more detail later in this chapter.

Getting Started: How Far in Advance?

Book a florist up to six months in advance of your wedding. In larger cities, some florists may even require more time. For most towns, however, many florists consider three to six months notice adequate. Remember that you can put down a small deposit further in advance and then talk specifics at a later date.

Figure 1: The Flower Council of Holland's site is among the web's best for flower pics, info and trends.

FIGURE 2: The Looking for bouquet ideas? Romantic-Flowers.com's gallery of magazine-quality bouquet pics is a good place to start.

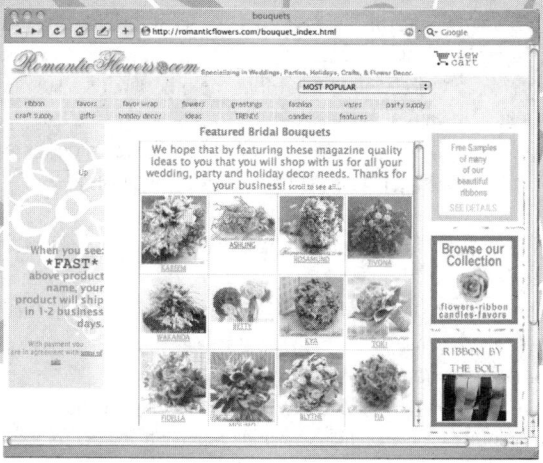

Step-by-step Shopping Strategies

♥ **Step 1:** First, you must have the time, place and apparel selected before you can get an accurate bid from a florist. The bridal gown is crucial—everything flows from this design element. The colors of the bridesmaids' gowns are also important.

♥ **Step 2:** Choose two to three florists to visit, using the sources mentioned earlier. Make an appointment with each and leave about one hour's time to discuss the details.

♥ **Step 3:** Be sure to bring swatches of the bridesmaids apparel and a picture of the bridal gown you have selected. A magazine ad or rough sketch will suffice. Give this to the florist so they'll remember what the dress looks like when they actually make the bouquet. Also, it will be helpful to bring any pictures of flowers/designs you like.

♥ **Step 4**: Look through actual photographs of previous work. Don't settle for FTD design books or floral magazines. Identify flowers and designs that fit your wedding's style—unadorned wedding gowns can be set-off by a lush bride's bouquet. Similarly, a simple bouquet may better compliment an ornate wedding dress. See if the florist attempts to understand your tastes and desires instead of merely telling you what you must have.

♥ **Step 5:** Get a written proposal specifying exact flowers to be used. Each item (brides bouquet, corsages, etc.) should be priced individually. Get this *before* you place any deposit with the florist.

♥ **Step 6:** Pick your top florist choice and ask to visit one of their weddings during set-up. On your visit, check to see if they are on time and organized. Also, look to see how fresh the flowers are. Do you find the designs pleasing (keeping in mind that the other bride's taste may be different from your own)?

♥ **Step 7:** If you believe an on-site meeting at your ceremony or reception site is necessary, now is the time. Finalize the details.

♥ **Step 8:** Get a written contract that spells out the following:

The date of the event (if it is not a Saturday, have the actual day noted, i.e. Sunday).
Set-up time and place.
Specific flowers for each item (roses for bridal bouquet, orchids for mothers' corsages, tulips for bridesmaids, etc.). Don't forget to list the colors chosen for each flower element as well—bridal white roses or red gladiolus.
Any special instructions. If you want open roses, include that in the contract. If you are ordering a flower girl hair wreath have the florist write down the girl's head measurements on the contract.
Emergency contact numbers for the florist (including cell phone).
Specific payment information including deposits as well as refund/cancellation terms.

As you get closer to your wedding, there may be some modifications (more corsages, etc.). Make sure any changes are in writing.

♥ **Step 9:** If you're having a large or complex wedding, a pre-wedding floral check-up may be necessary. Here you'll meet with the florist about one to two weeks prior to the date to iron out any last minute details/changes, etc.

Questions to Ask a Florist

1 **Is my date available?** If it is, check to see if a deposit is necessary to hold the date. Also ask if there is any consultation fee. Inquire as to whether you can receive a price proposal before a deposit is placed.

2 **Do you have actual photographs or samples of your past work?** It's important to see the work of the actual florist, not airbrushed photos from an FTD book. There is no better way to see if their style complements your tastes and verify just how skilled they are.

3 Is there a delivery or set-up fee? Watch out—this can be a substantial extra charge. Most florists will charge a delivery/set-up fee especially if you have either complex flower arrangements or a site that is a long distance from their shop. If the charge is high, consider finding a florist closer to the site or cut back on the complicated decorations.

4 Do you offer any silk or dried flower arrangements? This may be important to you if you want to save your bouquet or want an unusual look for a table centerpiece. Sometimes these two options may be less expensive than fresh flowers, especially for some exotics like orchids. A table centerpiece idea: dried rose topiaries (see right) double as an elegant keepsake.

5 How many weddings do you do in a day? The biggest problem with some florists is that they become over-extended—trying to do too many weddings in one day. A florist can probably do two or three weddings a day if the events are held at different times and/or the florist has plenty of help. If the florist's schedule looks crowded for your wedding date, they may arrive late or deliver the wrong flowers (or worse). Look for someone focused on your wedding . . . not just your wallet.

6 Are you familiar with my ceremony/reception site location? If not, will you visit it with me? It may be a good idea to introduce your florist to the ceremony or reception site if they've never seen it. Ask if there is any charge for this on-site visit.

7 What rental items do you have? How are they priced? Some things you may want to rent include candelabrum, aisle standards, or urns. The best florists don't over-charge on rentals. One way to find out is to compare prices with a local rental store. A common mark-up for florists is about 10% for their time to coordinate this detail. If you would prefer to rent the items yourself because you can get a better price, be sure you have the time to pick-up and return the items.

8 Can I attend one of your weddings during set-up for a look at your designs? Here is another way to determine how professional and talented your florist is. You'll need to visit during set-up and leave before the wedding party arrives. Try not to interrupt the florist or their staff while they work (save your questions for later). Look for timeliness, freshness and beauty of the flowers, and how well the florist and staff work together.

9 What time will you be at my ceremony/reception sites to set-up my wedding? Confirm this time constantly throughout your planning. Many florists set up weddings a couple hours in advance. If this is the case with your wedding, be sure the temperature at the site is not too hot for the flowers—you want them to look fresh at wedding time. Some ceremony sites might have a refrigerator to store personal flowers until you arrive. Confirm this detail with both your site and florist.

10 Will you merely drop off my flowers or stay through the ceremony? The degree of service here differs dramatically from florist to florist. Some just drop off the flowers at the ceremony and leave, while others stay to pin on corsages, make sure nothing is missing, etc. There may be an extra fee ($50) for this service—for large weddings; however, this may be a worthwhile investment.

11 What happens if the flowers I pick aren't available for my wedding? How will you determine what flowers to substitute? A related question: What is the policy if I want to add extra items (such as another table centerpiece or boutonniere) at the last minute?

Bridal Bargains Wedding Planner: Flowers

With all the minutiae that go into planning the flowers for a wedding, you need a detailed worksheet to keep track of all those roses, orchids and the like. Our new planner, the *Bridal Bargains Wedding Planner* has a five-page floral worksheet that lets you record every detail of the personal flowers, ceremony blooms and reception decor. Another worksheet lets you compare three florists side-by-side, contrasting prices, delivery fees and payment policies. See the back of this book for more details.

Top Money-saving Secrets

1 Don't use a florist who charges a consultation fee. Most florists do NOT charge a consultation fee, however, beware of those who do. You can find plenty of great florists who will talk to you for free; don't spend time with the few that charge such fees. (Some florists tell us they charge consulting fees to "weed out" brides who are just window shopping.)

2 Choose a wedding date that is not near a holiday. As you may well realize, all roses are outrageously priced in February thanks to Valentine's Day. So if you want roses, don't plan on a wedding at that time. Also, December is an expensive time to buy fresh flowers since the supply is limited and the demand from holiday events is high. On the other hand, brides have found Christmas weddings are less expensive for ceremony flowers since the church may already be decorated.

3 Seasonal and regional flowers can be great bargains. For example, in California, certain orchids and other tropical flowers grown locally may be available at affordable prices. Also, seasonality often affects floral prices. For example, tulips are abundant from December through April and as such are fairly inexpensive. If you want them in July, however, they will be extremely expensive (three times the price) if they are available at all.

4 Avoid exotic flowers. Of course, what's considered an "exotic" flower may vary from region to region. For example, in the Southwest, lilies of the valley (see picture) are very expensive and difficult to find. Yet in the northern part of the US, where they are common, they may be very reasonable. Exotic flowers such as pricey orchids imported from Hawaii are usually expensive no matter where you live.

5 Instead of big (and expensive) bouquets, carry a single flower. This is extremely elegant especially with long stem varieties like calla lilies and roses. If you (the bride) want to carry a bouquet, consider having the bridesmaids carry single flowers.

6 Use silk flowers to replace expensive, fresh varieties. Even dried flowers may be affordable alternatives. All-silk arrangements may not be much less expensive if you have them made by a florist—their charge for labor may be expensive no matter what type of flower they use. However, you can save money doing it yourself or substituting silk exotics (like orchids) for real ones.

Our readers came up with a few Internet discount sources for silk flowers. Their picks include Save-on-Crafts (save-on-crafts.com) and Annie and Company (annieandcompany.com). For dried flowers check out these two sites: Dried Flowers R Us (driedflowersrus.com) and Dried Flowers Direct (driedflowersdirect.com).

7 Limit the number of attendants. This is just basic math: the more attendants, the more flowers, the higher the final cost.

8 Spend your money where people will see it. Most wedding ceremonies are relatively short (about 30 minutes); therefore your guests will be spending most of their time at your reception. We suggest that you spend money on flowers at the reception rather than at the ceremony. You'll be able to enjoy them more at the reception and so will your guests. At a typical wedding, ceremony site flowers are the biggest expense, but you see them for the shortest amount of time!

9 Share and share alike. If there is another wedding scheduled for the same day at your ceremony site, share the floral arrangements with the other bride! Splitting the cost here could be a major savings.

Table centerpieces on the cheap

Talk with any florist and you'll quickly realize how table centerpieces can greatly inflate the final bill. If you have ten tables to decorate, the cost of flowers, greenery and a vase can easily run $55 to $80 per table. And elaborate centerpieces with extensive flowers and rented stands can soar above $110 or $170 each.

How can you save on this item without looking cheap?

♥ **Potted plants at Home Depot.** Five bucks goes a long way at Home Depot. One reader decorated her tables with $5 pots of spring flowers like daffodils and tulips. Obviously, what plants and flowers are available will vary depending on the time of the year. Tip: ask a Home Depot manager what flowers are set to arrive the week of your wedding. Ask them if they can order in specific colors or plants you want, plus set them aside when they arrive so you can get first choice.

♥ **Go with more foliage than flowers.** The more foliage you add to table centerpieces, the fewer flowers you will need. On average, foliage is much less expensive than flowers.

♥ **Baskets with gourds and silk leaves.** For a fall wedding, this would be a fitting theme. One bride in Massachusetts told us she found baskets on sale at Pier One for 50% off. By scouting out grocery stores, craft stores, and nurseries, she found gourds, mini pumpkins and silk leaves in fall colors to fill the baskets. Total cost: $21 per basket.

Use neutral hues like whites and creams to avoid any color clashes.

10 **Balloons!** Forget the florist and call a company that does balloon arrangements. You might be surprised at how inexpensive balloons can be. We priced balloon table centerpieces at $20 to $50 each—you'd have to spend twice or three times that amount to get a similar look from fresh flowers. One tip: balloon centerpieces look best in reception sites with high ceilings. For more ideas on affordable table centerpieces, check the box on the following page.

11 **Renting plants and other greenery as filler.** A great money-saving option, this may save you from buying tons of flowers for a reception or ceremony site that needs lots of decoration. Check local nurseries and party stores for rental greenery.

♥ **Fish bowls.** Go to a pet store and buy fish bowls and beta fish. Place them on mirrored tiles (available at any hardware store) and scatter votive candles nearby. The light will flicker off the water, creating a shimmering effect. Total cost: about $7 per table.

♥ **Edible centerpieces.** Instead of flowers, have your caterer stack piles of fruit (in coordinating colors, of course) in the center of the table. For example, an arrangement of strawberries with chocolate dipping sauce or powdered sugar would be nice. Another idea: cheesecake centerpieces. Elegant Cheesecakes of Half Moon Bay, CA (650) 728-2248 (web: elegantcheesecakes.com) sells cheesecake centerpieces that serve 10 to 12 guests for $110 to $240—not cheap, but since these elaborate designs double as dessert, you save on the expense of a wedding cake.

♥ **Cyber flowers.** Yes, you can order fresh flowers from the Internet delivered to you via Fed Ex the day before your wedding. You may not want to design and arrange all your flowers for your wedding, but you could buy 200 gerbera daisies from 2G Roses (freshroses.com) for $330, including shipping. Find affordable containers and you've got casual, fresh floral centerpieces (at just $11.65 per table, assuming 10 stems per arrangement). More on this option later in the chapter.

♥ **Watch the height of table centerpieces.** High table centerpieces often cost TWICE the price of low designs. Go with all low designs or mix up high and low to save.

Another idea: buy cheap greenery at places like Home Depot. Many sell large potted plants for a fraction of what a florist would charge. Use blooming plants as table centerpieces or larger greenery (trees) to fill in blank spots at the ceremony or reception sites. Best of all, at the end of the reception, you can give them away to guests or reuse them in your own garden. One bride told us she purchased an assortment of potted, flowering plants at a local nursery. The cost for 12 plants (covered in foil for a festive look) was only $100.

12 **Recycle!** Reuse some of the ceremony arrangements and bouquets at the reception. The bridesmaid's bouquets can be used to decorate the cake and guest book tables. Some altar arrangements can be moved to the reception site (although there may be a delivery fee).

13 **Consider arranging the flowers yourself.** It's not that hard, especially if you have a friend or relative who can lend a hand. An entire package of wedding flowers can be ordered online (see later in this chapter for sources) for as little as $250. Silk flowers are another option; many craft stores like Hobby Lobby (reviewed later) sell do-it-yourself supplies or you can use their in-house arranging service. Another source for do-it-yourself blooms: farmer's markets. We'll discuss this in tip #22.

14 **Scale-down the pew decorations at the ceremony.** Consider using just greenery or bows instead of fresh flowers. Some brides have eliminated this decoration altogether. Another option: craft stores will teach you how to make the bows yourself. One handy product is the EZ Bowmaker. This simple device enables you to make professional-looking bows for pew decorations, table centerpieces and more. The cost is $13 (instructional video $7). Why pay a florist hundreds of dollars when you can do it yourself for pennies? Made by EZ Bowz (call 800-311-6529 or 423-453-3060 for a store near you; web: ezcraft.com), the EZ Bowmaker is available in craft stores like Michael's (800-Michaels; michaels.com).

15 **Pick the general color scheme** and let your florist buy the most affordable flowers available the week of your wedding. Obviously, you must feel very confident in your florist to go this route. Specifically rule out any flowers you don't want but try to remain flexible—this isn't a tip for control freaks. Flower prices fluctuate so greatly from month to month; take advantage of this by having your florist pick the best bargains.

16 **Call a local horticultural school.** A bride in Ohio wrote to us with this great tip—she found that the students at a local horticultural school would arrange the flowers for her wedding for free. She paid for the flowers (only $200) and they did all the labor—a great deal! Check the local phone book for any schools in your area or go to Gradschools.com/programs/horticulture.html and click on your state.. Another idea: craft stores and community colleges often have classes in flower arranging. If you don't have time to take a class, see if the students will take on your wedding as a class project.

Another thought: hire an instructor from a local horticulture school to design your wedding flowers. They often moonlight for private parties and are very experienced as well.

17 **Surf the net.** Yes, you can order flowers at wholesale over the web. Check out the Spotlight: Best Buy later in this chapter for more info on this tip. You (or a friend or relative) have to do the arranging, but this can be a substantial savings.

18 **Check the church.** Yes, some churches arrange flowers. A reader told us at her Episcopal church in Chicago, the Altar Guild can make beautiful arrangements for as little as $100.

19 **Costco.** A great way to save! A reader from Atlanta sent us this tip about wholesale clubs: "Costco (costco.com) sells bouquets with over 2 dozen roses (approximately 25 or 26 roses) for $13 and bunches of 6 or 7 white calla lilies for $10. I purchased roses for my bouquet and my bridesmaids' from there. Great quality and great prices!" We'll take an in-depth look at Costco's wedding flower services later in this chapter.

20 **Local flower growers.** You might be surprised at the wedding services offered by local growers. For example, Flinthill Flower Farm in Maryland (301-607-4554) not only grows flowers but also offers a design service. Here's what reader Sara Markle told us about her wedding flowers from Flinthill: "I toured the farm to see what kinds of flowers were in season and had a good time working with the owner deciding on the arrangements. He was easy to work with and found ways to reduce my costs. I didn't compare costs with a regular florist, except that I got one quote from the florist who supplies my church. That person quoted $250 for one altar arrangement. I got *two* church arrangements from the farm for $150.

"In all, I spent about $1200 for my bouquet, a headpiece, 3 maids' bouquets, 7 boutonnieres, 4 corsages, 2 large church arrangements and one small church arrangement, 4 large arrangements for the reception, 21 table arrangements, and delivery and set up costs."

21 **Don't forget after Christmas sales.** We heard from one bride who found twinkle lights, bows and candles at 50% off and more. She recommended hitting Wal-Mart, Target and other discounters' after season sales to find gold candles, silver ribbon, bells and more. Use your imagination! Many "holiday" items can be re-used at a wedding.

22 **Farmer's markets.** This is a great resource for fresh, locally grown flowers. In our hometown, we found local growers selling flowers at prices that can only be described as a steal—a dozen roses for $6, a large mixed bouquet for $7. Pop into Home Depot for some containers (a steel watering can for $10? a galvanized bucket for $5 to $8?) and you've got ceremony or reception site decor on the cheap.

Some of our readers have hit the market the day of or day before the wedding and loosely arranged the flowers for a fraction of the cost of a professional florist. Be sure to have plenty of supplies on hand (like floral foam, rubber bands, ribbon, scissors and clippers). And don't forget to have a cool or cold place to store your creations before the wedding.

Another option: wholesale floral markets, which are held year round. One reader told us that the Los Angeles Flower District (laflowerdistrict.com) is an entire block of flower growers and importers. Yes, the main business of the district is wholesaling flowers to florists, but many vendors will sell direct to the public as well. The prices are phenomenal. For example, how about a bouquet of dendrobium orchids for $8? Or $3 each for japhet orchids?

23 **Ask your reception site if they have votive candles.** Sure, your florist can supply votive candles . . . but some charge up to $2.50 a pop! Instead, see if your reception site has votives. Most will let you use them for free or a nominal charge, typically much less than a florist.

24 **For bridesmaids bouquets, turn up the volume!** Choose flowers with large blooms—peonies in spring, for example. Why? You'll need fewer flowers overall to make a bouquet. Three or four flowers with large blooms will be much less than a bouquet of small bloom flowers like roses.

25 **Take a tax deduction**. If your church or temple requires you to leave behind altar decorations, check with your tax preparer to see if it is tax deductible. This is a gift-in-kind and may be deductible!

26 **Order candles online.** A reader from Seattle recommended this site for great deals on candles: CandlesJustOnline.com.

Spotlight: Best Buys

For some lovely yet affordable flowers that won't bust your budget, we've compiled a short list of flowers that can be used to fill out arrangements. Be aware that certain flowers may be more affordable in various regions of the US. Ask your florist for local recommendations. Also, seasonality may affect the prices of certain flowers.

♥ **Alstroemeria Lilies.** These are miniature lilies that come in over 20 different shades. Some flowers are even multi-colored. Because they are small, they look best in bouquets, hairpieces, on wedding cakes or in table arrangements.

♥ **Carnations.** Ah, the old standby. These are a great pick for altar arrangements since they stand out without great expense. They come in a wide variety of colors, but we don't recommend the dyed ones—stick to natural colors. Some varieties are also available as miniatures if you want to add them to table arrangements or bouquets. These are very "heat-hardy" too for those of you in hot climates.

♥ **Chrysanthemums.** More commonly referred to as mums, these flowers are also great filler for altar arrangements. They add oodles of volume to your arrangements without costing a great deal. These flowers are available in a wide range of colors from white to bronze. Some even look like simple daisies in pinks, yellows and white.

♥ **Freesia.** Another small delicate flower with a pleasant scent, freesia can be used as a wonderful substitute for the more expensive stephanotis (a traditional "bridal" flower). They come in white, yellow, pink, orange, lavender, and red.

♥ **Gerbera Daisies.** These giant-sized versions of common daisies make wonderful and colorful bridesmaids' bouquets. They also have long stems and can be used successfully in table and altar arrangements. They come in incredible colors from plain white to deep fuchsia. Pastels are also available; there are even "miniature" gerbera daisies that can be used in boutonnieres.

♥ **Gladiolus.** These long-stalked flowers are covered in bright blooms. They look especially nice in altar or buffet arrangements to add height. Individual blooms can be used as glamelias (ask your florist to see an example). Colors range from white to pink to deep, true red.

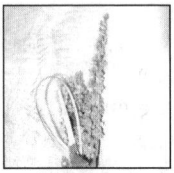

♥ **Heather.** This dusty-pink flower has tiny spikes of bell-shaped blossoms. Many florists use heather as an affordable boutonniere or in corsages. The price is about $1.50 per stem. Heather is a traditional flower at Scottish weddings.

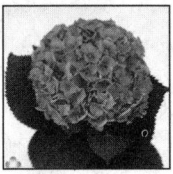

♥ **Hydrangeas.** Because hydrangeas are so large (6 inches across for just one!) they make excellent bouquets and centerpieces. You might need only three to five stems to create a full, lush look. They come in off white, blue and lavender.

♥ **Stattice.** Fabulous filler flowers for bridal bouquets, these clusters of tiny white or purple blossoms are reasonably priced. Other fillers that are inexpensive include Queen Anne's Lace and "stock," a long-stalked flower with copious blooms. Stock has another bonus: they have a great fragrance.

Biggest Myths about Wedding Flowers

Myth #1 *"My mother insists that we have lots and lots of flowers at my wedding. Is this really necessary?"*

Bridal magazines often picture weddings with flowers dripping from the ceiling and crawling along the floor. Some florists feed this perception by suggesting superfluous floral items like "cake knife corsages" (believe it or not, a special flower wrapped with a bow around the knife you cut the cake with), "hairpiece flowers" and arrangements for the gift table. We are not making this stuff up. Does the gift table really need a floral arrangement?

Among the more ridiculous examples of floral price gouging from our readers: $20 for petals for a flower girl's basket (that doesn't include

the basket, nor rose petals—just regular flower petals) and $50 for a small floral wreath for the flower girl's hair. Those were actual prices quoted to a Chicago bride by a Winnetka florist. The same bride told the florist to keep the quote under $1500. The florist's final bid: $1900.

Myth #2 *"I figured on spending only about $400 on my wedding flowers. Given the cost of arrangements I've sent friends, I assume this is a good estimate."*

Most flowers are cheap. Most florists aren't. What you are paying for is the florist's talent, skill and overhead. The manual labor needed to create beautiful bouquets and arrangements (not to mention delivery and set-up) is what costs big money. We should note that some exotic flowers (orchids, etc.) are pricey exceptions: they virtually guarantee an astronomically high floral bill.

Helpful Hints

1 Put your deposit and balance on a credit card. We have heard occasional stories of couples that hired a florist to do their flowers only to have the wrong flowers delivered. Or worse, the florist went out of business. Although these are rare occurrences, it's best to be safe. Special consumer protection laws protect deposits put on credit cards. See Chapter 2 (Apparel) for more details.

2 Keep an open mind. Instead of setting your heart on a particular design or flower, let your florist come up with some suggestions. Because florists work with flowers so closely, they may be aware of some options that are really terrific. Especially when choosing colors, listen to your florist's ideas and look at some of his/her past work before you make up your mind. You might be surprised!

3 Confirm any restrictions on flowers/decorations. Some churches prohibit candles and still others "request" that you donate the altar arrangement to the church. Reception sites may also have similar rules, especially regarding the throwing of birdseed or flower petals.

4 Go European. Check out European bridal magazines (available on some newsstands or in bookstores) for creative ideas. We've noticed those publications feature more unique designs than their American counterparts.

5 Mail order catalogs. These are great for tracking down hard to find items. An example: Oriental Trading Company (orientaltrading.com). They have numerous options for floating candles (snowflake floaters and even autumn leaves for a fall theme) $4 to $7 per dozen. They also sell tapers, votive candles and pillars. Another great option: Wax Wizard (waxwizard.com) and their sister store Bridal Shop Store (bridalshopstore.com). They sell the components for making centerpieces including floating candles, glass cylinders and bowls and votives. Best of all, they have quite a few pictures with great centerpiece ideas. Yet another site recommended by our readers for candles: genwax.com.

6 Head measurements for floral wreaths. One bride emailed us this tip: if you order floral wreaths for the flower girls or bridesmaids, make sure you give the florist head measurements so they have an idea how big (or small) to make the wreaths. Her florist failed to get this detail, and the resulting flower girl wreaths were so big they could be worn around the girls' necks.

7 Label the personal flowers. Here's a tip from a bride who learned this lesson the hard way: have your florist label the personal flowers (bouquets, corsages, boutonnieres) with the names of the intended recipient. That way you know who gets what at the wedding—and you avoid that messy scene when Aunt Bunny "accidentally" takes that special corsage you had made up for your mother-in-law. Don't laugh, this can happen to you.

8 Ask the florist to pin corsages and boutonnieres on your wedding party. One bride was frustrated that her florist just dropped off the flowers without taking a minute to help everyone pin on their flowers. Ask up front if your florist will be available to help—it's the least they can do when you're spending that much money.

9 Check out floral arrangement books. In the library or at the bookstore you can find many books on floral arranging or entertaining. You may find some great ideas that you can take to your florist or do yourself. You can also educate yourself a bit on types of flowers and good design tips.

Pitfalls to Avoid

PITFALL #1 THE MERCEDES SYNDROME

"I was at a florist the other day discussing my wedding when another bride pulled up in an expensive car. All the sudden, the florist's employees started chattering about how rich

Real Wedding Tip

Beware the Surprise Consulting Fee

A reader in Richardson, TX gave a florist a $100 deposit to hold the date for her wedding. The florist said she could work within the bride's specified budget, promising to mail a detailed proposal in short order.

Two weeks later, the proposal came in—at twice the amount the bride had budgeted. Obviously, the bride wasn't very happy. When she told the florist she was going elsewhere for flowers, the florist said she was keeping the $100, calling it a "consulting fee." To make matters worse, she had the gall to send the bride another bill for $62, for "additional labor" to prepare the proposal.

What's the lesson? Whenever you give a deposit, make sure you get a written receipt that states any refund/cancellation policies. Even better: put it on a credit card. Then, if the florist decides your refundable deposit is now non-refundable, you can go to your credit card company to dispute the charge. While it may be tempting to place deposits to hold dates, make sure you first get written documentation spelling out refund policies. Or better yet, get a detailed proposal or cost estimate before placing any deposit.

she was and how they'd have to triple the bill for her flowers! They were kidding, right?"

Maybe not. We once interviewed a florist who admitted charging more for wedding flowers depending on what type of car the bride drove up in! Apparently, brides who arrived at the florist's studio in a fancy ride looked like they could afford to pay more for their wedding flowers. While that sounds absurd, think about it—when you walk into a flower shop, do you see any prices for bridal bouquets? Nope, most flower proposals are worked up on the fly, where a florist "estimates" what items cost due to the flowers used. Or perhaps how deep the client's pockets appear.

We've never tested this theory scientifically, but we wonder what would happen if two brides arrived at a floral shop to price bridal arrangements. One drives a Mercedes; the other a Ford Focus. Guess who gets charged more? We sense this happens based on email we've received from readers. One bride in Oklahoma told us her florist's eyes lit up when the bride slipped and mentioned her fiancéé was a doctor. Suddenly, the florist insisted she fly in exotic Asiatic lilies for the wedding. And the bill soared concurrently.

A related story to this pitfall: the mom syndrome. Several brides we interviewed noticed that when they brought their moms with them to the florist, the final tab went up. The assumption: if mom is along, mom must be paying . . . so let's pile it on! One bride noticed her florist's proposal was much higher than a friend's, despite the same quantity/quality of flowers requested for both weddings. The difference? Her friend went alone; the first bride brought her mom to visit the florist.

So a word of advice when floral shopping: don't flash that big diamond engagement ring. Dress in baggy clothes. Don't bring your mom. And take the bus.

Pitfall #2 "FTD cookie-cutter" weddings

"I met with a florist for my wedding and was extremely disappointed. All they showed me were boring FTD design books. The few real photos I saw featured bouquets that all looked the same."

Some florists try to make every wedding fit a "cookie cutter" mold. Instead of keying on the individuality of the bride and groom, they merely suggest stiff, formulated designs that are uninspired at best and dreadful at worst. We find "cash and carry" florists most guilty of this offense—they simply don't care enough about weddings to try harder.

Pitfall #3 Plastic bouquet holders

"We attended a fancy wedding and were surprised at the bouquets. Beautiful flowers were stuck in plastic holders that just looked cheap!"

Plastic bouquet holders have become a crutch for many lazy florists. Instead of hand tying and hand-wrapping the bouquets, some florists simply stick flowers into floral foam inside plastic holders. Besides looking cheap, poorly inserted flowers can actually drop out of the plastic holder!

Some florists insist plastic holders are necessary since they provide a water source for delicate flowers. Other florists point out plastic holders are a cost-cutter for crescent or cascade bouquets, since they don't have to wire each individual bloom. That's great, but as they say, show us the money—we often found little savings with florists that use plastic holders.

If your florist uses plastic holders, insist the plastic be covered with green floral tape and/or ribbon. Another idea: you can camouflage a holder by wrapping it in satin fabric or by using leaves. Or choose a florist that hand ties and hand wraps the bouquets. A small tube of water can be attached to delicate flowers needing moisture.

PITFALL #4 HEAT-SENSITIVE FLOWERS.

"My friend got married last summer in an outdoor ceremony. Unfortunately, the heat caused the flowers to wilt and even turn brown."

If your wedding is in the summer, watch out for flowers that are vulnerable to extreme heat. Some flowers with this problem include stephanotis and gardenias (very expensive flowers to begin with). Ask your florist for flowers that can withstand the heat and still look fresh. As a side note, we heard from one florist who uses an "anti-transpirant" spray such as Bloomlife Plastic Wax or Crowning Glory (see right) on delicate blooms. These products seal in the moisture so flowers don't wilt as fast.

PITFALL #5 MARTHAHOLICS.

"I fell in love with a bouquet I saw in the Martha Stewart Weddings magazine. The flowers were phenomenal and I wanted my florist to copy it exactly. But when my florist called to find the source for the flowers, they told him they are from Martha's garden and not available commercially! Bummer!"

While Martha is still a major trend-setter these days (despite her legal woes), sometimes she forgets to let brides in on a secret: the supplies she uses are often hard or impossible to find. Or the "Martha look" may be impossible to replicate without hours of labor by a florist. If you've got your heart set on a Martha design, realize you may have to make compromises or shell out big bucks.

PITFALL #6 THE MARRIAGE MARK-UP?

"I went to a florist to price wedding arrangements. Among other items they quoted me $13.50 for a corsage with one rose and some alstroemeria. Later that week my sister called to order corsages for a charity event and they quoted her $8 for a corsage with three roses, filler flowers, greenery and a big bow! Why do brides have to pay more to get fewer flowers?"

Wonder if you say the word "wedding," and the price rises for flowers? We have always been suspicious of some florists, who seem to view brides and grooms as automatic cash machines. To test this theory, Boston NBC-TV affiliate WHDH called Massachusetts area florists to price wedding flowers for an undercover story. Then they called back to price flowers for a retirement party. Guess what? Eight out of 11 florists they called quoted them the "marriage mark-up." The same flowers, just a different event . . . and a different price. One example: a table centerpiece that is $30 for a retirement party, but $50 for a wedding. Another said flowers would be $25 for a party, but $80 for a wedding. "As soon as they hear wedding, they'll jack up the price," a Boston wedding planner told the TV reporter.

So, what's a bride to do? Well, while it is tempting to not tell the florist you are planning a wedding, this may not be very practical. Brides need items like bridal and bridesmaids bouquets that are hard to fake as decor for a birthday party. The best advice may be to just get several competitive bids. Not all florists charge a marriage mark-up. Our advice: take some time to get a few bids to make sure you are getting a good deal.

Trends

♥ **Pretty maids in a row.** Traditionally, bridesmaids all carried the same flowers, to match those identical dresses. But in a recent trend, maids are now carrying different bouquets. One may carry all gerbera daisies, another tulips and a third just freesia. You could choose similar colors or go all out and design each bouquet with a different color scheme.

♥ **Can the corsage.** Yes, the tradition for moms and grandmothers has always been the ubiquitous corsage, worn pinned to the chest or on the wrist. But that's always seemed awkward—you crush it when you hug someone or it itches your wrist and you take it off. So here's a new trend: mini bouquets for mom. Imagine mini gerbera daisies or roses tied up with ribbon to match the moms' dresses. And bouquets make a great keepsake when dried.

♥ **Color.** Brides are now choosing bouquets in shades of a single color. They may pick a variety of flower types, but all in a similar shade.

♥ **Single blooms.** Consider a bouquets consisting of a single type of flower. We've seen some stunning examples including a dozen hand-tied maroon mini calla lilies and a big puff of lavender hydrangeas accented by satin ribbon.

♥ **Bling for the bouquet.** Let's talk shiny! You can add in glittering broaches or pins to your bouquet, or wrap it with metallic ribbon and strings of pearls. We've even seen tiny faux gems glued to the centers of the flowers for a dash of sparkle. And don't forget the groom's boutonniere. It can incorporate a bit of bling to set your man off from the rest of the groomsmen.

♥ **Accent with flowers.** Flowers are not just for bouquets anymore. You can see them as hair accents, shoe accents or even on matching purses for the bridesmaids (if you don't want to ruin the purses, florists can design a detachable accent piece). One cool idea: a floral "pocket square" for the groom instead of a boutonniere. The florist glues tiny flowers to a cardboard form that will then slip into the groom lapel pocket leaving the flowers to peek out like a traditional pocket square.

♥ **SMALLER, COMPACT BOUQUETS.** Forget the loosely tied designs or the flowing cascades of the past. These days, brides want a tightly tied bouquet with a ton of blooms. If you want to add a bit of flair, some florists can add a few tendrils of greenery to soften the look.

Destination Wedding Tips

Our best advice when considering flowers for a destination wedding: go with what's available locally. Now you may expect that tropical destinations will be overflowing with exotic flowers. And in some cases you're right. Hawaii, for example, ships exotic flowers out to the US so you'll know they'll have plenty of choice for your wedding. However, a Caribbean island like Virgin Gorda (part of the British Virgin Islands), for example, doesn't actually grow flowers. It's basically a desert island—most flowers on Virgin Gorda must be imported.

So what's a bride to do? Here's where you'll have to rely on a local bridal consultant or the resort specialist. Be prepared because it can be rather expensive. Our recommendation: rely on the setting of your wedding site to supply the eye candy. A simple bouquet for the bride and bridesmaids is all you'll need. Don't get carried away with lots of flowers.

By the way, if you do choose a destination with a "flower tradition" go with it. For example, at a wedding in a Scottish castle, see about incorporating purple or heather, a popular local flower. Of course, if you want to be really authentic, purple thistle is the floral symbol of the Scots, but it's a bit prickly! In Hawaii, consider plumeria blooms. They smell great and look beautiful. You may even want to opt for leis instead of bouquets.

SPOTLIGHT: ROSES

Types of Roses

"Where do florists get roses? Will they look like roses at the grocery store? How can I be sure to get the best quality?"

Florists buy roses from wholesalers. Wholesalers, in turn, buy them from a variety of sources. California is the largest producer of roses for the US, but they also come from Colombia

(Visa roses) and Mexico (Vega roses). Another big supplier of roses to the US is Ecuador, not to mention Holland and France. Some of the best roses are Vegas, whose blossoms tend to be bigger than California roses and better shaped than Visas. Each florist typically has his or her own preference.

Roses also come in a variety of qualities, similar to eggs at the grocery store. California roses, for example, come in Select (the best), Extra Fancy (middle quality) and Fancy (cheap). Most of what you see in grocery stores are Fancy roses. Few professional florists sell Fancy roses, but it is difficult to determine yourself which grade your florist buys. If you are concerned about the quality, ask the florist which grade is used. Hopefully, they'll say Select. Select roses will be more expensive, but the quality will be better.

Color Options

"I requested bridal white roses from my florist for my bridal bouquet, but the bouquet I saw on my wedding day looked pinkish rather than white. Was my florist substituting the wrong flowers?"

Definitely not. One thing brides should understand about colors in the floral business is that they can be very deceiving. For example, a red rose isn't actually a true red. And a "bridal white" rose isn't really all white; rather it's a creamy white hue with a pink- or peach-tinged center. Gather several bridal white roses together in a bouquet and the overall look may be more pink or peach than you expected. If you have any doubts about color, request a sample of the flowers you are interested in to see the hue in person.

Here are some examples of other popular wedding roses:

♥ Champagne
A creamy, antique ivory colored rose.

♥ Candia
Creamy white with dark pink edges to the petals. This would be a truly unusual look.

♥ Darling
A creamy peach rose suitable for a touch of color in the bride's or bridesmaids' bouquets.

♥ Bridal Pink
These are definitely all-pink roses. Many brides assume they will be soft pink, but they are actually quite a bit brighter.

♥ Delores
This is a soft pink rose.

♥ Jacaranda or Purvey
A hot pink rose; perfect with the jewel tones of bridesmaids' dresses.

♥ Lady Diana
Named after the late Princess of Wales, these are pale peach roses. They are beautiful for bridal work and may even look pinkish rather than peach against a pink background.

♥ Sonia
A brighter peach rose with a little more vibrant color than the Lady Di.

♥ Jacqueline Kennedy
One of the few true red roses but tends to be rather small in size.

♥ Madame Delbard
This is a French rose with a rich velvety red color. It opens well but can be expensive.

♥ Sterling Silver
Also called an Elizabeth Taylor, the color is a lovely lavender. It tends to have a small blossom than other roses.

♥ Ranunculus
These flowers aren't actually roses, but they do look a lot like a fully open rose. They make a very inexpensive alternative to roses especially since they are available in February and March, the time of year when roses are most expensive. They come in reds, pinks, and yellows.

One interesting final note on roses: color has little or nothing to do with prices. You might expect more unusual hues (lavender, for example) to cost more, but in reality the wholesale price is often the same.

Unique Ideas

♥ Hold the rice. The traditional rice thrown at the newlyweds has been declared "environmentally-incorrect" (birds eat the rice; birds die). So, couples have been replacing rice with flower petals, bubbles and so on. Another alternative to consider: The Butterfly Celebration (800) 548-3284 (butterflycelebration.com) sells butterflies for live release as the bride and groom make their get-away. Prices start at $200 for 50 butterflies (plus a $30 shipping fee). Other sources include Amazing Butterflies (amazingbutterflies. com; $65 to $95 per dozen) and Butterflies in Bloom (butterfliesinbloom.com; $85 to $95 per dozen). A side note: releasing butterflies is controversial (environmentalists don't like it). Butterfly Celebration addresses this issue on their web site.

Please use your common sense and don't release them at a January wedding in Michigan—they'll all die! One site mentions that the air temperature must be at least 72°° for the butterflies to take off

A recent bride wrote to us with her idea for a dramatic send off. As wedding favors, she gave the guests printed matchbooks. They then used them to light sparklers (provided by the bride) at the end of the wedding as the couple left the reception. A few cautions: fireworks may be illegal in the city or town where you're getting married—check first. Also, if you live in a drought area, avoid any fireworks. And don't let small children play with sparklers. Finally, have buckets of water handy to douse the sparklers after you've left. (Check Chapter 7, Reception Sites, for more info about fireworks—we'll detail how one bride capped her reception with a mini-fireworks show).

♥ **Ribbon at a discount.** While both Michaels and Hobby Lobby (craft stores reviewed later in this chapter) have great prices on floral supplies like ribbon, sometimes you want better quality ribbon than what you can find at retail. Consider this web site: **RibbonTrade** (ribbontrade.com). They sell high-quality ribbon at great prices. Example: French wired ribbon at just $1.35 a yard! Yes, you have to buy 27 yards to get that price. But most wedding projects do require significant yardage. We also liked the site's iridescent and metallic ribbons. Other ribbon sites mentioned earlier: codwholesale.com and romanticflowers.com.

Spotlight: Best Buy

Wholesale direct from the growers

Ever wish you could order flowers at wholesale prices direct from the grower? Thanks to the 'net, you can. We (and our readers) have found a few options to choose from. Here are some tips before we review the different companies:

1. Do a small test order first, a few months before your wedding. That way you can evaluate the flower quality, color and delivery. You can also see how long it takes certain flowers to open. A multi-color bunch is a good idea to see variations in hues.

2. Plan in advance. You may need the flowers to arrive a few days before your wedding to insure they open in time. Warm water speeds this process, but it can still take a few days.

3. Be sure you have adequate supplies for arrangements. If you or a friend are arranging the flowers for your wedding, be sure to locate the appropriate supplies. From water tubes to vases to floral foam, the necessities are vast. Save On Crafts (save-on-crafts.com) is a great source for floral supplies as well as most craft and hobby chains.

4 Remember you don't have to go whole hog. If the thought of doing ALL your floral arrangements via the web is scary, consider doing merely the table centerpieces or other decor at the ceremony or reception site. Then hire a professional florist to do the personal flowers (bouquets, corsages, etc.).

Our round up of discount floral web sites:

♥ **2G Roses** *freshroses.com* 2G Roses was one of the first online flower wholesalers. The Watsonville, CA grower has been in business since 1974.

2G's web site is a floral bargain hunter's paradise. 2G sells much more than roses—you can order lilies, orchids, tulips or hundreds of other available varieties. And the prices? Roses start at as little as 60¢¢ each for short stems and $1 each for long stems. You can order flowers in individual bunches (say, mini calla lilies, 10 stems for $30) or select one of several bridal packages. For example, the "Standard All Rose Wedding" features enough roses, greenery and filler flowers to make eleven table arrangements, ten boutonnieres, six corsages, five bridesmaids' bouquets, one bride's bouquet and a head table arrangement (only available in three colors). Price: $392.50, including shipping (FED-EX overnight to insure freshness). Order that many flowers from a retail florist and you'd easily spend two or three times that amount of money. They also have a premium package ($504.5) which allows you to choose any color rose you want.

Items are also available a la carte. And you don't have to limit yourself to roses. We counted at least 42 floral varieties available in June alone.

2G's web site clearly explains their packages and how to order, or you can call for a brochure and price list. The also have a great FAQ to answer your questions. Most handy was a chart that listed flower availability by month—that way you can tell exactly what blooms are available for, say, an October wedding.

Here's what one bride told us who ordered from 2G Roses for her wedding:

"I used 2G Roses for all of my bouquets. The service and quality was excellent. They even confirmed my order over the phone before placing it. A friend and I made "hand-tied bouquets"...another tip out of your book. I would like to add that area florists started at about $85 a piece for one hand-tie bouquet. For about $350 I made my bouquet, 3 bridesmaids, 2 mother of the bride/groom corsages and I don't know

how many boutonnieres and other arrangements!"

We should note that we've had a few complaints about 2G on our message boards back in 2004. Many dealt with shipping snafus. Since then, the reviews have been mostly positive, so it appears the company has smoothed over any issues. Again, do that test order to make sure you are comfortable with how this process works!

♥ **Costco.com** *costco.com* Remember our advice about shopping for wedding items at stores that do NOT have wedding in their name? Here's a case in point: when you think wedding flowers, Costco (the membership warehouse chain) probably doesn't come first to mind. But the chain has moved big-time into weddings, so much so that they are now touting their bridal wares, both in the store and online. Go to Costco.com (click on Floral & Events) and you'll find both blooms and packages for brides (all flowers are shipped direct from the wholesaler to your home). For example, the White Rose Collection for $700 includes one bridal bouquets, one maid of honor and four bridesmaids bouquets, 2 mothers mini bouquets, 12 corsages, 12 boutonnieres, 6 centerpieces and 10 rose petal buds. They even throw in a Toss Away bouquet. Note these are FINISHED bouquets and arrangements, not loose flowers! If you need more flowers, you can always buy more loose blooms—125 roses run $139. Minor quibble: if you are not a member of Costco, there is a 5% surcharge on orders. A membership runs $50 for a year.

♥ **Fresh Petals** *FreshRosePetals.com* Also known as Obies Floral Design, Fresh Petal was first recommended to us by a reader. She told us she had found their prices to be excellent, as well as their service. Their long stem roses are 92¢ a stem and their shipping prices are less than 2G. A sample bunch of 25 roses was $35 including shipping. Of course, like 2G, Fresh Petal sells much more than roses. Their web site lists at least two dozen other flowers, including alstroemeria and tulips. New since our last edition, Fresh Petal has added a couple wedding packages. For $200 you'll get 50 long stem roses, 20 stems of spray roses, 20 stems of seasonal flowers and 2 bunches of greens (includes shipping). The larger package ($300 including shipping) adds another 25 roses, 10 spray roses, 10 seasonal flowers and one more bunch of greens. Wedding garlands are also available in ten foot lengths for $55 to $65 each. Great for decorating arches or tables.

One mother of the bride sent us this recommendation for Obies:

"After searching the web for Metalina roses, I finally found a grower in Northern California that will sell to consumers. ObiesFloral.com not only has one of the nicest web sites with great pictures, but their customer service is fantastic, as well as their prices being too good to be true. Each rose is only 84¢¢ a stem, with shipping being much more reasonable than even 2G Roses. Shipping to my location in Southern

California will run only $33, and that's for the 425 roses we'll need. I've ordered a sample bunch of 25 roses for $35 including shipping (and was allowed to specify exactly which roses I wanted - we're getting 13 different colors to compare!). They have plenty of other flowers available too, but my daughter wants only roses."

♥ **Sommer Flowers** *sommerflowers.com* Yet another recommendation from a bride, Sommer is a Florida wholesaler. Unlike other wholesalers, they don't offer wedding packages, but they do have a real person you can consult with to help you put together your own package. Individual flower prices were reasonable including roses starting at $1.10 per stem with a 100 stem minimum. They sell a wide variety of exotics and 9 different lily options. Mini callas were $3.50 per stem

FIGURE 3: Cut out the middle man and order your flowers wholesale! A sampling of web sites that you do just that.

with a minimum order of 50 stems.

Casey C of Key West wrote about Sommer Flowers:

"Sommer Flowers were great. The florist I first visited with wanted around $3000 total for everything (centerpieces and bouquets). I spent a total of $700 for ALL my flowers: my bouquet, bridesmaids, groomsmen boutonnieres, etc. Now, I just used roses, but the prices at Sommer were so reasonable, you could do anything. Plus the flowers were overnighted and arrived in perfect condition."

♥ **And more choices.** Readers of our past books have recommended several other online flower sources: **TheFlowerExchange.com** is a Miami-based wholesaler whose web site has detailed pricing info (click on product listing). A 100 roses run about 93 cents a stem; a box of 100 stock (filler flowers) are $66. **BridesNBlooms.com**, based in Tampa, not only sells flowers but also pre-made bouquets. Roses are around $1 a stem, while a pre-made rose bouquets are about $9 each (you have to buy a box of 15). **FiftyFlowers.com** imports its roses from Ecuador and has a detailed web site with four wedding packages that run $119 to $395. We liked their thorough advice on flower handling, shipping and more.

Spotlight: Craft Stores

Michaels Arts and Crafts Stores

(800) MICHAELS
michaels.com

One of the best sources for silk flowers and wedding supplies in North America has got to be Michaels Arts and Crafts stores. With over 899 stores in the US and Canada, Michaels provides not only a large number of attractive, affordable silk flowers, but they also have in-store arrangers who can do all the arrangements at affordable rates.

For example, when we visited a Michaels store, the floral department told us most custom silk bouquets range from $50 to $100. Pre-made silk bouquets are just $40 to $60. Wow! This is a great savings when compared with the average fresh bouquets from a retail florist—which can run up to $200 or more.

Michaels stores also carry other accessories for do-it-yourself brides. They have supplies with which to make veils and headpieces ($15 to $20), tiaras ($17 to $ 45) wedding cakes toppers, favors (Jordan almond 16 oz. bag $7), unity candles ($20-$40) and other wedding items. They carry accessories ranging from ring pillows to do-it-yourself invitations to cake knives as well.

FIGURE 2: Both Hobby Lobby and Michael's have free wedding project guides on their web sites. Michaels site (below) also offers online ordering, message boards and more.

If you have access to the web, check out Michaels excellent web site (michaels.com). Besides the standard store locator, you'll also find craft projects posted on-line, complete with supplies lists and instructions. We saw several bridal projects that could be used to make favors, table centerpieces and more. There's also a "crafts calendar" that lists in-store classes.

HOBBY LOBBY

(405) 745-1100 Web: hobbylobby.com

Hobby Lobby is an expanding national chain of craft stores with some attractive offerings. The stores carry all the usual bridal supplies like silk flowers and ribbon. We saw pre-made silk bouquets for $20 to $50 as well as headpieces for $10 to $45. Unity candles were $25 and cake toppers were $15 to $75.

But don't limit yourself to the wedding aisle at this store. We discovered clay pots (for garden style table centerpieces) for only $1. Looking for gifts for children in your wedding party? Don't pass up the funky picture frames and craft kits for kids. Overall, we think Hobby Lobby is one of the best do-it-yourself wedding resources you'll find in the country.

Floral Dictionary

Lilies

- **Calla**
  Huge, long white flowers on thick stalks (as in Katherine Hepburn's ". . . the calla lilies are in bloom.") Smaller versions (called posy calla lilies) come in a variety of colors.
- **Rubrum**
  Star flowers come in colors from white to peach to deep maroon.

Rubrum Lily

- **Lily of the Valley**
  Small, white blooms that look like tiny bells. This flower is affordable in northern climates but quite expensive in other parts of the U.S. For a picture, see "Top Money-saving Secrets" earlier in the chapter.

Orchids

- **Dendrobium**
  Miniature orchids that come in sprays, may be used individually or as trailing pieces.
- **Cymbidium**
  Smaller than Japhet orchids with a curly edge only at the center.

Dendrobium Orchid

- **Japhet**
  Large orchids with a curly edge all over, often have yellow throats.
- **Phalaenopsis**
  These are round-edged orchids that are white with reddish throats. Their delicate nature makes them best for corsages as opposed to bridal bouquets.

Miscellaneous

- **Stephanotis**
  Small, white flowers with star-like petals and a deep throat (we've been told that these can discolor in extreme heat.)

Stephanotis

- **Anthuriums**
  One of the few "true red" flowers, this has a heart-shaped bloom with a large stamen.

Chapter 6

Invitations

In this chapter, we'll tell you about a printing process that can save you 50% or more on your invitations. Then, check out discount sources for invites, from catalogs to web sites. Next, we'll show you the five-step shopping process for finding invitations, and share several of the latest invite trends.

What Are You Buying?

Buying invitations is a little like buying a meal at an a la carte restaurant. In other words, everything is priced separately: the appetizer, salad, entree, and dessert. With invitations, the entree is the basic invitation design itself (the paper style and the printing). Thankfully, the price does include the envelopes (two for very formal invitations or one for more informal options).

There are also other "accessories" available but these are priced separately in addition to the original invitation. Here are some options and a short description:

♥ **Reception cards** announce to the guest the location and time of the reception.

♥ **Response cards** (also known as R.S.V.P.'s) are just as they sound—a card that asks guests to tell you whether or not they can attend. An envelope (with your return address printed) is included with each response card. Most brides put postage on the response card envelopes to encourage their guests to respond.

♥ **Colored Ink** is available from almost every manufacturer (you can often choose among as many as 30 or more hues). Some low-priced printers will charge an additional fee for colored ink (say, $7 additional per item with colored item). High end printers usually don't charge an extra fee for colored ink.

♥ **Envelope linings** add a little flair and color to invitations.

♥ **Your return address** can be printed on the back flap of the envelopes.

♥ **Informals**, used mainly as thank-you notes, are blank cards with your names printed on the outside.

♥ **Programs, pew cards, and other enclosures** may be additional items you'll see in invitation books. Programs ($30 to $100 per 100) list all the participants in the wedding ceremony and tell guests the order of the service. Pew cards are used to differentiate between guests who are to be seated up at the front of the church (reserved seating) from those who should be seated farther back (general admission). Maps are included for weddings with many out of town guests or if guests are going to a separate reception site after the ceremony.

A word on invitation sizes. Most wedding invitations are rectangles; a typical size is 5" by 7". In recent years, new hip styles include square invites (7" by 7" or their smaller cousins, marquis 5.5" by 5.5") and something called "tea length" invites that are the size of this book (4" by 9"). Remember that larger square invitations may require additional postage.

Average total costs. The average couple pays about $426 for invitations and other stationery needs (for a wedding with 150 guests). But you can spend as little as $100 . . . or as much as $1000 for top-of-the-line engraved options. The average deposit is 50% down with the balance due when you pick up your order.

Where to Buy Invitations

Fortunately, there is no national shortage of wedding invitations; not only are the styles endless, but the suppliers are equally plentiful. How does this process usually work? Well, big, national printers print most wedding invitations. Some of these printers have a network of retail dealers (stationery shops, department stores, etc.). Others market invitations online and through the mail—they print up full-color catalogs and do business over an 800-number or web site. You can also buy invitations through discount buying services or online.

Here's a little secret about the invitations industry you won't hear from anyone else. Ironically, the same one company owns both the major web sites/mail-order catalogs *and* many of the invitation brands sold through retail stores. Taylor Corp. is the 800 lb. gorilla in this business—this private printing company with $1.4 billion in annual sales has over 80 subsidiaries in the US, Europe and Australia. We guess that Taylor long ago must have realized brides don't want to buy their invitations from some giant company. So instead, Taylor has a Byzantine collection of brands and catalogs that operate more or less like autonomous business units.

Taylor owns such major invitation brands as Regency (and its upscale division Elite), Carlson Craft, Celebration, Chase, Nu Art/Pacific Thermographers, Stylart, Royal, Masterpiece and Tatex among others. Taylor also owns major mail-order invitation catalogs like Rexcraft and the American Wedding Album. Taylor even owns Current, a mail-order specialty catalog. And here's the crazy part: you can often find the very same Taylor invitations styles sold through retail stationer shops in a Taylor-owned mail order catalog or web site at HALF the retail price.

Of course, you can bypass the standard invitation brands entirely if you wish—all you need is a computer and printer. More on this later. Here are some common (and not-so common) places to find wedding invitations:

♥ **Retail sources.**

1 Stationery shops. Look under "Invitations" or "Wedding Invitations" in the phone book and you'll find a smorgasbord of places, from party stores to gift boutiques. As dealers for the major invitations printers, they carry a selection of sample books containing examples of each invitation. Brides choose a design from these sample books and then place an order. Hands-on service is one of the chief advantages to this route—most stores can help you with etiquette/wording questions and, perhaps more importantly, deal with any problems that crop up with the printer. Of course, you pay for this service with full-retail prices and few discounts.

2 Places you wouldn't think of. Some churches and synagogues offer invitations at discounted prices as a fundraiser. We've even heard of several companies that offer invitations as a perk for their employees. One bride who worked at Xerox told us she was able to order invitations through the company at a substantial discount.

Another great source is "out of home" stationers. These businesses operate from home-based offices and, thanks to low overhead, usually pass along savings from 10% to 20%. You still get service with these stationers, just no fancy retail shop. As with any merchant you deal with for your wedding, you'll want to make sure the company is reputable by calling the Better Business Bureau, checking references, etc.

Some department stores with bridal registries also sell invitations, as do offset printers. Some local printers actually print their own invitations; while most send the orders along to the same national printers you'll see in stationery shops.

♥ Online (Mail-Order Catalogs)

Of course, you can also order wedding invitations from the comfort of your home. Over 20 companies have sprung up in recent years to offer wedding invitations via mail and online (later in this chapter we'll review some of the best).

How do the catalogs work? First, you call the 1-800 number and wait two to four weeks for the catalog to arrive. The glossy four-color publication will have pictures of invitations, accessories and generic etiquette/wording advice. Most will also send along a sample or two of various invitation styles.

Ordering from the catalogs is rather easy. Prices (at least on the invitations) are hard to beat; we've found the same designs in catalogs for 40% less than at retail stores. Yes, we are talking the SAME invitation. Most take credit cards and are quick to fill the order—it takes as little as two to four days (plus another week shipping time). Expedited or overnight delivery may be available, but at a steep extra cost.

Later in this chapter we'll go into more details on mail-order invitations, including pitfalls to avoid.

Don't forget the Internet either. You can both browse the catalogs of major printers and order online from their retailers. And small, custom designers are using the web to attract customers by offering the offbeat and the unusual. You'll see some of these sites later in this chapter.

We do have to admit using the 'net to shop for invitations is often exhausting work. With a few exceptions, most major catalogs' web sites are hard to navigate. Slogging through page after page of invites to look at tiny thumbnails is a pain. We wish we could standardize the categories of invitation styles at all the web sites. This would certainly make the search for invitations a little less time consuming.

♥ Discount buying services.

Later in the chapter, we review several discount invitation sources. What do they discount? Basically, the same premium brand names you'd see in full-price stationery shops (examples of such brands are reviewed later in this chapter) at discounts from 15% to 25%!

Discount buying services are a hybrid between mail order and retail dealers. They don't have any catalogs—you do the shopping and then call them for a price quote, once you've decided on the invitation (a

page or style number will work). You place the order over the phone or online, the invitations are mailed back to you within a few weeks time. In a way, discount buying services offer the best of all worlds—the high quality of premium brands at discount prices, combined with the convenience of mail order.

Sources to Find Stationers

♥ **Friends.** Recently married couples may be your best resource to find a good stationer.

♥ **Bridal shows.** Bridal shows are a great place to find little-known stationery companies. You may be able to look through some of their sample books at a show too.

♥ **Other bridal businesses.** Many other bridal businesses such as photographers, florists and bridal shops may be able to suggest a good local stationer. Some wedding vendors even sell invitations at steep discounts as a perk for their customers.

Brides in Cyberspace: What's on the Web?

eInvite

Web: eInvite.com

What it is: An online invitation source (see Figure 1 on the next page).
What's cool: This site with its 1000 invitation designs (from Traditional to Ribbons & Bows to Affordable Choices and more), offers a cool option: "display proofs." Called "Check Mate Preview technology," this system allows you to select any design, enter your personal wording, choose an ink color and letter style, then click on "display proof." Immediately you'll see a life size version of your wedding invitation exactly as it would be printed. If you like it, it's simple to order the design online. Or, eInvite will send you a sample in the mail if you want to touch it yourself. And you can email it to your best friend or mom or save your changes to an account for another day.

If you have any etiquette concerns eInvite offers a wedding etiquette guide, FAQ, glossary of terms and email access to human experts. They offer four shipping options from UPS Ground to Next Day Air. When we visited the site, they were offering free ground shipping for orders over $200.

Prices seem to have improved. When we last reviewed eInvite, we complained that a basic panel invitation was $229 per 100. Now you'll find a similar look for as little as $80 to $90 per 100.

By the way, the promise to correct any errors on your order for free. But the best part, they say "If you receive your cards and need to change

FIGURE 1: eInvite's cool "online proof" lets you create and customize invites to your heart's desire—but at a stiff price.

the information or have simply changed your mind, we will re-do your order at 50% off." Nice guarantee!

Needs work: There really isn't much to complain about this site. It's easy to use and we love the display proofs. We still recommend you ask for a physical proof of your invitation when you buy it and we think it's prudent to ask for a sample of invites you're interested in before you place your order.

By the way, eInvite has a sister site, EasyInvite.com. You can buy EasyInvite blank paper stock (find it under "Print at Home" on eInvite's site), and then go to their web site, input the item number for your invites and design your invitation wording. Then you'll be able to preview it with a full color online proof, download a PDF and print your invitations with any desktop printer. Your only cost is the paper!

Costco

Web: costco.com

What it is: The online site for their wholesale warehouse. Click on Floral & Events.

What's cool: As we noted in the flower chapter, Costco has made some big moves to weddings—and invitations is part of their bridal push. We were impressed with Costco's invites—they offer 4 different collections

of invitations (traditional, latest trends, floral accents and lavish looks) for 25% to 30% off. Example: a simple cream panel from Birchcraft was only $53.13 per 100, a 30% discount off the $75.90 retail.

But don't think it's all boring cream cards. Costco also sells invites with vellum and ribbon accented designs, tea length styles and more. One example was the Paper Damask invite from Checkerboard ($261.75 per 100, a 25% discount). The outer paper wrapper is printed with an elegant swirling damask pattern which opens to a cream center card. All this is tied with a matching satin ribbon.

Each invite style is listed on Costco's site with a graphic and details like paper weight and approximate shipping time, Costco also sells engagement party and bridal shower invites, announcements, blank printable invitation paper and printed napkins. Click on Bridal Accessories for pens, pillows, and more from Beverly Clark.

Needs work: You don't have to be a member to order online from Costco, but non-members are charged an additional 5%.

♥ **Other web sites to consider.** Our readers have also recommended these invitation sites, based on their positive experiences:

Wedding Invitations 411 (weddinginvitations411.com)
Custom Shots photo invitations (customshots.com)
Sand Scripts (sandscripts.com)
Invitations by Karina (invitationsbykarina.com)
You're the Bride (yourethebride.com)
Let's Party by Jake 418 (letspartybyjake418.com)

FineStationery.com is among the best-designed invitation sites online. You can search by brand (they carry three dozen of the top brands, including William Arthur, Cranes and more) or by design (floral, religious, formal, etc). We liked the clear pricing info—prices for thermography, flat printing and engraving are listed for each invitation depending on what options are available. Even if you are just browsing, this is a good place to start.

Getting Started: How Far in Advance?

There are five steps in the shopping process for invitations: Overall, we recommend you order invitations at least three to four months before your wedding.

1 Shopping. Take a couple of weeks to visit two or three stationers in your area. If you are interested in mail order, remember it takes two to four WEEKS (or more) to receive most catalogs. Yes, you can browse online sites 24/7, but sometimes it is easier on the eyes to have a printed catalog in front of you.

2 **Ordering**. This varies greatly by printer. Generally, it can take anywhere from ten days to two months to order invitations. Most orders take two to four weeks, although some companies offer rush service.

3 **Mistakes**. We suggest you leave a two-week "buffer zone" in case your invitations come in with errors. One stationer told us that one out of every three orders comes in with mistakes from the printer. "Quality control" seems to be a fuzzy concept with some invitation printers.

4 **Addressing**. Considering how busy you probably are with work and wedding planning, leaving four weeks here is prudent. If you choose to hire a local calligrapher, most take between one and three weeks to complete a job.

5 **Mailing**. Everyone knows how wonderfully efficient the US Postal Service is. Give yourself plenty of time. Mail invitations to out-of-town guests at least six weeks before the wedding. For in-town guests, mail at least four weeks before the event. If your wedding is on or near a holiday, consider mailing even earlier so your guests will have time to make plans.

Step-by-step Shopping Strategies

♥ **Step 1:** Determine the number of invitations needed. Here's a quick quiz: if you're inviting 200 people to your wedding, do you need 200 invitations? Answer: no—you send only one invitation *per household*. And since most of the folks you invite will be couples, you probably need about 100 invitations. (There is one exception to this rule, however: if a guest's child is over 18 and living at home, he receives his own invitation.) This step, of course, involves the groom. You must compile a guest list of his, yours, theirs (parents' friends) and ours.

♥ **Step 2:** Confirm the place and time of the wedding and reception. Also, verify the spellings of the facilities and names of participants. (We heard one story of a bride who didn't know how to spell her fiancé's middle name—the resulting invitation was misspelled! Doing your homework here is obviously helpful.)

♥ **Step 3:** Determine your overall wedding style. For example, an outdoor afternoon wedding followed by a barbecue reception will probably not have a formal, engraved invitation. On the other hand, a formal wedding with a sit-down dinner reception at the Waldorf-Astoria isn't the time for embossed hearts and flowers on parchment paper. The invitation is your guests' clue about what to expect. To decide how formal your wedding is, consider time of day, formality of dress, and reception style. At the same time, you and your fiancé's personalities should also be reflected in the wedding invitation.

♥ **Step 4:** Decide on an invitation budget. Prices range from $25 to $900 per 100 invitations, so have some amount in mind.

♥ **Step 5:** Once you find a stationer (either retail or mail-order), look at their sample books or catalog. First, decide on the paper. Forget the wording, type styles, and ink colors. Instead, look at the paper design and quality. (If you are shopping mail order or online, request a sample of the paper to see it in person). Any style of type, wording and colors can be put on any paper design, so focus on the paper first. Paper grades and weights largely determine the price–inexpensive mail-order catalogs use lightweight 24 lb. paper, while more expensive brands use heavier (up to 80 lb.) stock. Papers made of 100% cotton are usually more expensive than wood pulp options, but give a more elegant look.

♥ **Step 6:** Next, consider the printing. Decide on the ink color, lettering style and printing method (engraving or thermography). Sometimes the design of the invitation limits the choice of printing method.

♥ **Step 7:** Given the paper design and printing that best fits your reception, choose an invitation in your price range. Don't forget to factor in the cost of extras including napkins, place cards and maps if you want them.

♥ **Step 8:** Order at least 25 more invitations than your actual count in case you decide you need more later (you may want a few for keepsakes, etc.). Also, order extra envelopes in case of addressing goofs (calligraphers often ask for 10% extra for mistakes). After the order is written, proofread very carefully before the order is sent off. This is a critical step to catch any errors.

♥ **Step 9:** When the order comes in, proofread again and count the number of invitations to be sure you received the amount you ordered. Do this before you leave the store or as soon as the invites arrive by mail. Stationers have only a three- to five-day window allowed by printers to catch mistakes. Mail order catalogs have varying return policies, but most only allow 10 to 15 days.

Questions to Ask a Stationer

1 How many different lines do you carry? A wide assortment of styles and brands not only gives you more choices (and price ranges) but also a clue to how serious the retail stationer is about her business. Since stationers must purchase those sample books (at a cost of $35 to $250 a book), the number they carry indicates their commitment to wedding invitations.

2 Given my wedding and reception, what is your opinion of having response cards? Response cards (an extra expense) encourage your guests to let you know whether they will attend the

Real Wedding Tip

How many people should you invite?

Here's a classic dilemma: Your reception site holds 150 people . . . so, how many guests should you invite? 200? 175? Or just 150?

This issue points up one of the mysteries of wedding planning: estimating possible response rates to a wedding invitation. The answer . . . it's anybody's guess.

Your response rate will be based on several factors. How many out of town guests are invited? Odds are you'll have a higher rejection rate from folks who have to travel a great distance. What about the time of year? Weddings near major holidays may also suffer from lower response rates, since guests may be out of town on vacation.

A parallel issue to this is the response (or RSVP) card, where folks are asked the simple question "will you be attending?" Yes or no? Heck, they even get a postage-paid envelope that makes a response painless. The sad fact: many guests simply don't pay you the courtesy of using them. Perhaps they're too busy; perhaps they don't want to offend you by saying no. Whatever the reason, it can be very hard to tell just HOW MANY people will actually show up to your wedding.

We think it's fair for the bride and groom to contact wayward guests to see if they are coming. Blame it on the caterer, who needs an approximate count two weeks before your wedding. If the acceptance rate seems lower than expected, consider sending off a second wave of invitations to those friends or relatives on the B list.

wedding. However, in some regions of the country (parts of the South and Southwest) guests often don't send in their response cards because they prefer not to "disappoint" the bride by saying no. In other regions, particularly the Northeast, response cards are considered a must and are routinely returned by guests.

A retail stationer in your area should be able to give advice on this if you are uncertain. Even if you do choose to send response cards, you may only receive as few as 30% back. We recommend response cards when you are inviting a large number of guests and/or are having a very expensive meal. If you are only planning a cake and punch reception or are having fewer than a hundred guests, response cards may not be needed. Remember that response cards also require their own stamp, raising your expenses accordingly. Yes, you can put your email address on the RSVP card, but always give guests the option of responding by mail.

3 Can I see some samples of actual invitations? This is one way to separate the part-time stationer from the full-time professional—the latter typically has many actual samples on hand. The best mail order and web sources also provide samples of invitation designs upon request (either for free or at a nominal charge). Don't look at the style or color of the samples. Instead key in on the wording and the overall composition. Is the effect pleasing? Are the lines of type proportionate to the paper size? Is the type correctly aligned on the paper? If the invitation wording looks awkward, you may not want to trust your invitation to this business.

4 Who is responsible for any errors that occur? Some retail stationers may not offer to fix errors, whether you made them or they did. The true professional will take care of anything that goes wrong, regardless of who is responsible. If ordering from a catalog, be sure you get a written copy of the return policy and guarantee offered.

5 Can I see a proof of the invitation? Some printers offer this at a very small cost (about $10). If you have a large order or complex invitation, this might be a prudent way to go. One trade-off: requesting and approving a proof will add more time to the process, but still may be worth it for the peace of mind.

Bridal Bargains Wedding Planner: Invitations

How do you word a wedding invitation? While we don't have room in this chapter here to go into that detailed subject, we do pick up that topic in the *Bridal Bargains Wedding Planner*, our new planner. You'll find sample wording—including advice on how to deal with divorced parents, if you are throwing the wedding yourselves, etc. Then you'll find a worksheet that will let you work out the exact wording your invite, plus other stationery needs (reception cards, RSVP's and more). Finally, we take a look at how to properly assemble and address a wedding invitation, with detailed advice and tips. Use *Bridal Bargains* to find the best deals on invites, then follow up with the *Bridal Wedding Planner* to get the wording and addressing just right.

Top Money-saving Secrets

1 Choose thermographed invitations instead of engraved. Right about now you may be wondering what is thermography. Let's take a quick look at the difference between the two printing processes. Note: we aren't talking about the style of script or the quality of the paper; this is just the actual printing process.

Engraving is the Rolls Royce of printing. Until the 1970's (when thermography became widespread), this was your only choice for invitations.

Both engraving and thermography create raised printing. However, with engraving, a copper or steel plate is etched with the type and design. These etchings fill with ink and are forced against a die, lifting the ink out of the plate and creating a raised image on the paper. The paper is left with an impression from the back (called a "bruise").

Thermography is often used to simulate engraving. A resinous powder is dusted over the ink while it is still wet. The paper is then heated, the powder melts and fuses with the ink, swelling to create a raised surface. While metal plates may be used, this process is much less expensive (up to 50% or even more!). Another advantage to thermography: this process also allows you to use a wide variety of ink colors and type styles. Thermography has become extremely popular, thanks to better production quality. The process is virtually indistinguishable from engraving, except there is no dent (or bruise) on the back of the invitations. All the mail-order catalogs/web sites listed later in this chapter offer thermographed invitations.

2 Order from a professional stationer who discounts. See the discount sources later in this chapter.

3 Check the local newspaper for sales. Some professional stationers have periodic sales.

4 Don't buy all the extras. As you've read above, there are quite a few different accessories and extras available to match your wedding invitation. Instead of ordering separate reception cards, consider printing "Reception Following" at the bottom of your actual invitation (obviously, this only works if you are having the wedding and reception at the same location!). This could save about 15% off your bill. Also, skip envelope linings and response cards if you don't see a need for them. To see how all these charges add up, let's look at the sample costs for an invitation with black ink from Regency, a major brand we'll review later in this chapter.

INVITATION PRICING EXAMPLE

Regency Invitation

(PRICE FOR 100 INVITATIONS)

Basic Invitation	$77.90
Return Address on Flap	32.90
Reception Card	54.90
Response (RSVP) Card	62.90
Lined Envelopes	21.00
Informals (Thank You Notes)	54.90
TOTAL	$304.50

As you can see by this sample, the original invitation is a fraction of the total bill; note how the "options" can double or triple your final tab.

5 Buy an embosser with your return address instead of paying extra to get this printed on the back flap. The cost of an embosser is about equal to or less than the return address charge in many cases—the advantage here is you can use the embosser again. You can order an embosser at most office supply stores.

Here are a few on line sources to find embossers as well:

Officedepot.com

Livingvictorian.com/embosserhome.html

Stampco.com/embosser.html

6 Order all your stationery needs all at once. Many printers offer quantity discounts if you order an invitation and any extras (thank you notes, RSVP cards) at the same time.

7 To save on postage, don't buy an oversized invitation. Oversized invitations require more postage. Also, an invitation with lots of enclosures (reception cards, response cards, maps, etc.) will be more expensive to mail since it will probably exceed one ounce in weight. (A smart tip: before you do the mailing, take one invite to the post office to get an actual weight with all enclosures). Remember that response cards require their own stamp, too.

8 For engraved invitations, consider alternatives to Crane. The Cadillac of engraved invitations, Crane (see review in the next section) charges about $800 to $1000 for 100 engraved invitations. But what if you desire engraved invitations, yet can't afford the Crane price? There are several affordable alternatives. For example, the Reaves Engraving mail-order catalog (877-9REAVES or 910-369-2260; web: reavesengraving. com) charges just $377 for 100 engraved invitations on Crane paper. (It's even less for engraved invitations on their own in-house stock—$268.25 per 100). FYI: Reaves also offers calligraphy service for $1 per set of envelopes. See box below for a reader's feedback on Reaves.

Another alternative: use a discount buying source like Invitation Hotline (800) 800-4355 (see review later in this chapter). They offer a variety of manufacturers with engraving options for up to 30% off.

9 **Postcards**—a great way to save on money and postage for RSVP's! Instead of a response card (which needs a separate envelope and a first-class stamp), consider a response postcard. One bride told us she whipped up a response postcard on her computer and had it copied on double-sided cardstock at a local copy shop. Total cost: $15 per 100. And then the postcards only require a 24¢ stamp. A basic response card with envelope costs about $50 per 100 and requires a 38¢ stamp. Your savings: $49.

10 **Design it yourself on a computer.** Got a computer and printer? Check out the Best Buy later in this chapter for info on software that lets you design invitations on the cheap. We'll also discuss sources for laser-compatible invitation paper. Another good source for do-it-yourselfers: *Crane's Wedding Blue Book* by Steven Feinberg. This 150 page paperback answers just about every wedding etiquette question there is when it comes to invitations—wording, addressing, assembling and more. The book is available in libraries or online at Crane's web

Real Wedding Tip

Engraved invites without the engraved price

A reader in Maryland found Reaves (reavesengraving.com) saved her big bucks over Crane engraved :

"I saved $900+ on my engraved wedding invitations thanks to Reaves. I used their card stock verses Crane's (I couldn't tell the difference) because the watermark wouldn't show anyway. I was so pleased with their work, service, prices and overall GREAT attitude!"

site (crane.com/social/weddings/WeddingBlueBook). See figure 2 below.

ED-iT software products (ed-it.com) offers a wedding invitation software program that allows you to design and print invitations, announcements, response cards, pew cards, reception cards, place cards, maps, thank you notes, programs and even envelopes. The software helps with wording, offers "perfect typesetting" and has a built-in guest list manager. Six invitation fonts are available or you can use your own fonts. This Windows-only program costs $30. They also offer a Try-Before-Buy feature that allows you to use the program for 30 days free (the only trick: they add "for evaluation use" to every print out so no, you can't really use it without paying). Finally, ED-iT also helps you find paper with some recommendations for vendors on their site. The only downside, the site is still stuck in the late '90's. They really need to upgrade the site with a little more zazz.

Yet another do-it-yourself software option called Printing Press is available from Mountain Cow (mountaincow.com). This kit offers a built in address book as well as original fonts for a wide variety of looks. It will help you design invitations, guest cards, place cards and more as well as address envelopes. Printing Press also keeps track of RSVPS automatically and allows you to import

FIGURE 2: How do you word a wedding invitation? Address envelopes? Crane's online wedding blue book provides excellent advice and tips.

Crane's - The World's Finest Stationery Since 1801.

ONLINE STORE

Order Personalized Holiday Cards and Receive this Complimentary WATERFORD Ornament.

Sign In • Customer Service • Find a Retailer • Events • Contact Us • Shopping Bag

SEARCH by keyword or item number GO

JOIN our e-mail list GO

To sign up, type your e-mail address above.

WEDDINGS
- **Idea Center**
  - Classic Traditions
  - Wedding Trends
  - More On Color
  - A Crane Sampler
  - A Crane Sampler pg. 2
- **Express Yourself**
  - Design Palettes
  - Paper Styles & Sizes
  - Typestyles
  - Engraving
  - Ink Colors
  - Borders
  - Motifs & Monograms
  - Envelope Linings
  - Ribbons & Bows
  - FAQ
- **Planning Your Big Day**
  - Wedding Planner
  - The Engagement
  - For The Wedding
  - At the Reception
  - After the Wedding
  - FAQ
- **Wording**
- **Where To Buy**
- **Wedding Invitation Design Center**
- **Wedding Etiquette Blue Book**

Crane's WEDDING BLUE BOOK — The Style and Etiquette of Announcements, Invitations and Other Correspondence — STEVEN I. FEINBERG

Addressing the Envelopes

After the Wedding

Anniversaries & Reaffirming Vows

Assembling the Invitations

Before the Wedding

Enclosure Cards

Postponement & Cancellation

Responding to Invitations

Wedding Announcements

From announcing the engagement to writing that final thank-you note, Crane's Wedding Blue Book has helped thousands of brides prepare for, and create the mood for, their special days. Now, the must-have reference for brides-to-be is right at your fingertips. With Crane's Online Wedding Blue Book, every bride can have a private consultation with the best in the business. Among the topics included in the Online Blue Book are:

- Etiquette for all wedding invitations, announcements and correspondence
- How to choose wedding papers, ink colors and lettering styles
- How to handle new and unusual circumstances
- The anatomy of a wedding invitation - the significance of each and every line and enclosure card

Using Crane's Online Wedding Blue Book To make browsing quick and easy, we've organized the contents into eleven different sections, such as Wedding Invitations, Addressing the Envelopes, and After the Wedding. Each section contains a number of related topics from which to choose. For instance, the Wedding Invitations section contains such topics as Selecting Your Wedding Invitation, Divorced Parents and Late Receptions, to name just a few. Using the menu provided to the left, you may access a different section at any time.

photos. The price: $30 for the standard option, $60 for a basic version and $130 for an deluxe option dubbed "Extreme." Extreme includes the ability to create patterned text, diamond and circle monograms, patterns and borders and more (see picture on previous page).

71 Cut the second color. Sure, it might be tempting to set off a small embellishment on your invitation in a second color, but watch out! Two colors add dramatically to the cost of any invite—raising the price by 50% or more. One trick to achieve the same look: choose a different SHADE of the same color, instead of a second color. Some custom printers and invitation designers can use a darker hue of the same color to give that second color look . . . without the second color price.

72 Get creative on the accessories. When you buy invitations, you're more than likely to be pitched on buying all those little bridal accessories like guest books, plume pens and other doo-dads—at high retail prices.

Our advice: to save, get creative. One reader from Toronto told us her inventive idea for a guest book. She went to an arts and crafts store and purchased a picture matte (16x20) and an archival-quality gold pen. "At the wedding, each guest signed their name on the matte. I used the matte to frame a photo of us and got a beautiful and unique keepsake." Total cost: $12. Compare that to fancy guest books that can run $30 to $50.

Another idea: Reader Mary O'Rourke wrote to tell us that they forgot to take their guest book to the wedding—so they grabbed some permanent markers and had guests sign a table cloth! She said, "The idea was a hit. Our guests wrote such nice messages, much more than they could have in a guest book. Today, we have it hanging in our office room of our apartment and we read it constantly."

Looking for a source to print maps? A reader emailed us with a recommendation for Wedding Maps (weddingmaps.com). The site has an online proof for your map and allows as many revisions as you need. The cost: $198 to design the map (including 100 maps and up to four locations) with an additional 25¢ per map over 100.

Instead of using traditional invitation printers to print her napkins, one reader searched the Internet for a cheaper alternative. Her bargain find: Oceans of Roses (OceansOfRoses.com—click on Miscellaneous) sells 100 personalized cocktail napkins for about $20.

73 Compare prices on mail order invites. Many of our readers notice that mail order companies often sell the exact same invitations at different prices. In one case, a bride noticed that The American Wedding Album offered a floral invite at $65.95 per 100 while the *exact same design* from Wedding Invitations by American Stationery was

$46.95, a savings of 30%!

The same parent company, American Stationery, owns both catalogs! Our guess for the reason behind these price differences: perhaps different catalogs are targeted toward different audiences? The lesson: it pays to shop around with mail order.

14 Check out warehouse clubs. An example: some Costco warehouse stores (web: costco.com) offer name-brand invitations at a 10% to 30% discounts. We discussed Costco's invites earlier in this chapter.

Helpful Hints

1 For large weddings, engraved invitations may be a better bargain. While thermography is generally cheaper than engraving, there is an exception. After you get beyond 300 to 350 invitations, the reverse is often true. For example, we priced 400 thermographed invitations from a major printer at $575. The same number of engraved invitations from a discount buying source was $566. Not only is it cheaper, but you also get a bonus: some printers like Jenner (see review later in this chapter) will fold and stuff the invitations into envelopes—that's no small task. Another tip: while mail-order catalogs have great prices on orders of 100 or 200 thermographed invitations, their price advantage drops as the quantity grows. You may find a better deal on large orders (over 300) from a local stationer.

2 Consider addressing options. Many stationery shops and even mail order catalogs today offer envelope addressing services for busy brides and grooms. They'll take your guest list, feed it into the computer and then voila! Addressed envelopes ready to stamp and mail. While some services use a pen-based addressing machine (like Inscribe), more and more are turning to computerized output from laser and ink jet printers (occasionally a stationer will offer hand calligraphy—check to verify). Which is best? Consider the paper type before making a decision. If your envelopes are not made from paper that is laser-printer compatible (ask the stationer or catalog to find out), go with an ink jet printer service. Why? The laser printer toner might rub off at the post office, making the invitation undeliverable. Ink jet printing is preferable since it sticks to the envelope better.

3 Recognize the limits of the postal system. Invitation printers love to sell brides all sorts of new looks. But before you pay, make sure your invitations are post-office friendly. An example: wax seals.

They sure look neat on envelopes, but they can gum up the post offices' processing machines. The result: at best, the wax will smudge. At worst, the invitation gets jammed in the machine, shredding it beyond recognition. The best advice is to only use wax seals on the *inside* envelopes.

Along the same lines, watch out for invitation fads. Example: bows, ribbons and fabric appliques that extend off the card. Sure, they look neat . . . BUT they have to be stuffed into an envelope and sent through the postal system. The result may look nothing like those glossy catalog books.

Finally, ask the post office to hand cancel your stamps. That way your invitations aren't machine canceled with an ugly post mark.

4 Beware of brazen bridal registries. In the category of overzealous marketing hysteria, some bridal registries are providing brides with special cards that they're suppose to include with their invitation. Online registries offer to send emails to your guests. The cards/emails "inform" guests where the bride is registered, with a handy web address or phone number. Nifty, eh? No, it's in bad taste. You are NEVER suppose to send guests an invitation that suggests or demands a gift. Even for us etiquette minimalists, we're appalled at the attempt of bridal registries to shamelessly shill for business. Guests should find out where you are registered the old-fashioned way—by word of mouth. Trust us, if they want to know, they'll ask.

Another idea: some couples include registry info on their wedding web sites. That is fine, of course.

5 If you don't like the flimsy paper from mail order catalogs, check out single panel cards. The card stock used to make single panel invitations is much more substantial than many of the papers used for the folded designs in mail order catalogs. You'll give your guests the illusion of better quality invitations and spend a fraction to do it. Rexcraft, reviewed later, sells a simple single panel invitation for just $47 per 100.

Biggest Myths About Invitations

Myth #1 *"My aunt, who is a real stickler for etiquette, says engraved wedding invitations are the only option to consider. She says the quality of thermographed invitations is awful."*

Unfortunately, your aunt has been reading too many outdated etiquette books. In reality, thermography printing has improved so much in recent years that even Crane, the number-one seller of engraved invitations, now offers thermography. The only visible difference between thermography and engraving is the dent on the back of your invitation—and in your pocketbook.

MYTH #2 *"I thought it would take 15 minutes to write up my invitations order at the stationer. Boy was I surprised when it took nearly two hours!"*

That's right! Many folks think writing an invitation is easy—until they actually try it. In reality, finding the right combination of words and type styles that make an aesthetically attractive invitation is challenging. That's why just writing up an invitation order can take an hour or more. Using a professional retail stationer or calling a catalog's customer service department will make this process go easier. As we mentioned earlier, *Crane's Wedding Blue Book* (available in stores or online at crane.com) is a good source for wording advice.

MYTH #3 *"I assumed when we ordered our invitations that extra envelopes would be included—is this true?"*

Nope, many printers send the exact compliment of envelopes as invitations ordered. If you want extra envelopes, they must be ordered in advance (there is a small additional cost). Why is this important? Well, if you're addressing your own invitations, it pays to have extra envelopes in case of mistakes. Even calligraphers will request you supply extra envelopes.

Pitfalls to Avoid

PITFALL #1 UNDER-ORDERING OF INVITATIONS.
"When I first ordered invitations, I ordered exactly enough for the people on my list. Later, my mother came up with some long-lost relatives, and I had to go back and reorder another 25. I was shocked at the extra expense!"

If you guess wrong and need more invitations, the set-up charge to reprint more invites will be tremendous. For example, let's look at a sample invitation order from a popular brand. The total for 100 invitations is $204.50. Let's assume you're a smart bride and decide to order extras, say 125 invitations. The total would be $246.20—a $41.70 difference. However, if you order only 100 now and find out later you need 25 more, the total cost will be $363.50. Wow! Ordering 125 in the first place would have saved you $117! As you can see, ordering extras in your original order is much more cost effective. That's because the set-up charge for additional orders is the same as for the original order. There is no cost savings on invitations if you go back later to order more. Also keep in mind that if you "go back to press" later, the ink color and paper may not match the original order.

PITFALL #2 MAIL-ORDER SNAFUS.

"I ordered invitations from one of the catalogs advertised in a bridal magazine. Boy, am I sorry—the order came in with several mistakes and the whole design looked out of whack."

Sure, mail-order invitation catalogs offer great prices, but do you get what you pay for? We've heard stories from brides who felt burned when their invitations arrived, looking nothing like they expected.

The reasons for this are many. In some cases, the composition (how the type is aligned) is off, due to a mistake in the printing process. Other times, the catalog made a goof with spelling or wording. Later in this chapter, we'll review the companies we think are most reliable—including those who offer an unconditional guarantee, the best bet for getting what you want.

Of course, the mail-order companies sometimes have themselves to blame. At some catalogs, quality control is so bad they actually send out samples to prospective customers that include spelling errors and bad composition! In other cases, we've seen catalogs recommend invitation wording that is awkward at best.

PITFALL #3 WHEN INVITATIONS ARE JUST A SIDELINE.

"The bridal shop where I bought my gown offers invitations at a 10% discount. However, the salesperson who helped me didn't seem to know much more than I did about how to write up the order or word the invitation."

Competition in the invitation business is intense. Many bridal businesses (particularly bridal shops and tux shops) now offer discounted invitations as an enticement to order a gown or purchase photography. The discount is usually 10% to 20% off retail. The problem: many of these businesses are inexperienced with invitations. Their selection and knowledge of invitation printers is limited and service by low-paid clerks is lackluster. Many also lack the skills to word the invitations correctly.

Another twist on this pitfall are stores that advertise "up to 50% off" wedding invitations, as one bridal shop in Ohio recently promoted. As it turns out, you have to order five bridesmaids dresses (or rent five tuxes) to get the discount, which only applies to the invitation itself—response cards, maps and other accessories are full price. Hence, you might get a better deal on the *whole* invitation order from a mail-order catalog or retail stationer who discounts.

Nancy Gresl from Milwaukee wrote to us about her frustrating experience ordering invitations at a local tux store:

"We first planned to order our invitations from the tux store, as they offered us a 30% discount since we are getting our tuxedo rentals from them. I had already decided on an invitation I found in the Now and Forever catalog (N&F), but since the tux shop offered 30% off, I thought I would try that.

"First, 30% is off of *the store's* price. But the *regular* price in the N&F catalog was almost equal to the *discounted* price at the tux shop. Bottom line: the total savings was only about $20 for 225 invitations with inserts and thank yous! Plus, the tux shop had a $35 shipping fee! Their selection of font types was also not as broad as N&F, and I was told I could not adjust the font point size for various parts of my wording. After trying three proofs with the tux shop, I canceled my order—wasting almost three weeks. I then called N&F and was told that if I sent/faxed a detailed description of my invite wording with the point sizes noted, they had no problem printing my invitations in various font sizes. I faxed an order, had my proof a day and a half later, approved the proof on Thursday, and had my entire order the following week using their two-day shipping! My invitations look wonderful. And this was so easy to do."

PITFALL #4 LAST MINUTE CHANGES.

"My church just called to say that we have to move up the time of our ceremony by one hour. The problem is I've already ordered invitations. Can I make a change?"

Candles at a discount

Yes, candles do add ambience to a wedding or reception. But many invitation catalogs sell candles at obscene prices. Of course, our smart readers never pay retail. Here are their picks for best discount candle sites:

- **Little Cindy Candles** (LittleCindyCandles.com): floating candles and votives
- **Candle Comfort Zone** (CandleComfortZone.com): unity candles, votives.
- **Printed Candle** (printedcandle.com): unity candles, wedding favors.
- **Rosewood Candle and Craft** (RoseWoodCandleAndCraft.com): unity candles, floating candles, votives.
- **Oriental Trading Co. (orientaltrading.com):** votives, unity candles floating candles.
- **Wax Wizard (waxwizard.com):** floating candles, votives.
- **Gen Wax (genwax.com):** floating candles, votives, unity candles.

Not without incurring some big charges. First, understand that most invitations orders are faxed/emailed to the printer within 36 hours. Once received by the printer, it is very difficult to change or stop the order. If changes can be made, there is always a charge. For example, one big printer we researched charges $10 "per inquiry" and another $10 per change.

PITFALL #5 CRANE SWITCHEROO.

"I ordered Crane invitations from this store in the mall that was advertising a special deal. Yet, when the invitations came in, they didn't feel anything like what I expected. Did I get ripped-off?"

It's possible. Crane is one of the best known (and most expensive) brands of wedding invitations. This notoriety has a downside–some Crane dealers, desperate to compete with lower-cost alternatives, use tricks to discount the brand to brides. One common example is the "Crane envelope switcheroo:" sure, you get Crane engraved invitations, but the stationer substitutes cheaper, non-Crane *envelopes* without telling you. How can you spot this? Most (but not all) Crane envelopes have the distinctive Crane watermark–check for this when you pick up the order. Also, make sure you specify in writing that you're to get Crane envelopes.

Another Crane scam: we've documented several cases of stationery dealers who use Crane's "commercial" stock instead of the 40 lb. social paper more commonly used for wedding invitations. Why? The commercial stock is thinner and less expensive, enabling the dealer to give a "discount" on the order. Our advice: don't use it–this stock just doesn't look right for wedding invitations. Ask the dealer what type of stock they use for their Crane orders.

PITFALL #6 THE REVENGE OF THE ETIQUETTE POLICE.

"I just got in my invitation order and got a big surprise. With no warning, the printer had changed my order to fix an alleged 'etiquette error' in the wording! This is ridiculous."

Hard to believe, but it is true that some printers will change the wording on invitations to conform to "proper etiquette" as they see it. The only way you can avoid this problem is to tell the stationer or catalog that you want the wording (and any capitalization) to be printed exactly as you specify. Checking a box on the order form or noting it in some other way usually accomplishes this (which can be in very small type buried at the bottom). You must also indicate if unusual spellings of names (like Henri instead of Henry) are correct. That way the printer won't substitute their etiquette rules or spelling corrections for your finely crafted prose.

PITFALL #7 PET POSTAL PEEVES.

"My stationer told me the invitations would cost just 37¢ to mail. However, after I added two maps and took the invitations to the post office, they said it would be 60¢. As a result, we have to shell out another $50 in postage. Is that fair?"

This is why we recommend taking your invitation (and all the enclosures) to the post office and getting it weighed before you buy all those cute "love" stamps. Start adding maps, response cards or other enclosures and you'll notice the postage bill soars.

Another interesting twist on this problem is a story we heard from Austin, Texas. A local wedding company there was advertising an "addressing, stuffing and mailing" service for just $1 per invitation. Sounds great, eh? The problem was the service didn't tell brides they were mailing their invitations *bulk rate*. The post office treats bulk rate mail as a very low priority, to put it charitably. As a result, some of the brides' invitations arrived six weeks after the wedding—others didn't arrive at all. As it turns out, it's illegal to mail invitations (or any personal correspondence) bulk rate and the post office may have confiscated the invitations. The best advice: *always* mail invitations first class.

PITFALL #8 OUTRAGEOUSLY PRICED ACCESSORIES.

"I was so excited with the savings on invitations from a mail-order catalog, I decided to order a slew of accessories too. Yet when I visited a local shop, I saw some of the same products at much lower prices. What's going on here?"

Ah, you've discovered the secret moneymaking machine behind the mail-order invitation catalogs. While the invitation itself is very affordable (perhaps as much as 50% less than retail), the prices on accessories can go through the roof.

Look through any of the mail-order invitation catalogs and you'll see plenty of superfluous stationery items (pew cards, save-the-date cards) as well as pictures of "suggested accessories," including matching napkins, programs, unity candles, cake toppers, toasting glasses, garters—even swizzle sticks printed with the bride and groom's name. Yet the prices can be amazingly high. We found much better deals on these items online, at party stores, gift shops or other local stores. And then there's the whole question of whether you really need a matching "gold guest-book pen with heart-shaped, rose-etched Lucite base" for $20. The best advice: comparison shop before you buy. See previous chapter (Chapter 5 Flowers) for affordable accessories such as candles, decor and more.

Reviews of selected invitation brands

Based on our research, we have identified a few "best brands" in wedding invitations—these are printers who sell their designs through retail dealers. *These printers do NOT sell directly to the public; nor do they have catalogs for consumers. We provide their web sites and phone numbers so you can find a dealer near you who has their sample books.*

The Ratings

A	Excellent . . . .our top pick!
B	Good . . . . . .above average quality, prices and creativity.
C	Fair . . . . . .could stand some improvement.
D	Poor . . . . . .yuck! could stand major improvement.

Birchcraft Customer service is what makes Birchcraft a long-time invitation brand favorite. They're fast (printed invites ship in as little as 48 hours) and affordable. Most Birchcraft designs run $100 to $150 for 100 invites. They are similar in style to Carlson Craft (see review below)—we noticed plenty of embossing and ribbon accents. We found the quality to be quite good. *For a dealer near you who carries check Birchcraft, go to birchcraft.com.* **Rating: B+**

Carlson Craft One of the largest invitation printers in the country, Carlson Craft has something for everyone. Their catalog features a wide variety of styles that range from $65 to $590 per 100. Some range! In fact, Carlson Craft has really upped it's prices and added some high end fancy designs. They used to offer invitations in the under $100 range (for 100). But along with the new higher prices, their designs have improved. We see a lot more sophisticated styles with translucent overlays, unique paper textures and colors and a variety of ribbons. One example of their paper textures, Laid in Stone ($180 for 100). This square invite is embossed with a cobble stoned border. Show with gold ink on rich chocolate brown paper this is quite an unusual look. Carlson Craft also offers a line of "Imprintibles" for couples that want to print their own invites off the computer. *For a dealer near you who carries Carlson Craft, call (800) 328-1782. Web: carlsoncraft.com.* **Rating: B-**

Chase Paper From plain traditional to glitzy contemporary, Chase Paper has a wide selection of unique papers. The quality of the thermography is top-notch, say our stationery experts. Prices run $60 to $140 per 100 invitations. Best of all, the lower-priced options are a definite step up in quality compared to other companies. Chase also offers an upper-end line of exclusive paper designs called the Chase Collection, with prices

ranging from $180 to $400. This group featured current fads like invites with ribbons and bows, as well as printing on velum paper. While we liked the look of this collection, if you plan to spend that much money, you might as well go with an even better brand like William Arthur. Shipping takes about two weeks. By the way, Chase is now part of The Consortium Invitations company that also owns Janssen and Elite. *For a dealer near you who carries Chase, call (508) 478-9220. Web: consortiuminvitations.com* **Rating: B**

Checkerboard Invitations Checkerboard's sample book features a wide assortment of designer invitations—you can even mix and match type styles (most printers don't let you do this). We saw designs with splattered ink, Mylar prisms and marbled paper; they even have several recycled paper designs. Funky envelope linings complete the looks. Checkerboard's prices aren't for the faint at heart: they average $290 per 100, but range from $100 to $590. *For a dealer near you who carries Checkerboard, call (508) 835-2475. Web: checkernet.com* **Rating: B+**

Crane Pull out a dollar bill and you'll feel some Crane paper. Yes, this is the same company that provides Uncle Sam with stock for greenbacks. Their wedding invitations are equally legendary—"Crane engraved" invites were the preferred (some say only) method for announcing a high-society wedding in the past. Today, 200 year-old Crane bows to modern times by also offering thermography. No matter which printing method you choose, however, a Crane order will require bushel loads of those aforementioned greenbacks. The average engraved invitation runs $800 to $1000 per 100 invitations (thermography is about 20% less). Add in pricey extras like response and reception cards and you can easily see how the average order for Crane tops $1200! So, is it worth it? Well, the paper (heavyweight 100% cotton) is exquisite, and they've added some new styles over the years. There are 72 different typefaces, 30 ink colors and nine new paper colors including azalea and sea glass green. And we found Crane prices vary dramatically from dealer to dealer (see Pitfalls to Avoid earlier in this chapter for more info). If you do decide Crane is right for you, pick a dealer that has their "Paper Emporium" system, a computer that lets you (and the store) word the invitation in perfect etiquette and see a preview of it on screen, letting you swap typefaces, paper options and more. Then, you get a laser print of your invitation, composed exactly as it will be printed—that's a concept other printers should (but don't) offer. Or now you can do it yourself on Crane's web site. They have about 20 designs on line to choose from. Then you can customize your choice with traditional wording, ink color choices, envelope linings and more. Print out your own sample and you can even order it (at full retail) on line. *For a dealer near you who carries Crane call (800) 472-7263. Web: crane.com* **Rating: B**

Elite Elite is Regency's sister division that offers high-end invites that are equal parts quirky, elegant and stylish. Of course, this comes at a price. Pearlized, embossed and beribboned designs can cost as much as $950 for 100 invitations (they start at $225, and range up to $450). Elite's designs are always on the cutting edge: their current catalog features many mixed media invites, combining fabrics, ribbons, translucent papers, embossing and more. All invitations are engraved or thermographed on 100% cotton paper. If you want something more conservative, the Infolio "Fine Papers" designs are more restrained both style and price wise (starting at $158 per 100 for thermography, $248 for engraved). While we like Elite (it's hard to believe they're even related to Regency), the print quality and customer service are a few steps behind rival brands like Encore. And if you're looking to buy on the 'Net, you have to call most online dealers for prices—they're not printed online. *For a dealer near you who carries Elite call (800) 354-8321. Web: elite.tc* **Rating: A-**

Embossed Graphics If you're planning a large wedding, Embossed Graphics should be at the top of your invitations shopping list. That's because the company has incredible prices for large quantities of thermographed invitations. For example, 400 invitations from Embossed Graphics cost just $366! Compare that to Carlson Craft or Regency, where the same quantity would set you back $400 or $500—on paper that's much lower in quality. In fact, it's Embossed Graphics heavyweight paper that is the star here; the type styles (45) are good but the extra options are more limited compared to the competition. And if you want inner envelopes, you'll have to pay extra. Yes, they've tried to jazz up the line in the past few years (new styles feature embossing, foil borders and bonded envelope linings), but this line is still more the understated than glitzy. Prices range from $125 to $200 per 100 invitations (an excellent value for a quality product) and shipping is fast. *For a dealer near you who carries Embossed Graphics, call (800) 362-6773 or (630) 236-4001. Web: embossed.com* **Rating: A**

Encore Cutting-edge invitation printer Encore combines the best of both worlds: high-quality paper, innovative designs and, most of all, excellent quality. If you're going to spend $400 per 100 invitations (Encore's average order), you might as well go for the gold standard—choose from designs trimmed with ribbons, flecked paper overlays or round borders with gold or silver edges. Want flowers? Choose from embossed lilies, roses and more on textured papers and card stock. We can hardly do their designs justice; you have to see them to believe them. All Encore invitations There are three collections) are thermographed and a wide variety of ink colors is available. Encore's prices range from $140 to $1095 per 100—no bargain. Stick with the Classic collection and you'll find prices more reasonable. Of course, the top-of-the-line Encore Edge collection is breath taking, but at a minimum of $595 per 100 *just* for the invites, you'll need oil money to swing this. Encore line still offers it's envelope calligraphy service that matches the typeface on the invitation. Brides and grooms can download a calligraphy database program off Encore's web site for free. Also available: a translation and typesetting service for foreign languages and peel-and-stick envelopes—no more licking. "Encore's quality is the best in the industry," an industry source tells us. "They have an artistic flair when it comes to typesetting—and they rarely make mistakes." *For a dealer near you who carries Encore, call (800) 526-0497. Web: weddinginvitations.com or encorestudios.com* **Rating: A**

Jenner Here's a little secret of the invitation business: if you want Crane engraved invitations, there are other sources than just Crane itself. For example, Jenner, a Kentucky-based printer, engraves invitations on Crane paper . . . and for much less than Crane. 100 engraved invitations on Crane paper from Jenner are $395 (that's about 50% less than Crane's prices). You can save even more by using Jenner's in-house stock, which runs $299 for 100. Best of all, Jenner includes folding and stuffing of invitations into the envelopes (most printers don't offer this service). The printer also offers thermographed invites as well. (The only bummer: some states like California have very few Jenner dealers; call the company for a list of local dealers). *For a dealer near you who carries Jenner, call (502) 222-0191.Web: jennerco.com* **Rating: A-**

NuArt Unimpressed with the flimsy, boring designs of the low-cost printers—but you can't afford the fancy designs of the super-expensive brands? Here's a solution: check out NuArt.. This printer offers excellent printing on incredibly heavy paper. And best of all, the prices are very down to earth—just $62 to $500 for 100 invitations (most are around $200 per 100). Their catalog features intricate embossing, linen and silk-finished papers and a choice of over 50 type styles. Fool your friends into thinking you spent hundreds of dollars on invitations! With both stylized and traditional paper designs, NuArt/Pacific is definitely a best buy. *For a dealer who carries NuArt, call (800) 653-5361. Web: nuartinvitations.com.* **Rating: A-**

Regency This invitation printer behemoth has just about something for everything. Their six invitation books (some of the names of which—Flower, Breeze and Rainbow—sound like '60's love children) feature just about every style known on Earth. Prices range from $64 to $295 per 100. New to the line are several combo letter style looks that combine two typefaces for no extra charge. You wont see lots of fancy ribbons or bling here. And the quality of this line (paper, printing) is only average. *To find a dealer near you who carries Regency, call (717) 762-7161. Web: regencythermo.com.* **Rating: B-**

William Arthur Our pick as a best bet for invitations is Maine-based William Arthur. Their fabulous collection of thermographed invitations offers a sophisticated and classic look for brides who want an alternative to the plain, traditional invitation. With a variety of unique type styles and card-type designs, Arthur's line runs $190 to $835 per 100 invitations. Upper end designs are usually only available with engraved printing. Unlike Crane's limited offerings, Arthur's engraved invites feature delicate touches like an embossed design on the envelope, different ink colors and hand-lined envelopes. You'll also find letterpress accents, die cut designs and unique ribbon accents (often, there is an additional charge for the ribbon—kind of unfair, in our mind, when they show the sample with the ribbon). We especially like the two color ink samples we saw. Arthur's customer service is excellent, according to stationers we interviewed. "They're in a class by themselves," one told us, adding that their shipping (24 hours for thermography, 7-10 days for engraved) is incredibly reliable. One and two day rush service is also available. *For a dealer near you who carries William Arthur, call (800) 985-6581 or (207) 985-6581. Web: williamarthur.com.* **Rating: A**

Do-It By Mail

When we first researched this topic for earlier editions of this book, we were not very impressed with the mail-order wedding invitation catalogs. The designs were bland and the samples we viewed left much to be desired.

Well, there is good news to report. In the last several years, the catalogs have improved their offerings and quality. And, not too surprisingly, their popularity has soared—now nearly 50% of all wedding invitations sold in North America are through the mail order catalogs.

The big reason: price. Catalogs sell some of the very same designs you see in the stores for 40% less than retail! How do they do that? Well, here's a little secret of the wedding invitation business: the same giant company (Taylor Corp.) that owns most of the big invitation brands sold in stores (such as Regency and Carlson Craft) also produces the catalogs. Sneaky, eh?

How they get away with this is beyond us—why would anyone walk into a store and order invitations at full retail when the very same design can be had for 40% less through the mail or online? Well, the invitation printers tell us some brides like the "hand-holding" (that is, etiquette advice, wording suggestions, etc.) they get from a retail stationer. It comes down to personal choice.

So, here's our research on the best mail-order invitation catalogs—and some comments on how we came up with this list. First, we pored over samples and catalogs from 20 mail-order companies. Then we looked at the feedback we've received from brides over the past several years (our e-mail address is in the back of the book, by the way). Finally, we think we've come up with a list of the best resources for discount mail-order invitations.

A couple of thoughts before we get to the chart on the previous page. We noticed many of the catalogs carry some of the same designs. Yet comparing prices can be difficult—some catalogs charge more for fancy type styles, while others throw this in for free, for example. Also, the prices can be all over the board: some catalogs offer great deals on small quantities, while others give better discounts on large orders.

The big bummer with most mail order invitations: paper quality, or lack thereof. Most catalogs sell invitation papers that are quite thin (24 lb. is a common stock weight). If you want a heavier weight, you may have to go with a brand we review earlier that is sold through retail stores.

Even more offensive than paper weight were the samples from some of the catalogs—one had printing that was off-center and the wording was incorrect (etiquette-wise). And this is an example of their best work?

On the other hand, the prices were hard to beat—sometimes 40% below retail for the exact same invitation. Mail order (and the web) is also a convenient option for many brides; you can shop in the comfort of your home and don't have to drag the groom to yet another wedding-related appointment. New this year in some of the catalogs are "seal 'n send" invitations. These informals offer an affordable alternative for invites to engagement parties and showers. They don't include an envelope; you just fold them over and seal them. Also, a few web sites sell blank paper for do-it-yourself invitations (more on this later in this chapter).

Our advice is to shop carefully. Request a sample of the design you're thinking about ordering. Visit retail stationery shops to compare paper quality and prices. Make sure the mail-order company has an unconditional guarantee that allows you to return the invitations for a refund, no questions asked. Finally, we recommend paying with a credit card (in case a dispute develops, you may be able to get a refund from your card issuer).

Our round up of the best mail-order invitation catalogs can be found on a chart on the next page. The prices quoted are for invitations with black ink and regular lettering.

Mail order Invites

Catalog	Taylor?	Price*	Turnaround
American Wedding Album (800) 428-0379 TheAmericanWedding.com	No	$76.95	3-4 days plus shipping
Dawn (800) 361-1974 InvitationsByDawn.com	Yes	$41.80	2-3 days plus shipping
Heart Thoughts (800) 648-5781 Heart-Thoughts.com	No	$76.00	2 days Plus shipping
Now & Forever (800) 521-0584, (800) 451-0610 Now-And-Forever.com	Yes	$39.90	2-3 days Plus shipping
Precious Collection (800) 537-5222, (800) 553-9080 PreciousCollection.com	Yes	$63.90	3 days Plus shipping
Reaves Engraving (877) 9REAVES or (910) 610-4499 ReavesEngraving.com	No	$126 (in-house paper)	4-5 weeks for engraving
Rexcraft (800) 635-3898 Rexcraft.com	Yes	$46.95	2 days Plus shipping
Willow Tree Lane (800) 219-1022 WillowTreeLane.com	Yes	$81.90	2-3 days Plus shipping

***Key: Taylor?** *Is the catalog owned by giant printer Taylor?* **Price:** *Single panel price is*

Guarantee	Comments
10 days	A nice mix of traditional and contemporary styles. Customer service is OK
Return within 30 days	Both US & Canadian version. More traditional and frilly. This catalog does carry laser-compatible blank invites. New themes: Disney, asian, destination weddings.
Return within 10 days	Web site does not include catalog photos or prices. Must order catalog to see the line. Allow one extra day for invitations with ribbons.
Return within 30 days	Carry a large selection of square cards and other unusual shapes and sizes. About 88 different invitations.
Return within 15 days	Lots of layered invitations and bow accents. Floral motifs abound. Up to three free samples.
Return within 30 days	$377 for engraved invites on Crane paper, a 50% discount. Good buy for engraved options.
Return within 30 days	Huge catalog and excellent web site. Great customer service and decent prices.
Return within 15 days	Some of the cheapest invites around. Improved web site now includes "Value Packages" that include invitations and extras.

the cost for 100 single-panel invites thermographed (printed) with black ink.

Destination Wedding Tips

A save the date card is a must for destination weddings—consider sending this out six months or more to give folks a heads up!

Remember when we said you should mail invitations to out of town guests at least six weeks in advance? When you're talking about a destination wedding, you're going to have to back it up quite a bit. We recommend sending out invitations a couple *months* before the event.

If you only plan to include your closest friends and family at your destination wedding, but want to announce your marriage after you get back, you'll be shopping for wedding announcements. Remember, they are worded differently—you're not asking anyone to attend the wedding, just letting them know you've officially tied the knot.

Finally, you may decide to have a big party back at home for friends and family who couldn't come or weren't invited to your destination wedding. The tips throughout this chapter will apply to invitations to an after-wedding party.

Trends

♥ **Color and more color.** Gone are the old days of simply white or cream invites. Now color is the rage: from jewel-toned envelope linings to colored ink for the printing itself. Some invitation printers are now doing TWO ink colors on one design. For example, one William Arthur design features alternating lines of text in peach and charcoal hues. Add a peach envelope liner for an even cooler effect.

A big part of the color trend: colored papers. From chocolate brown to copper to baby blue, the choices are endless. Add a metallic ink like gold or silver (especially to dark colors) and the designs really pop. And look for reversed color pallets with reception cards. For example, you might choose a chocolate brown invite with cream ink—then this is paired with a cream reception card with brown ink.

♥ **Motifs.** A motif is a small leaf, swirl or flower bud that might be used to separate text on your wedding invitation. This can be repeated on all your stationery, napkins, engraved champagne glasses and more.

♥ **Unique paper for do-it-yourself kits.** **Invitesite** (invitesite.com) offers brides unique papers in a do-it-yourself kit. Kits include handmade papers, printable papers, instructions and accessories. For example, Lauren's Bouquet comes with gate-folded platinum velum with a light lavender mulberry paper sash. To complete the look, a sprig of pressed blue larkspur decorates the design for $2.50 per invite (minimum order of 50). What makes this unique: the designs look hand crafted rather

than mass produced. What excited us most about Invitesite: finally, a company has made sets of invitations that are compatible with laser or inkjet printers but also look truly unique. If the kits don't interest you, Invitesite can create a one-of-a-kind design.

♥ **Ribbon.** More than just a tied bow, ribbon accents are being employed on invites in creative ways: a decorative banner, ribbons with texture (organza, for example) and more.

♥ **Small custom designers.** The web is a great place to find small, custom invitation designers. One reader emailed us about **Dreamland Designs** (dreamland-designs.com), a custom invitations designer in Minnesota. She told us owner Gina Selesky hand draws all her invitations and announcements. She praised Gina's calligraphy and hand coloring. New this year you can see a few samples on line and you can order a sample box of 20 invitations for a $100 refundable deposit. While they aren't cheap ($4 to $20 per invitation including the invite, envelop and response post card), the quality of the work might be worth a look.

♥ **Belly Bands.** Yes, invitations are still layered with vellum and wrapped in paper folders, but a new trend is to add "belly bands." These accents, often vellum strips, wide ribbons or contrasting paper, wrap up your invitations. Some belly bands printed with the couples names. Just remember, as with most ribbons, belly bands and other accents, *you'll* be the one assembling them. Be sure you order them with plenty of enough time.

Spotlight: Best Buy #1

Wedding Invitation kit

Like the idea of doing your invitations yourself on a computer, but feel a bit intimidated? After all, maybe you're not a graphic artist. Even if you could track down laser-compatible invitation paper, what's the correct way to word an invitation, etiquette-wise?

We found a great answer to those questions: the Wedding Invitation kit, made by Masterpiece and available online at several site (go to easytoprintpapers.com and click on "buy more product"). What does the kit include? Some kits come with 50 invitations, envelopes, overlays and fold overs for $36 to $38. Others have as few as 25 invitations and 25 note cards for $18. Depends on how many you need and how fancy you'd like them. As an example, the Pearl Border panel card kit, includes 50 flat cards and envelopes, 50 notes cards and 50 seals for $34. At last count, we saw 21 different papers available.

So once you've bought the paper, what next? Couldn't be any simpler. You go online to EasytoPrintPapers.com and log on with the product code (included with the kit). You'll need to register as a new user and choose a password. Then, follow the steps online to input your invitation data, see a copy of it online and print it out. The site automatically generates a PDF file so you don't have to worry about fonts, margins or other printing requirements.

One gripe about the Wedding Invitation Kit: the web site is very sketchy on info on the different designs and options. That means you have to go Office Max or Office Depot in person and see the kits for yourself. In an age when you expect to be able to see it all online, this was disappointing.

Another option: Gartner's "Do-It-Yourself Printables" (uprint.com). Available in Office Depot and Target, these kits of 50 invitations and envelopes go for $33. Matching response cards are $15 for 50 ; there are also matching place cards, programs and thank you notes. These invites work the same as the Wedding Invitation Kit–you go online at Uprint.com, input the keyword or SKU on the box and start writing your invite. You will need a Flash plug-in to print the invites.

Bottom line: these print-it-yourself invites are a great alternative for affordable invites . . . especially for smaller weddings.

Spotlight: Best Buy #2

Online Invitation Discounters

Here are our picks for best online invitation discounters:

♥ **Invitation Hotline.** If you love the quality of designer wedding invitations but not the designer price tag, consider the Invitation Hotline (800) 800-4355, (732) 536-9115, fax (732) 972-4875 (invitationhotline.com). This Manalapan, New Jersey-based company offers a 25% discount on such well-known brands as Carlson Craft, Elite/Infolio, Encore, Embossed Graphics and more. Over 90 albums are available to choose from, including such premium brands as Arlene Segal and C'estpapier. Owner Marcy Slachman told us the company also moved into calligraphy and other custom accessories (maps, seating cards) in recent years.

You can submit an online quote request from Invitation's Hotline with pricing–just include the book name and style number. Slachman will help troubleshoot any etiquette or wording questions. Delivery takes about two weeks from the date the order is placed. Faster delivery is available via overnight services.

The Invitation Hotline also carries favors, including a few more eclectic offerings. For example, we noticed their price list included a silver-plated dolphin bottle opener ($2.70). Other wedding accessories and calligraphy are available as well.

♥ **Invitations 4 Sale** (invitations4sale.com). Our readers report success with this discount invite source. A sample email from a recent bride: "I just wanted to report that I had a very good experience ordering my invitations from invitations4sale.com. The invites were 40% off, they were extremely prompt in answering my emails and helped guide me through the process." Free samples of invitations from Carlson Craft and Regency are available up to four per vendor—nice touch.

♥ **YoureTheBride.com** had "great prices and very honest service," says a reader who said the site saved her $300 on her invites. The well-designed site sells Regency, Birchcraft and other brands. Owner Tracie Morris of Garden City, MI is also a wedding planner.

♥ **Elegant Brides Invitations** (ElegantBrides.Invitations.com) offers a big 35% discount off NuArt, Checkerboard and Carlson Craft, as well as 25% off other brands like Encore and Elite. A reader who used this Michigan web site praised their service and lack of minimum orders. You can view an invitation proof online and get a proof mailed to you for a small fee. "Efficient, quality service," said another reader.

Spotlight: Best Buy #3

Paper sources for do-it-yourself invitations

If you have a computer, laser printer and desktop publishing know-how, you can easily design your own invitation. But how do you find the appropriate paper?

There's good news: laser-compatible papers (called "imprintables") are now one of the hottest-selling items at stationery stores and copy centers like Kinko's (with prices as low as 20¢ per invitation, including envelope). If you can't find imprintables through a retail source, check these mail order catalogs:

Paper Direct (800) 272-7377 (paperdirect.com) has an amazing collection of laser-compatible stationery, note cards, placards, and more. For a rehearsal dinner, bridesmaids' luncheon or informal wedding invitation, Paper Direct's "Themes" collection has several fun options.

Our readers have also recommended these sites for invitation paper:

Art Paper	artpaper.com
C&J Papers	cjpaper.com
First Base	first-base.com
Geographics	geographics.com
Grafcom	invitation-supplies.com
LCI Paper	lcipaper.com
Marco's	marcopaper.com
Paper Zone	paperzone.com
Southworth	southworth.com
Paper & More	paperandmore.com

For a bargain on vellum, check out the web site **Drafting Deals** (DraftingDeals.com). You can buy vellum in packs of 100 8 1/2x11 sheets for only $11.

Spotlight: Favors

Like many wedding traditions, favors have a colorful if not somewhat mysterious history. Here is some background:

Where did favors originate? Popular mainly on the East Coast and in California, wedding favors have had a long, rich history. When we say rich, we really mean royal. In fact, in France in the 16th century, nobility and royalty gave valuable gifts (usually of porcelain) to their wedding guests as mementos of the occasion.

In the middle of the 16th century, almonds came to Italy from the Far

Do yourself a favor—and save money

If there is one aspect of a wedding where you can put that do-it-yourself energy to work, consider making your own favors. Heather Remer of Pittsburgh told us she "didn't want to give my guests a dust collector that they throw away. I wanted something simple and sweet—chocolates! Yet, when I looked at the prices some places were charging for a box of chocolates, I thought I would have to starve for a month (okay a little drastic) just to scrounge up the money. Then I got an idea—why not make them myself? A few weeks before the wedding, my four bridesmaids and I had a "chocolate party" to make my favors. The molds, chocolate and netting are all inexpensive—I figured my total savings to be $150."

East. These almonds were very expensive and became popular to give as favors to guests at royal weddings. To preserve these almonds, a sugar-coating was added—Jordan almonds were born.

In the 17th century, three almonds, painted in bright colors and wrapped in bridal veiling, were given to guests as a symbol of fertility. Why three almonds? From the union of two comes one—a baby. The veiling meant that the guests shared the couple's happiness.

What about favors in the US? Favors in America are most popular with ethnic communities (particularly Italians). Favor manufacturers tell us that nearly 25% of their orders come from just three states, Pennsylvania, New York and New Jersey. Couples there order more expensive favors with almonds inside a porcelain swan or champagne glass—these can cost as much as $20 each! In other areas, potpourri is a more popular choice. While favors are also common in the Southeast (Georgia, Florida, the Carolinas in particular), brides in the Midwest, Northwest and Southwest rarely give favors to guests.

Here are top sources for favors on a budget—as well as some unique ideas for favors submitted by our readers:

♥ **Nashville Wraps** (nashivillewraps.com) offers amazing wholesale prices on items like metallic favor bags, tulle, ribbon, candy boxes and more. How about a sheer mini bag in pastel colors 12 pieces for $2.57. Fill them with treats and you've got an affordable favor. Look for close-outs at even better prices.

♥ **Fairy Tale Brownies** (Brownies.com) offers a bit different take on favors. You can buy their brownies (a single favor is $6.00) complete with a monogrammed box. Sounds yummy to us!

♥ **Hercules Candies** (800) 924-4339 or (315) 463-4339 (web: herculescandy.com) is a New York-based candy maker that's been selling handmade chocolates for 90 years. Their extensive brochure lists dozens of chocolate favor options. Each is customized with the bride and groom's name and wedding date on the box holding the chocolates. Prices start at $1.50 per box for the 2-piece versions. Other options are available. The samples we tasted were great.

♥ **Eco ideas.** An Ohio bride told us she gave away flower seed packets as favors to her guests. Cost: 17¢ per packet. One source: the Tender Seed Company (web: tenderseedcompany.com) sells customized seed packets, some with ribbons and pearls, for $1.79 to $2.29.

♥ **Candy Wrappers.** And what about candy bar wrappers with the bride and groom's name and wedding date? Moosie Wrappers (web:

moosiewrapper.com) sells the wrappers for only 80¢ each for 36 to 149 wrappers. Discounts on larger quantities are available. You buy the candy bars then slide the wrappers over them. If you want the bar and wrapper together, the charge for a minimum of 24 bars starts at $1.50 each.

♥ **To the Moon and Back** (moonfavors.com) If you're tired of the same old favors, Moon Favors seems to have hit on a twist: hand pained votives, tins, spice bottles and more. For example, for an Asian themed wedding, give your guests hand-painted silk fans. Now they aren't cheap (fans start at $8), but they are different. If that's a bit much, hand painted glass ornaments start at $4. And no, you don't have to imprint the favors with your names and wedding date. You can opt for a simple flower or even snowflake theme.

♥ **CD Favors:** A bride wrote to us with this suggestion: "You can burn your own CD's with your favorite songs—or even make multi-media CD's with pictures and text. Office Depot sells a 100 pack of CD's for $35, and then you can purchase some inexpensive CD labels to personalize and decorate them. Avery makes a 50-label pack available at Office Depot for $16. And Memorex sells label-making software for only $23. So, you can make some very cool, personalized CD's for your guests for less than $1 each. If they like your taste in music, this will definitely not be a favor that just collects dust." A quick note on this favor idea: while "fair use" laws let you make a few copies of copyrighted music for your personal use, burning 200 CD's with tunes probably crosses the line.

♥ Bride Elizabeth Jaust suggested an altruistic wedding favor: **give to your favorite charity.** "I am making a donation on behalf of the wedding to the Susan G. Komen Breast Cancer Foundation. They give you a card to place at each table. It just seems nicer than giving out 100 little wine bottles that nobody keeps. Also, my mother passed away from cancer and this seems like a nice way to celebrate her. And you don't have to give a large gift. It can be like 50 bucks or so. Contact the foundation at komen.org."

♥ Kathy LeFevre invented a great idea for wedding favors: **a family recipe cookbook.** She started a company called Friends and Family Cookbooks (friendsandfamilycookbooks.com) that creates custom cookbooks. Just hit up all your relatives for their favorite recipes and send them to the site (you can enter the recipes online via their web site). You can also add up to 60 family photos. Friends and Family will put it all together for you starting at $7 each for the first 100. Yes, it's a bit expensive, but they will take all those recipes, organize them and design the book for you. And, Kathy points out, you'll only give one cookbook out per family, not per person, so the cost isn't as much as you think. The result is a unique favor that folks won't toss after the wedding is over.

♥ **eBay**. Reader Joely Macheel sent an email about buying favor supplies on eBay: "I purchased 72 undecorated bubbles (3 boxes of 24) for $6.00, a favor-maker for $11.50 and 144 ribbon roses for $3.50. eBay is my savior!"

♥ **Ribbons, at a discount.** As we mentioned in the floral chapter, RibbonTrade.com sells high-quality ribbon at a big discount. We're talking the $2 a yard stuff you see in fabric stores, at half price or less. Example: Morex Swiss Double Face Satin Ribbon (5/8 inch) for 56 cents a yard.

♥ **Two words: Oriental Trading.** Their famous web site (OrientalTrading. com) is the mother lode of cheap favors. Examples: 50 white organza wedding favor bags for just $10. Or two-dozen wedding bubbles for $7. The site will even personalize items. The only caveat: watch out for shipping costs, which can sometimes run more than the items!

Notes

Part 2

Your Reception

Chapter 7

Reception Sites

The choice of a reception site can make or break any wedding budget. In this chapter, we'll explore 13 ways to save—including some ingenious places that brides have discovered to hold their receptions. Plus, we'll give you the five most common pitfalls with reception sites and how to avoid them. Finally, we'll take a candid look at the pros and cons of the five most common sites.

What Are You Buying?

There are two basic categories of wedding reception sites: places where you just rent the hall (and bring in an outside caterer) and others that have on-site catering, like hotels, country clubs or catering halls. Therefore, you are basically buying the following services:

♥ **EXCLUSIVE USE OF THE FACILITY.** Either you are charged a flat fee for a certain period of time or there is an hourly rate. Obviously, rates vary with the amount of ambiance. An historic restored mansion will cost much more than a local union hall. Most places require a booking deposit, which can be several hundred (or thousand) dollars. A second deposit (to cover any damage or clean-up) may also be required at some sites.

♥ **Catering** (food, beverages, service and rentals). You typically have two choices: use the site's in-house caterer or bring in an off-site caterer. When a site has an in-house caterer, there is often no "room charge"—the facility makes its money from the catering. Unfortunately, some sites not only charge you for the catering but also tack on a facility rental fee. We cover wedding catering in-depth in a separate chapter later in this book.

The Big Trade-off: Ambiance vs. Great Food. In a perfect world, a reception site would offer both a beautiful setting AND great food. In reality, there are typically trade-offs. A restaurant may offer a stunning view of the city, but only mediocre food choices. On the other end, catering halls may have a sterile "wedding factory" atmosphere, but they have receptions down to a science. A site that lets you bring in an outside caterer (and hence, allows you more control over food quality) may be the perfect compromise, but these sites can be hard to find.

Average costs. What a wedding reception cost? As you might remember from Chapter 1, we quote the average cost as $9286 for 175 guests. That figure covers not only the facility but also all the catering (food, beverages, labor, rentals, etc). What makes this confusing is that some sites include the site rental fee with the catering (hotels, for example). Of course, you often have to meet a rather hefty minimum spending charge. Other sites charge you a flat or hourly fee and let you bring in your own caterer. Prices for those types of sites are all over the board, from free (a church hall in some cases) to thousands of dollars for a historic inn or home.

The basic rule is that money buys you more ambiance—the prettiest sites always cost more than a nondescript hall.

Sources to Find a Reception Site

Finding the right reception site for your wedding may be the most challenging task you face. That's mainly because of the big bucks involved here—the reception (and, specifically, the catering) is the most expensive part of getting married. Here are some top sources to find affordable sites.

♥ **Wedding coordinators at your ceremony site.** Yes, these folks probably have talked to hundreds of brides over the years. They might be able to give you the "word on the street" for several reception sites.

♥ **Caterers.** Most off-site (or independent) caterers are well aware of the best local wedding reception sites. That's because their livelihood depends on the existence of facilities that let outside caterers come in for receptions. Call around to a few local caterers to find leads.

♥ **RECENTLY-MARRIED COUPLES.** Ask your co-workers or friends if they know anyone who was recently married. These couples are often more than willing to share their research and experiences about reception sites.

♥ **VISITORS/TOURISM BUREAUS AND LOCAL PARKS DEPARTMENTS.** If you are looking for a civic site (such as an historic home), your local

REAL WEDDING TIP

How to get reception sites to call *you*!

One Minneapolis bride found that her local visitors' bureau went way beyond the call of duty to help with her wedding plans:

"I don't believe your book does enough justice to this great resource that I tapped into—the local Convention and Visitor Bureaus (CVB)! This is an especially great resource if you are having a lot of out-of-town guests. I called the Minneapolis CVB several weeks ago, first to ask if there was any major convention or event going on the weekend of my wedding. Then they asked what type of event I was planning, so I broke down and told them. Lo and behold, the representative said she would transfer me to the CVB's "wedding coordinator." This woman was a God-send! She immediately asked for key info about my event—the dates, how large a space I would need, type of reception—and most importantly, how many hotel rooms I would need. (This is the key here because the goal of any CVB is to fill hotel rooms!)

Then, the wedding coordinator said she would create a blast e-mail to all the hotels in the area, effectively putting my event "out for bid." Since all the hotels would know other hotels got the same information, it creates a bit of competition. Sure enough, hotels started calling and emailing ME, instead of the other way around! They gave me great room rates, room blocks, reception space info, etc. I settled on a large downtown business hotel that offered me room rates of only $109 with free guest parking, and a full reception package at $43 per person, including an open-bar cocktail hour, hors d'oeuvres, champagne toast, seated dinner, and free parking for the guests. I even negotiated a lower food and beverage minimum and a $3 per person discount on the wedding package.

I would have never thought to even call this hotel, because it is upscale, and I thought it would be way out of our budget! I'd urge all brides to call their local CVB—especially if you tell them you need a block of hotel rooms. They also can give you free city guides and maps for out-of-towners. Please pass this tip onto other brides, especially those getting married in large metro areas!"

visitors/tourism bureau or chamber of commerce may have some suggestions. Many local parks departments book civic sites (like gardens and parks). See the following box for one bride's experience with the visitor's bureau in her town.

♥ **The Web.** Yes, you can find amazing site info online. One good site: UniqueVenues.com, with over 7000 sites in the U.S. and Canada. Enter your state (or Canadian province), event size and other requirements and you get a list of sites, some of which have an online video tour.

Once you come up with a list of possibilities, query local brides about their experiences. Our message boards (BridalBargainsBook.com, go to message boards and then local) let you question other couples in your area about which sites are best and which to avoid. Don't overlook this resources—sometimes other brides can be your best source to find a hidden reception site gem. And our message boards are ad and spam-free. Unlike other wedding web sites that take ads from reception sites, you can be assured our boards are free of such conflicts.

♥ **Bridal shows.** Yes, bridal shows can be a source for reception sites. Large expos with many vendors are your best bet. Reception sites often set up booths and hand out food samples and menus.

Brides in Cyberspace: What's on the Web?

Yes, the big wedding portals like the Knot.com and the WeddingChannel.com have large databases of reception sites and other wedding vendors. But how do you find unique and unusual sites like restaurants with banquet facilities, historic homes or other off-the-beaten track facilities? Try these sites:

♥ **CitySearch.com** has detailed listings for restaurants and catering facilities in over 50 cities. Click on "wedding resources" for site possibilities.

♥ **DigitalCity.com** (AOL's City Guide) allows you to access incredible information for over 60 cities. A good site to find venues, bridal shops, photographers and more.

Getting Started: How Far in Advance?

Don't delay the search for your reception site. As soon as you have confirmed your ceremony site, start the search for a reception facility. Time is of the essence. Most cities have a shortage of great reception sites; prime dates in the spring and summer often go quickly. In the South, December can book up to a year in advance for popular Christmas weddings. For spring/summer dates, booking a site nine months to a year in advance may be necessary.

Of course, the city you live in can require even more advance planning. Case in point: Washington, DC. DC brides and grooms not only compete with other weddings for scarce sites, but also political and charity events. No wonder that hotel receptions in DC book up to a year or more in advance. Historic sites in the Capitol are an alternative, but most are small in size. Another challenge: photographers. Since they can only be in one place at one time, in-demand photographers also book up a year or more in advance in Washington DC. And don't forget about the limo—one major political event can book up all the limos between DC and Montana. Again, advance planning is crucial.

Step-by-step Shopping Strategies

♥ **Step 1:** Figure out how many guests you want to invite. Then look for a site that fits that capacity. Many brides make the mistake of doing this the other way around—picking a site first and then having to adapt their guest list around its size.

♥ **Step 2:** Using the above sources, make appointments with three to five of the top prospects. Confirm the availability of your date before making any trip. Bring a friend or your fiancéé along to help inspect the facilities.

♥ **Step 3:** When you visit a reception site, look carefully at the facility. Can the room really hold all your guests comfortably or does it look cramped? Is the lighting on a dimmer system? How will guest traffic flow around buffet tables, the dance floor, etc.?

♥ **Step 4:** Ask for the manager! Try to meet the catering manager (if the catering is done in-house). Honestly discuss your budget and suggest the manager custom-tailor a menu for your reception. Read the catering chapter to make sure you cover all of those details. Get a detailed price breakdown—in writing—on *everything* (food, beverages, service, centerpieces, linens, china, etc.).

♥ **Step 5:** Ask to see the site set-up for a wedding. It's sometimes hard to imagine an empty ballroom dressed to the nines for a wedding reception. Here's a good way to get a more realistic impression. Ask to visit just before a reception is about to start. Check the traffic flow—for buffets, see if the lay-out of the food stations makes sense. Does the staff seem organized, or are they running around at the last minute like chickens with their heads cut off?

♥ **Step 6:** If the site has in-house catering, ask for a taste-test of the food. The quality of food varies greatly from site to site, so asking for this is a wise precaution. Most sites offer taste tests at no charge; of course there are exceptions. Some brides have emailed us with stories of sites that refuse to do tastings. We usually wonder what those facilities are trying to hide.

♥ **Step 7:** After visiting several sites, make your decision and put down as small a deposit as possible. Sign a contract that includes the date, hours, rental fee and any other charges and approximate guest count. Be very careful to get any verbal promises by the site ("oh, sure we can decorate that landing with flowers for no charge") in writing in the contract. As with any wedding, details may change. Make sure you get any alterations to the original menu or site plan in writing (keep a log of conversations, send/email a letter to confirm changes, etc.).

♥ **Step 8:** Get the site coordinator/catering manager's name in writing in the contract. Confirm that this person will be there at your reception. If there are problems, you'll need this contact to troubleshoot any last minute issues.

♥ **Step 9:** Keep the lines of communication open. Remember you might book the site up to a year (or more) before your wedding. Checking back periodically with the site's manager (a call every couple months or so) is prudent to avoid any surprises (oh, did we mention we sold the facility to the Society of Professional Motorcyclists last month?).

Questions to Ask of a Reception Site

1 How many guests can the space accommodate? Typically, the capacity is given in two numbers, one for a buffet/hors d'oeuvres (or standing) reception and one for a sit-down (seated) dinner. Be careful about these figures–sites often fudge capacity numbers or give "approximate" guesses. Don't forget to account for any buffet tables or dance floors; these all take space.

2 How many hours does the rental fee cover? What are the overtime charges? Be sure to ask about whether set-up and clean-up time is included in the stated hours. Some sites don't count this time "on the clock," while others do. Because some sites do more than one wedding a day, be careful there is adequate time between events. A money-saving tip: book the time you realistically need for your reception and avoid costly overtime charges.

3 Is there an in-house caterer or a list of approved caterers? Or can you bring in any caterer? Obviously, hotels have in-house caterers (that's how they make the big bucks). But many other sites are also picky about this–after a sloppy caterer burns them, a site may restrict brides to a list of "pre-approved" caterers. In case you can't find a caterer on their approved list that meets your specifications, ask if you can bring in another one.

4 Are there any cooking restrictions? For a site where an outside caterer is brought in, check the kitchen facilities. Some sites restrict caterers from cooking on-site and just allow the warming of food that is prepared elsewhere. Make sure you confirm with your caterer to see if the kitchen facilities are adequate.

5 Is there a piano available? How about a dance floor? Obviously, bands don't cart around a baby grand with them to every reception, so ask the site coordinator. Don't assume anything is free. Ask the site about any extra charges to prevent surprises.

6 What else is happening at the site the day of my wedding? Greed drives some sites to book multiple events during one day, even when the site can't realistically handle that many people. And we're not just talking about hotels. We've even seen smaller sites (restored mansions, catering halls) try to cram two or more weddings into a facility. Any site that tries to do more than one wedding a day is a wedding factory; approach any such facility with caution. Will you have to compete with a noisy convention of insurance agents that has a 10-piece band in the next room? Will your party have to share a bathroom or other facilities with the other party? Press the catering rep to give you exclusivity over the facility. Or at least, insist on a layout of the parties that minimizes overlapping noise.

7 Are there any union rules we must follow? In some states (particularly the Northeast), union work rules may force certain restrictions on sites, including the serving of food and set-up of any audio equipment.

8 What are the minimums? Watch out–some sites may require you to pay for a minimum amount of catering, no matter how many guests you have. Such minimums are common during peak wedding months (typically, May through September).

9 How late can we play music? Some facilities have a curfew for music. Be sure that doesn't conflict with your plans to dance the night way.

10 Are there any insurance requirements? According to our reader email, there are some reception sites out there that require other wedding vendors present at your event (DJ, band, photographer) to carry liability insurance. We're not sure why this is the responsibility of the bride and groom to check out, but it might be a good question to ask. If a vendor you want doesn't have liability insurance, inquire as to whether your (or your parents') homeowner's insurance will cover the event.

11 Are there any "caterer surcharges"? Some sites that let you bring in a caterer will slap that vendor with an extra surcharge that is a percentage of what you are spending on food and beverage. This fee is a major rip-off and rarely disclosed—that is, until the caterer passes it along to you in the form of an additional charge of 7% to 15%. We'll discuss this more in the Pitfalls section later in this chapter.

Bridal Bargains Wedding Planner: Reception Sites

Now that you've learned the above questions to ask a reception site, use those queries to compare three sites side-by-side in a worksheet we have in our new planner, the *Bridal Bargains Wedding Planner*. Once you've selected a site, you may need to map out just where the dance floor, tables, buffet and more will go—yes, we have a worksheet for this, plus detailed to-do lists on equipment rentals, the schedule for your reception and more.

Top Money-saving Secrets

1 City Sites. Fortunately, most sites run by municipal governments aren't trying to make a killing on weddings. Hence, city sites are the most affordable reception sites you can find. For example, in one town we researched, a nice city-owned clubhouse in a park that offered stunning skyline views was available to rent for just $500 for 7 hours. That's no typo—$500 and you bring in your own caterer. Another similar-sized facility run by a private company in the same town cost $1500 to rent for four hours. Obviously, the ambiance of these city sites (clubhouses, recreation centers, parks, gardens) is different than a downtown hotel or catering hall, but, hey, they are great bargains.

2 **Choose a site where you can bring in a caterer.** In every city we've researched, there are always a handful of sites where you can rent the facility and then bring in an "off-site" caterer. Often, this is where the big savings are found—see our chapter on catering for more details.

3 **Ask for the manager**. Skip the sales rep and head to the top—ask for the manager at a venue to get the best deal. If you want to haggle (or even simply ask "is this your best price?"), it's best to deal with the manager or owner of a venue. The manager may go under different titles—at a hotel, this could be director of catering. At a country club, it might be food and beverage manager . . . you get the idea. Yes, that friendly sales rep may be all smiles . . . but it is the manager who can really cut you the deal.

4 **Consider an off-peak time.** Everyone wants to get married on a Saturday night in June. Now, if you pick a time with less competition, you can often negotiate better rental rates. Many sites have stated discounts for Friday or Sunday weddings. (The down side to this tip: some wedding vendors like photographers may charge an extra fee to work on Sundays). If you still have your heart set on a Saturday wedding, consider less popular months of the year (basically anytime other than the summer). Many sites have stated discounts for such off-months. A reader in Seattle did point out a negative to having a wedding on a Friday night: traffic. She was a bridesmaid in a Friday night wedding and she wrote to say that "even the photographer who left way earlier, was late because of traffic." Keep this in mind when you schedule your wedding.

5 **Your house.** Hey, at least the facility is free. But be aware that you may have to rent chairs, tables, etc. and this will add to the tab. You may also have to pay a mover to store your furniture for the weekend. If you plan to pitch a tent in the backyard, the expense can go even higher (see the next page for the box Tent Rental 101 for tips and advice). Of course, even when you factor in all these expenses, the savings of a home wedding instead of holding the reception at a pricey hotel may put you ahead overall. Between 10% and 20% of all receptions are held in private homes.

6 **Consider your ceremony site.** Many houses of worship have attached reception halls. In fact, almost one-quarter of all receptions occur at churches or temples. One key reason: rental rates are particularly affordable. We'll have more on this option later in this chapter.

Tent Rental 101

Yes, renting a tent for a home wedding can be pricey, but there are some basic points to remember:

♥ There are four types of tents: frame tents, pole tents, pop-ups and party canopies. **Frame** tents have no center poles, using a lightweight metal frame covered with vinyl for support. Since they require minimal staking, frame tents are best for decks and patios. **Pole** tents are more traditional, with pole supports both on the perimeter and in the center. These types of tents require extensive staking. Some folks think pole tents are more festive looking; pole tents are probably the best option for large receptions. **Pop-up** and **party** canopies are do-it-yourself alternatives to pole tents with collapsible frames and offer shelter against sun or light rain.

♥ Which is the most affordable? Pop-up and party canopies are the cheapest options. Frame tents tend be more expensive than pole tents. A large company that rents tents in New England charges $625 for a frame tent that is 30' by 60' feet (this would hold 144 people seated for dinner). The same size pole tent is $545. Other elaborate pole tents with sidewalls can top $1000 and even $2000 depending on the options. At the top end, in the Northeast, it can cost $6000 to $9000 to rent a 50x70 tent that holds 200 guests—that includes lighting, flooring, heating, delivery, set-up and tear-down. While it might run $4000 for the same tent without all the extras, remember that a tent for large crowds will probably be more expensive than holding the same event in a hotel or catering hall.

♥ How big of a tent do I need? A good general rule is to leave 15 square feet per guest at receptions; for ceremonies the suggested size is eight square feet per person (assuming chairs, a center aisle, podium and/or stage).

♥ Accessories can add comfort—for a price. Sidewalls with windows are an option for larger tents, as are air conditioning and heating. If a tent is placed on a lawn, sub-flooring and carpeting can protect sod. Most folks rent a dance floor and add some basic lighting to create a mood.

♥ Key questions to ask: What exactly is included in the price? What are the extras? Some companies include set-up and take-down in their fees; others price this separately. Be sure to confirm any extra charges for weekend delivery and special fees like a "drying charge" should it rain on your event. Also ask: Are tents deodorized? How early is the set-up? Do you have insurance? Get a written agreement that covers ALL these details.

7 **Have a reception lunch or brunch instead of dinner.** The biggest expense of most receptions is catering, and the most expensive meal to serve is dinner. Wedding lunches or brunches often are much more affordable. What's the cheapest time of day to tie the knot? A two o'clock wedding—guests will already have eaten lunch and are not expecting dinner. Hence, a reception with cake, punch and light hors d'oeuvres is all that's needed . . . and 40% to 60% less expensive than a full dinner. Check the catering chapter for more tips to save money on this big budget item.

8 **Restaurant receptions.** Many restaurants have banquet rooms, some that can hold large crowds. These may be a great alternative to pricey hotels or catering halls. A bride in Chicago provided us with some cost comparisons: she priced a reception at a gourmet French restaurant in Des Plaines at $55 per person. That's for a chicken or filet mignon dinner. Compare that to fancy Chicago downtown hotels, where a similar reception starts at $75 and can go up to $200 per guest. Another bonus: most restaurants don't charge "room fees" or other bogus charges that pricier facilities do. And the food may be higher quality than a hotel or catering hall.

9 **Join the Navy.** Just kidding. But, do you have any relatives or friends who are active duty or retired military? If so, you may have access to a wide range of possible reception sites at military bases. One bride in Cape May, NJ discovered she could rent a wonderful Officer's Club of the local Coast Guard base since her father was a retired naval officer. The cost? A mere $25 per hour.

10 **Check nearby small towns.** A bride in Lexington, Kentucky emailed us this tip. She found a reception site in nearby Paris (a 15 minute drive) that was charging 40% cheaper rates than in-town options. "The historic building offered the outdoor intimate garden we were looking for," she said. Another tip for historic sites: barter. If you've got any skills, offer the caretaker of these sites a trade. One groom offered to fix some broken doors and shutters on a historic site and received a reduced rental rate.

11 **Tell them you are planning a retirement party.** A Connecticut bride called in this tip: she found a restaurant with a nice banquet room that was perfect for her 50-guest reception. Instead of telling them it was a wedding reception, she said the party was a family reunion. The result: she was able to get a great price for a complete sit-down luncheon, estimating she saved about 20% off a similar "bridal" package. Two weeks before the reception, she told the restaurant it was actually a wedding—too late for the restaurant to raise the price!

72 **Consider a business hotel.** If you like the convenience of a hotel reception but not the costs, check out hotels that cater to business travelers. Why? Most are dead on the weekends . . .and may be willing to cut a deal for a wedding reception. A bride in Los Angeles discovered the savings could be dramatic. She priced a 250 guest reception (four-course sit-down dinner, cocktail hour with open bar and appetizers, beer, wine and a champagne toast) for $7500 at a Wyndham hotel that caters to business travelers. "That's pretty amazing considering that this is in Los Angeles," said the bride, adding, "I don't feel that we are giving up on the quality either. The food is excellent." An additional bonus: she got a special weekend hotel room rate of $100 for out of town guests, which is a steal in LA.

The Marriage Mark-Up

Do you wonder if the price suddenly goes up when you mention the word "wedding" to a reception site? We've always been suspicious that folks planning retirement parties, birthdays or any other type of event get quoted LOWER prices than brides and grooms.

Our suspicions were confirmed when Boston NBC affiliate WHDH-TV did a story on the "Marriage Mark-Up." The TV station did a simple test—they called eleven Boston-area reception sites and asked how much they charge for a wedding. Then they called back and asked for a retirement party. Now, to be fair, the station made sure it was asking for the same size party on the same date.

The results? Eight out of eleven places quoted the station the "marriage mark-up." One site said a retirement party would be $65 per person, but $90 for a wedding. Another said brides and grooms have to shell out 20% more. And those prices didn't include any special wedding-only items like a cake, just food and beverage.

In Atlanta, one major hotel quotes a $10,000 minimum for a wedding, but just $7500 for retirement parties. Another facility in San Francisco quoted us an $18,000 estimate for a wedding with 125 guests; the same size party for a family reunion was just $9000.

So, what can you do? While most couples don't want to perpetuate a major hoax on a site, it is rather tempting. Perhaps the best path would be to just "forget" to mention you are planning a wedding when you request menu packages. Just say you are planning a party or event. It's clear that hotels and other reception sites have special "bridal package" menus that are quite pricey. What they DON'T show you is their regular menu packages with lower-cost food options (these go to other non-wedding event planners). You'll be in a better position to negotiate a deal if you have ALL the facility's menu and pricing info, not just the expensive "bridal" options.

Real Wedding Tip

Frequent flier nuptials; Zoo I Do's

We never cease to be amazed at the sheer creativity of brides who unearth some very amazing reception sites. Like the airport in Chattanooga, TN. Apparently, it's not so busy, so the airport rents the brand new terminal for weddings at affordable rates.

Museums (like the Museum of Life and Science in Durham, NC or the Museum of Natural History in Cleveland, OH) make a creative backdrop and are usually very affordable. Finally, don't rule out oddball places like . . . breweries. In Memphis, the Coors Brewery (901-375-2100) has two large rooms available for receptions (the Texas Deck and the Coors Belle). Meanwhile, a bride in Apple Valley, MN found the Minnesota Zoo to be a great reception site bargain:

"The Minnesota Zoo (612) 431-9215, www.wcco.com/partners/ mnzoo/rentals.htm) has various rooms for weddings, including Discovery Bay, an area surrounded by dolphin tanks. So you feel like you are under a huge coral reef. The rental is $1850, which includes tables, chairs, linens and china (for a Saturday night)! You bring in your own caterer."

13 **Go to college.** Got a university or college in town? If so, that's a great place to look for reception site bargains. Many such institutions have alumni halls, faculty clubs and other facilities that are available at very affordable rates. And you don't always have to be a student or alum to book a site.

14 **Get creative.** We're constantly amazed at the inventive sites couples can find to hold their receptions—aquariums, airports, zoos, laundromats, you name it, it might be possible. If you want an offbeat site, the web is your best friend. Brides say they've found great site possibilities from web sites such as FieldTrip.com (which focuses on such Eastern states as Connecticut, New York, New Jersey, Delaware, Maryland and Pennsylvania) and HereComesTheGuide.com (California). By using FieldTrip.com we actually found a site in Monkton, MD called Ladew Gardens (www.ladewgardens.com), a phenomenal topiary garden that rents out for weddings (you have to be a Garden Friend to rent the site—a $100 fee). See the Real Wedding Tip on the next page with details on how one reader found a bargain deal on a wedding reception at a baseball stadium.

Real Wedding Tip

Take me out to the . . . wedding?

Here's a bargain idea that's definitely out in left field—literally. Lisa Touye of New York City was aghast at the cost of wedding receptions in the Big Apple, where $200 per-plate dinners are considered "routine." Her solution: get married at Shea Stadium during a Mets game. She rented the Left-Field Terrace, a luxury box that seats 144. For $44 per person, her guests had a choice of two entrees, dessert, wedding cake, beer, wine, soda and the "best hot dogs we've ever had." Sure, she also had to pay for tickets to the game ($18 per guest), but hey, they also got to take pictures down on the field before the game and the bride and groom's names were flashed on the stadium's big screen monitor. Instead of a guest book, guests autographed baseballs for the couple. For more info, contact the Mets' Coordinator of Group Sales (718) 565-4332 (web: newyork.mets.mlb.com).

15 **Write it off.** Many reception sites are non-profits that will allow you to write off some or all of your rental fee as a charitable donation. One bride told us that her contract with The Chapel of our Lady in Cold Spring, New York specifically noted that the donation required to use the site ($300) was tax deductible because the fee "helps to preserve the beauty" of this historic restored building. We should note that the key to deducting these dollars is HOW the site refers to the fee—if it is a donation or contribution, it may be tax-deductible. If the fee is a rental charge (where a service is provided), the fee may not be tax deductible.

16 **Get historical.** Speaking of historic sites, don't overlook historical societies. Many rent out their facilities as a way to further their preservation mission. Elizabeth S. of Texas said she found an incredible bargain by going this route—a local historical society rented her their rose garden, covered gazebo, reception hall for four fours for a grand total of $180. Nope, that no typo. $180 for the complete site and she could bring in her own caterer. Now that's a great deal.

Destination Wedding Tips

With all the resorts offering destination weddings today, how do you choose? Here are our tips:

♥ **Find real user reviews.** Sites like TripAdvisor.com have consumer reviews of resorts world-wide. Yes, sometimes folks can go off on a rant about the most minor issue, but these reviews do give you a relatively accurate snapshot of a resort's service.

♥ **Get a good local guide book.** We know it is low-tech, but a well-written local guidebook can provide more insights into destination than a zillion web sites. Example: Wizard Publication's guides to Hawaii (Maui Revealed, Ultimate Kauai, etc). These excellent guides give you the low-down on hotels, restaurants and more—all with the frank, candid writing you'd expect from locals who live there. Web: Wizardpub.com.

♥ **Do recon.** If you can, do a pre-wedding trip to the destination to confirm details, talk with vendors, etc. Yes, you can do much of the planning for a destination wedding online—but it is one thing to email a vendor in Aruba about rehearsal dinners . . . and another to actually visit the restaurant in person to confirm menus, ambience, etc. Hint: do the recon trip AFTER you've confirmed the guest count. It will be easier to talk about details once you know how many guests you are expecting.

Pitfalls to Avoid

Pitfall #1 Unwritten promises.

"I booked my wedding and reception at an historic home. The wedding coordinator there told me all the wonderful things they would do for my reception at no charge. For example, they said they would decorate the gazebo for free if I brought them the fabric. Then, wouldn't you know? My contact person left and the owner of the site refused to fulfill the promises she made! I was furious! The only problem was I couldn't prove a thing since nothing was written down!"

Well, this is perhaps the most common complaint we hear about reception sites: unfulfilled promises. To get you to book the site, some unscrupulous site managers will make wild promises they never intend to keep. Another problem: the person you first meet with quits or is fired before your wedding. This happens more than you might think (catering and site managers hop from job to job like rabbits). A word to the wise: get every last promise and detail *in writing* in the contract. This protects you from dishonest salespeople or from changes in personnel. If promises are made after the contract is signed, get them to write a note (a fax or email will do) putting the promises in black and white.

PITFALL #2 MENU GOOFS.

"My wedding and reception was at a popular hotel in our town. We spent hours going over the menu but what was served at the reception in no way resembled what we ordered. Worse yet, then we couldn't find anyone from the catering department to fix the problem! What happened?"

Sometimes the bloated bureaucracy at hotels and other reception sites can lead to snafus. Perhaps the catering manager "forgot" to inform the kitchen of your menu. Maybe the chef just had an extra 200 Chicken Cordon Bleus left over from a banquet the night before. In any case, you deserve a refund or the site should offer a fair reduction in the bill as compensation for their mistake.

As for fixing a problem the night of the wedding, good luck. While you might be able to have the maitre d' contact the catering director, there may be little that can be done at that moment. Another wise idea: if the catering director or representative won't be at the reception, get their home phone, pager and cell phone numbers.

PITFALL #3 KICK-BACKS AND CATERING MANAGERS.

"I picked a band for my reception based on the recommendation of my site's catering coordinator. It was a disaster—the band was a flop! To add insult to injury, I later found out the catering coordinator received a 'commission' from the band!"

One scam we uncovered in this field is catering managers/coordinators who take kick-backs from bands (or other wedding merchants) they recommend. In California, one musician blew the whistle on a site that was charging a $200 fee to get on their "recommended list." We've also encountered this on the East Coast. Protect yourself by thoroughly checking out any of these "recommended" services before hiring them.

PITFALL #4 BETTER SAFE THAN SORRY.

"My fiancé and I wanted to book this civic site since it had sentimental meaning to us. The site coordinator told us we 'had dibs' on the site because we had inquired about it first. They only book one year in advance, but we were told we didn't have to get our deposit in immediately. Guess what? We just discovered they then booked our date to another bride who came in on the first day it was available!"

Some site coordinators may tell you "there's no need to rush" to put a deposit on a site, but you might want to do otherwise. There's no guarantee that a date will be held for you . . . especially when another bride shows up with deposit money in hand. The best advice: book it now, show them the money (place the deposit) and get it in writing.

Pitfall #5 Catering surcharges

" I was perturbed to learn recently that the reception site I have booked for my wedding charges caterers a percent fee for "use of the site." In other words, once the total catering fee is determined, an extra 7% of this total must be paid to the reception site. This cost of course, is passed on to me. This was nowhere reflected in my contract with the reception site and it seems pretty underhanded to me. The caterer I'm working with however, explained that technically the fee is imposed on the caterer as the price of doing business at the site, that all sites do this and that in fact 7% was very reasonable. Is this typical? Is this LEGAL when I've already paid $2000 to rent out the space!"

The words "sneaky, underhanded and unethical" have been used by brides and grooms to describe these new surcharges and we agree—many sites "forget" to disclose this fee when booking. It also appears nowhere in the site's contract. And, of course, many caterers simply pass this fee along to you as an extra charge. (In one case, a caterer simply refused to work with a bride at a site that charged a 15% commission, since she didn't want to pay it either).

How can you prevent this from happening to you? Be sure to ask about any catering surcharges or commissions BEFORE you book a site that allows outside catering. And if a site fails to disclose this fee, you should be entitled to a full refund on your deposit if you decide to cancel. From a legal point of view, such sites are on very shaky ground. The sites cannot impose a fee on a third-party (the caterer) because you've contracted with the site for a reception. What's next? Charging the DJ a "electricity fee" when he plugs in a CD player? Slapping the baker with a "cake fee" because they are delivering a wedding cake to the site?

Pitfall # 6 Cookie Cutter Reception Sites

"My friend was convinced to have her wedding at a 'one stop shopping' wedding emporium.' They touted their experience with weddings and promised that my friend wouldn't have to lift a finger—everything would be done for her. But the meal was only mediocre, the band played the music too loud (and too much disco) and we all left early. The $105 a plate price seemed a waste."

Popular on the East Coast, wedding halls like to promise the moon, but often deliver much less. Our advice: comparison shop these sites on an apples to apples basis. The bride who wrote that email noted she was able to price out an elegant reception at the Four Seasons with spectacular food and great service for much less than the wedding emporium was charging. While it may be convenient to go with a wedding emporium, the better deal may be to steer clear of such establishments.

PITFALL #7 BALLROOM SWITCHEROO

"We reserved a hotel ballroom for our reception six months before our wedding. When we went to put down the deposit, we were told "Oops! Sorry...we moved you to a smaller ballroom to make room for a convention that day." The hotel's contract has a clause that states they retain the right to change the ballroom, even up to a day before the wedding. Is it just me, or does this policy seem absolutely ridiculous?"

Yes, this is certainly a problem with hotels and other sites with multiple ballrooms. Our advice: if they can't guarantee you a specific room, don't show them the money. Never sign a contract with such a clause.

Helpful Hints

1 Kids' buckets. If you plan to have children at your wedding, consider doing what one reader did: she made up kids' buckets (cheap, plastic sand buckets) and filled them with 99¢¢ coloring books, crayons and small games. "They were waiting on the tables at place settings for kids. As a result, moms and dads didn't have to entertain their kids. I still hear thank you's to this day!"

2 Check back occasionally. Bridal shops aren't the only ones to go out of business suddenly; sadly this can happen to reception sites too. We heard from a Michigan bride who reported two reception sites near Ypsilanti closed during a recent six-month period; couples were left scrambling to find alternatives. While this is still rare, it might be prudent to call your reception site every other month to make sure they're still around.

3 Box up meals of guests that don't show up. If you paid for 100 prime rib dinners and only 97 guests showed up, then ask the caterer to box up those extra meals! If not, they go into the trash (or into the mouths of waiters). Note: some county health department rules may prohibit you from taking food off the premises.

4 Choice can be a pricey option. Some folks like to give their guests a choice of entrees—say fish or chicken. That's nice, but watch out: some sites will charge you the HIGHER meal price no matter what option the guest chooses. It might be less expensive to just pick one menu and forget the choice.

5 Practice your poker face. Just like when shopping for a home or car, don't appear too excited when visiting reception sites. Many sites are willing to negotiate their prices if they know what your exact budget is. But if you act as though you *must* have the site for your wedding or else, they may think they've got you and don't have to negotiate.

One reader told us that she was surprised that so many hotels she visited were willing to meet her budget to get the business. Don't be afraid to haggle. Just because a site's price sheet says their weddings cost X doesn't mean it's the price *you* have to pay!

6 **Check with a local convention or visitor's bureau** to make sure a major convention or event is not scheduled during your wedding weekend. Many visitor's bureau web sites have convention calendars.

A Look at the Six Most Common Reception Site Types

This section will explore the pros, cons and costs of the six most common places for receptions: hotels/catering halls, private and country clubs, civic sites, home weddings, church weddings and (our favorite) miscellaneous sites.

Hotels/Catering Halls

Catering halls and hotels may seem like an obvious choice as the site for a reception—both have spacious banquet rooms and full-service catering staffs to take care of every detail. On the East Coast, catering halls host as many as half of all wedding receptions. Meanwhile, in the South, hotel ballrooms are often the only choice for a bride who is inviting 300 or 400 guests. While hotels may only account for 10% to 20% of receptions nationwide, they often host the biggest and most lavish receptions in many cities. Here are the pros and cons of having your wedding reception at a hotel or catering hall.

The Good News

♥ **All-inclusive packages.** When you have a reception at these facilities, all the rentals (tables, chairs, serving pieces, bars, dance floors, etc.) are generally included in the price.

♥ **Large weddings.** For large weddings, hotels or catering halls may be the best choice. That's because their big ballrooms can accommodate large parties up to or over 1000 guests. Most other sites have peak capacities at about 200 to 300 guests.

♥ **Climate control.** In areas of the country with harsh weather, climate-controlled ballrooms are a plus.

Real Wedding Tip

Catering insider dishes the dirt on hotels

A bride-to-be emailed us with her "in the field" stories about hotel consumer abuse:

"I worked as a waitress/bartender for weddings in a five-star hotel in a major city and witnessed some incredible rip-offs. Examples: it was customary to remove an appetizer platter when it was only half-empty. The left-over food would be served in the employees' cafeteria. In the bus stations, it was not uncommon to see busboys and wait staff having a drink on the customers' tab. In addition, the customer would be charged a tip on those drinks as well. Think you can complain to the management? Forget it. When working a large party as bartender, the food and beverage (F & B) director came up to my bar and asked me to fill several large pitchers with frozen margaritas. I thought he was going to deliver them to another bar. When I had to go into the kitchen for additional supplies, I saw the F & B director with the margarita pitchers. To whom was he serving them? The catering director, the chefs, the general manager. All on the customer's tab."

♥ **Discounts on room rentals, honeymoon suites.** Most hotels are willing to negotiate a discounted rate for a block of rooms. If you have many out-of-town relatives, this may be a big plus. Some hotel packages also throw in a honeymoon suite gratis—a nice touch. One caveat: make sure to double-check the hotel's "special" rate to see if you're really getting a deal. More than one bride has told us they discovered the "special group rate" was no different than the regular room fees available online.

♥ **Special wedding reception packages.** Many hotels and catering halls have special catering packages for wedding receptions. Unfortunately, these are sometimes more expensive than their a la carte choices! Why? The extra labor needed for a reception versus other functions might be one answer. Or maybe it's just extra profit (call it a "bridal" package and the price rises 30%). Be sure to crunch the numbers for different packages to see which is the best deal. On the other hand, some facilities aggressively pursue weddings by offering many freebies—you'd be surprised at the big difference in costs from one site to another.

♥ **Dietary restrictions.** For those couples that need Kosher catering, hotels are often a best bet. Hotels must meet certain standards before they are certified Kosher. Call a local synagogue or rabbi to get a list of approved facilities.

♥ **I Do too.** Some hotels and catering halls can also host a lovely ceremony. One West Coast hotel we researched has an outdoor garden and gazebo for ceremonies. At a catering hall we visited in New Jersey, lush gardens offered several ceremony site options. The convenience of having everything at one location may be a big plus.

♥ **Advice on entertainers, florists, bakers, etc.** Catering managers at hotels and catering halls often have their pulse on the best wedding bands and entertainers. Use their experience, but be careful of unscrupulous managers who take kick-backs from "recommended" services. (See Pitfall #3 earlier in this chapter for more info.)

The Bad News

♥ **Drab interior decor.** Some sites look like they were decorated in Early Eisenhower.

♥ **These sites can be darn expensive.** While hotels and catering halls

Real Wedding Tip

Don't pay rack rate!

A recent bride had advice on working with hotels for accommodations for guests:

"Even if you don't need ANY banquet/catering services, most hotels will happily negotiate a group room rate for your hotel guests. When my Matron of Honor got married four years ago, she talked the Omni in San Antonio into a fantastic group rate for her wedding guests. For my wedding, she made a bunch of calls on my behalf and did the same thing at a Houston Marriott: our rate was less than half the best weekend rate and was valid for the entire week of the wedding. Business hotels are dying for business on weekends. Also, remember December and January are really good times to get deeply discounted room rates at many hotels—the holidays are busy for banquets/parties, but not for room occupancy. Just make sure your guests are really coming BEFORE you guarantee a room count—most hotels charge steep penalties if you use fewer room nights than you guarantee."

offer all-inclusive packages, you definitely pay for this convenience. Case in point: sky high minimum food and beverage fees for premium nights. A bride in Chicago told us one exclusive hotel there has a $30,000 minimum charge for a Saturday night in May! Another famous Michigan Avenue hotel charges $150 to $250 per guest just for food and beverages. And that's before they slap you with an 18% mandatory gratuity and 9.75% sales tax. Even if you don't get married at the most chic hotel, your wedding budget at any hotel can suffer death by a thousand cuts. Hotels are skilled at taking $12 bottles of wine and charging you $80 in their "bridal package" Another famous hotel chain charged couples $35 for a gallon of fruit punch.

♥ **Frozen Food.** Perhaps the biggest problem that plagues many hotels and catering halls is poor quality food. These sites often buy frozen food that can be quickly prepared. Ever seen those mini-quiches at a hotel wedding reception? Hotels can buy these and other popular buffet items in bulk. Pop them in an oven and presto! Dinner's ready! Obviously, pre-fabricated, frozen hors d'oeuvres simply don't compare to freshly-prepared dishes.

♥ **Bureaucracy of catering departments.** From busboys to waiters to captains to catering assistants to managers, the multi-layer management of catering departments can be vexing. Ask if the catering manager (or the contact person you planned your event with) will be at your reception.

♥ **Weddings can be low on the priority list.** Especially in December, hotels are distracted with corporate holiday parties on large budgets. Competition with convention and reunion business can also be a headache.

♥ **Remember the catering representatives are on commission.** The more money you spend, the more money they make. Hence, we find many hotels and catering halls pushing exotic (and expensive) foods to jack up the tab. Many hotels also "suggest" expensive wines and other liquor.

♥ **Be careful of nickel-and-dime charges.** Never assume that anything is free. Extra charges could include valet parking, special table skirting, ice carvings, a dance floor, corking fees, cake cutting charge (see catering chapter), food station attendants, and any audio equipment (a microphone for toasts, for example). Also, silk flower table centerpieces and special linens or china may be extra. Compare the estimate on centerpieces with your florist's bid to get the best deal.

What Does a Hotel/ Catering Hall Reception Cost?

Reception packages vary widely (particularly when the economy is less than healthy). Hotels and catering halls in downtown areas tend to be the most expensive (and also expect to pay extra for valet parking). In suburban areas, rates are somewhat less and these sites tend to be more aggressive in their competition for wedding business (since they can't rely on downtown convention traffic). In our research, we've found packages that start as low as $20 per person for a buffet at an Oklahoma hotel and go up to $250 per person for a complete sit-down dinner at a posh New York City catering hall. In general, most sites are in the $30 to $75 per person range for basic receptions (not counting liquor). In the biggest cities (New York, Los Angeles, Chicago, Philadelphia), you can expect to pay twice to three times more. Add in a big liquor tab and you'll see the total costs soar. In Chicago, we hear some top hotels now charge $15,000 to $20,000 minimums for food and beverage. And considering those same hotels charge $150 to $200 per guest for reception dinners, you'll be hitting those minimums real fast.

Private/Country Clubs

Think you have to be a member of those fancy country clubs and private clubs to hold a wedding reception in their facilities? Not always. In fact, many clubs welcome non-members with open arms! That's because weddings often bring in badly-needed revenue. We define private and country clubs as any site that has membership requirements or restrictions. While you may have to be a member at some sites, others just require a "member-sponsor." Still others don't have any requirements at all.

Types of Clubs

1 **Business clubs.** Located downtown on top of skyscrapers,.some business clubs have a restaurant open for lunch each day and space to host meetings and receptions. Various professional organizations (i.e., Engineers' Clubs, Doctors' Clubs) may own and operate these facilities. Such sites vary widely in appeal (we saw one Engineer's Club that looked like it was decorated by, well, engineers) but are generally more open to wedding receptions. Most likely, you must use the club's in-house catering.

2 **Military clubs.** If someone in your family is a retired or active duty military, you may have access to a military club facility in your area. Rates are usually very affordable.

3 Country Clubs. These sites normally have a golf course and several acres of landscaped grounds. Here, the clubhouse is the focal point for receptions. Some of these sites can be quite stuffy, with the snob appeal often spread rather thick. Nonetheless, lush grounds can make beautiful backdrops for photos. These sites may be the most restrictive; many require a member (who can be a friend or just an acquaintance) to at least "sponsor" the reception. Sometimes, this sponsorship is just a token technicality where the member assumes responsibility in case you don't pay the bill and move to Peru. In most cases, you must use the country club's in-house catering.

4 Civic/Social clubs. Elks Clubs, Garden Clubs, Federation of Women's clubs, Junior Leagues, Junior Forums—each of these organizations may have facilities they rent for receptions. Typically, you must bring in an outside caterer. Prices and quality are all over the board: Elks Clubs and Veterans of Foreign Wars (VFW) Posts, for example, are often quite affordable but offer rather Spartan decor. Other clubs are located in historic buildings that are beautiful but also carry a hefty price tag. Membership requirements are usually non-existent.

The Good News

♥ **More personal service.** These facilities have less of that "wedding factory" feel you find at hotels or catering halls. One reason: less bureaucracy. Many sites have fewer people to deal with and this sometimes improves customer service.

♥ **Better Ambiance.** Unlike the drab and sterile decor of many hotels, country and private clubs are usually set on beautiful sites—golf courses are definitely easier on the eyes than parking lots. Downtown business clubs perched atop skyscrapers may offer spectacular skyline views.

♥ **Some clubs permit outside caterers.** While business and country clubs usually have in-house catering, some clubs let you bring in a caterer of your choice—this can be a fantastic savings (see our catering chapter).

The Bad News

♥ **You may have to be a member.** Frequently this depends on the local economy. If the club is in need of funds, they may let non-members in to boost a sagging financial situation. However, if the club is flushed with members, they will limit the use of the club to members only.

Discount chair covers

Yes, most rental places rent chairs, but what if you want a fancier look? Some folks like the look of chair covers. But the price? A reader in New Orleans was stunned when she priced out chair covers from a local party store. Her suggestion: BBJLinen.com, a Chicago-based company that rents chair covers and other linens at very affordable rates. BBJ Linen's rates are often HALF the price of other rental companies. Also try Be-Seat.com, another site with great prices (they service Texas, Washington, DC and several other states).

Another tip: when shopping for chair covers and table linens from local companies, watch out for shipping. Some companies charge for this, others don't. "Many times I found a company that wanted to charge me $7.50 for a chair cover, another $3 for a sash and then slap shipping on top of that," a reader emailed us. By shopping around, the same reader found chair covers for $2.50 each—with a free sash and free shipping.

♥ **If you aren't a member, some clubs require you to have a member-sponsor.** Here, a member of the club must "sponsor" your reception, agreeing to attend the event and pay for it if you skip town. If you have a friend who is a member, great. If you don't, some clubs may negotiate around this point—perhaps by requesting a larger deposit. We know one club that will find you a sponsor if you don't know one!

♥ **Food quality can vary widely.** Some clubs have gourmet chefs on staff that create wonderful dishes. Other clubs may not be as lucky and their food quality is, at best, as good as that of an average hotel. Ask for a taste test to confirm this detail.

♥ **Expensive receptions.** Some clubs can be just as, or even more, expensive than hotel weddings. Overpricing of liquor is a common problem. Just like hotels, club catering managers receive commissions based on the total amount you spend—giving them an incentive to inflate the tab. Many clubs also add on a high gratuity, similar to hotels.

What Does it Cost?

Well, it depends. Fancy country clubs may be just as expensive as the prices we quoted above for hotels and catering halls. Other clubs, that don't have in-house catering, just charge a rental fee for the facility. These can be a major bargain.

Civic Sites

A "civic" site is any reception facility that is owned and administered by a city or municipal agency. Almost always, you must bring in your own caterer. Some civic sites have a recommended list of caterers that you may have to choose from. Be aware that some sites may have time and beverage restrictions (no liquor) and others require you to hire security officers. Civic sites are usually the best bargains. Why? Subsidized by taxpayers, these sites aren't out to make big bucks like private facilities.

Types of Civic Sites

1 **Parks, gardens, amphitheaters.** Often quite affordable, these sites are usually administered by city parks departments. Some sites even have clubhouses. If you decide to have an outdoor ceremony or reception, make sure you have a backup plan in case of inclement weather.

2 **Recreation centers, civic centers, town halls, conference centers.** Quality varies greatly with these sites (some are spectacular while others are dumps), but they are usually quite affordable.

3 **Sites owned by universities or colleges.** These sites include faculty clubs, alumni halls, chapels, etc. You might be surprised at the sheer variety of spaces available for rent on a college campus—they are rarely advertised and can be great bargains. One limitation: you may have to be an alum (or know one) to book the site. Also, many of these facilities will require you to use their in-house caterer.

4 **Museums**. Rare but available in some cities, these sites may be quite expensive and even require you to be a "museum patron" (i.e. make a hefty donation).

The Good News

♥ **Low cost and Unique locations.** Most of these sites are very affordable.

♥ **Bring in an outside caterer.** Off-site caterers can save oodles of money and offer creative, delicious menu options. However, you may be required to pick a caterer off an "approved" list.

The Bad News

♥ **Very popular sites book up quickly.** Since civic sites are so affordable, they are also very popular. Many book months in advance.

♥ **Equipment rental expense can be high.** Some of these sites might require you to bring in tables, chairs, serving pieces, etc. This could be a significant expense.

♥ **Make sure the caterer is very familiar with the site.** Some brides find hiring and dealing with an outside caterer challenging—increasing the complexity of the event by adding another person in the loop. Another limitation: civic sites' lack of kitchen facilities may affect a caterer's ability to do the function.

Home Weddings

Yes, we can always tell when it's wedding season in Boulder, Colorado. Pick any road that winds its way up into the foothills and you'll see several handmade signs directing guests to a remote location for the nuptials of "Spense and Lisa," "Cheyenne and Bob," and so on.

Home weddings are big here, as they are in other parts of the Rockies. While only accounting for 6% to 10% of all receptions in the US, Boulder seems to be the center of the universe for home nuptials and receptions—half of all weddings here are at home, according to our estimates. Perhaps it's the nice summer weather or the views of the Continental Divide that convince brides and grooms to tie the knot at home. Or maybe we're just cheap—the price ($0) is right for many folks.

The Good News

♥ **Affordable receptions.** Let's be honest: home weddings can be had cheap. Whether you have friends and family help with the food or order a meal from a restaurant or catering service, home weddings are a fraction of the cost of receptions at traditional sites like hotels, catering halls and private clubs.

♥ **No scheduling conflicts.** If you want to have a wedding in June on a Saturday night, you may discover that so do many other brides in your area. The competition for reception sites during popular months may lead you to consider a home wedding.

♥ **Small weddings.** Unless you live in Bill Gates' house, the average home can only hold a minimal number of guests (usually under 100). This is a plus and a minus. While you may not be able to invite everyone you'd like to, you do have the perfect excuse for cutting down that guest list.

Real Wedding Tip

An Amazing Send-off

We are impressed with the resourcefulness of our readers and none more than Robin Holzer of Houston, TX. She was determined to have real fireworks at her wedding reception and shared her story:

This one may be beyond the scope of Bridal Bargains, but I managed to arrange a five-and-a-half minute professional fireworks display (set to music) for the end of our wedding reception. The process was fraught with red tape, but here's a summary:

In most jurisdictions, all pyrotechnic displays are strictly regulated by state and local fire codes. Conveniently, the Texas state code is available online. In Texas, only licensed professional operators may legally discharge fireworks. The operator must carry minimum liability insurance ($1 million) for the event.

A fire marshal must review the site plan prior to issuing a permit for the fireworks display, and one or more fire marshals must be onsite to monitor the actual display and sweep the area for fallen embers afterwards. Fourth of July fireworks displays are typically "aerial" and go upwards of 400 feet. A "close proximity" display is smaller and goes only 150 to 200 feet in the air. Outside of city limits, we could get a five-minute display with 200-250 shells/minute for $1000. Inside the city, the same close-proximity display ran $2500-$3500.

Brides on a budget should consider "gerbs," which are small (4 to 6 feet) "fountains" of shooting, colored sparks (see the end of "My Best Friend's Wedding" for a visual). Remember that even tiny sparklers and gerbs require a permit from the fire marshal in many jurisdictions.

We found licensed operators in the Yellow Pages—there were only three in Houston. The big operators are considerably more professional than the small independent guys, though the little guy IS cheaper. And the big guys WILL do small displays (except around July 4 and January 1) as long as they feel the display site is adequate/large/safe. Make sure that the permit is for the exact street address where the display will occur. Also check how long the permit is good for and what are the contract terms if it rains on your wedding day. (It may be reasonable to pay a nominal fee for trucking the explosives/charges back and forth and setup/break down, but you shouldn't pay for the shells since they can use them for another event)! Have a blast on your wedding day!

The Bad News

♥ **Rentals, rentals, rentals.** Planning a home wedding for 75 guests but you don't have tables and chairs for the crowd? You'll need to rent them, along with plates, silverware, glassware, serving pieces, bar set-ups and more. Afraid it might rain on your parade? Renting a tent can set you back $500 for a simple tent or $5000 for a fancy model with air conditioning, lighting and more. As you can see, the money you save on catering with a home wedding may be partially eaten up by a big rental bill.

♥ **Surprise expenses.** Home weddings may entail several unexpected bills. At one home wedding we attended in Austin, Texas, the bride and groom hired a van service to shuttle guests back and forth because of limited parking—this cost an extra $250. You may also need extra insurance to cover liability at the event—call your homeowner's insurance provider to see what's covered.

Church Receptions

The classic mid-America wedding typically has a low-cost reception that follows in a church fellowship hall. Yes, they are cheap, but fellowship halls can look more Spartan than fairy tale. A mother of the bride in a small Arkansas town came up with some thoughts on how to make this work: "Beg, borrow, use that church family! If people want to lend stuff and help, then let them! Give them a list! We borrowed almost all of the decorations from church friends whose daughters have married in the last three years. Lattice work, columns, lights, artificial ivy, and flowers were used to cover up an ugly fellowship hall. We have friends who own a large restaurant and are letting us borrow silver serving pieces and 12 candelabras! We have other friends who are decorating the sanctuary and fellowship hall with tulle (very cheap yet a great bridal look), ivy, loose flowers, ferns, azaleas, etc. We have other friends who used to be caterers who are cooking all of the food at cost. We have another friend who is in food distribution who gave us free food for the reception. That's what friends are for!"

And everywhere else

Yes, you can have a wedding reception just about anywhere—theaters, ranches, private estates, chartered boats and yachts, bed and breakfast inns, and so on. Anything goes!

What's the message here? Don't think you must have your reception in a hotel or club just because all your friends did that. Every city has many romantic and beautiful settings for receptions—it may just take a little creative searching.

In fact, that's perhaps the biggest challenge to using a "non-traditional" site—finding one! (Perhaps the second biggest challenge is convincing parents and relatives that the site is better than the traditional options!) To find a non-traditional site, surf wedding message boards for ideas. Ask local caterers for suggestions. Often you must bring in your own caterer.

Now that you've found yourself a reception site, what to do about the food? Read on and you'll find tips on how to save on catering no matter where your reception is!

Chapter 8

Catering

If you read just one chapter in this book, make it this one. That's because we give you 20 ways to cut your catering budget, the biggest expense area for any wedding. Wonder what to ask the caterer? Check out our 18 questions to ask, plus six pitfalls to avoid with wedding catering.

What Are You Buying?

Wedding catering varies dramatically across the country. When food is the topic, the United States of America is hardly united. And such variations make weddings in one part of the country much different than another. Sometimes the differences are also social in nature. For example, in the Northeast, nearly all receptions are sit-down dinners—folks there like to have their own space to enjoy the meal. While in the South and West, almost all weddings have buffets or hors d'oeuvre receptions—people there like to mingle, instead of being in one chair for the entire reception. No matter where you have your wedding, however, here are the four basic things you buy from a caterer:

♥ **Food.** Everything from hors d'oeuvres to dessert. The typical method of calculating the cost of wedding catering is based on a figure per guest. Costs can range from $5 per guest for a simple "cake, punch and mints" reception in North Dakota to over $250 per person for a full sit-down dinner with open bar at a posh hotel in New York City.

As you can see, food costs can vary dramatically from region to region. Yes, prices are less in the middle of the country and tend to be higher on the coasts and in major cities. In Oklahoma City, for example, a *simple* buffet dinner reception runs $15 per guest. In Seattle, that same meal is $42. But entry-level reception packages in catering halls in the Northeast can run at least $75 per guest.

In the mid range, a more elaborate meal (say a heavy hors d'oeuvre buffet or sit-down dinner of prime rib) is about $35 to $65 in a place like Houston, TX. On the coasts and major cities, you can see the tab soar to $70 to $150 for such a reception.

And what about the upper end? Once again, it depends on where you live. In Oklahoma, $50 per guest will buy you one fancy reception and open bar. Expect to shell out $100 to $175 for a top-end reception in Atlanta, up to $250 per guest in Boston and New York City.

In Chicago, a bride recently emailed us to say that she got proposals from six independent caterers for a meal consisting of six hors d'oeuvres per guest, salad, and a chicken entréée. The cost? Nearly $100 per guest. Rather amazing since that didn't include any appetizer, dessert, wedding cake OR the alcohol. Most fancy downtown hotels in Chicago charge $150 to $200 per person just for food and beverage.

According to the *Washingtonian* magazine, the starting price for most weddings (whether seated dinner or buffet) in the Washington DC metro area is $80 per person. Fancy events from top caterers run $100 to $175 per guest. Hotels in DC charge $60 to $85 per guest as a minimum, with prices up to $200 per guest at four-star properties. No surprise that the *Washingtonian* quotes the average wedding in Washington DC as $50,000!

♥ **Beverages.** Whether your reception will just have punch and coffee or a full open bar with premium well brands, the cost of beverages can be a significant part of the catering budget. For one hors d'oeuvres reception at a posh hotel with a full open bar serving premium liquor, the total bar tab for 300 guests came to $9200—almost half the $19,000 total cost of the evening!

Why are beverages so expensive? Sure, alcohol isn't cheap . . . but the real reason is profit margin. This is where any caterer (or restaurant) makes the bulk of their profits. A caterer will take a $15 bottle of wine and charge you $65. A simple glass of fruit punch is $2. You get the idea.

(Now, we know that's America—businesses like caterers can only survive if they make a profit. BUT . . . nothing says you have to pay such a steep mark-up for your wedding!).

Of course, the charge you'll end up paying for beverages at your wedding depends on what you serve and how the reception site accounts for this. An open bar of modest-grade beer, wine, sodas and champagne (for a toast) averages about $15 per guest, according to national averages. That's for the entire reception. Of course, costs can quickly soar above that for bars with mixed drinks and premium liquors—hotels in Washington DC regularly charge $25 to $35 per guest for drinks. In Boston, an open bar runs $10 to $18 per guest *per hour*, depending on the site.

Beverages can be priced one of several ways. One common method: the consumption bar. What your guests drink, you pay for. This can be by the drink or by the bottle (or tenths of a bottle consumed). Some sites have a flat charge for soft drinks and juices. If your guests aren't big drinkers, a consumption bar might be the most affordable way to go—just be sure to place a cap on the bar tab and get in writing that you are to be asked before they exceed that amount.

Another alternative method of beverage charging: flat pricing. Some sites might offer all-you-can drink packages for a specified period of time (an hour or so). This is a common option at sites that offer cocktail hours before a seated dinner. If your guests are heavy drinkers, this might be the way to go. Ask the site to only charge you for *adult* guests. If you have 100 guests but 10 are children, be sure to get a flat pricing

Real Wedding Tip

Open vs. Cash Bars: Don't charge your guests for drinks.

One big controversy in the world of wedding etiquette is whether bars should be open or cash. In the latter case, guests pay for their drinks. Given the big expense of liquor at most reception sites, this can be $15 to $30 each guest must shell out at the bar. As you can imagine, open versus cash is a hot topic in the bridal world. Yes, we realize some couples simply don't have the funds to stock an open bar for several hours. Some couples compromise by having an open bar for an hour at the beginning of the reception and a cash bar for the rest of the evening. This also discourages guests from getting smashed toward the end of the evening when they might get behind the wheel. The liability issue is also forcing many couples (and reception sites) to rethink serving alcohol altogether. Yet, despite all the pros to limiting alcohol consumption, our advice is simple—skip the cash bar idea. If you can't afford even a simple beer/wine/champagne bar, don't charge guests for drinks. Go non-alcoholic with creative ideas like coffee drinks, exotic teas, etc. If you insist on going the cash bar route, the least you could do is warn your guests in advance (perhaps putting notice of this on a personal wedding web site when you discuss the reception details).

package that just covers the 90 adults.

Finally, you can sometimes bring in your own liquor at some sites—but quite a few sites slap on a "corking fee" to chill and serve the booze. This can be $10 or more per bottle, plus a gratuity and (in some states) sales tax.

♥ **Labor.** Hey, don't forget those folks who actually serve the food. Of course, most sites won't let you forget to pay the staff—they impose a mandatory gratuity of 15% to 20%. This applies to the food and sometimes the liquor served at the reception. If you serve a buffet that costs $8000, you may pay as much as $1600 extra for the servers, bus boys, etc. Frankly, we think a percentage gratuity is slightly deceptive—most sites don't pay their staff anywhere near the amount of money they collect for "service." They pocket the difference as pure profit. For example, in the above case, let's assume the reception was for 150 guests. Using an industry rule of thumb of one server for 25 guests at a buffet reception, we would need six servers. Hence, each server would theoretically receive $165 of a $1000 service charge for the evening. If the reception lasts four hours (plus another two for set-up and clean-up), do you really think the site is paying the servers a wage that totals nearly $30 per hour? In most cities, we wouldn't bet on it.

Perhaps a more equitable way of paying for service is a method adopted by some independent caterers. This involves paying a flat per hour fee per waiter at the event—say, $15 to $20 per hour per server. No matter what the total tab of your function, you pay only for the number of people actually serving your guests.

How many bartenders do you need? It depends on whether you plan a full bar or just beer, wine and soft drink service. The latter is much faster as you can imagine and requires less staff, say one bartender to 75 or 100 guests. A full bar might require a one-bartender-to-50-guest ratio.

♥ **Rentals.** Certain reception sites may lack tables, chairs, silverware, china, glassware, table linens, etc. All these items must be rented separately and brought to the site. Some caterers have an in-house supply of rentals while others arrange the needed rentals through an outside company. Charges for this service vary greatly—sometimes the caterer will charge you what the rental company charges them. Other caterers may tack on an extra fee of 5% to 10% of the rental bill to cover the administrative expense of dealing with the rental company. Some caterers (who charge this fee) also absorb any charges for broken or missing rental items. However, in other cases, you may be responsible for any breakage.

♥ **Coordination of the reception.** In the past few years, many caterers have added a new service: coordination of the entire reception. This can range from simply referring names of good florists or entertainers to actually booking and negotiating with other services. Some caterers offer such coordination as a free customer service; others charge fees that are similar to that of a professional wedding consultant. The degree you will want your caterer to coordinate your reception will depend on how much you trust them.

♥ **Average catering costs.** So, what's the total tab? As we pointed out above, it highly depends on where the wedding reception will be. The exact menu (food and beverage) that costs $25 per person in Albuquerque could be as much as $90 in Detroit. For example, one bride told us she had to move her reception from Dallas, Texas to Washington, DC. In Dallas, she priced her complete reception at $32 per person. A very similar menu at a comparable hotel in Washington, DC cost $73 per guest!

According to industry estimates, we peg the national average cost for wedding catering at $9286 for 175 guests—about $53 per guest. This includes everything: food, beverages, gratuity/labor, rentals and any fees for the reception site. Of course, that "average" combines both lower-cost areas like the Midwest with expensive major metro areas. If you are planning a wedding in a big city, the average is closer to $85 per guest (or a total of $14,875 for 175 guests).

Most caterers require a deposit that is as much as 50% of the total bill to hold a date. The balance is customarily due a week or two weeks *before* the date—some caterers will let you pay the final balance the day of the wedding. Get all payment policies in writing before you sign the contract.

Types of Caterers

1 In-house or on-premise caterers. These are catering operations that exclusively provide the catering for a site. Examples are hotels and many country clubs. Unless they're really desperate, most of these sites won't allow outside or "off-premise" caterers. (The exception to this rule: the cake. Most sites let you bring in a wedding cake produced by an off-site baker).

2 Off-premise caterers. These caterers bring in food to an existing site. The caterer's services can be limited to just providing the food or include the coordination of the entire event. Here, caterers become more like party planners or wedding consultants—either providing or contracting out for services like decoration (table centerpieces, table skirting, for example) and entertainment (DJ's, musicians, etc.).

Sources to Find an Affordable Caterer

♥ **Ask friends and other recently married couples for suggestions.** Finding a good, affordable caterer is by far the biggest challenge faced by engaged couples. The best caterers work strictly by word of mouth and hence, don't do much high-profile advertising.

♥ **Reception sites that don't have in-house caterers.** Most will have a list of local caterers they recommend. This will be an invaluable time-saver. Ask them for their opinions as to which caterer offers the best service or most affordable prices. Also, we have found some photographers can recommend caterers (they usually sneak a taste during receptions!).

♥ **Forget about ads.** Most caterers don't do any big advertising in bridal publications or online. Most work by word-of-mouth.

♥ **Our message boards.** On BridalBargainsBook.com (click on message boards and then local), you will find specific message boards tailored to local metro areas. Use the board for your area to ask other readers about great local caterers. Swap tips and get advice on the boards, tailored for where you will have your reception. Best of all, there are no ads or spam on our boards . . . just readers helping other readers save money!

Brides in Cyberspace: What's on the Web?

NACE

Web: nace.net

What it is: Home of the National Assoc. of Catering Executives.

What's cool: While much of this site is focused on the association, you can click on "Resources" and then "Chapter Directory" to find a caterer in your area. Or check out their extensive links to other catering-related sites.

Needs work: It'd be nice if you could search their membership directory on line to find caterers within X miles of your zip code. Instead, you just get the contact info for local chapters—you then have to call or email the chapter president for member listings.

Getting Started: How Far in Advance?

Book your caterer as soon as you confirm your reception site. Many book up far in advance (as long as a year) for popular summer wedding weekends. Also, December is extremely busy for caterers, thanks to holiday parties.

Step-by-step Shopping Strategies

♥ **Step 1:** Using the sources above, set up appointments with at least three recommended caterers. When you call for an appointment, notice how promptly the caterer returns your call. Within the business day is good—if it takes them more than a day, that's a red flag. Prompt attention is your first clue to the caterer's commitment to service. Before your meeting, discuss with your fiancéé your likes and dislikes for catering.

♥ **Step 2:** Ask to see photos of each caterer's previous work. Look for colorful and creative presentations of food. Are hors d'oeuvres artfully arranged with flowers and garnishes or just piled up on mirrored trays?

♥ **Step 3:** Ask for sample menus. These may list some popular hors d'oeuvre choices or sit-down options. Hopefully, prices will be listed to give you a better idea of costs. While most caterers customize menus for each reception, they should provide basic cost parameters for certain items.

♥ **Step 4:** Be honest about your budget. If you're not sure, give them a range of costs per guest that you feel comfortable with. What one caterer will offer you for $30 per person may be vastly different from what another may propose. Also, be specific about your menu likes and dislikes as well as any dietary restrictions.

♥ **Step 5:** Ask for a proposal that details possible menu options. Also, the proposal should clearly identify costs for liquor, rentals, and labor. Call the caterer back and ask them to clarify any part of the proposal that isn't clear. Don't assume the proposal includes extra items like glassware, china, linens, etc.—always confirm that detail. One bad sign: caterers who promise to send you a proposal and then fail to do so.

♥ **Step 6:** Confirm any "minimums." Some caterers require you to purchase a minimum amount of food (in dollars or meals). Hence, you may have to pay for 125 meals even if only 100 people show up to your wedding. While some of this is negotiable (depending on the date and time of your wedding), never book a caterer who has a minimum you don't think you'll be able to meet. Check to see if the wedding cake will count toward the minimum—sometimes that helps put the figure within reach. Also ask the caterer about the opposite case: when more guests show up than expected. Most caterers make 5% to 10% more food than is ordered, but confirm this to be sure.

♥ **Step 7:** Given the different proposals from each caterer, pick the one you most like and ask to visit one of their weddings during the set-up. Look for how organized they are and how the staff is dressed. Just observe.

♥ **Step 8:** Ask for a taste test of proposed menu items. You are most likely planning to spend several thousands of dollars on catering, so this is the least caterers can do. You may be able to combine the taste test with a visit to one of their weddings. Another suggestion: take pictures of the food at the tasting, in case the chef or catering manager changes before your wedding. That way you'll be able to show the new staffers what you expect.

♥ **Step 9:** Once you select a caterer, get everything in writing—down to the very last detail. Food, labor, beverages, and rentals (if necessary) should be clearly stated in a written contract. Make sure you understand any price escalation clauses (where the caterer has the right to up the price within a certain time period) and get any price guarantees in writing. Also get a drawing of the physical layout of the room (placement of the tables, dance floor, buffet tables, etc.).

♥ **Step 10:** Before you sign anything, take the contract home to read it. Pore over any fine print—note any refund policies and cancellation fees. Remember that just because the caterer's standard contract has certain boilerplate provisions doesn't mean such rules are set in stone and can't be changed—ask the caterer to alter or change any wording that makes you uncomfortable. Make sure any modifications or cancellations are made in writing.

Questions to Ask a Caterer

1 **Can we have a taste test of the foods on our menu?** We positively loath caterers who expect you to pay thousands of dollars for food on faith. Equally reprehensible are caterers that ask "why do you need to taste such basic items? Hors d'oeuvres are hors d'oeuvres." We suggest you find another caterer if you get this line. Should there be a charge for taste tests? Well, some caterers (especially restaurants) may have a minimal fee for tastings, which we can understand. While we'd prefer it to be free, it's better to pay for a taste test and know what you're buying. Ever better: taste two or three options for each course (if you plan a sit-down dinner).

2 **Can we see a wedding during set-up?** A truly organized and professional catering company should have nothing to hide.

3 **Do you provide a written estimate and contract?** Verbal agreements are a prescription for disaster. Make sure every last promise and detail is in black and white.

4 **Are you licensed?** Almost all municipalities (or counties) require caterers to be licensed. Local standards will stress clean and adequate facilities for food preparation and storage. Liability insurance on liquor and food may also be part of the requirements. Ask the caterer about insurance. Operating a catering business out of a residence is often illegal.

5 **Tell me about a wedding you did where something went wrong—how did you handle it?** Even the best caterers have things that go wrong—a crisis, accident or other unforeseen event that throws a wedding reception into chaos. How they handle the situation separates the professionals from the amateurs. We're always suspicious of caterers who say they "never" have problems with their weddings.

6 **Do you specialize in certain cuisines or types of menus?** Although they may claim to handle all types of weddings, caterers usually specialize in certain receptions (smaller versus larger, finger hors d'oeuvres versus full sit-down dinners). Some caterers may have chefs who specialize in certain cuisines (Mediterranean, Southwestern, Indian, etc.). What about vegetarians? Can you prepare a complete vegetarian menu (vegan, ovo-lacto, pesca-vegetarian, etc.)? A few veggie dishes? What about a Kosher meal? Are you certified?

7 **Where is the food prepared?** Will you need additional kitchen facilities at my site? Make sure these details are confirmed by the caterer to prevent any last minute surprises.

8 **When is the menu "set in stone?"** How close to the wedding can we get and still make changes to the menu? Trust us, there will be changes. Different family members, friends and relatives will add in their two cents on the perfect wedding menu.

9 **How is your wait staff dressed?** The key here is professional attire. Don't assume the wait staff will be wearing tuxedos (the exception is hotels that always have uniformed servers).

10 **For cocktail or buffet receptions, how often will the food be replenished?** Will the servings per guest be limited? Who makes the decision on when to stop serving?

11 Given the style of my reception, how many waiters do we need? For seated receptions, one waiter per 16 to 20 guests is adequate. For buffet or cocktail receptions, one waiter per 25 guests is standard.

12 How is the charge for labor figured? Is the clean-up (dishwashing, etc.) extra?

13 How much does a dessert table cost? Is the wedding cake price included in the package? Dessert or Viennese tables are popular in the Midwest and in parts of the Northeast. Be sure the cost of a dessert table is clearly identified.

14 What are your cancellation/postponement policies? Since catering is the biggest expense area, confirming this aspect would be prudent.

15 Do you have a liquor license? How is the cost of the beverages calculated? What brands of liquor will be served? Most caterers offer both "premium" (or "call") and generic or "house" brands. Can you taste the house brand of wine? If you plan to serve alcohol, you'll want the caterer to carefully explain what brands you are buying and how the cost is calculated. Per drink charges are often the most expensive, although per bottle charges can be just as costly.

16 Are you familiar with my reception site? If not, will you visit it with me? For off-premise caterers, don't assume they know your facility. Confirming details such as the kitchen facilities and the clean-up rules are very important if you want to get your security/damage/cleaning deposit back from the reception site. The site will hold you responsible for any damage or rule violations by your caterer.

17 Do you receive any commissions from services you recommend? Caterers may recommend bakers, florists or musicians but watch out! Some take "commissions" (we call them kick-backs) from the businesses they recommend. Don't just take their word—thoroughly check out any "recommended" services before contracting.

18 Will you guarantee price estimates? Many caterers raise their prices at the beginning of the year. Since we urge you to plan in advance, your reception may be several months away. Our advice: negotiate a price guarantee in writing (or at least a cap on future increases). Most caterers will be willing to do this to get your business. One couple we interviewed in Colorado learned this lesson the hard way—the site they booked raised their prices 15% just weeks before their event. Their wedding budget was thrown into complete disarray.

Bridal Bargains Wedding Planner: Caterers

Okay, we realize planning the catering for a wedding can rival the logistics of climbing Mt. Everest. Use the handy worksheets in our new *Bridal Bargains* wedding planner to cut down on the stress—we have a worksheet that lets you compare caterers, plan the menu, budget the liquor and more. If you follow our advice and book a site that let's you bring in your own caterer, you'll probably need the special worksheet on rentals—this will help you keep track of items and quantities needed.

Top Money-saving Secrets

1 Find a site where you can bring in an outside caterer. Outside caterers are not only more affordable but many times offer higher-quality food and beverage service than caterers at hotels or other sites. The big savings for you is the caterer's lower overhead. Outside caterers may let you buy liquor at wholesale, provide rentals at cost and basically provide more food for the dollar. Best of all: outside caterers usually don't have lots of "nickel-and-dime" charges.

2 Hold the reception in mid-afternoon. A wedding reception at one or two in the afternoon will be much less expensive than evening affairs. Why? Guests will already have had lunch and won't be expecting a six-course, sit-down meal.

3 Go ethnic. Surprisingly, certain ethnic cuisines are affordable alternatives to traditional wedding fare. Chinese, Mexican, Italian and barbecue are crowd pleasers and, happily, 20% to 30% less than

Alcohol Alternatives

With the soaring cost of booze and worry over drunken driving, many couples are looking for alternatives to the standard-issue open bar at receptions. In San Diego, one wedding we attended featured an espresso bar with a selection of flavored coffees. Other couples are forsaking hard liquor for bars that serve a selection of micro-brewed beers, sparking waters, and other creative ideas. Go to any wedding in San Antonio, Texas and you'll probably see a frozen margarita machine humming away. All of these ideas are less expensive than the traditional open bar.

fancier, haute cuisine. Dress up an ethnic buffet with food stations (a design-your-own quesadilla bar or pasta station, for example) that lend some pizzazz to the meal. Instead of an open bar, tie in affordable alcohol alternatives (a margarita machine for a Mexican buffet, bottles of Chianti for an Italian meal) to save even more money.

4 Consider a wedding brunch or luncheon. Ever been to a restaurant and noticed the exact same menu is less money at lunch than dinner? The same rule often holds true for wedding receptions. Brunch or breakfast is often less expensive because the food/beverage items are less pricey than what's served at dinner. Portions are also smaller too, as is alcohol consumption.

5 Have a dessert reception. Why not skip all those other boring courses and cut to the chase: have a dessert-only reception. A Chicago bride told us how she pulled that off: her late evening ceremony (9 pm) was followed by a reception for 200 guests that featured a lavish buffet of desserts. On the menu: a fondue of fresh fruits, torts, cheesecakes, an ice cream bar, and favorite dessert recipes from relatives, along with the traditional wedding cake. An espresso bar with flavored coffees provided refreshments. Sounds expensive? Not really. Since there wasn't a full meal served, she saved $2500. (To avoid any confusion, it's appropriate to add on your invitation or reception card "Dessert Reception Following.") This tip might work best at a civic or independent site where you can bring in your own catering; facilities with large catering minimums (hotels, country clubs) may balk at this concept, especially during peak wedding months.

Real Wedding Tip

Yeah, it's a family function! That's the ticket!

A Boston bride emailed this story about using our "family function" tip when approaching caterers: *"Your tip to approach the reception sites as a 'family function' made an incredible difference in options for food and drink at the site we chose. We are getting the reception for $35 per person instead of their 'bridal package' of $70 per person! Turns out the site had a ten-page itemization for food and drink if you are planning a regular function, but a two-page brochure for weddings. This way, we had more information to CHOOSE what we wanted instead of having to go with their idea of what a wedding should be."*

6 Avoid Saturdays, if you can. Some caterers have reduced rate-packages for Fridays and Sundays with 10% (or more) discounts. (The only bummer: some rental places may charge extra fees or overtime charges to deliver on Sundays.) Another way to save: some caterers have discounted rates for off-peak times of the year like April or November. One groom in New York City told us their reception site on Long Island had an off-peak rate that saved them $16 per guest for the very same menu. By moving their wedding date back one weekend, they were now in the "off-peak" zone—and saved 20%. A tip: most sites don't advertise their "winter season discounts." You have to ask.

7 Negotiate. Yes, you can haggle with most caterers and reception facilities. Those written menus aren't cast in stone. If the caterer gives you a proposal for $48 per guest, ask what he or she can do for $40. If a competitor offers you a great freebie, ask if the facility will match the competition. Like all negotiations, you want to be reasonable and recognize that your leverage to get a good deal may depend on the date/time of year for your wedding.

8 Ask for the manager/owner. The best way to negotiate a deal is to go to the top—ask to speak to the manager or owner of the facility. Yes, that smiling salesperson says she can get you the best deal . . . but it is often the manager or owner of the facility that makes the final decision.

9 Avoid "budget-busting" menu items. Certain food items are extremely expensive and can bust your budget. Two common examples are shrimp and beef tenderloin, while chicken is almost universally affordable. If you still want to have a "budget buster," get creative. Can't afford cocktail shrimp? Go for shrimp toast or a shrimp salad. Another tip: stay with fruits and vegetables that are in-season. Putting chocolate-dipped strawberries on the menu for a December reception will cost you a pretty penny.

10 Choose items that aren't "labor intensive." Certain hors d'oeuvres may be made of simple ingredients but require painstaking labor to assemble. For example, hors d'oeuvres like "Boursin cheese piped into Chinese pea pods" take a long time to prepare since the cheese has to be hand-piped into the pea pods. Caterers pass along that labor cost to you.

11 Tell them it's a family reunion. As we mentioned in the reception site chapter, you can save money by telling a caterer that the event your planning is a "family function" (reunion, anniversary, etc).

That way, you get to see the "regular" menus, which (surprise) may be much less expensive than the "bridal packages." See the previous Real Wedding Tip for more details.

12 **Forget the "bridal packages."** Most contain pricey items you don't need. One conference planner (who was also a bride-to-be) gave us this tip: it may be much more affordable to buy items like hors d'oeuvres a la carte. A good rule of thumb is eight to ten hors d'oeuvres per guest (less if your reception is outside standard meal times). If you've got 100 guests, then you need 800 to 1000 pieces of hors d'oeuvres. Our reader said she saved 25% by ordering a la carte (100 egg rolls, 200 beef skewers, etc.). Remember that what's considered an hors d'oeuvre can vary from region to region. In the Northeast, these may be tiny items (like cheese puffs) served during a cocktail hour before a sit-down dinner. In the South, they may be more substantial selections ("heavy hors d'oeuvres"; an example—Virginia ham on baking powder biscuits).

13 **For buffet and hors d'oeuvres receptions, have the caterer's staff serve the items instead of letting the guests serve themselves.** This will control the amount of food served (and hence, the cost). When guests serve themselves, the food always seems to go much quicker (wonder why)!

14 **Buy your own liquor, if possible.** While most hotels, catering halls and country clubs don't let you do this, other sites may permit you to buy your own liquor. The savings of buying liquor at or near wholesale prices will be tremendous (perhaps 50% to 70% off "retail" prices). Ask the caterer if they will refer you to a good wholesaler in your area. Or check out wholesale clubs like Sam's, Costco or BJ's—many sell beer, wine and spirits by the case at fantastic prices (see the box later in this chapter for more detail). When you buy by the case load, you can normally negotiate lower prices than retail. Some liquor suppli-

Do-it-yourself ideas

If you are planning to cater your own wedding, consider the vast troves of recipe ideas on the web. A good example: About.com. Their wedding section (weddings.about.com) has an excellent archive of links to hundreds of web sites with appetizer, entréée and cake recipes. Another source: The Food Network (foodtv.com) has a large free recipe section. And we can't forget about Martha. MarthaStewart.com has two areas of interest to brides and grooms—weddings (which has advice on everything from cakes to favors and receptions) and a recipe section and search engine.

ers may even let you return unopened bottles for full credit. (Check to see if they will allow the same return of unopened beer and wine bottles; some may not allow returns because of damage that might occur when beer or wine is chilled). Wonder what wines are best buys? Check out the *Wall Street Journal's* "Weekend Journal" section—each Friday they review and rate a selection of wines, most of which are very affordable. One note of caution: most beverages must be chilled prior to the reception, so plan ahead.

15 **Provide your own bar service.** In some cases, "free-lance" bartenders are cheaper than the caterers' own staff. If the caterer allows you to have your own bar service, do a cost comparison between the two options. On the other hand, some caterers may not allow free-lance bartenders because of liability concerns. What about having a friend or relative tend bar? We don't recommend tapping Uncle Joe to do bar service. An amateur will waste more in booze than you'd save in bartender fees; skilled bartenders are more efficient at the task.

16 **Don't move those hors d'oeuvres!** Having hors d'oeuvres passed on silver trays may look elegant but watch out! One Florida wedding planner told us sites there charge exorbitant prices for "passed hors d'oeuvres." The more affordable alternative is to keep them stationary—scattered about the room at "stations" in chafing dishes. Of course, these exorbitant prices aren't the rule everywhere. A Wisconsin wedding planner says there is no premium price for passed hors d'oeuvres in her area; as a result, she highly recommends them to keep guests from over-indulging at a buffet table. The bottom line: compare costs for these two options carefully to get the best deal.

17 **Steer clear of course overkill.** For sit-down dinners, do you really need to serve both hors d'oeuvres and an appetizer? Or soup and salad? Some brides eliminate a dessert course and let the wedding cake suffice. Another money-saver: DON'T offer a choice of entrees at sit-down dinners. Some sites will charge a premium for this option.

18 **Slash the alcohol bill.** If you still want to have that traditional open bar, there are a couple ways to save money. First, use only house brands instead of pricey "call" brands for hard liquor. Here's another smart tip: if you're having a cocktail hour, serve affordable hors d'oeuvres to lower alcohol consumption (people drink less when they're munching egg rolls). Finally, close the bar early, say an hour or so before the reception ends. Have less expensive soft drinks or punch (or a coffee bar) available for the rest of the reception. Some couples only have an open bar during a cocktail hour; then wine is served with dinner and coffee/soft drinks are available thereafter. Another idea: some hotels and catering halls offer flat-rate packages for beverages. Instead of being billed per drink ordered, you pay a flat fee per guest. This might be a more affordable alternative.

19 **Hire a student.** Got a culinary school in town? See if you can hire a student(s) to cater your reception. A bride in Illinois called the Cooking Hospitality Institute of Chicago (888) 295-7222 (Web: chic.edu) and found graduate students will do her wedding for a fraction of what "professional" caterers charge. Sometimes these schools have their own restaurants, which might be another contact point. CookingSchools.com and Petersons.com/culinary are two web sites for finding a cooking school near you.

Deals at Wholesale Clubs and Gourmet Supermarkets

Liquor prices too much for you to swallow? Full-service catering charges too high to stomach? Consider two alternatives that offer great deals: wholesale clubs and gourmet supermarkets.

Popping up in most major cities, wholesale clubs like Sam's, Costco and BJ's offer cut-rate prices on everything from electronics to groceries. Best of all, some of the clubs have fully stocked liquor departments where you can buy in case quantity at fantastic discounts. Costco has prices 15% to 30% below regular liquor stores. Name brands of wine, beer and spirits are available by the case at fantastic prices. If you're hiring a caterer who will let you purchase your own liquor, be sure to get a quote from a local wholesale club.

To find a location of a wholesale club, look at their web sites: Sam's (samsclub.com), Costco (costco.com) and BJ's (bjswholesale.com). Another tip: in some states, you do not even have to be a member in order to buy liquor from a wholesale club. A reader in California pointed out that state law there forbids the charging of a membership fee to purchase liquor at such clubs. So, at a Costco or Sam's in California, all you need is an ID in order to get an "alcohol pass" to shop the store.

While many wholesale clubs have been adding liquor and groceries, supermarkets have remade themselves into "gourmet markets" with full-service catering departments. We've spoken to brides who have found affordable catering options for small at-home receptions at a local gourmet supermarket—and they found the quality to be excellent. Many markets also have pastry chefs on staff that can whip up a respectable wedding cake. With full-service floral departments as well, some markets offer an affordable one-stop shopping service. Prices for catering, cakes and flowers tend to be about 10% to 20% below retail.

20 **Go for a keg.** A keg of beer is equal to about SEVEN cases of beer. The bottom line: you save about 50% on beer if you use a keg instead of bottles. Worried a keg will give your reception all the ambience of a college frat party? Don't worry. Most caterers can hide the keg behind the bar and use a carbon dioxide tapper system to draw the beer. Another caterer trick: boxed wine. Pour boxed wine into carafes and you'll save 50% over bottled wine. Avoid having multiple selections of wine available on tables; that adds dramatically to costs since much of it is wasted.

21 **Just do a champagne toast.** Even the cheapest champagne is very expensive—bubbly has a higher cost per portion than even a mixed drink using premium liquor. Offering champagne throughout the entire evening is a budget buster for most couples. A better alternative: just do a champagne toast (that is a single glass per guest at the appointed time). Or skip it altogether.

22 **Buy your champagne December 30th.** Sara M. of Camanche, Iowa discovered this great way to save: she bought all of the champagne for her wedding right before New Year's Eve. She paid just $10 for a box of three bottles of champagne at Sam's Club. Stores often do champagne sales right before New Year's Eve at prices you won't find after January 1. Buy it in advance and save! FYI: if you follow this tip, store the champagne in a cool dark place around 55 degrees. It should not be refrigerated until just before the wedding.

23 **Cap it.** If you want an open bar but don't want to go bankrupt if your guests drink like fish, consider capping the bar amount. That is, you have an open bar until you hit X dollars in spending (the bartender keeps a running tab), after which the bar is closed. You can serve soft drinks or coffee after that point in time.

24 **The signature drink.** Instead of a full open bar, just serve ONE signature drink that best matches the evening's menu. A mojito? An appletini? The signature drink is a clever way to put your personal stamp on a reception . . . and save money at the same time. It's much cheaper to serve the signature drink (and perhaps a few non-alcohol alternatives) than a full open bar. One bride in Seattle told us she saved $1700 with this tip alone!

25 **Go magnum.** A magnum is a wine bottle that's twice the size of a regular bottle. If are bringing in your own wine and paying a corking fee, go for a wine that's in these larger bottles. You'll save on corkage fees and the wine will be cheaper to boot (the price per ounce is less in magnums, as you might guess).

Destination Weddings Tips

When planning the food and drink for a destination wedding, consider these tips:

♥ **Go local.** You didn't drag your wedding party and guests to a tropical island to eat burgers, right? Keep the menu simple and incorporate local flavors, ingredients and drink. Avoid the big expense to

Real Wedding Tip

Tips on tipping

Boy, this is a perennial question—who do you tip? How much? First, understand that many wedding vendors (the caterer, limo, etc.) add a mandatory gratuity to the final tab. As a result, you don't have to tip anyone. However, if you believe an individual staffer has gone "above and beyond the call of duty," it may be nice if you slipped them an extra $20 or more. A server who tracks down a missing special dietary meal for a relative, a limousine driver who makes a special return trip to your house to retrieve an errant bridesmaid, a catering manager who works miracles with a cake that's collapsed—these are examples of extraordinary service that you may want to reward with an extra tip. You may also give a tip to the band or disc jockey if they turn in a stellar performance.

We've noticed there are some regional differences when it comes to tipping. Brides in the Northeast (particularly Long Island, New York and northern New Jersey) tell us it's standard practice to "grease" all wedding vendors with a $25 or $50 tip on the day of the wedding. Some bridal vendors can be darn pushy about this; one Long Island bride told us she was informed by her photographer that he expected her to tip his assistant 10% of the bill. And the catering manager told her that even though a labor charge was built into her $60 per plate reception, an additional tip would be nice. Our take on that: it's rude for a vendor to demand a tip, either for themselves or their workers. We say ignore them.

If you really want to give a tip, give it directly to the worker(s). One waitress who works for a catering hall in Cleveland told us their staff never sees extra tips that are paid with the final tab. Apparently, the owner of the facility pockets these as extra profit. Hence, don't give that tip to the owner or maitre'd—hand it directly to the people you want to receive it. And there's no law that says you have to give cash: consider handing out gift certificates or a bottle of wine as a thank you to wedding vendors.

import in items that are not in abundant local supply.

♥ **Be realistic.** If you are getting married on a tropical island in the Caribbean, be realistic about the catering for your reception. On many islands, it's hard to source certain food items that we take for granted here in the U.S. And folks tend to move on "island time." Set your expectations accordingly. True story: on a recent trip to British Virgin Islands, we found the only market on the island had run out of milk. The next delivery: in about three days!

♥ **Use our hotel tips as a guide.** Most destination weddings are in resort hotels–see the tips on hotel wedding receptions later in this chapter for guidance.

Biggest Myths about Catering

Myth #1 *"Maybe you can settle an argument I'm having with my mother. If I invite fewer guests, will my catering bill will go down dramatically?"*

Well, yes and no. Obviously, fewer mouths to feed will have an impact on your total bill. However, if you invite fewer guests, the price *per person* may go up. Why? That's because a large part of the per-person price caterers quote you is "fixed." Fixed costs include the caterer's overhead, kitchen facilities, etc. No matter how many guests you invite, caterers still have to pay these administrative expenses. Hence, you're paying for more than just the food. Most caterers have an unwritten base price or minimum that engaged couples must pay—no matter how many guests they want to invite.

Myth #2 *"Buffets are always less expensive than sit-down dinners."*

How to feed 100 for $100

How much food do you need to feed 100 guests? 200 guests? You can find the information on line at angelfire.com/bc/hobbyhorse/. The page offers impressive tips on "feeding 100 for $100," as well as calculations for how much you need to serve at a buffet and how to figure beverage amounts.

Also recommended: a book called *Secrets From a Caterer's Kitchen* by Nicole Aloni ($18.95; available at Amazon.com). Bon Appetit magazine called this book a winner, saying "The chapter called 'What Every Caterer Knows' and the detailed food-quantity and beverage-service charts make it invaluable!"

This is one those great debates that has no right answer. The bottom line: the cost of a reception is often *what* you serve rather than how you serve it. Hence a basic sit-down chicken dinner will be cheaper than a fancy buffet with shrimp, sliced beef tenderloin and other pricey dishes. Conversely, a five-course lobster sit-down dinner may cost several times more than a simple buffet with hors d'oeuvres like fruit, cheese and sandwiches.

We've noticed that caterers tend to steer couples toward the type of reception they do most often. Therefore, a caterer who frequently does buffet receptions will tell you a sit-down dinner is too expensive. In the Northeast (where sit-downs dinners are most common), caterers will advise just the opposite.

Of course, you can combine both types of receptions if you prefer. A "seated buffet" is set up like a sit-down dinner, with tables and chairs for every guest. Waiters serve the salad or first course at the table, while the main dishes are served buffet style.

Real Wedding Tip

Affordable linens

Reader Virginia H. found a way to cut her rental bill for her reception linens by 40%:

"I checked with several party rental companies regarding rental of table linens, and I kept looking at a bill of about $600 to $800. I couldn't believe that companies in my area wanted at least $22 to rent a single tablecloth, or $2 to rent a napkin. I was certain I could buy them for the same or less.

"I finally found DeNormandie linens (or 773-731-8010). Boy, are they a find. It is a small company based in Chicago, operated by the same family for over 100 years. They custom made me new tablecloths for both my five-foot rounds and eight-foot rectangular tables for about the same price as I could have rented cloths. Delivery took one week. Plus I had a huge choice of colors to choose from. The quality is nice, too..... a non-wrinkling wash and wear fabric, but very nice to the touch. As for napkins, the DeNormandie representative sold me 100 lightly used damask napkins in sage green for $1 each. I thought they would go nicely with the cloths, but DeNormandie told me that if I didn't like them together, just to ship them back for a refund. I ended up spending a total of about $450 on my table linens."

MYTH #3 *"Given the expensive prices caterers charge, you get the feeling these guys make big, fat profits off weddings."*

Gosh, it may be hard to believe, but most don't. Profits for caterers only range from 8% to 15% of the total bill. In the past few years, food and insurance costs have soared for most caterers. Don't shed too many tears for them, though. Since the average business only earns a 5% profit on sales, caterers' profits aren't all that bad. Different caterers make more money in different areas. For off-premise caterers, the biggest revenue area is the food. For on-site or in-house caterers (like hotels), the biggest moneymaker is the alcohol.

MYTH #4 *"Aren't plastic plates more affordable than glass?"*

Nope. In many cases, the cost of renting glass is actually almost as affordable as using plastic! Besides looking nicer, glass doesn't have the negative environmental impact caused by throwing away plastics. Ask your caterer to do a cost comparison between plastic and glass.

MYTH #5 *"Guests always drink and eat more at weddings than any other party."*

REAL WEDDING TIP

Liquor prices soar

Recent bride Samantha Day of Canton, Michigan was amazed at the cost of liquor when she priced her reception:

"What is it with liquor prices? I almost fell out of my chair when I contacted a restaurant in Wyandotte, Michigan (just outside of Detroit). The reception costs were average for the area, however the bar costs almost made me want to elope.

"I was informed that their bar costs were done on a 'per bottle' basis and they would also pro-rate any bottles that weren't completely used. So far, it doesn't sound bad. However, then came the price per bottle—starting at $90 PER BOTTLE! My next question—how big are these bottles? The site said they were just average size bottles. Say what?! They wanted to charge me $90 for a bottle of alcohol, that I could buy in a store for anywhere from $15 - $20! That's outrageous!"

This myth is used by caterers to justify higher prices for weddings than other types of parties like corporate events, retirement parties and the like. We don't buy it. Why? Almost any host today (whether a bride or corporate party planner) buys catering packages based on consumption. That is, you buy 100 pieces of an hors d'oeuvre, 125 chicken dinners, etc. Most bars are also billed on consumption (per drink). Therefore, when a caterer says they charge more for weddings because guests are pigs, it rings hollow to us. Why is the same chicken dinner for a wedding 30% more than a corporate party?

Helpful Hints

1 Make sure the catering representative who planned your reception will be there the night of the wedding. Hotel catering staffs are frequently guilty of not showing up to make sure everything is right. If you contract with a smaller, off-premise caterer, make sure the owner is there. Obviously, the owner may not be able to be at your wedding reception every minute, but there should be a clear chain of command in case a problem arises.

2 Have the caterer prepare you a going-away package. Believe it or not, you probably won't get to taste any of the food at your reception. You'll be too busy shaking hands, giving hugs, posing for pictures, etc. Considering the amount of money you're spending, ask the caterer to prepare a going-away package with a sample of the evening's menu (don't forget to include the cake!). You and your fiancéé will probably be starved when you leave the reception!

One reader pointed out that some cities and counties have laws that prohibit caterers from allowing you to take home leftovers. Rebecca, a bride from Minnesota, noted that it wasn't allowed in her state because the caterer could be held liable for any illness that results from the consumption of that food. Check with your caterer to determine the regulations in your area.

3 Carefully budget food and liquor amounts. No, guessing how much food or beverage you should budget for a reception is NOT an exact science. For hors d'oeuvres, one caterer suggested budgeting eight to ten hors d'oeuvres per guest for a one-hour cocktail reception. A Wisconsin wedding planner provided us with this rule of thumb to budget how many drinks guests will consume at an open bar: 2.5 drinks the first hour, 1.5 drinks the second hour and one drink per hour thereafter. Hence, for a four-hour reception, you should budget five drinks per guest. Wow! Do people really drink that much at wedding receptions? No, the caterer told us. Remember that you are charged for the number of drinks *ordered*, not consumed. "So, when Uncle Joe can't remember what he did with his nearly full drink, he figures it's 'free' and he just gets another one," the caterer said. One scam that inflates liquor tabs: wait staff that clears half-full glasses before guests can finish them. As you'll read later in the Pitfalls to Avoid section, this is but one way some sites can boost the beverage bill.

Pitfalls to Avoid

PITFALL #1 FROZEN FOOD.

"We went to a friend's reception last weekend at a hotel. I know the bride spent a lot of money, but the food was just so-so."

In our opinion, too many hotels have mediocre food. The culprit? The freezer. Bought in bulk, frozen versions of mini-egg rolls and mini-quiche are mainstays on some reception site menus. Obviously, it is cheaper (and hence more profitable for the site) to buy these items frozen and quickly warm them in chafing dishes than to painstakingly make the same items from scratch. The problem? Besides obviously tasting "frozen," caterers who use frozen food often aren't any less expensive than those who hand-make food from scratch ingredients. If the food at your reception is one of your high priorities, shop carefully for a caterer who doesn't use shortcuts.

PITFALL #2 THE INFAMOUS CAKE-CUTTING FEE

"Boy am I steamed! The reception site I chose for my wedding said they would charge me $1 per person to cut my wedding cake. After spending thousands of dollars on food and liquor, I think they're trying to wring every last nickel from me!"

WE COULDN'T AGREE MORE! Boy, this is our number one pet peeve with caterers and reception sites. Some of these guys have the audacity to charge you a ridiculously high fee to cut your wedding cake. Ranging anywhere from 50 cents to $3 per guest, this "fee" supposedly covers the labor involved to cut the cake, as well as the plates, forks, etc. The real reason some reception sites charge this fee is to penalize you for bringing in a cake from an outside baker (instead of having the site bake it for you). Even more amazing are some sites that don't even bake wedding cakes themselves but still charge cake-cutting fees! Talk about abusive.

We say if you are spending thousands of dollars on food and liquor, the caterer or reception site should NOT tack on $100 to $400 more just for the privilege of cutting and serving the wedding cake! First of all, you are already paying a mandatory service gratuity to have a staff present at the reception. Hence, the cake-cutting fee is double charging. Secondly, do you really think they pay the cake-cutter $100 to $400 for

30 minutes of work? We suggest you try to negotiate away this charge—don't forget that everything is always negotiable.

(Note: some caterers or sites try to sneak in the cost of serving coffee into the cake-cutting fee. We suggest you tell the caterer to forget the cake-cutting fee and just price the coffee out separately. If the site still insists on a cake-cutting fee, try to negotiate a flat fee, say $50 or $75, instead of a per guest charge.)

Another inflated price we've discovered: the cost of punch. One hotel in Denver charges brides and grooms a whopping $45 per gallon of punch! Since a half-gallon of Minute Maid Fruit Punch goes for $2 to $3 at grocery stores, you can see how outrageous this charge is.

PITFALL #3 CORKING FEES AND THE LIQUOR THAT RUNNETH OVER.

"My friend had her reception at a country club that seemed to push liquor on the guests. Every five minutes, they went around to the guests and pitched more drinks. I also understand they charged the couple for every bottle that was opened! Isn't this a bit excessive?"

Not only excessive but also quite expensive. When couples are charged based on the number of $60 bottles of wine or champagne that are opened, one mad staffer with a corkscrew can inflict heavy financial damage. Such charges (called corking fees) are perhaps one of the biggest cost pitfalls of any wedding reception. That's because couples must pay for any opened bottles whether or not they were poured! Think you can just re-cork the bottles and bring them home? Think again—most sites prevent the removal of liquor from the premises.

In a different twist on the same problem, some sites push drinks on guests when the bar is "open" (that is, the engaged couple pays for each drink). Why would sites or caterers do this? BIG PROFITS! Liquor is the biggest moneymaking area for sites like hotels and catering halls, and hence the temptation to push booze or open unneeded bottles is too great for some.

The solution to the corking fee pitfall is to give the caterer or reception site a LIMIT on the number of bottles they can open. Tell them to confer with you before they go beyond that limit. Get that detail in writing.

Another version of this scam surfaced in California. We spoke with a former employee of a catering company who admitted they brought *empty* bottles to receptions! Since the liquor charges were based on the number of empty bottles at the end of the evening, the caterer was able to make a killing. Solution: if you are paying by the bottle, we recommend you count the bottles at the beginning of the evening and again at the end. If there are 100 full bottles at the start, there better not be 125 bottles (80 empty and 45 full) at the end.

Real Wedding Tip

Liquor slight of hand

Lisa M. of Phoenix, Arizona wrote to us about a scam she encountered at her wedding: her caterer "forgot" about the paid-for bottles of wine the couple provided for guests and instead charged guests for drinks:

"We arranged with our caterer to buy 24 bottles of wine for our guests to enjoy at no charge to them. We followed your advice about counting the bottles before and after, and a good thing. The problem: our caterers hid the free-to-our guests bottles of wine below the bar shelf and sold people $5 glasses of boxed wine from clearly visible boxes! They obviously made more money from selling the wine by the glass instead pouring the $10 bottles we had agreed to buy. So, only five bottles of our 24 were opened, but the caterer had an invoice for 24 bottles ready for us to pay at the end of the evening. Luckily, I had followed your advice, had a friend count the open bottles, and only paid for what we drank. HOWEVER, by charging our guests for their wine, they made us look cheap, as if we hadn't provided wine for our guests, and made more money for themselves. I guess in the future, brides should stipulate with the caterer that the wine provided by the bride and groom be clearly visible, and that other wine be hidden away, to be served only if the guests specifically request it."

Good point—never ASSUME that instructions like this will be followed at your wedding reception. Get it in writing!

Sites can also inflate the liquor tab by picking up half-full glasses, forcing guests who have just returned from the dance floor to go back to the bar to get something to drink. One wedding planner we spoke to suggested couples should explicitly tell catering managers to make sure the wait staff is not overzealous in clearing half-full glasses. If you see specific examples of this behavior, you should be able to negotiate a 10% to 20% reduction in the beverage bill.

Pitfall #4 Gratuitous gratuities and sales taxes from hell

"When we saw the final bill for our reception, the facility charged us a 'gratuity fee' on everything including the room charge! Is this fair?"

Many facilities look at the gratuity as "extra profit," not something that is paid to the staff. One bride in California called in the above story, where the facility was charging an 18% gratuity on the *room rental fee*, of all things (this worked out to an extra $300). In our opinion, the gratuity should only be charged on the food and beverage. (We should note in some states it is illegal to charge a mandatory gratuity on the liquor tab—as an alternative to the gratuity, facilities often charge bartender or bar set-up fees.) Placing a gratuity on other charges (like room rental, valet parking, coat check) is price gouging.

Another similar rip-off is the "double-charging" of labor. In Denver, for example, many caterers charge both a gratuity and a "labor fee." While the staff generally gets the gratuity, the owners usually pocket the labor charge. As a result of this double charging, couples are being socked with an effective 25% gratuity rate on receptions—an outrage in our opinion! (No, double charging for labor isn't illegal, but it still stinks).

What about sales tax? In some states, food and beverage is taxable. A few cities or counties even slap sales tax on labor charges like the gratuity and other services. Since the sales tax rate can be nearly 10% in some locales, this can add to the bill in a hurry. Be forewarned: some brides have told us that their sites have slapped sales tax on items like room rental that were clearly *not taxable*. Why? Maybe it's just sloppy bookkeeping. Or they may be pocketing the tax to pay for that Mercedes parked out front. If you have any questions on what's taxable and what's not, check with your local city or county government.

The state of California (always on the forefront of taxing everything that moves) has an inventive way of viewing this controversy. California law draws a distinction between a voluntary "tip or gratuity" and a mandatory "service charge." Basically, the state determines that voluntary tips are NOT subject to sales tax—but mandatory service charges (those 19% whoppers charged by California hotels) are. Adding insult to injury, the state also considers such items as corking fees and cake cutting charges as mandatory (and hence, taxable).

The best advice: watch out for all these sneaky charges and taxes. Be sure to question any item that looks strange.

PITFALL #5 PRICE RISE SURPRISE!

"I booked my reception site a year in advance and we agreed on a certain price per guest. One month before my wedding, the catering manager informed me of a 20% price increase and pointed to the fine print in their contract. Is this fair?"

Our office has received several complaints from brides and grooms who believe they were stung unfairly by "surprise" price increases. Ironically, their own advance planning may trip up these couples—they booked their wedding site so far in advance that the facility wouldn't

guarantee a price for food and liquor.

Instead, these couples received a written proposal and contract that included a "price escalation" clause. This enabled the site or caterer to raise the price with little or no notice. Obviously, that can be a painful lesson for brides and grooms who get socked with unexpected extra costs.

Certainly, the best course of action is to get a firm price guarantee. If that's not possible, try to negotiate a "reasonable" price increase cap in the contract—paying a small 5% increase isn't fun, but it's much better than being surprised with a 20% whopper.

Never agree to a menu where the price for an item is "market price" at the time of the wedding. That leaves you exposed to a huge bill in case the item's price skyrockets for whatever reason.

Also look out for clauses that let the caterer substitute food items. Insist in the contract the caterer get your written approval *before* any changes to the menu are made by the facility. You want to be reasonable, of course. While a sudden frost in Florida might change your plans for Mimosas, you don't want your caterer or reception facility to start making wholesale substitutions to the menu without your approval.

PITFALL #6 DO-IT-YOURSELF NIGHTMARES

"My family did all the catering for my sister's wedding. What a disaster! When we arrived at the reception site, the doors were locked so the food had to sit out in our hot cars. The potato salad spoiled and over 100 guests got sick from food poisoning."

Yep, that's a true story from a reader in Corpus Christi, Texas. While it's an extreme example of what can go wrong for those who want to go the do-it-yourself route, there are some important lessons—consider how BIG this task is before taking the plunge. Do you have time to prepare that much food? What about the delivery/set-up and refrigeration of the food before the reception?

If you want to do-it-yourself, you may want to compromise: have a restaurant cater the food. Or pick up prepared items from a grocery store or deli. Yes, this isn't as cheap as whipping up 400 canapes yourself . . . but it may be smarter in the end. Instead of serving the food from plastic trays or containers, dress up your buffet with some nice (rented) silver serving pieces.

Now that you've been inspired to slash the catering bill for your reception, what about photography? After the reception, the cost of photos is a big expense for most couples. In the next chapter, you'll learn how to preserve your memories without going bankrupt!

Notes

Chapter 9

Photography

Ever hire a professional photographer before? For most couples, the answer is no. And with over 27,000 wedding and portrait photographers out there, choosing the best one for you and your budget may seem daunting. From key questions to ask to important pitfalls to avoid, this chapter will give you a clear and concise guide to finding a great photographer at an affordable price.

What Are You Buying?

When you hire a professional wedding photographer, there are three main areas where your money goes:

1 Candids: These are the pictures taken at the wedding and reception that are assembled into an album for the bride and groom. Photographers often assemble candid packages for the parents (referred to as parent's albums) and gifts for attendants (usually two or four pictures in a gift folio). Note that parent's albums (usually 20 to 60 pictures) and gift folios are extra and are not included in our average photography tab.

2 Albums: Most photographers offer a wide selection of albums to hold the candids. The best are Art Leather (ArtLeather.com), Leather Craftsman (LeatherCraftsmen.com) and Capri (CapriAlbum.com). Unfortunately, they are also the most expensive and are sold only by professional photographers. Art Leather albums (more on these later in the chapter) are guaranteed for a lifetime. With Capri or Leather Craftsman albums, the pictures are mounted to the pages, which are permanently bound in the album. Some photographers skimp by using cheap, vinyl albums with plastic-covered pages. We'll explain later why these cheaper albums can damage your pictures.

The biggest trend in albums: digital albums. Instead of printed photos inserted into album pages, digital albums print the photos right on the album page. See the following box for more details.

3 Portraits: Pictures taken prior to the wedding day fall into this category. A bridal portrait is a formal portrait of the bride in her wedding gown. Particularly popular in the Southern U.S., bridal portraits are taken in an indoor studio or on location, typically four to six weeks before the wedding. An engagement portrait is a more informal picture of you and your fiancéé. This portrait is often used to announce your engagement in the local newspaper.

Two expenses are involved with portraits: the sitting fee and the portrait print itself. Sitting fees are a charge for the photographer's time and range from $50 to several hundreds of dollars. The most popular print size is 16x20 and this can cost $500 to $2000 depending on the photographer and city.

Digital albums

Digital has made a big impact on photography; now digital has staked a claim on wedding albums. The result is a major sea change to how albums look and we're happy to report it's all for the better. In the past, if you looked at one wedding album, you looked at them all—sure you could change the color of the cover, but the album looked the same . . . printed photos slipped into page sleeves with little gold frames.

Digital has turned that world upside down. Now, you can combine photos, text and graphics on a single page. The result looks more like the pages of a glossy fashion magazine than a wedding album. More and more photographers are offering this option and the cost isn't much different from old style print albums. (Hint: see the money saving tips later in this chapter for advice on how to create an affordable digital album yourself).

Photography customs and traditions vary greatly across the U.S. and Canada. For example, in Sacramento, CA, many couples have a formal portrait taken *after* the reception at one of the area's many parks. In the South, a formal portrait of the bride taken a month before the wedding is often framed and displayed at the reception. Several Colorado photographers bring studio-quality lighting systems to the wedding in order to do portraits of the bride and groom before the ceremony. A new trend for portraits: virtual backgrounds. Some photographers are using computer-generated backdrops to add sizzle to their portraits. The bride stands before a green background onto which a computer generated image is projected.

Average total costs: In most U.S. cities, the average tab for professional wedding photography—you might want to sit down—is $2000.

So what does that buy you? That figure just covers your album of candid coverage at your wedding and reception. Keep in mind if you add all sorts of extras (parent's albums, bridal portraits) or if you hire a "celebrity" photographer in a larger city, you could spend several times more than the average ($4000 and up). Brides in the DC area report that many wedding photographers charge $3000 to $6000 on average for their pictures.

No matter where you are, however, the process of selecting pictures is relatively the same. We should note that photographers don't usually talk in plain English, so here are three typical terms you will come across and their simple translations:

♥ **Exposures**: Basically this is every time the camera goes click. At least 150 to 200 exposures are taken at the typical wedding and four-hour reception. Be careful of packages that limit the number of exposures below that level. FYI: This is more of an issue with photographers who still shoot on film instead of digital. Digital photographers don't worry about using up expensive film since there isn't any! Hence, they may be willing to take more images at your wedding. One wedding photographer told us he used to shoot 500 images in four hours with a film camera; with a digital camera, he now shoots 800 to 1200 shots in the same period of time.

♥ **Proofs:** Digital photography has transformed the way proofs are handled today. In the past, film exposures were developed into proofs. The proofs were often 5x5 pictures from which you chose the final prints that would appear in your album. Unretouched, the proofs chronicled all the pictures that the photographer took at your wedding.

Digital technology has changed this in several ways. Some photographers give a couple a CD with proofs; others present the proofs via a slideshow in their studio. An increasingly popular method is online proofing: Pictage.com and EventPix.com are two of the biggest online proofing sites for weddings. Visit each site to get a feel for how this process works. EventPix.com, for example, has a helpful online demo.

Some photographers use a hybrid method for proofs—they take digital proofs and can create a "magazine proof" book. Here, a photographer prints 12 images on a 10"x15" page and bounds them into a book, creating a mini-magazine. That makes it easier to preview the larger number of images that most photographers take with digital cameras.

♥ **PRINTS:** The proofs are enlarged into final prints. For photographers who use medium format cameras (we'll explain this later), popular enlargement sizes are 5x7, 8x8, 8x10 and 10x10. The final prints are assembled into the album. (As a side note, some photographers offer to sell you the proofs, either individually or incorporated into the wedding album). As you'll read later, we recommend purchasing an album package that includes 60 to 80 prints to adequately tell the wedding story. Some of those pictures (say 10 to 20) would be enlargements (8x10 or 10x10). The balance would be the smaller 5x5 or 5x7 prints. Exactly how many enlargements you want is a personal preference, but additional enlargements obviously tend to add to the final tab. As we discussed earlier, digital albums are changing the way photographers present their prints—see the box earlier in this chapter for details.

Can you just buy a disk of your wedding photos from the photographer and print them yourself? The answer is typically no. Nearly all photographers make their money selling your finished prints in a fancy album. Giving you a disk would eliminate most of that revenue.

Okay, so now you know the basics of what you are buying. But how do you find a competent, yet affordable, professional wedding photographer in the first place?

Sources for Finding a Photographer

Photographers generally fall into two categories, commercial and portrait. While commercial photographers work for advertising agencies and other industrial clients, portrait photographers concentrate on weddings, special occasions, and (as you might guess) portraits. The best wedding photographers are those who specialize in just weddings and portraits, with several years of experience. They should do at least ten to 15 weddings per year. Here are three sources to find the very best wedding photographers:

♥ **RECENTLY-MARRIED COUPLES.** Yep, word-of-mouth referrals are key to finding the best photographers. Ask them how happy they were with the

Are wedding photographers overpaid?

What are the ten most overpaid jobs in America? Sure, you could pick the obvious suspects—professional athletes, movie stars, Fortune 500 CEOs . . . but MarketWatch.com went one step further by identifying which *common* professions are over-compensated. And what was #10 on the list? Wedding photographers. (For the curious, others on the list included airport skycaps, orthodontists, and real estate agents who sell high-end homes).

Here's how the site described wedding photographers:

> "The overpaid ones are the many who admit they only do weddings for the income, while quietly complaining about the hassle of dealing with hysterical brides and drunken reception guests. They mope through the job with the attitude: 'I'm just doing this for the money until Time or National Geographic calls.'
>
> "Much of their work is mediocre as a result. How often have you really been wowed flipping the pages of a wedding album handed you by recent newlyweds? Annie Leibovitz and Richard Avedon they're not, but some charge fees as if they're in the same league. Photographers who long for the day they can say 'I don't do weddings' should leave the work to the dedicated ones who do."

As you can imagine, wedding photographers were not thrilled at this. Several lit up message boards with posts, defending their profession's honor and compensation.

Their points? Wedding photography is hardly a one-day job—the prep work does take hours, including those pre-wedding meetings to go over logistics, etc. The actual wedding day is five to eight hours of work, standing on your feet, paying an assistant, etc. Then, thanks to digital technology, there is more post-production work then ever—processing images, designing an album, etc.

But MarketWatch.com has a point when it comes to arrogant photographers—yes, these folks are artists, but they are also providing a service to you, the CUSTOMER. For the big amount of money most photographers command, you should expect professionalism and respect, not attitude and sneers.

And, when it comes down to it, brides and grooms determine the market price for photographers. There is pressure to get the best, because you can't have a "do over" when it comes to the pictures. Even MarketWatch.com acknowledges this: "A lot of people are overpaid because there are certain things consumers just don't want screwed up," he said. "You wouldn't want to board a plane flown by a second-rate pilot or hire a cheap wedding photographer to record an event you hope happens once in your lifetime."

photographer and final prints. Was there anything they would change?

♥ **Wedding coordinators at ceremony and reception sites.** What an incredible resource! These people have seen hundreds of wedding photographers come through their door. Ask them who they thought were the best. Of course, their impressions are limited to the photographer's behavior at their particular site. Site coordinators rarely see the final photo album. Nevertheless, their opinions are valuable.

♥ **Bridal shows.** These shows (sponsored by local bridal shops and reception sites) often have several exhibits by local photographers. Be aware that these shows may feature young or new photographers who are looking to build their business. Unfortunately, bridal shows also tend to showcase large photography studios whose quality can vary greatly from associate to associate (we'll discuss these studios later). One tip: don't make a snap decision to book a photographer right there at a bridal show. Instead, visit with the photographer after the show at their studio and see more of their work.

♥ **Our local message boards.** Go to our site (BridalBargainsBook.com), click on message boards and then local. There you'll find a list of special message boards for local metro areas. Check the buzz on the best local photographers in your town or post a query about a studio you are considering. Get other reader feedback on prices, packages and more.

Where not to look. Unfortunately, the phone book is *not* a good source for wedding photographers. Many of the best wedding photographers do not invest heavily in this type of advertising. In fact, many don't advertise at all, working exclusively by word-of-mouth referral. Some photographers will also put an album of their work in local bridal shops. However, whose work is displayed has more to do with politics than merit. Another place that is a poor source: wedding advertising publications, both print and online. Most good photographers avoid having anything to do with them.

Brides in Cyberspace: What's on the Web?

The web can help with wedding pictures in several ways. First, you can search for a photographer. Second, you can put your wedding pics on the web for guests to see them and order reprints. Let's look at each use in depth:

♥ To find a photographer, we suggest two sites: **The Professional Photographers of America** (ppa.com) and **Wedding and Portrait**

PHOTOGRAPHERS (wppionline.com). Each let you search for local photographers by city, zip or area code.

Brides and grooms tell us they have had success with **CRAIGSLIST.ORG** in finding affordable local photographers. As you probably know, CraigsList.org is an online classified site, with different versions for 30+ cities. (When you first log on, you will see the San Francisco area—look to the right to see a list of other cities). Click on Services/Creative to read ads from available photographers; or post a query to Gigs/Creative for what you are looking for. Best of all, it's free (our favorite word). Hint: you can also use Craigslist to find more than just photographers; we've also seen hair/make-up artists listed here, as well as other wedding vendors!

♥ Getting your wedding pictures online is simpler than ever. Of course, most folks have two types of wedding photos—those snapped by guests and others taken by a professional photographer. Let's look at each type:

1 Guest pictures. Did your guests use single-use cameras (discussed later in this chapter) to help you fill out the candids from your wedding? If so, getting these pictures on the web is relatively easy. When you drop them off for developing, most processors given you an option to get digital images like AOL's "You've Got Pictures (pictures.aol.com) or Kodak's Easy Share Gallery (kodakgallery.com). Then simply send your guests an email with the info on how to access the photos. Another source: Photoworks.com, which scans and stores your pictures online at no additional charge.

Other options to share your photos with guests include free sites like PictureTrail (picturetrail.com) and Shutterfly (shutterfly.com). Most let you password-protect your photos so only your friends and relatives can view them. The only bummer? You have to do the scanning yourself with these sites. If you don't have a scanner, you can usually use one at a local Kinkos.

Of course, if you are tech-savvy enough, you can post an online album yourself. Most Internet service providers (ISP's) give you a certain amount of server space to upload files, including pictures. You just scan the pictures, FTP them to your ISP and create HTML pages that let your friends and relatives view them. If all that went over your head, then it might be best to leave this to one of the services listed above.

2 What about the professional pictures? As with guest photos, you may want to post professional photos online for family and friends to view and order prints. Yes, this service is available, but in the case of professional photographer, your photographer has to set up the picture preview.

Professionals use several web sites including PhotoReflect.com, Pictage.com, EventPix.com, and Collages.Net. See Figure 1 on the next page.

FIGURE 1: PhotoReflect.com's main business is to sell wedding picture reprints—but you can also search for photographers.

All of these services work much the same way. A photographer uploads the pictures to the site, which creates a password-protected web page for your wedding. You email guests with the site address and password. Guests can then view the pictures online and order reprints right from the site. Most of these sites are free to photographers; they make their money by taking a cut of the reprint revenue.

A few caveats: while some sites have interactive features like guest books, you can't print or email the pictures to others. If you try to save the image to your hard disk, a watermark that says "proof" appears on the image. And beware that some photographers mark-up the reprint prices to sell online. If you or your guests plan to purchase more than a single print online, you might consider contacting the photographer directly for a better price.

Understanding Wedding Photographers: Some Basics

As you shop for a good wedding photographer, there are three key areas that you must always keep in mind:

1 **Equipment.** Obviously, the quality of equipment the photographer uses is directly related to how good your wedding pictures will look.

No matter how talented and personable the photographer is the resulting pictures will be a disappointment if he or she uses an inferior camera.

"I visited a wedding photography studio yesterday that said they use medium format cameras and shoot on film. They said this is better than digital cameras. Is this true?"

Well, that isn't necessarily true or false.. To understand why, let's look at the three types of cameras mainly used for wedding photography: digital, medium format cameras and 35 millimeter.

♥ **DIGITAL CAMERAS.** Not more than a few years ago, most wedding photography was shot on film with a medium format camera. No longer—the majority of wedding photographers now shoot with digital cameras.

The digital revolution has radically changed the photography biz, in both big and small ways. An example: lighting. One of the first things photographers learn with digital cameras is that it is easier to work with an underexposed image than overexposed (it is the opposite with film). Why? Software can compensate for underexposed pictures and fix other glitches that previously required expensive manual re-touching.

Speaking of software, the biggest change for wedding photographers in the digital world is using image manipulation software like PhotoShop, as well as electronically transferring the images to album makers for output.

As we discussed earlier, digital albums are opening up a wide range of design possibilities, combining text, graphics and photos in an infinite number of ways. The challenge: the photographer now has to be a graphic artist, using software to create those nifty album pages. Yes, many album companies offer templates and other shortcuts, but there is still a level of design skill required.

Finally, let's talk about the prints. While your album may be digital, you still may want printed photos to frame, give as gifts, etc. In the early days of digital photography and inkjet printers, there were many concerns about print quality and how long prints would last. Good news: in the last few years, professional inkjet printers now produce prints that are of "archival quality"—in English, that means they will last for 100 years without fading. That may even outlast machine prints from film cameras, where the average life is 80 years.

♥ **MEDIUM-FORMAT FILM CAMERAS.** No, not all photographers have gone digital. Some are still more comfortable with film cameras—and the most popular type of film camera for weddings is medium format.

The main distinction between medium format cameras and 35mm is their negative size: a medium format's square negative is usually $2^1/_4$ by

$2^1/_4$ inches. This provides much clearer photos when prints are enlarged. Medium-format cameras produce pictures that have richer depth, warmer colors and sharper contrasts than 35mm cameras. (To be technical, the warmth of a photograph is determined by the amount of flash light. However, medium-format cameras deliver pictures with more color saturation than 35mm. Color saturation relates to the richness of color in the print).

The Hasselblad is apparently the Mercedes of medium format cameras. This camera (which was the one NASA used on the moon for astronaut snapshots) is still incredibly popular among the best wedding photographers, apparently for the beautiful pictures it takes. Another popular medium-format camera is the Bronica.

We should note in passing that there are also several larger-format cameras that produce even bigger negatives (and hence, greater color saturation) than standard medium-format. Cameras such as the Mamiya RB67 are considered the ultimate camera in this category. That camera takes a negative that is 6cm by 7cm.

One final tip about cameras: the best medium format cameras for weddings have a "leaf" shutter, instead of "focal plane." This enables flash-fill outside in the bright sun and prevents the bride's white dress from washing out. The leaf shutter allows a photographer to properly balance shadows. Most medium format camera makers sell both types of shutters, so it might be worth it to ask the photographer which type he uses.

Proofless Studios: How Some Photographers Use the Net to Speed the Delivery of Wedding Albums

In the ancient days of wedding photography (like before 1995), brides and grooms first had to look at dozens of printed "proofs" to assemble their albums. Trying to judge what a picture would look like cropped or enlarged was difficult—and the wait to get the proofs and the final album sometimes stretched into weeks. Or months.

New digital technologies have made this process quicker and easier, for both photographers and consumers. Thanks to digital proofing and online ordering systems, final albums can be delivered to couples in a matter of days, instead of weeks or months.

Here's how it works: after the wedding, a photographer sends his film to a lab. The lab then scans the film negatives and creates digital pictures which are downloaded by the photographer off the 'net—all in a matter of days. (Of course, if your photographer shoots with a digital camera, he or she doesn't have to go through the above process.) Next, the photographer uses a software program like

♥ **35 MILLIMETER FILM CAMERAS:** This type of camera is being rapidly replaced by digital for wedding photography, but you still may find a few die-hard photojournalists using 35 mm film cameras. Why?

Photographers who are fans of 35mm point out that the quick action of the shutter on 35mm cameras lets them take more candid-style pictures (so-called photojournalism-style). They also say the equipment and film has improved dramatically in recent years, closing the quality gap with more expensive cameras.

The biggest rap on 35mm is the negative size—the smaller negative size means pictures blown up bigger than an 8x10 look grainy. Other photographers also say 35mm pictures look flat and the colors are not as vibrant.

This debate is becoming increasingly moot, however, as more photographers shift to digital.

For the curious, how do photographers who shoot on digital blow up their pictures to wall portrait size? Most use a PhotoShop plug-in called Genuine Fractals (lizardtech.com) that enables digital photos to grow without losing resolution.

"Well, now I'm confused. Should I hire a photographer who uses a digital or medium format camera? Or 35mm?"

The key is to look at the pictures. As we'll discuss later in this chap-

ProShots (proshots.com) or Montage by Art Leather (an album company) to create your album. Then, the pictures are shown to you. Most photographers will create a slide show (on a big screen or computer monitor) with all your photos. Then you are presented with a suggested album layout (again on computer), complete with possible enlargements, mattes, crops and so on.

Many digital photographers use online proofing or even give you a CD of the proofs or suggested album. As we mentioned earlier in this chapter, other photographers are using online reprint web sites to let your guests view and order pictures off the 'net. The days of passing around a proof book are numbered.

One caution to this "proofless" system: some photographers try to up-sell you by presenting a virtual album of, say, 100 pictures when your package just includes 75 shots. Photographers know showing you the possible album with all the enlargements and extra pictures convinces many consumers to pony up more money. If you want to stick with your budget, tell the photographer to construct the proposed album with the number of prints in your package—and no more.

ter, there are several ways to evaluate photographs and some key questions to ask the photographer.

Also, consider the *style* of wedding photography you want. If you'd like a heavy emphasis on candid or spontaneous pictures, a photographer with a digital or 35mm camera might be a best bet. Traditionalists who like a more posed look should consider a photographer who shoots on medium-format. Since most formal bridal portraits are enlarged to 16x20 (or larger), these should always be shot with a medium-format camera.

Why do some wedding photographers use digital or 35mm cameras? One reason: money. These cameras cost several hundred dollars. Medium format cameras cost several *thousand* dollars—each. For example, a completely outfitted Hasselblad (camera, lenses, lights, flash) can cost from $10,000 to $15,000. Obviously, amateur photographers opt for the cheaper digital 35mm when they are starting out. What is most disgusting, however, are large studios that use low-quality cameras in order to cut corners. While the studio makes a few extra bucks of profit, engaged couples can be left with inferior-looking photographs.

Of course, some professional photographers PREFER 35mm and digital cameras. Why? Because these cameras are smaller and less obtrusive. This enables the photographer to achieve that hip "photojournalist" style now the rage. One such photographer told us she uses a Leica RangeFinder, which is sort of like the Hasselblad of small format cameras. "It looks like a toy but it costs a fortune ($3000 for a body and lens) because the lenses are so great. This makes it perfect for shooting during the ceremony, toasts or other quiet private moments. It is also great in low light because it can be handheld at slower shutter speeds." Her point is well taken: negative size and image sharpness is not everything. Capturing the moment as it happens may be more important and smaller format cameras provide that flexibility: "From my point of view, a big camera, a big flash, and an assistant or two to hold them just makes the photographer intrusive," she said.

Just as important as the camera is the lighting equipment. Lighting techniques often separate the amateurs from the pros. Amateurs will use only a flash mounted on the camera—the resulting pictures are flat and of poor quality. Professional wedding photographers will use a powerful flash placed about 45 degrees to the side of the subject. The resulting light provides shadows and depth. Some photographers will add one or more flashes aimed at the background. A California photographer told us he even puts light behind posed groups and dancing couples to give his pictures additional depth.

Who holds all these extra flashes? Usually it's an assistant. Many pros have one at their side the entire day. Not only does the assistant hold the additional flashes, but he or she also makes sure the photographer doesn't miss any detail. In Dallas, Texas, we found one expert photographer who brings *two* assistants to each and every wedding.

2 Skill: Equally as important as having a high-quality camera is knowing how to use it. Photographing a wedding takes a tremendous amount of skill. This is not something that can be taught in a classroom. Only by actually going out there and clicking the camera can anyone learn how to be a good wedding photographer.

Skill involves not only knowing where to stand to get the best shot of the couple as they are showered with birdseed, but also how to coax a reticent flower girl into that perfect pose. The best wedding photographers learn how to work around adverse lighting conditions and, perhaps, adverse relatives.

The only way to tell a wedding photographer's skill is by looking at many albums of his or her work. After seeing hundreds of wedding albums, we are convinced that you can tell the skilled pros from the unskilled amateurs. One key: posing. Does the photographer creatively pose his or her subjects or are they lined up against a blank wall (like police mug-shots)? And not every church looks like the Sistine Chapel—the best photographers mask ugly backgrounds with creative posing and lighting.

One last caution about skill: don't believe studios that tell you that every one of their associates is trained in the same style. This has to be the biggest lie told by wedding photography studios. True, studios may have a professed quality standard that they strive for, but what matters most is the talent and skill of the individual photographer who will actually photograph your wedding. Despite the smooth sales pitch, quality can vary widely from associate to associate.

3 Personality: Besides professional equipment and the skill to use it, great wedding photographers also must have great people skills. This isn't nature photography where the photographer patiently sits out in a field for six hours waiting for that perfect photo of the yellow-finned butterfly. Wedding photography involves real people.

Obviously, this doesn't come as a surprise to you, but apparently this is news to some wedding photographers. Communication is key. Besides a sixth sense for good pictures, photographers must be persistent in getting the shots the engaged couple requests. Controlling large crowds of unruly bridesmaids and groomsmen for a group shot can be trying on even the best of nerves. Wedding photographers walk a fine line between being gentle conductors and absolute dictators. In the latter case, some fall victim to director's disease: barking orders at the bride and groom (or their guests) and turning the wedding and reception into a military exercise. (One good question to ask a photographer's references: how did he treat your guests? Was he polite and professional?).

Photographers must also work with other bridal professionals at the wedding, especially the videographer. Clashes between these two vendors have been legendary and sometimes nasty; we'll talk about this later in the chapter.

Remember that you will spend more time with your wedding photographer than any other merchant. For example, you won't see your florist or baker during or after the wedding. Not only do you meet with the photographer prior to the wedding, he or she will follow you around the entire wedding day. Then, you may spend several more hours with him viewing proofs and ordering prints. Make sure you like this person. We mean you need to *really* like this person. If anything makes you the slightest bit uncomfortable, consider hiring someone else.

Getting Started: How Far in Advance?

Obviously, photographers can only be at one place at one time. This limited capacity leads to a spirited competition between brides to book the best photographers. Once you reserve the ceremony site (and therefore confirm your date), consider shopping for a photographer. While some photographers can be had on short notice (a few weeks to a couple of months), booking nine to 12 months in advance of your date is prudent. That way you won't have to settle on a third or fourth choice. During the wedding season in your town, prime dates will go quickly.

Step-by-step Shopping Strategies

♥ **Step 1:** Once you have booked your ceremony site, contact three to five wedding photographers you have identified by using the sources we listed earlier in this chapter. Make an appointment with each studio. Request to meet the actual photographer who will be available on your wedding day.

♥ **Step 2:** On your visit, view as many pictures as possible from the photographer's past work. Be sure that you are looking at the photographer's own work, not a compilation of the studio's greatest hits. Also, ask to see a proof book from a recent wedding. See complete albums, not just greatest hits collections.

♥ **Step 3:** While looking at the work, decide if the pictures strike an emotional chord with you. Is the posing natural or do the subjects look uncomfortable? Are the pictures in-focus and well-framed? Check for any over or underexposed prints—a common problem among amateur photographers. Look to see details in the icing of a wedding cake and delicate lace in bridal gowns—if these subjects look washed out then the pictures are overexposed. Also check out the various poses a photographer uses. Are there any you'd like the photographer to mimic for your wedding?

♥ **Step 4:** Ask to see photos taken under low-light conditions, especially if you are planning to have a candle-lit ceremony. This is good measure of the photographer's skill, since low-light photography is a technical challenge for even the most experienced.

♥ **Step 5**: Ask the photographer the questions we list later in this chapter. Get a good reading on the photographer's style and personality.

♥ **Step 6:** After visiting with several photographers, pick the one you think offers the best quality for the most affordable price. Be sure to compare prices on an apples-to-apples basis, accounting for differences in package sizes and prices. Don't let any photographer pressure you into a quick decision.

♥ **Step 7:** Once you make your decision, get a written contract from the photographer. Before signing it, take it home and read it thoroughly. A good contract should specify:

The name of the actual photographer who will be at your wedding.
When the photographer will arrive and how long he or she will stay.
A minimum number of proofs to be provided.
The exact number of prints and the type of album.
The exact dates the proofs and the final album will be delivered.
Provisions in case the photographer gets sick or can't make the wedding.
A specific schedule with due dates for deposits/final balance payments.
Any additional charges for travel time, overtime costs, or other fees.

♥ **Step 8:** A few weeks before the wedding, set up another meeting with the photographer to go over details. Discuss your expectations of the photography and clearly state the types of pictures you want. Identify on a written list any special friends or relatives that you want photographed. The more explicit your instructions to the photographer, the better the odds your wedding photography will meet your high expectations. Frankly, you're paying a ton of money to this person so the least they can do is take the pictures you want. Bring a copy of this list with you to the reception. After taking all the time to make this list, you want to be prepared in case the photographer forgets his or her copy.

A word on shot lists: you should make TWO lists. The first list is must-have shots. The second list is for relatives you want the photographer to photograph in moderation. That way if you have an uncle who is a camera hog, you don't end up with 62 pictures of him.

♥ **Step 9:** In "Chapter 15: Last Minute Consumer Tips," we recommend you pick a trusted friend or relative to be a surrogate bad cop. This person ensures all the vendors are doing their jobs correctly, while letting you enjoy your wedding day. Introduce the photographer to this contact person early on the wedding day so the he or she knows whom to turn to for help when trying to take all your requested photos. Give your bad cop a copy of the list of requested photographs to make sure the shots are taken.

Questions to Ask a Photographer

1 Who exactly will be photographing my wedding? This is perhaps the most important question to ask. Don't settle for vague answers like "one of our expertly-trained associates will do your wedding." Avoid wasting time by making sure your appointment is with the actual photographer, not the studio's marketing representative or bridal consultant. Another good question to ask: does the photographer have an assistant who comes to weddings? This helps a photographer concentrate on the event instead of worrying about his equipment, tripod placement and so on.

2 Can I see a complete album from one wedding you photographed? By viewing a complete album from one wedding, you can see how the photographer tells a story from beginning to end. Even better: try to look at several complete albums.

3 Can I also see a proof book or disc from a recent wedding? This is the best way to see what you are buying. Proofs are an unedited and uncensored look at what you will receive after your wedding. Good wedding photographers probably have at least one proof book or disc that is waiting to be picked up—ask to see it.

4 Describe to me your philosophy and approach to wedding photography. Ooo, this is a good question. Sit back and listen to

What size album should we get?

Most photographers offer two sizes: a 5x5 album or a 10x10. The latter holds both small and large prints. If you have a choice, go for the larger album. Even if you don't purchase enlargements from the photographer, you may want to include a "memory" page at the front of the album with your wedding invitation and other mementos. These won't fit into a small album as easily. What about all those guest candids you might get as well? It's probably best to put those in a different album, separate from the professional pictures. We'll discuss a mail-order source for albums later in this chapter.

what they say. How active a role do they take in the direction of the day's events? Obviously, some photographers may have a canned speech for this question, but you can shake them up by asking good follow-up questions.

5 What is your shooting schedule during a wedding? When do you arrive and what is your general order of shots? How long does it take to do the traditional pictures after the ceremony? This is a real controversial area of wedding photography. See "The Great Before or After Controversy" discussion later in this chapter.

6 Will you come to my rehearsal? Some photographers will do this; others don't. Photographers who do attend the rehearsal get a heads up on the different players for the wedding, meeting key relatives in advance.

7 What is the balance between posed and candid shots? Some photographers prefer to stage most pictures by formally posing the subjects. Ask the photographer's opinion about whether pictures should be posed or candid. A recent trend in wedding photography is photojournalism. Here the photographer documents the wedding as it happens without any formal posing.

8 How many exposures will you take at my wedding? Is there a limit on the number of exposures or your time? Be careful of photographers who limit either one. Too many times we have seen weddings shift into fast-forward because the photographer's clock was running out. Limiting the number of exposures is also a problem since it restricts the possible choices for your album. About 150 to 200 exposures should be taken to provide enough choices for an album with 60 to 80 prints (our recommendation to adequately cover the day's events). FYI: Photographers who shoot digital don't have this problem, as they don't have to worry about using up expensive film.

9 Do you bring any backup equipment? What will you do if you are sick and unable to shoot my wedding? Cameras (even expensive ones) are just machines. Sometimes they break. Good photographers should have backup cameras and lighting systems ready in case of a mechanical problem. Having an associate on call in case of emergencies is also prudent.

10 Can I see the actual album that comes with my package? A favorite trick of wedding photographers is to show you their past work lovingly bound into leather albums. Then they forget to mention that their packages come with cheaper vinyl albums with plastic-covered pages. And, oh yes, after the wedding, the photographer casually mentions that the leather albums are available at an extra fee. Besides the deceptive nature of this practice, some vinyl albums with plastic pages are also problematic since the chemicals in the plastic can damage the prints over time. (Some plastic is okay if it is of archival-quality; that is, free of damaging chemicals). Insist on seeing the actual album that is mentioned in the package before you sign the contract. For more on albums (and one popular brand, Art Leather), see the box below.

77 Describe to me the most difficult wedding you ever photographed. How did you handle it? We love this question. It can

Art Leather Albums: The Inside Story

Elmhurst, New York-based photography album maker Art Leather (artleather.com) seems to have a lock on the bridal market—if you visit a handful of photographers, odds are you'll see their albums. In business since 1925, Art Leather sells only to professional photographers. Here's a look at some of their offerings.

♥ **Futura albums.** This is Art Leather's most popular line of wedding albums. The covers come in three varieties: Onyx, Hi-Key and Metro. With these albums, you pay for the album and page inserts.

♥ **Perma-Bound albums.** These albums feature pages with permanently mounted pictures (by contrast, the pictures are slipped into inserts in the Futura albums). Interestingly enough, the prices for Perma-Bound albums (covers, inserts) are just about the same as Futura. But we've noticed some photographers will charge higher prices for Perma-Bound albums, which do look fancier than a Futura.

♥ **The Mezzo Album.** These less expensive albums feature simpler pages (no gold edges) and covers.

be fascinating to see what the photographer defines as difficult.

Another related question: how does the photographer deal with camera hogs? You know, the relative who just has to be in every shot. Think about giving the photographer a list of relatives who should be photographed in moderation.

12 How long will you keep the negatives/digital files? Can I buy them? If money is tight, don't purchase a large number of prints right after your wedding. Instead, buy the minimum now and wait a year or two to finish out the album. Most photographers store negatives (or archive digital files) for a few years after the wedding and

♥ **Image Box.** Introduced in the last couple of years, the Image Box is designed as an add-on that lets you display the best images of your wedding. Basically, it is a box that holds 12 to 24 mattes that are unbound (so they can be individually removed from the box).

♥ **Digital albums.** Art Leather offers a wide range of digital albums (Montage Art Books, pictured at right), which combine photos, text and backgrounds. The prices for these are all over the board, depending on the design and number of photos. Art Leather's digital albums include the Cache and iMount Deluxe. New this year: Art Leather has introduced "Demi Books" a miniature copy of the bride's album intended as a gift or. Also new are "Urbans", soft leathers with a distressed feel. Art Leather even has a line of Ostrich Leather photo albums (warning: not appropriate for the PETA activist).

♥ **Extras.** Art Leather sells a surprising number of extras and accessories for their photography albums. Want a gold oval frame (for a picture) on your album cover? How about a panorama photograph that runs across two pages in the center of your album? What about your names and wedding date (or monogram) printed on the album cover? These are all pricey extras. Besides albums, the other big part of Art Leathers business is gift folios.

You can get more info on Art Leather (as well as preview some of their new products) on their web page at artleather.com. Art Leather does not sell directly to the public, however.

will be happy to do reprints later when you have more money. Yes, some photographers will even sell you the negatives/digital files for a small fee (granted, the majority do not sell them, but it doesn't hurt to ask!).

The photographer who shot our wedding called us five years later and offered to sell us the negatives for $1 each (an offer we accepted). You may want to ask how long the photographer will store the negatives, whether you'll have an option to buy them and so on. Get it in writing. One caveat: while most photographers will keep your negatives/files on hand for a year or two, don't expect them to archive them for over five years. Most photographers have a limit on how long they'll keep them. (Hint: send the photographer a forwarding address card in case you move after the wedding; if they can't reach you, the photographer might eventually destroy the negatives/digital files).

13 If you shoot with a digital camera, will the prints be of archival quality? You can't just go down to Best Buy and purchase a $50 ink jet printer, expecting to get top-notch prints. Most professionals who shoot digital use expensive in-house printers or send their work to an outside lab. Ask the photographer how your pictures will be printed and make sure you are getting archival-quality photo prints.

14 If you shoot with black and white film, do you do your own developing of the pictures? A photographer who does his own in-house processing of black and white film is able to get the contrast just right. Many photographers we interviewed insist such in-house processing is the only way to insure black and white photographs are high quality. Interestingly enough, this doesn't seem to be a big deal with color film (most photographers send this out to a lab for processing). It is probably still best to use black and white film (which shows more subtle hues of gray) than to use tricks to turn a color negative into a black and white image. Of course, if your photographer uses a digital camera, this is less of an issue. Software programs can transform a color picture into black and white with appropriate contrast.

15 How soon will my photographs be ready after I submit my order? You might be surprised how slow photographers can be when it comes to delivering a final album—sometimes measured in MONTHS not weeks. Photographers who value customer satisfaction should always quickly process albums and reprints. Another measure of customer service: how quickly are your phone calls returned? Messages should be returned within one business day. Taking days to return a simple voice mail is a red flag.

16 What rights do I have to the digital files? With more wedding photographers going digital today, don't assume you'll be able to get a disk with image files after the wedding. Most shooters want to keep the high-resolution master images in order to sell enlargements—but some might give you a disk of lower-resolution images for you to view on a computer screen. Confirm the rights you will have to any digital files before you sign a contract.

Bridal Bargains Wedding Planner: Photography

Yes, wedding photography is big bucks. But comparing photographers on an apples-to-apples basis can be tricky—use the worksheets in our new planner, the *Bridal Bargains Wedding Planner*, to point the way toward the photographer who will give you the most value for your photography budget. Once you've selected a photographer, our planner can help you organize this area of your wedding by tracking expenses, balances and payments due. Finally, we have a detailed shot list you can copy and give to your photographer to make sure he/she doesn't miss any key pictures on your wedding day.

Top Money-saving Secrets

1 Get married any time other than Saturday evening. Many photographers offer discounted packages for weddings held during Saturday afternoon or any other time of the week. Savings typically range from 10% to 20%. As a side note: some photographers charge extra to work on Sundays, although that is the rare exception. We find this kind of strange: some brides report that photographers tell them Sunday is "family time," but if you want them to work, they charge an extra fee. If Sunday really was family time, why work at all?

2 Hire a photographer who works out of his or her home. When you walk into a photography studio in a fancy office complex and see all that plush carpeting and furniture, who do you think pays for all that? That's right, you do. No one has ever explained to us how designer wallpaper translates into great wedding photography. Our advice: seek out a photographer who works out of his or her home. Quite simply, the lower overhead of a home studio/office is often passed along in the form of more affordable prices. Believe it or not, after visiting with 200 wedding photographers, we found some of the best work was from home-based professionals. Savings here can range from 20% to 40% off our photography average.

3 Skip the extra frills. Forget about the extras that photographers will suggest you buy. Gift folios (pitched as the perfect gift for wedding party members) are fluff at $100 a pop. Bridal and engagement portraits are expensive extras. Instead, if you really want a portrait, take a candid from the reception and have it enlarged to a 16x20. You'll save the sitting fee (anywhere from $50 to $300) and the print is often less expensive too. Forget about ordering a frame from the photographer; this service is grossly overpriced. Instead, go to your favorite framing store.

4 Hire a professional for the ceremony only. Then let your guests capture the reception candids with their own cameras or single-use cameras (see tip below for more information). Many engaged couples don't realize photographers offer a ceremony-only (two hours or less) package for small weddings. Of course, there is no law that says couples must have a small wedding to use this package. A no-frills ceremony-only package might run $600 to $800, depending on the photographer. One bride in Ohio told us she found a ceremony-only package there from a reputable studio for just $450—that was $1000 LESS than their five-hour plan. Obviously, prices will vary depending on the city you are in, but you can expect a savings of anywhere from 40% to 70%. (Note: beware of studios that might assign less-experienced photographers to shoot the ceremony-only packages.)

5 Get your guests involved. Supplement a professional photographer's pictures with shots taken by your guests. Single-use cameras are ideal for this—and you'll find a wide variety of options out there.

Kodak sells half a dozen single-use models, from a basic "Fun Saver" model with flash ($5) to a camera with a digital option (Plus Digital; $14). Since each camera has 27 exposures and it costs about $7 to develop each roll, your total cost is 44 cents per picture.

Fuji has a QuickSnap Wedding pack with four cameras for $20 (CameraWorld.com). Each camera has 15 exposures, so you get 60 pictures per pack.

Of course, many sites sell generic single-use cameras. The Ultimate Online Wedding mall (ultimatewedding.com) sells wedding single-use cameras for as little as $6 each for orders of 35 or more. Check your local warehouse club for bargains as well. Readers have spotted Kodak single-use use cameras for $10 for a two-pack at Costco (costco.com). Sam's club was offering a similar deal.

One tip: be sure to place a small sign near the single-use cameras asking them to be returned at the end of the evening. That way guests don't think the cameras are a party favor! (If this worries you, an alternative to the single-use camera trick is to just buy film or storage cards for several guests you know will have cameras.)

Another tip: you might designate one guest at each table to be the single-use photographer. Other brides say they have even provided a list of suggested shots. This prevents a dozen shots of the guest's wife or kids.

Should these cameras replace professional photographers? Of course not. Instead, we suggest hiring a professional photographer to cover the ceremony and let the guests snap away at the reception (they'll probably get pictures your photographer wouldn't take anyway).

Worried about the quality? Pictures from single-use cameras have dramatically improved in quality the last few years. If you still have doubts, buy yourself a camera and do a little experimenting. Is there any difference among the brands of single-use cameras? We've noticed the bridal magazines are stuffed with ads from mail order companies offering single-use cameras (one offers a 27 exposure camera for $10 with free developing). We'd suggest sticking to the name brands (Fuji is our top pick) unless you can confirm the quality by shooting a few of these generic cameras first. With professional photographers charging as much as $20 to $40 for a single print, single-use cameras offer an affordable way to hold down the photography bill.

Real Wedding Tip

Beware of re-loaded disposable cameras.

Reader Nia G. had this tip and warning for brides who want to use disposable cameras at their wedding:

"I have worked in a photo lab for several years and I've seen all kinds of film and disposable cameras come through. What most people don't know about disposable cameras, especially Kodak's Wedding Pack, is that they reuse them. This may sound like a good idea to recycle, but it can effect your picture quality. What happens is because they are reused, the cameras are not as light-tight as the original and thus your pictures are not as clear! Kodak's wedding cameras are all reloads! So are the other cheaper Kodak disposables in boxes (they disguise the reused plastic camera with a box). Fuji and Agfa DO NOT ever do reloads, so I highly recommend using their disposable cameras! Just thought I'd pass this on to other brides, cause I've seen Kodak wedding disposables come in looking awful and grainy very frequently."

6 Buy the album somewhere else. Chances are you will get a photo album as a gift. If your budget is tight, forget the fancy leather album. If the photographer includes the cost of the album in the package, ask him or her what the discount would be for an album-less package. The retail price of an album from photography studios ranges from $150 to $400. Where can you find a great album for your wedding pictures without spending those kind of bucks? Check out the Real Wedding Tip below for a mail-order source. Another hot trend for wedding pics: scrap-booking. Many arts and crafts stores like Michaels (michaels.com) and Hobby Lobby (hobbylobby.com) have jumped on the scrap-booking bandwagon, offering a myriad of supplies, albums and ideas to the do-it-yourself crowd. Check their web sites for free projects and supply lists.

Real Wedding Tip

Mail-order albums can cut costs

Our favorite catalog for photo albums is Exposures (800) 222-4947 (exposuresonline.com). They features albums, frames and accessories . . . and many are perfect for wedding photos. An example: the "Our Wedding album" in black leather holds 50 pages and runs $59.

Most Exposure albums use album pages made from archival quality Mylar that does not contain chemicals that damage pictures. Other albums are scrapbook-style, where you use old-fashioned photo corners to mount pictures to the acid-free pages, separated by protective tissue.

Other scrapbook albums from Exposures cost $50 to $90, not cheap but still much less expensive than albums from professional photography studios. You can also add in invitations, newspaper clippings and other mementos from your wedding. Frames and other accessories are equally intriguing—great gifts for bridesmaids, friends and other relatives.

Of course, there are more options out there for photo albums than just Exposures. Our readers recommend Albums and Frames (albumsandframes.com) for their professional-quality albums at affordable prices. Sample price: a 12-page "Renaissance Removable" 10x10 album is just $124, with other sizes available. If you want something fancier, check out the "Renaissance Library Bound" albums that start at $295. These prices are HALF what professional studios charge!

7 Consolidate your orders to take advantage of quantity discounts. Okay, you've decided which pictures you want but hold it! Now your parents want a few extra prints. And Aunt Bea wants an 8x10 of you and your spouse exchanging vows. By consolidating several small orders into one large one, you may be able to take advantage of quantity discounts offered by your photographer. Also, you'll be able to avoid the service charges some photographers slap on orders after the bride and groom's album is delivered. One photographer we interviewed charges an extra 20% service fee on such reorders. In addition, we found several photographers who offer discounts if you turn in your order within a certain number of days after the wedding. Read the fine print.

8 Buy the proofs at a discount. What do photographers do with all those nice 5x5 proofs of your wedding? Apparently, not much. That's why you can sometimes negotiate to buy ALL the proofs for one low price. One bride in Atlanta bought 100 proofs for just $350. She then used them to fill in spots in her albums and as gifts for friends.

9 Delay your purchase. Photographers will apply big pressure to purchase lots of prints NOW! Yet, if cash is tight, we say wait. Many photographers will keep negatives and digital files on hand from your wedding for a specified period of time (sometimes a year or more—be sure to confirm the exact details). You can buy your wedding prints when YOU (and your bank account) are ready. One bonus to this tip: after a few months, you might realize you don't really need all those extra shots of your bridesmaids whooping it up at the reception. Hence, you might order less than you would right after the wedding.

10 "You get the film" packages. You just pay for the photographer's time; at the end of the evening, you get the film (or digital storage card) and handle the developing yourself. Obviously, these packages can be big money-savers—even if you pay a photographer $100 to $200 per hour for their time, the result is much less than what complete album packages run. But . . . there are some pitfalls to this strategy, which we'll discuss later in this book.

11 Hire a student. Call a local photography institute or college to see if they can recommend a student or recent graduate. Most will photograph your wedding at rates far below those of so-called "professionals." One reader said she hired a recent grad from a local photography school and saved $1000 over the going rate for wedding pictures in her city.

To help you with this tip, we've posted a list of photography schools (and web site links) on our site BridalBargainsBook.com (click on "Bonus

Material.") Also: check local community colleges, as they may have a photography curriculum. Email or call the folks in charge of the photography program and tell them you are looking for a student to photograph your wedding. Some schools may be able to forward your email to interested students; other schools may ask you to post a flyer with the details.

Try to find a student who is at least in his or her second year (sophomore or later). Just like any other photographer, ask to see their portfolio. They may not have a sample wedding album, so ask to see other portraits and candids. Insist on a written agreement that covers all the basics outlined earlier in this chapter.

The Great Before or After Controversy

Ever attended a wedding where it seemed like the bride and groom took forever to make it to the reception? Where were they? Was their limo hijacked by an alien life force? More than likely the bride and groom were hijacked by a wedding photographer who took an amount of time equivalent to the Creation of Heaven and Earth to do the after-ceremony pictures.

So what exactly are the after-ceremony pictures? Basically, these are pictures of the bride and groom with the officiant at the altar, with the bridesmaids, with the groomsmen, with the whole bridal party, with their various relatives, etc. Also, since some churches restrict photography during the actual ceremony, several events from the ceremony (exchanging rings, lighting of the unity candle, the kiss, etc.) may be re-staged for posterity. All told, we are talking quite a few pictures here.

Photographers often mislead couples about how long this process takes. Sometimes photographers sound like a cartoonish version of Name that Tune. (Yes, Bob, I can take those after-ceremony pictures in 20 minutes. Well, Bob, I can do those same pictures in 15 minutes.) In reality, we have known several couples that took one to two *hours* to make it to their reception thanks to the after-ceremony photo session.

Of course, some bright person recently came up with a solution to this problem. Hey, why not do all those pictures before the ceremony? The only problem: this would require the bride and groom to see each other before the ceremony on the wedding day. OH NO! How can you break such a sacred superstition? they screeched.

Well, lets take a closer look at the prohibition of seeing each other before the ceremony. As far as we know, this started back in the year 1008 A.D. when all marriages were arranged and couples didn't see each other until the wedding day. Keeping them separate was intended to prevent Thor the Viking (the groom) from running away in case Freya the Bride was not the beautiful Viking goddess he was promised. Or vice versa.

72 **Hire a newspaper photographer.** Call your local newspaper to find a photographer who might be able to moonlight at your wedding. Why is this a money saving tip? Such photographers are very experienced but aren't interested in selling you a fancy album or expensive reprints. Instead, you just get the pictures (probably digital files) and you go from there. The cost? We'd estimate this would be $500 to $1200, depending on the city and the photographer. Yes, more expensive than a student, but you'd getting a more experienced photographer in the bargain. The downside? Most newspaper photographers aren't experienced in doing formal posted portraits, so you'd have to willing to

Today, brides and grooms not only know each other before the wedding, they also probably share the same tube of toothpaste. It seems a little silly that you wouldn't see your fiancéé the day of the wedding when you were just sharing the same pint of Ben & Jerry's 24 hours earlier.

Furthermore, brides today are taught to believe that the groom stands at the end of the aisle and looks down toward his beautiful bride, all the while thinking, "Wow! Isn't she beautiful? Aren't I lucky?" In reality, most grooms are thinking, "Thank God she's here. Now we can get this over with."

We're not trying to take away from this special moment, but there are several advantages to doing the after-ceremony pictures before the wedding (i.e., seeing each other before the ceremony):

♥ **Everything is perfect:** Hair and makeup are fresh prior to the ceremony and hence those important pictures will capture you at your best. After the ceremony, all the hugging and crying can alter that perfect face, hairdo, etc.

♥ **You can leave immediately after the ceremony for the reception:** You will have more time seeing relatives and enjoying the party you spent so much effort (and money) planning.

Here's our recommendation: Get to the ceremony site two hours before the wedding. After everyone is dressed, clear out the church with just the groom at the head of the aisle. Then, with appropriate music playing, the bride emerges and walks down the aisle. After this initial meeting, all the formal group pictures are taken before the guests arrive.

Or here's another variation: in a private room at the ceremony site, have the bride and groom meet prior to the ceremony. Here, you and your fiancéé can exchange gifts, marvel at each other's dapper appearance, gaze at the gown, etc. What's especially nice about this approach is that you actually get 15 minutes alone, just you and your fiancéé. For the rest of the day, you'll be surrounded by friends, relatives, and that ever-present photographer. On a day that's supposed to celebrate your relationship, it is ironic that most brides and grooms have their first private moment in the car leaving the reception—after the whole shebang is over.

have more of a photojournalistic spin to your photos.

13 Create your own digital album. Like the look of digital albums . . but not the price? Yes, this is a hot trend—but in some cities, the only photographers offering digital albums also happen to be the most expensive shooters. Our suggestion: do it yourself. The web site MyPublisher.com lets you create a digital album on the cheap, using software you download from their site. Albums run $30 to $40, depending on whether you want a linen or leather cover. There's even an iPhoto plug in for Mac users.

Destination Wedding Tips

Booking photography for a destination wedding is much like that of a regular wedding—with a few twists. First, we've noticed photographers who work in places like Hawaii, the Caribbean or Mexico are not likely to have the latest bells and whistles. Example: your wedding will most likely be shot on film, not digital. If possible, see if you can get the film for processing at home. If you want a digital album, consider the do-it-yourself tip earlier in this chapter (you scan the photos, upload them to a digital album web site like MyPublisher.com, design the album, etc.).

But the basic advice remains the same: meet the actual photographer who will be shooting your wedding, get his or her name in a contract and be sure to pick a package with adequate coverage. For a destination wedding, there is typically an on-site bridal portrait and other photos. You'll need to budget the time to take all these photos—which can be significant, time-wise!

Biggest Myths About Photography

Myth #1 *A photographer I visited told me he has won several awards for his portraits. Should I be impressed?*

Not necessarily. To understand why, lets look at how photographers win these contests. According to an article in a professional photography magazine, some photographers hire models to pose for these portraits and then take hundreds of exposures to get just the right pose. Then, an army of professional retouching and PhotoShop artists "enhances" the image into an award-winner. The final work presented before the judging panel bares little resemblance to the original print or negative, the article stated, adding that many award-winning photographers create exceptional prints specifically for competitions, while exerting little effort toward producing the same caliber of images for customers. That's why you need to see examples of actual wedding albums, not just the glossy prints produced to win competitions.

MYTH #2 *I always see those photography specials advertised by big department stores. You know, the ones for $19.95 that include several dozen prints. Shouldn't wedding photographers be similar in price?*

Sorry to say, but no. Stores that set up these portrait specials hire an amateur to shoot 35mm or digital pictures in a high-volume operation. Unfortunately, professional wedding photography ain't cheap. The time involved in shooting a wedding is one big factor. Weddings take hours of time, shooting on location with expensive professional equipment.

MYTH #3 *The best bridal portraits are those that are mounted on canvas.*

Yes and no. Studios like to pitch canvas-mounted portraits as top-of-the-line, but there is a catch. In fact, a bride in Alexandria, Virginia alerted us to this rip-off. She spoke with a professor of photography who does *not* recommend canvas-mounted portraits for a couple of reasons. First, in order to be mounted on the canvas, the print must be

Should you feed the photographer?

A bride emailed us this question the other day: should she provide a meal for the photographer? She asked because the photographer had not only required a meal in his contact, but requested a meal for his assistant as well. While that written demand is rather unusual, many brides and grooms wonder if they should feed the vendors at their wedding. We've seen this argued both ways. On one hand, you could argue that your boss doesn't pay for your lunch, so why should you do the same for a photographer? The other side is obvious—a well-fed vendor probably works better than a starving vendor. Photographers often work non-stop, five to eight-hour days for most of their weddings and may find it difficult to fit in a meal. Of course, if you do decide to feed the photographer, that does NOT mean you have to feed them the $75 per plate filet mignon dinner the guests are getting. First, ask your caterer if they would help—perhaps there would be no charge if the photographer (and vidoegrapher and DJ or band) eats after all the guests since the leftovers might be tossed anyway. There is always extra food at most buffets. Or perhaps the caterer can do a half-price vendor meal. Or the caterer whips up some sandwiches or alternative fare that doesn't cost $75 per person. That way you can make everyone happy—the vendors get fed and you don't get stuck with the bill.

peeled. As a result, the portrait may crack and reveal the canvas beneath. Second, canvas-mounted portraits must be oiled periodically to preserve the print. And guess who pockets these hefty re-oiling fees? You guessed it, the photographer. All in all, the extra expense of canvas may not be worth the hassle.

Helpful Hints

1 Photographers pricing methods may be as easy to understand as the federal income tax code. We are not quite sure why this is. One possible explanation is that photographers want to give you maximum flexibility in choosing prints, albums and portraits. The only problem is that every photographer approaches pricing with a different philosophy that ends up confusing you, the consumer.

Another, more Machiavellian explanation is that photographers want to make comparison-shopping more difficult. The lack of a pricing standard makes it very difficult to compare apples to apples. Instead you have one photographer who offers a complete package with an album of 50 8x10s for $1800 and another has an a la carte system. The only way for you to make sense of this is to try to equalize the prices, in the same way the grocery stores often display the price per ounce of certain products. We do this by asking ourselves "how much does the photographer charge for a four-hour package with 50 5x5s and 20 8x10s in an Art Leather album?" This package provides adequate coverage for most weddings. You may have to take a photographer's package and add a few prints (from an a la carte pricing list) to come up with that above example.

2 Watch out for personality clashes. One common problem: photographers and videographers who step on each other's toes. Since both are trying to document the wedding, there can be conflicts. One such clash occurred at a wedding in Wisconsin, where a photogra-

The Package Game: Are you bronze, silver or gold?

Those cutesy names used by photographers to describe their packages aren't by accident. Many studios cleverly use psychological tactics to get couples to spend more. For example, some photographers use precious metals for package names: from bronze (the least expensive) to gold (top of the line). But what bride and groom just wants "bronze" wedding pics? Isn't daddy's little girl worth at least silver or gold?

Our advice: don't get caught up in all the clever marketing. Just pick a package that meets your needs and forget what the photographer calls it!

pher ordered a video company NOT to shoot any of the formal picture sessions. He claimed the formal poses of the bride and groom were his protected copyright images. Of course, that's nonsense. But . . . you may want to play it safe and tell the photographer you plan to have a videographer at your wedding—and find out how they can both work together without grabbing for each others throats.

3 Consider going with a woman-owned photography studio. Yes, men have dominated the profession of wedding photography for years. The only women at studios were secretaries or the wives of photographers who came along as assistants. Fortunately, today more and more women are actually behind the camera. While they may be harder to find, we suggest giving women photographers a look-see. Yes, we realize good wedding photography isn't dependent on the gender of the photographer . . . but we can't help but notice how many woman photographers seem better at capturing the emotional aspect of weddings on film. Perhaps this is because sometimes the guys are caught up in the technical end of photography, missing some of the emotion while focusing on f-stops. We know that might be an over-generalization, but don't overlook women photographers just because they are outnumbered 10 to 1 at local bridal shows.

4 Have a photographer wrangler. Designate a friend to round up the photographer, helping him or her find a wayward relative. Give this person your must-shoot and shoot-only-in-moderation lists. You enjoy your wedding, while your friend makes sure the photographer gets his job done.

Pitfalls to Avoid

PITFALL #1 BAIT AND SWITCH AT LARGE PHOTOGRAPHY STUDIOS AND CELEBRITY PHOTOGRAPHERS.

My friend who recently got married contracted with a well-known, large studio to do her wedding. Everyone was shocked when the photographer arrived—the studio had sent out a person who had never shot a wedding before! The pictures were a disaster! How can I prevent this from happening to me?

Bait and switch is probably the biggest consumer complaint with wedding photographers. Unfortunately, some large studios bait engaged couples with a great reputation only to switch them by delivering less-than-great wedding photography. How does this happen? Basically, some studios farm out their weddings to poorly trained associates or (even worse) stringers. Stringers are free-lance photographers who are often amateurs working on the weekend for a few extra bucks.

The work of these photographers can be far inferior to professional wedding photographers.

A famous photographer in our town has taken many pictures of celebrities. Since the studio also does weddings, I assume my fiancéé and I will get the same high quality photography.

Don't bet on it. Here's how it works in this case: every city in the U.S. probably has at least one celebrity photographer who attracts engaged couples to her studio based on her famous name. But *who* would actually shoot your wedding? Instead of the famous photographer, weddings are often assigned to a no-name associate or a stringer. Hence, couples are baited into the studio by the famous photographer and then switched to a less-famous associate. While an associate may do good work, this is obviously deceptive since couples are duped into paying a hefty premium for celebrity photography.

Solution: You can prevent these problems by doing one simple thing: make sure the name of the actual photographer who will shoot your wedding is specified in writing in the contract. Most importantly, *before* you sign the contract, meet with the actual photographer who will do your wedding and view several albums of his or her work. Don't let the studio show you a few slick sample albums and feed you the line "all our associates are trained in the same great style." Remember your wedding pictures are dependent on who is behind that camera, not a fancy name that's embossed in gold on the studio's stationery.

PITFALL #2 HIDDEN CHARGES.

I really liked my wedding photographer. Yet, when the final bill came in, we were charged an extra $200 for travel time at $3 a mile! When we protested this fee, the photographer pointed to the fine print in his price list. And if we didn't pay the extra $200, he said he wouldn't give us our pictures!

Beware of fine print or hidden charges for travel time, over-time, special handling and other services. Sometimes, these fees are mentioned only in fine print on the price list, not your contract. One photographer charged an out-of-town bride a $500 penalty fee when she returned her proof book three days late, thanks to a delay at the post office.

This is why we recommend taking the photographer's contract home first and reading it thoroughly before signing. As we mentioned earlier in the catering chapter, you can request a change in the wording of any clause that makes you uncomfortable. Be wary of any requirements that may be unreasonable and ask for an adjustment to fit your needs.

PITFALL #3 SMALL PACKAGES AND HEAVY SALES PRESSURE.
I contracted with a photographer for one of his small wedding packages that had 20 8x10s in an album. After the wedding, the studio tried to pressure me into buying more prints than the original package—at those high reprint prices! My only problem—I never realized how many more pictures I would want for my album! Help!

Ah, this is a common deceptive practice. Here, the studio attracts wedding business with low package prices like "Just $795 for complete coverage and an album with 20 8x10s!" Sound like a great deal? No, it isn't. That's because most weddings generate dozens of great pictures—photographers often snap 40 to 50 pictures before the ceremony even begins!

The result is that most albums need at least 60 to 80 prints to adequately tell the story of an average wedding. Of course, photographers are well aware of this and realize couples will want to order many more pictures than those packages with just 20 prints. The result: the $800 package ends up costing $1200, $1500, or even $2000 by the time the total order is placed. We have talked to photographers who admit this deceptive practice is commonplace. Some studios even make matters worse by adding some heavy sales pressure after the wedding to increase the size of the order.

The most blatant example of this practice was one studio we visited that offered a package for $995 that included just 40 5x7s. The price list then went on to say that brides and grooms may purchase additional 5x7s or 8x10s to create a more complete story. Those additional prints cost $25 for a 5x7 and $45 for an 8x10. *Each.*

You can prevent this practice by selecting a package that offers the amount of coverage that will realistically tell the story of your wedding. For small weddings (under 100 guests with a short reception), this might be just 40 to 60 prints. Most will require 60 to 80 and some large weddings (with big bridal parties and long receptions) may require 100-plus prints.

In Milwaukee, a photographer was criminally charged with violating deceptive trade practice laws after several couples alleged he tried to pressure them to buy more wedding photos—if not, he refused to give them any pictures at all! The photographer's defense: he was an "artist" and the couples needed to buy "more pictures" ($1000 worth) because that was the only way to show their complete wedding story. While that guy was an obvious scam artist, it points up that even if you have a written contract for a reasonable number of pictures, you can still get heat from a photographer who thinks *his* artistry demands more of *your* money.

The bottom line: be prepared for at least some sales pressure when you select your wedding photos. But . . . don't get hooked by low-price packages that only give you a minuscule amount of actual pictures.

PITFALL #4 UNREASONABLE TIME LIMITS.

I recently attended a wedding where it seemed like the reception moved at the speed of light. Apparently, the photographer was in quite a hurry.

We can't tell you how many weddings we've seen where the reception looked like a sped-up film because the photographer's clock was ticking. After researching this book we now know why: photographers often sell packages with unreasonable time limits.

For example, we interviewed one photographer whose main package had only two and half hour's coverage. Since most photographers start their coverage one hour before the ceremony and because the ceremony itself can take up to one hour (including those pesky after-ceremony pictures), this would leave just 30 minutes to cover all the reception activities! No wonder the bride and groom seemed in a frantic rush to cut the cake, throw the bouquet, toss the garter, and so on! Instead of enjoying the reception, the couple was racing to get everything on film before the photographer's clock expired.

You can prevent this from happening to you by selecting a package with reasonable time limits, or better yet, no time limits at all. In the latter case, the photographer stays at the reception until both of you leave. However, some photographers argue their time is precious and want to impose some time limit. In that case, select a package with at least four hours coverage for an average wedding. You'll need more coverage (perhaps five or six hours) if you have a long ceremony or a large wedding party (all those pictures take more time).

Of course, it shouldn't come as a surprise to you that those same photographers who have those unreasonable time limits also offer overtime at a pricey charge per hour!

We should note that a close kin to this pitfall are photographers who limit the number of exposures they take at a wedding. Ask the photographer about any such limits before you sign a contract.

PITFALL #5 GREATEST HITS ALBUMS.

I visited a photographer who only showed me an album with pictures from several weddings in it. Shouldn't this person have shown me more work?

Yes. This problem is what we call the Greatest Hits Album. Even lousy photographers can occasionally take good pictures. In order to convince you of their excellence, these photographers compile all those greatest hits into one album. Obviously, you are only getting a tiny glimpse of their work.

When you visit a potential photographer, try to see as much work as possible. The best photographers should have *complete* albums that chronicle a single wedding from beginning to end. This allows you to see how the photographer will tell the story of your wedding. Another helpful album to look at is a proof book. Unedited and uncensored, proof books will let you see what the photographer can (and can't) do.

PITFALL #6 FRIENDS AND RELATIVES.

A friend of mine decided to let her uncle, who is a shutterbug, photograph her wedding. What a disaster! His flash didn't work for half the pictures and the other half weren't that exciting anyway.

As most brides and grooms realize, having friends and relatives do various part of your wedding can save you a tremendous amount of money. While you might have a talented aunt who can help alter your gown and a helpful friend who bakes great cakes, you may want to draw the line at the photographs.

Photography is typically high on everyone's priority list and its no wonder—the pictures are all you have left after the wedding. Investing the money in professional photography is a wise choice. Trying to save money by using an amateur is tempting but we say resist the urge—at least when it comes to your ceremony, the most important pictures of the day. Well-meaning friends and relatives who are amateur photographers often bite off more than they can chew when they shoot a wedding. Adverse lighting conditions and other technical challenges can vex even the most talented amateurs.

If you are on a tight budget and can't afford a professional photographer, consider some of the money-saving tips mentioned earlier. Specifically, hire a professional for the ceremony only and have friends and relatives cover the reception with their own cameras or single-use cameras you provide.

Also be aware that many photographers' contracts specify that they must be the only photographer at the ceremony or reception. They claim that friends who snap pictures of the bride and groom compete with their work and equipment (their flashes may prematurely set off the photographers' flash, for example). Ask your photographer about any such prohibitions.

PITFALL #7 YOU GET THE FILM PACKAGES.

I met a photographer at a bridal show who told me that he could save me money by giving me all the film after the wedding. Then I go and get the pictures developed. Is this a good deal? What's the catch?

The catch is that you have to develop the film, which in most cases is from a medium format camera and much more complicated that it sounds. Unlike 35mm film (which you drop off at Target and then a day later—POOF! you have pictures!), medium format negatives must be developed by professional labs. These labs produce negatives that must be cropped and masked to make final prints. We won't go into more detail on cropping and masking, but we can say that we did this for some publicity pictures and it was quite challenging.

The other main problem is dealing with the lab. As a consumer, you may not know the photo-speak that photographers use to communicate with the lab. For example, many labs offer two choices: less-expensive machine prints or custom prints, which include touch-ups and artwork. We found communicating with the lab that did our publicity pictures difficult. Furthermore, you have little leverage over the lab in case the developed pictures have quality problems, since you are a one-time customer.

Of course, these problems are lessened if your photographer shoots a "you get the film" package with a digital or 35 mm camera. Still, you don't want to trust your wedding pics to K-Mart, so you might end up at a professional lab anyway, insuring quality development.

PITFALL #8 HERE TODAY, GONE TOMORROW?

My friend took some pictures of our wedding with his digital camera. We printed these out on an ink-jet printer and they looked great—UNTIL they started to fade just six months later! What happened?"

Here's a nasty surprise for those who like to be on the cutting edge of technology—digital prints that are here today and gone tomorrow. Cheap ink-jet printers produce prints that will start to fade after just six

REAL WEDDING TIP

Spam! Spam! Spam!

Reader Pauline B. wrote to us with this warning about spam and wedding photographers:

"Last year I attended a friend's wedding in the Bay Area of California. The couple provided a web site where you could see and buy photos of the wedding. To access the photos, you had to provide an e-mail address. I provided a disposable address with the photographer's name in it, and guess what: after the wedding, I started to receive spam e-mail (having nothing to do with weddings) at this address. The photographer (or the picture web site) must have sold the guests' e-mail addresses to spammers within weeks of the wedding. Luckily I could disable this address so I wasn't bothered by more spam. I was annoyed, but if I were the bride I would be mortified if my guests' e-mail addresses were abused in this way"

months. After a year, the image might be gone. Contrast this to conventional wedding photographs, which can last a generation or more when printed on special archival paper.

Fortunately, ink-jet printer manufacturers are working on a solution to the disappearing ink. Both HP (hp.com) and Epson (epson.com) have been rushing to roll out printers with longer-lasting ink. The latest Epson models, for example, have ink that will last six to 26 years, depending on the paper used. The company is also targeting professional photographers with new large-format printers that produce prints that can last 100 years when printed on special paper.

Sure, you can always output a digital photo again if the first print starts to fade out . . . but that's a hassle. If you decide to have a friend take digital pics (or hire a professional photographer who shoots with a digital camera), a word to the wise: confirm the subsequent prints will be of "archival quality." Find out what type of printer will be used to output the pictures and go to that manufacturer's web site to confirm how long the images will last.

PITFALL #9 PADDING THE BILL BY SPLITTING GROUPS

Our photographer insisted on NOT taking any big group pictures; instead all the relatives were shot in small groups. Was this done to increase his total bill?"

Yes, it was, in our opinion. One photographer admitted as much in a trade newsletter for professional wedding photographers: "By shooting the family in group shots, you are eliminating the possibility of extra sales. Taking (separate) groupings of relatives will produce as many as six portraits sold rather than the usual single group picture. It is almost forcing the parents to buy all of them rather than just the big group."

The same photographer also advised his fellow shooters that "grandparents are the real money makers." He makes sure to include the grandparents in many shots, knowing this increases sales. "God willing, all the grandparents are alive and still married," said the photographer since this adds to the profit dollars.

Trends

♥ **ODD ANGLES, BLURRY SHOTS, OFF-CENTER COMPOSITIONS.** That's how the *Wall Street Journal* described the hip trend of photo-journalistic wedding photographers. And they're right: these aren't your mother's wedding pictures. From celebrity photographers in Beverly Hills to the average wedding shooter in Des Moines, what's in is offbeat pics. What's out? Stiff, formal posed photographs. Instead, couples opt to make fun of their professions (a county prosecutor bride and her highway patrolman groom posed in handcuffs) and generally go for a lighter touch.

♥ **Black and white photography:** Yes, its back. Some couples are rediscovering the contrast and beauty of black and white photography. We've seen several truly striking albums that mix black and white and color photography—à la *The Wizard of Oz.*

Special Touches to Make Your Photography Unique

1 **Add a memory page to your album.** This is a page at the front of the album with a copy of your invitation. We've seen couples add a few of the dried flowers from the bride's bouquet and some lace from the bridal gown to this page.

2 **Personalize your wedding photography.** Instead of an engagement portrait in a studio with a boring blue background, have the picture taken at a special location. Perhaps the place you first met or had your first date. Obviously, photographers will charge a little more to go on location, but it is a nice way to personalize the portrait.

3 **Chronicle your engagement with pictures.** With your own camera, document the wedding process (trying on gowns, tasting cakes, visiting various reception sites) from the proposal to the big day. Undoubtedly, you will receive a photography album as a gift, so here's a use for it. Add your honeymoon pictures in the back to complete the album.

Chapter 10

Cakes

It's the centerpiece of your reception—all eyes will be on your wedding cake. But how do you get one that tastes as good as it looks? We'll explore that issue, plus give you nine money-saving tips to cut your cake costs. And what about that mysterious white icing you see on so many cakes? We'll explain the secret ingredient that bakers use to make white icing white, plus three other pitfalls to avoid.

What Are You Buying?

Wedding cakes have come a long way over the years. Once a dry, white tasteless confection with globs of sugary icing, wedding cakes have morphed into gourmet desserts that are truly "to die for." Across the country, we have found a dazzling array of gourmet flavors and high-style designs that turn the pedestrian wedding cake into a culinary work of art. No matter how fancy the design, however, there are four basic elements to a wedding cake:

♥ **THE CAKE, ITSELF.** Traditionally, wedding cakes were vanilla-flavored confections. However, today anything goes. Gourmet cakes are the rage, with options like you'd see from a four-star restaurant or top pastry chef.

♥ **THE FILLING.** In addition to cake flavor possibilities, many bakers also offer a variety of fillings. Fillings used to be fruit jams or butter cream icing, but have expanded today to include liqueurs, fresh fruit, custards and mousses. The traditional wedding cake has two layers of cake with one layer of filling in each tier. Lately, we've seen more European torte-style cakes: confections with four or five layers of cake and filling. This torte-style cake tends to be richer than an American-style cake.

♥ **THE FROSTING AND DECORATIONS.** The options for wedding cake icing are numerous. Some bakers opt for the traditional butter cream icing (to which liqueurs are often added) while rolled fondant or marzipan is also popular. Whipped cream icings and meringue icings are yet more options. No longer are you limited to the typical white icing; many brides want their cakes tinted to match the bridal party colors or merely prefer the antique look of an off-white icing.

Wedding cake fads come and go like fashion. In the 1970's and 80's, hip brides had wedding cakes adorned with gurgling fountains and plastic tiers. The taste of the cake was secondary, if not ignored completely. In the 90's, simpler weddings ushered in the simpler wedding cake, more likely adorned with fresh flowers than plastic brides and grooms. In the last few years, cakes are changing again—this time to make a "personal" statement for the bride and groom. Bottom line: wedding cakes are expected to both look AND taste good today.

♥ **DELIVERY AND SET-UP.** Another element you are buying is the delivery and set-up of the cake. This means the actual engineering of the cake with its several layers, possible separations (or stacking if you prefer the tiers to sit one on top of the other) and decoration, if you want flowers and greenery. Rental items like the columns and plates for separating tiers are another cost. Some bakers have actually made a special stand for their cakes, which they rent to couples for the day.

Average total costs. What's our favorite scene from the Steve Martin remake of *Father of the Bride?* It has to be Steve Martin's shock at cake prices. After Martin Short's wedding consultant says that $1200 is a reasonable price "for a cake of this magnitude," Martin rejoins: "Franc, a cake is made of flour and water! My first car didn't cost $1200!" To which, Short replies: "Welcome to the 90's!"

Yes, they are just made of flour and water, but the average wedding cake still runs hundreds (if not thousands) of dollars. Cakes are typically priced per serving. We peg the average wedding cake at $525 for 175 guests—that's about $3 a slice. Prices are lowest in rural areas and the Mid-West. But, as Steve Martin learned, cake prices can be much higher. We noticed Palm Beach, Florida bakers expect $5 a serving for their creations, while some wedding cakes in Boston fetch $8 per guest. And New York? Fugetaboutit! A cake from renowned bakers like Gail Watson or Sylvia Weinstock *start* at $10 a slice and quickly go up from there.

The average deposit for a wedding cake can range from $50 to 50% of the total bill. The balance is due usually a week or so before the wedding.

Trends

What's new with wedding cakes? Here is a round up of the latest trends:

♥ **In a word: color.** Forget the white! From pale celadon to bold Tiffany blue to a scrumptious chocolate brown, color is the trend for wedding cakes. Even white frosted cakes are decorated with boldly colored fresh flowers or bright sugar accents.

♥ **Personalized.** Instead of the old-fashioned cake topper, Swarovski crystal encrusted monograms, sculptured glass or silver and gold metal designs are popular. Pictured at right is a topper from Toppers With Glitz (topperswithglitz.com).

♥ **Deconstruction.** Picture the standard wedding cake. Most folks would envision a stacked layer cake. Times have changed and cakes no longer are "constructed." In North Carolina, bakers put cakes on separate "floating" cake stands of varying heights.

♥ **"Mini-cakes."** When they first hit the scene a few years ago, we thought this was a "here and gone" fad. But we're still seeing mini cakes as an option to replace the traditional wedding cake. How does it work? Each guest gets an individual wedding cake instead of a slice of a larger cake. Since these are all the rage at celebrity weddings, you can be assured the price is high. In Boston, bakers sell elaborately decorated mini cakes for $10 a pop! In Manhattan, mini cakes can run $15 to $20 each. We don't quite see what all the fuss is about-isn't a mini-cake simply a cup cake by any other name?

Another take on this is small cakes placed as centerpieces at all the guest tables. This way, brides can decorate the table with dessert.

♥ **Dr. Suess.** Oh, the places cakes can go! Symmetrical cakes are out; asymmetrical is in. Bakers are now creating wacky "Dr. Suess" cakes with eccentric angles, lopsided corners and other Cat in the Hat-inspired images. If you don't want to go all out wacky, instead consider using different shapes for each tier.

♥ **Different flavors in different tiers.** If you can't decide between flavors, some bakers make it easy for you—they'll whip up a different flavor for each tier.

♥ **Ribbons.** Ribbons are the hot accent for wedding cakes today. Some are draped across the cake and gathered with real or sugar flowers; others are laid flat against the layers like satin ribbons or tied in bows to top the cake. Ribbon accents may be made of fondant, white chocolate or even real satin fabric.

♥ **Matching the invitation.** Use to be, wedding cakes were designed to match the bride's gown. But with the advent of funky, unique wedding invitations (even stalwart Crane is selling colored paper invites) we're seeing brides and bakers gravitate toward the invitation as inspiration. Some cakes now echo the invite's paper color, patterns or accents.

Sources to Find an Affordable Baker

There are three types of bakeries that do wedding cakes. Here's a breakdown:

1 **Cake factories/grocery stores.** Better know as commercial bakeries, these folks bake and deliver over ten cakes per Saturday. These businesses may be less personalized than the other two types of bakers. Grocery stores fall into this category, too.

2 **Reception sites and/or caterers.** Quality is sometimes great, sometimes not.

3 **Small bakers and pastry chefs**. These are the hardest to find, but often the best and most creative cake bakers. Some work out of their home; others are pastry chefs that might also have a small cafe business.

Here are our sources for finding great bakeries:

♥ **Florists.** Because they often work with bakers to help coordinate the floral decorations, florists may have great contacts.

♥ **Photographers.** Since they attend many receptions, photographers see the best and worst creations of local bakeries. They also often hear praise or criticism about cakes from guests.

♥ **Reception sites.** Besides helping set up the cake, as well as serving it, catering managers notice whether guests like the cake or not.

♥ **BRIDAL SHOWS.** Most bakeries offer samples of their cakes at bridal shows, so here's a great opportunity to taste without any pressure to buy.

Brides in Cyberspace: What's on the Web?

♥ You gotta love the web. Where else can you find a home page for the **INTERNATIONAL CAKE EXPLORATION SOCIETÉ** (ices.org), an association of cake bakers? Check their links section to find local chapters and bakers' home pages. Also click on the newsletter link, which features pictures of creative cake designs (see Figure 1 below).

♥ **SUGARCRAFT.COM** has just about every supply for the do-it-yourselfer, including edible flowers made of gum paste or royal icing. "The prices are great," says a reader who emailed this tip.

♥ **WILTON** (wilton.com) is the undisputed leader in cake decorating supplies. Their crisply designed web site is fun to visit, complete with an online store and a "recipes and ideas" section. The latter featured a half dozen wedding cakes, complete with instructions, needed supplies and a picture of the final product.

FIGURE 1: The International Cake Exploration Societé has a great web site (www.ices.org) with all sorts of wedding cake pictures.

♥ The web is also a great place to find small artisans that make cake toppers. If you don't like the sometimes cheesy wedding cake toppers you see in discount stores, check out **Portraits in Clay**, created by Burlington Vermont artist Adele Dienno (portraitsinclay.com). This company creates "fine heirloom sculptures" that are individually designed and fabricated in porcelain. Okay, this isn't cheap at $400 and up but it *is* unique. And a keepsake you can hand down in the family.

Another unique cake top designer was recommended by a reader: **Designs by Dorian** (designsbydorian). They offer handcrafted "fantasy" cake tops with spun glass or hand blown glass figures, porcelain dolls, sea shells, coral, miniature lights and much more. Many of the design are in the "awww . .how cute" vein, but if you've got a favorite animal (a pair of pandas, anyone?) this is the designer for you. Prices range from $65 to $245. Each design does take about eight weeks to make plus shipping so plan ahead.

♥ **What is the best bakery in your town?** Ask other brides in your area this question by surfing our ad-free message boards at BridalBargainsBook.com (click on message boards and then local). Compare notes, ask questions and query other readers about their cake shopping.

Getting Started: How Far in Advance?

Because bakeries can make more than one cake on a Saturday, brides may only need two to four months to plan. With some of the large commercial bakeries, you may even need less time (as little as a week's notice). Popular bakeries and popular dates may require more advance planning (between three and six months) and you may want to do this part early anyway to get it out of the way.

Step-by-step Shopping Strategies

♥ **Step 1:** Before visiting a baker, you will need to have an estimate of the number of guests invited. Final exact numbers won't be required until a week or two before the wedding date; this will allow you to get a basic price for a cake. Also, knowing your wedding colors will help guide the baker. How formal is the wedding? This will also influence the cake design.

♥ **Step 2:** Given the resources above, identify two to three bakers who have skill levels and style ideas to fit your needs. Make an appointment with them and ask if you can have a taste test. Time the appointment to make it easier for the baker to give you a sample (like Friday while they are decorating cakes for Saturday weddings).

♥ **Step 3:** At the baker's shop, be sure to look at *real* photos of their past cake designs. Some bakeries use standard cake-design books and tell brides they can make anything from these publications. Be skeptical. It is preferable to see actual photos of what they can do!

♥ **Step 4:** Given the size of your reception, ask the baker for a proposal or estimate of the cost of a cake based on one or two of their styles. Also ask for suggestions on how much cake to buy. The amount of cake to order will depend on several factors: if you will be having a groom's cake or sweets table; how much other food you will be serving (sit-down dinner vs. hors d'oeuvres); the time of day; and the size of the slices (paper thin up to birthday cake size). Some bakers think a wedding cake slice should be four inches wide; others think just two inches.

♥ **Step 5:** Make sure you taste a sample of their cake. There is no substitute for having actually tasted it before buying. If a baker doesn't offer taste tests, you should be very cautious. You may have to buy a small six-inch cake from the baker in order to get a taste, but we prefer bakeries that offer free samples—these are usually the best.

♥ **Step 6:** Choose the baker and ask for a signed proposal detailing the design, flavors of both cake and filling, any rentals (like columns or stands), delivery and set-up fees, and deposit information. Don't forget to have the date, place and delivery time clearly written on the proposal. If you are planning far in advance, you may have to adjust the number of servings you will need—find out the last possible moment when you can change numbers.

♥ **Step 7:** Confirm any last-minute details and pay the balance on the cake a week or two before the wedding.

Questions to Ask a Baker

1 **Do you have any photos of previous designs?** The idea is to see the bakery's actual work, not to look through generic picture books with designs they may never have created.

2 **Can we have a taste test?** You may have to wait for a day when they are making cakes, but the best bakeries will offer free taste tests.

3 **Are there any extra charges?** Some bakeries prefer to break down the charges for almost everything. These items may include:

fillings, complex decorations, silk or fresh flowers, delivery, set-up, cake plates and columns, and more. Find out exactly what these items will cost and get a written proposal.

4 Who will decorate the cake with fresh or silk flowers? If you prefer this type of decoration, find out how the flowers will be provided and who will decorate the cake. Some bakers can purchase the flowers and decorate it themselves. Others will get the flowers from your florist. In some cases, the florist is totally in charge. (Another tip for flowers intended for cake decoration: make sure you pick blooms that have not been sprayed with pesticides or preservatives).

5 How far in advance is the cake prepared? This may be a delicate question to ask, but you will want to know how fresh the cake is that you are buying. Almost all bakers must bake the cake a few days prior to the wedding, and then freeze it before applying the decoration. Of course, no one wants to have a cake that has been frozen for more than a week. Unfortunately, some high-volume bakeries may do just that.

Top Money-saving Secrets

1 Do the cake "switcheroo." Here's a clever way to cut costs. Instead of buying a huge wedding cake to feed your guests, get a small cake for photos. After the pictures, wheel that cake out of view... and have the caterer cut up sheet cakes in the kitchen. Out come slices of cake for the guests, who probably won't know the difference (a slice of cake looks like a slice of cake, right?). But you'll notice the difference in your wallet. Sheet cakes cost 75% less than wedding cakes (as little as 50¢¢ a serving). Why? Much of a wedding cake's cost is the labor to decorate it, which sheet cakes omit. This trick gets you the best of both worlds—a nice wedding cake for photos and the ceremonial cake cutting, while giving your guests some cake as dessert at a price that doesn't break the bank. Another twist to this tip: fake the cake. You can buy fake wedding cakes (decorated to look like a real cake) from a site like DesignerdDsplayCakes.com—most run $200 to $250. Put the fake cake on display and serve guests from economical sheet cakes. Then sell the fake cake on ebay or Craigslist after the wedding!

2 Pass on your caterer's cake offer. Many banquet halls, hotels and caterers will suggest you buy a wedding cake from them. Do they bake the cakes? Nope, they go to an outside bakery and order one of their cakes—and then mark it up to sell to you! Avoid the cake markup and contract directly with a baker. One caveat: some sites won't let you bring in an outside cake, so check first. Others slap brides with a "cake cutting fee" ($1 to $2 per guest) to discourage the use of outside bakers. We discuss this rip-off in our catering chapter; try to negotiate away this fee.

3 **Go simple and decorate with flowers.** All those fancy cake decorations (from gum paste flowers to fondant icing) cost a fortune. A better money-saving strategy is to get a plain, basic cake and decorate it with flowers. Blooms are more cost-effective than a baker slaving away for hours to create an icing masterpiece. Use the bridesmaids' bouquets to decorate the cake's base. And use our flowers-at-wholesale from the 'net tip from Chapter 5 to buy roses on the cheap to complete the look. You'll save 25% to 40% by going plain and dressing it up with flowers. And the cake will look just as beautiful for photos.

4 **Order less cake than the number of people.** If you have a sweets table or groom's cake, consider fewer servings. Also if you will be eating a heavy sit-down meal or have a crowd that doesn't eat a lot of sweets, consider cutting back.

5 **Choose an independent or out-of-home baker.** This could mean as much as $1 to $2 difference in cost per serving. Out-of-home or small bakeries often have lower overhead, which they pass on to brides. Caution: Local health laws may prohibit bakers from operating out of their home. Each city is different, so you may want to check with your local health department.

6 **Skip the anniversary cake top** (see pitfalls later in this chapter for more details).

7 **Roll the sides in nuts.** One bride emailed us an interesting idea—she found a wedding cake from her favorite bakery was $4.50 a slice. But . . . if she opted for a cake with sides rolled in nuts, the price was $1.50! So, she saved $3 per guest by going with that option! The complete story is in the Real Wedding Tip on the next page.

8 **Hire the teacher.** A bride in Iowa phoned in this tip. She called a local crafts store to see if they had cake-decorating classes. They did—and she hired the teacher to do her wedding cake. She estimated she saved about 30% off what a commercial bakery would have charged her for a similar cake.

9 **Consider offbeat places for cakes.** For example, Wal-Mart isn't exactly the first place brides think to look for wedding cakes. But one reader found the discounter to be a great deal: "My wedding cake was just $110! That's right—$110 for a 3-tier cake that feeds about 100

Real Wedding Tip

That's nuts!

Here's one way to save money with wedding cakes, from a reader in San Francisco:

"Since I have a favorite bakery that sells reasonably priced cakes, I assumed their wedding cakes would be too. Wrong! They were $4.50 a slice! Eek! But when I tried to cut costs, it was difficult. I made it clear that they didn't need to make frosting ribbons and roses, didn't need to have a balancing act with stacked tiers on little pillars, etc. But that made no difference in price. Why? Because, they explained, the majority of the labor to make a wedding cake is in getting the frosting smooth on the sides of the cake. Their wedding cakes are frosted, frozen, re-frosted to smooth, re-frozen, and so on. And the labor is most of the cost. So, we ended up buying our cakes with the sides rolled in nuts for $1.50 a slice. That way they don't have to have smoothly frosted sides, we don't have frostbitten cake, and we save a bundle! I just hope none of our guests have severe nut allergies . . ."

people! The new Wal-Mart Superstore in my town has everything including a bakery. The wedding cakes are beautiful and very affordable."

10 **Cut the groom's cake.** Instead, have a chocolate wedding cake. This eliminated the expense of a separate cake, yet gives your guests that chocolate fix.

11 **Deconstruct the cake.** A wedding cake is just several white cakes stacked together. But who says they have to be stacked? Katie, a reader in the San Francisco Bay Area, found she could save 50% off the price of a "wedding cake" by ordering three separate cakes (frosted white, of course) and displaying them on tiered cake stands. Where did she find the stands? eBay. And after the wedding, she sold the stands on eBay to another couple, recouping her $100 investment. Katie's total savings by using this trick: $200. Now that's clever!

72 **Buy it wholesale.** Can you buy a wedding cake at wholesale? Sure! Just look in your phone book to find Bakeries—Wholesale and give these listings a ring. An example: Food Attitude (800-427-5370) is a wholesale baker in Washington DC and New York City that supplies those cities top gourmet shops and hotels with wedding cakes. But shhhh! You can buy the same cakes direct from them at half the retail price (you pay $5 to $7 per slice). Their web site (weddingcakeonline.com) features over two-dozen cake styles and ten flavors, with detailed info on how to taste free samples and order.

Biggest Myth of Wedding Cakes

Myth #1 *"At every wedding I've ever been to, the wedding cake was tasteless and dry. It's impossible to find a good-tasting cake."*

Wrong. This fallacy is based on all those tasteless white cakes with Crisco-based icings that wedding guests remember from years past. Today brides and grooms can have a cake that tastes as good as it looks.

Pitfalls to Avoid

Pitfall #1: The Revenge of Martha: Cakes that taste like sand paper! And cost thousands!

"I fell in love with a cake design from Martha Stewart's magazine that featured rolled fondant icing. My baker warned me the cake would taste terrible! Not to mention cost 30% more. What's up?"

Martha sure makes pretty cakes, but look out—her current fave (cake with rolled fondant icing) has some major drawbacks the diva of domesticity forgets to mention.

First problem, taste. Yes, fondant iced cakes have an ultra-hip smooth finish but don't ask how it tastes (some folks think fondant tastes too sweet or is like eating gum paste; some claim it's much better than it used to be). To understand why fondant lacks in the taste department, consider how it is made. Developed by British and Australian pastry chefs as a replacement for rock-hard royal icing, fondant is a mixture of sugar, gelatin and corn syrup. The result is a dough-like pastry. All the labor that goes into making and rolling out fondant onto cakes (not to mention hand-tinting) means higher prices—most bakers charge at least $1 to $2 *extra* per serving for fondant cakes. That's a 30% hike over average prices.

If you have your heart set on the fondant look, consider a couple of tips. Ask your baker to add a layer of butter cream frosting under the fondant to add flavor (guests can knock off the fondant icing and still have cake and icing below). Also, consider fondant look-alikes. One Texas baker we interviewed mixes butter cream and cream cheese to give a fondant look with better taste.

PITFALL #2 ANNIVERSARY CAKE TOPS

"The baker I visited told me that 'of course you will want to save the top tier of the cake for your first anniversary.' This sounds like a silly tradition!"

Yes, we agree. Saving the top of the wedding cake to eat on your first anniversary is a common tradition in many areas of the country. This entails having mom or someone else remember to take the top home, wrap it very carefully, and put it in your freezer. Even supposing you have room in your freezer, the taste of the cake after 12 months may leave much to be desired. In fact, if you serve the cake at your wedding instead, you may be able to save 10% to 20% off your bakery bill—a much better deal than a stale year-old cake! If you want to follow this tradition, we recommend calling up your baker in a year and buying a small, freshly made cake to celebrate with on your first anniversary.

PITFALL #3 MYSTERIOUS WHITE ICING.

"We attended a wedding last weekend that had a beautiful wedding cake. But, when we tasted the cake, there was this terrible, greasy aftertaste. Yuck! What causes this problem?"

The answer lies in what makes white icing *white*. Well, a key ingredient in icing is butter—which creates a problem for bakers. Most butter made in the US is yellow, which gives icing an off-white or ivory color. To

Disappearing Deposits

Reader Julie H. e-mailed us this interesting story about a disappearing deposit—a good lesson for all brides. *"Our baker charged us a $75 deposit for the Lucite tiers used with our wedding cake—he told us we had one month to return them or we'd lose the deposit. Well, after the wedding, we had our maid of honor drop them off since we'd be on our honeymoon. Unfortunately, she forgot about the deposit and didn't ask for any money back. The bakery also wouldn't give her a receipt. Well, you can guess what happened next—we got back, asked the bakery for the money and they claimed they gave it to the maid of honor. It took three visits to the bakery before the manager agreed to refund our money."*

get pure white icing, bakers must use expensive white butter (imported from Europe). Unfortunately, some bakers use a less expensive short cut to get white "butter cream" icing—they add white *shortening* like Crisco. Yuck! That's why some cake icing has a greasy aftertaste. If you want white icing, you might ask your baker how they make their icing white. For example, some bakeries offer a meringue icing (made from egg whites), while others do fondant, a paste of sugar, water and corn syrup that's rolled over the cake. Yet another trick: adding one drop of blue food coloring to the batch of icing, which turns off-white icing into a pure white hue. Each of these methods achieve a white look without the Crisco.

PITFALL #4 WELL-MEANING FRIENDS AND RELATIVES.
"My aunt has offered to bake my wedding cake. She's good at baking basic cakes but isn't a wedding cake much more complicated?"

REAL WEDDING TIP

Small versus large bakeries: an insider view

Recently, a bride who has worked in the bakery business wrote to us about our contention that "cake factories" (that is, large bakeries) don't make cake that tastes as good as a small bakeries. Her thoughts:

"Yes, many large bakeries do use mixes. Just like a cake mix that you would use at home. . . add water, oil, eggs, etc. Some bakeries have their own recipes converted into mixes. Although it is very cost effective, it's not something I personally approve of. I think that mixes often leave an aftertaste as opposed to a cake that is made from scratch.

But, your readers should be aware that cakes made from scratch are more expensive. So they should consider which is most important: flavor (better from small bakers) or design (often technically superior at large bakeries). These are the two trade-offs with wedding cakes.

Finally, advise your readers to beware when using home bakers. Although many do know what they're doing, the potential for disaster is high. Putting together a stacked/tiered wedding cake requires knowledge. Making a cake that is structurally sound is a bit more complicated than make a small birthday cake. I've heard so many horror stories about home bakers who offered to do wedding cakes because they thought they could handle it. The heartache may not be worth the savings."

That's right. Offers like this are made with the best possible intentions but, if accepted, can be disastrous. Baking a wedding cake is far more complex than baking a birthday cake from a Betty Crocker box mix. You need engineering skills required to stack a cake and keep it from falling or leaning. Unless you have a friend or relative who is a professional baker or pastry chef, politely refuse their offer. Consider telling them you've already contracted with a baker to make your cake if you don't want to offend them.

PITFALL #5 EARLY DELIVERY AND COLLAPSING CAKES.
"My baker delivered my cake nearly five hours before my reception. In the interim, someone or something knocked the cake over and destroyed it! How could I have prevented this?"

This is a problem that often occurs when large bakeries deliver many wedding cakes on a single Saturday. The cake is dropped off (and set-up) hours before the reception and left unattended. As you can guess, Murphy's Law says that an unattended wedding cake is a collapsed wedding cake. No one at the reception site may admit to knocking it over but you can imagine how "things happen" during a wedding reception set-up. Prevent this problem by insisting the baker deliver the cake within two hours prior to the reception. You may want to coordinate with the catering staff to limit any scheduling snafus. Be sure someone (the catering manager, a maitre d', etc.) is there when the cake is delivered so they can keep an eye on it.

Unique Ideas

1 Ethnic Traditions. Many couples incorporate ethnic traditions into their wedding cake. For example, traditional French wedding cakes are actually cone-shaped confections made of cream-filled puffed pastry stuck together with caramelized sugar. Guests serve themselves by merely grabbing a cream puff from the cone!

2 Cheesecake. You gotta love this idea: cheesecake wedding cakes. Available in many different flavors, cheesecakes can be frosted with cream cheese icing (to look more like a traditional wedding cake) or left plain and decorated with fresh fruit or flowers. Yum!

Chapter 11

Video

Lights! Camera! Money! Wedding DVDs and videos are big part of any wedding budget. In this chapter, we cut through the technical mumbo-jumbo to give you a practical guide to finding an affordable yet talented videographer.

What Are You Buying?

Basically, there are two things you are buying when you hire a videographer: the cameraperson's time, and the DVD /video itself.

♥ **THE CAMERAPERSON'S TIME.** Many videographers will charge you for their time first and foremost. Most offer packages with a time limit of three, four, or more hours. Overtime is charged on an hourly basis. Some videographers will charge a flat fee for the whole wedding and reception; others offer "multi-camera" shoots as an extra option.

Besides hiring a cameraperson for a certain amount of time, you are also buying his or her talent and personality. As with photographers, it is very important to find a videographer who is not only skilled at camera work but is also easy to work with. You will be working with him as much as with the photographer. And, of course, the videographer's investment in equipment is important too—we'll discuss this later.

♥ **THE FINAL PRODUCT.** The most important item you're buying is the video footage (whether put on DVD or VHS tape). There are several styles of wedding videography. Here's an overview:

Raw footage. This video simply starts at the beginning of your ceremony and runs, uninterrupted, to the end of your reception. There is no editing or post-production graphics. Raw footage videos are the least expensive option, typically offered by amateur videographers. Professionals more likely will offer one of the next two options.

Edited "in camera." This type of video also does not have post-editing or added graphics. However, the videographer edits your video "in-camera." This means the cameraperson shuts off the camera during any uninteresting moments or rewinds and copies over any unnecessary footage. If done by a professional, this option can work very well. It will usually be moderately priced in comparison with other types of video.

Post-edited. This category of wedding video is the most common—and the most expensive because the videographer spends the most time on it. Videographers "post-edit" footage after the wedding and reception (most of this is done by computer today). During this production, the videographer will take raw footage, cut out the boring parts (if there are any!), smooth the transitions, and add in titles and music. Some videographers add still photos (baby pictures, honeymoon photos) to give the tape a truly personal feel. If you have multi-camera coverage, post-editing blends the footage from several cameras to make for a more interesting DVD. Many videographers charge an additional hourly fee for post-editing, while others may have packages that include editing and special effects.

Highlights. In addition to videos that cover the entire wedding and reception, some videographers offer brief highlight DVD's that condense the day's events into a short montage that is 10 or 20 minutes long. Set to music and crisply edited, these videos are perfect when you don't want to torture your friends with the full-length version of your wedding video.

Copies. Most wedding video packages include one copy of the DVD or videotape. Extra copies often cost more; however some videographers have packages that include copies for parents.

Average total costs: The average wedding DVD/video costs about $1000, although prices are all over the board depending on what you get. In small towns, a one-camera, unedited video could cost as little as $500 to $750. The mid-range in most cities, $750 to $1500 will buy you a one or two camera shoot, some editing, music and a few copies. Want to go whole hog? You could pay $2000, $3000 or even $5000 for a complete "movie" of your wedding, shot with multi-camera coverage and heavily edited with added music, titles and other special effects. In general, more money buys you more camera coverage (two versus one camera) and extra frills like special effects, highlight montages and artsy editing.

In recent years, videographers have started to get creative with selling all sorts of add-ons, like a "love story" (a five to 20 minute video that reenacts how you met, the proposal, etc.). The extras can start at $800 and go up from there, depending on how elaborate the production. Another option: the "retrospective" which is a post-wedding video where the bride and groom reminisce about the day (see the Trends section later in this chapter).

Most videographers require a deposit for one-third to one-half of the contract amount to book a date. Some require another one-third payment on the day of the wedding with the balance due when the completed video is picked up.

We should note one troubling trend with videographers and deposits: increasingly, we see video companies demanding complete payment UP FRONT, weeks before the wedding. Obviously, we have a problem with that. When a videographer receives ALL their money before your wedding, there is no incentive for them to deliver the final product on time. We prefer a small balance that remains to be paid until the video is delivered—try to negotiate this point if a videographer demands total payment up front.

Sources to Find a Videographer

Wedding videography is a relative newcomer to the bridal market. Only in the 80's did the videotaping of weddings really take off. Despite its current popularity, finding a good videographer can still be a challenge. Here are some of the best sources:

♥ **Recently married couples.** These folks can give some of the best advice about videographers. Look at friends' videos to decide what styles, editing and extras you might want. Don't have any recently married friends? Ask other brides in your area for advice—log on to the local talk part of our message boards (BridalBargainsBook.com). Compare prices and get the buzz on the best video companies.

♥ **Professional associations.** The Wedding and Event Videographers Association International (WEVA; 800-501-WEVA; weva.com) has 5000 members, both domestic and international. (We do have some concerns about WEVA; see the following box for details). Another source: you can also check with national videographer franchises like Videomasters (800) 836-9461 or (716) 381-9240 (web: videomasters.net). With over 200 franchisees, Videomasters has been in business since 1978.

♥ **Television stations.** Many camerapersons at TV stations moonlight on weekends shooting weddings, using high-quality (broadcast) cameras. In Ft. Worth, Texas, for example, one of the most popular videographers for weddings is the chief videographer for the NBC affiliate. One tip we heard from a reader: when you call a TV station, bypass the receptionist and ask to speak directly to a cameraperson. Why? Some stations don't like their camera people moonlighting at weddings and instruct receptionists to tell callers that this service isn't available.

♥ **Wedding photographers.** This can be a good source. Photographers will be able to recommend good videographers they've seen at other weddings. Yes, some photographers and videographers have conflicts. You can avoid this by choosing two people who have worked together

The dark side of WEVA?

We have mixed feelings about recommending brides contact The Wedding and Event Videographers Association (WEVA) for referrals to local videographers. While WEVA has done a good job at helping educate videographers and improve the quality of wedding videos, some of the association's activities have been questionable if not outright anti-consumer.

First, WEVA holds numerous "town meetings" and even a national convention for videographers. One common theme at these get-togethers: videographers need to RAISE their prices. WEVA's thinking here is that the profession of wedding videography is sullied by amateurs who offer cheapo prices. The mantra of "raise your prices" is repeated again and again on WEVA's online message boards (which are hidden from view of brides).

Our take on this: while it is understandable that a trade association like WEVA wants to improve the professionalism of its industry, advocating such fee hikes smacks of price-fixing. The Federal Trade Commission has ruled that such collusion by trade associations runs afoul of anti-trust laws, so WEVA is skating on very thin ice.

Our second beef with WEVA: their web site offers a "Member Referral Service" that promises to pair you with a videographer, but has some hidden pitfalls for consumers. Brides and grooms are supposed to fill out an on-line form that asks for your name, email, wedding date, city and state. All that's fine, of course. But the problems begin when WEVA requests you list your ceremony and reception sites.

According to private emails posted on WEVA's industry-only message boards, videographers use this info to then "cherry-pick" customers. If you put down the fanciest church or the Four Seasons as your sites, the videographers leap at your business. Not so if you plan a wedding at a budget location, where you'll be singing the country tune "If the phone don't ring, it's me!"

before. Don't, however, feel obliged to use a photographer's suggestion without checking out the videographer carefully to see if he or she fits your needs. Another caveat: some photographers have video divisions, so, of course, they will recommend *themselves* to do the video. Just because you hire the photographer doesn't mean you must go with their video package—check out other videographers before you make a final decision.

♥ **CEREMONY SITE COORDINATORS.** These folks often have first-hand knowledge about videographers since they are responsible for reciting the rules to camerapersons. Site coordinators can recommend people familiar with the site who are also easy to work with. And they may also hear back from brides about how good (or bad) the finished video is.

Understanding Videographers: Some Basics

When shopping for a professional wedding videographer, keep in mind these five elements:

1 Lighting. As with photography, lighting is key to a good DVD/video. Often, existing room light is not bright enough to get a good picture. In the past, videographers would need to flood a room with light in order to get good video, spoiling the ambiance of a candlelit reception hall.

Well, we have good news on this front. Advancements in technology have led to new professional video cameras that are sensitive enough for use with only available room light. If they do require any extra light, videographers can use smaller, low-wattage lights that are less distracting and still get good video.

2 Sound. Especially during your once-in-a-lifetime wedding ceremony, it is vital to get perfect sound on your video. Thanks to new technology, great video sound is possible without the use of giant boom microphones hanging over your head.

There are basically three ways to capture sound at the ceremony. The least effective is through a "boom" microphone. This is attached to the video camera and often picks up every sound in the room, including your vows. If you don't want to hear your seven year old nephew Joey squirming around in his seat and fidgeting, the boom microphone is not for you.

The next option is the "hard-wired" microphone, connected to the camera via a cord. The other end, typically a small clip-on mic, is attached to the groom's lapel, the official, the podium or the kneeling bench. This may not be ideal for some weddings, especially if there is a lot of movement during the ceremony. The sound quality is usually average to good.

The final (and most common) option is a "wireless" microphone. This microphone sends sound to the camera via a radio transmitter (about the size of an iPod) attached to the groom's waist.

One caveat: wireless microphones that are "low band" may pick up interference from police radios or other radio equipment. "High band" microphones, on the other hand, can weed out most interference and produce a clean, clear "I do."

Remember that audio is as important as video. When looking at samples, listen for rough transitions or conversations that are cut off. Sloppy audio can keep you from following the sequence of events on the video. Another clue: check to see if the audio is in sync with the video.

3 Equipment. *"All this video camera stuff is so bewildering—I hear there are digital cameras, Super VHS, HDTV. . . I'm so confused! I can't even stop my DVD player from blinking 12:00! Help!"*

Well, you're on your own with the DVD. But we can help you to understand the different cameras used for wedding videography.

The majority of wedding videographers shoot with digital cameras on digital video (DV) tape today. Until a few years ago, Super VHS was the standard, although a few videographers shot with Hi-8 (8mm) cameras.

Why did digital become the standard? The format lets videographers easily edit video and add special effects. Digital also lets companies easily transfer footage to DVD's. Of course, not all videographers have gone digital yet, thanks to the high price of editing equipment and other technological hurdles.

No matter what format they use, the actual cameras most videographers use are far different from (and more expensive than) the kind of camcorders you see at Best Buy. Most are professional-grade (or "prosumer"), which provide a sharp picture and vibrant colors. Today's prosumer cameras use advanced computer technology to produce better video. A typical prosumer Panasonic camera used by professionals at weddings today runs about $2700.

What about industrial cameras? This category includes broadcast-quality cameras used by TV stations. These ultra-high priced cameras need bright light to produce good video and, hence, are rarely used by videographers who shoot weddings. Perhaps they're just overkill.

Finally, let's talk about high-definition TV (HDTV). Many folks have invested in these new TV's, which have more lines of resolution than a standard TV. The good news: many digital video cameras shoot at a resolution that will look crisp and sharp on high definition TV. But . . . ask your videographer about this. Some videographers are still using standard-definition (SD) cameras, while others have migrated to high definition (HD).

We should note that high-definition cameras shoot a bigger picture (16:0 ratio) than standard-definition cameras. That means videographers have to re-tool their shooting style a bit—and HD cameras require more sophisticated editing equipment, more hard-drive storage, etc. One hint: if you are being shot in high definition, be sure to double-check your bridal make-up—these cameras show every pore!

So, what does this all mean? Well, don't get bogged down in this technical mumbo-jumbo. What makes this even more challenging is the fact that video technology (cameras and formats) changes so quickly. The key is to look at the final product—the camera skills of the videographer are just as crucial as the type of equipment he or she uses.

4 The DVD/videotape *"Can I get my wedding video on DVD?" "Should I future-proof my video and get it in high definition?"* DVD is the standard format that most videographers use. What if you want your wedding video on a VHS tape? Obviously, most videographers have no problem with that request as well.

DVD's have two key advantages over plain old videotape: first they are more "archival" than videotape, which can be susceptible to heat, dust and other problems. Another advantage: sharper pictures. As most folks realize, DVD's offer much better picture quality than video tape.

Of course, there are some problems with DVD's. We'll discuss those later in this chapter in the Pitfalls section.

As for "future-proofing" your video, we can understand why some couples want a high-definition (versus standard-definition video). After all, most TV's are going HD. BUT . . . you'll need to have a HDTV and high-end DVD to really make it worthwhile. So if you aren't big into gadgets, a standard-definition wedding video should work fine. Another factor: HD wedding videos cost more then SD videos.

5 Camera Angle *"Some sample videos I've viewed show the bride and groom only from the back or from strange angles in the church. Is there any way I can avoid such problems?"*

Some of the responsibility for these strange angles and shots belongs to your church or synagogue. Many don't allow the videographer to move once the bride begins her walk down the aisle. They may also assign the cameraperson to a particular part of the sanctuary (like the back balcony). This is why it is important to check with the policies of your ceremony site. Also, you can ask the clergy if your videographer can get a better view (they might respond more to a bride and groom's request than that of the cameraperson).

It is crucial to have your videographer visit the ceremony site before the wedding (even attending the rehearsal) to see where he or she will be setting up. This advanced preparation may help avoid those camera angle problems. Be aware that some videographers will scout out the ceremony site for free–others charge a fee.

Many videographers today offer multi-camera shoots with two or even three cameras at the ceremony. So does that mean you have to pay three camera people to shoot your wedding? Not always. Some of these cameras may be remote-controlled from the back of the church. The different views are edited together on the final product to provide a much more interesting video than single-camera coverage.

Getting Started: How Far in Advance?

As with photographers, good professional videographers can book months ahead of the date. Popular summer months are often spoken for by January or February in many major metropolitan areas. In New York City, videographers are commonly booked up to two years in advance! We recommend you hire your videographer six to nine months before the wedding (as soon as or even before you book a photographer).

Step-by-step Shopping Strategies

♥ **Step 1:** Using the sources discussed above, make appointments with two to three video companies. Ask to see

Wedding Videos: the good, the bad and the ugly

View a few wedding videos and you'll see quality that's all over the board. Yes, there are some wedding videographers who do truly stunning work. And, there are others that should stick to taping high school choir performances. After viewing literally hundreds of wedding videos, here are some points that separate the good from the bad:

♥ **Good**: The best videos have a mix of close-ups and far-away shots. You'll see plenty of TV-style production tricks, including shots that "link" one scene to another. The best videographers also bring a small ladder to make sure their shots aren't blocked by the backs of guests' heads.

♥ **Bad**: Jerky movements and too-fast pans are signs that a videographer needs to go back to video school. We've also seen demos where the video and audio portions were not in sync (they looked like the dialogue in a bad Kung-Fu movie). Another bad wedding video sign: the cameras in a multi-camera shoot are all focused on the same image.

a demo or a video of a recent wedding. If you contact a studio with several associates, make sure you will be meeting with the person who will videotape your wedding. As with photographers, each videographer's style is different, so meeting the actual cameraperson is key.

♥ **Step 2:** See the sample or demo tape of each company. View more than just "highlight" tapes–ask to see complete weddings. Even better, ask if they can show you any wedding videos shot at your ceremony/reception site.

♥ **Step 3:** Check for sound quality and lighting–are there any awkward moments? Make sure you can hear the vows. This is the most important aspect of the video–isn't the exchange of vows the whole reason you are planning this wedding and reception anyway? If the lighting is extremely bright, guests may squint or turn away. You want everyone to feel comfortable so watch this aspect carefully.

♥ **Step 4:** If this is an edited video, ask yourself if the editing is smooth and professional. Does it have a home-movie feel or a raw-footage quality? Or is it seamlessly edited with a smooth flow? Is the DVD/video enjoyable or boring? Decide if the special effects (if any) add to or detract from the video.

♥ **Step 5:** Make sure the personality of the cameraperson is pleasant. If you don't feel comfortable, shop for another videographer.

♥ **Step 6:** Get references from previous customers. Ask these recent brides if they were satisfied with their tapes. Did they meet their expectations? If they had to do it over again, would they choose that same company? How did the videographer deal with adverse conditions? Did they bark orders at guests or members of the wedding party? Checking references here is especially important since many video companies are still new to the business world and some lack professionalism.

♥ **Step 7:** Once you have decided on a videographer, get a signed contract. Specify the date, time, place, editing and other issues. Make sure they note any preferences too: will there be any interviews, for example.

♥ **Step 8:** Meet with your videographer again closer to the wedding date to discuss any special people you'd like on your video. It may even be a good idea to draw up a list of names. Also go over the sequence of events and talk about any changes or additions.

Questions to Ask a Videographer

1 Are you familiar with my ceremony/reception site? If not, will you visit the site before the wedding or attend my rehearsal? These are critical questions since the videographer must determine the best angle, lighting options and sound needs for each site. Many ceremony sites have specific rules about where the videographer can set up. Some sites may also present sound or lighting challenges—the more familiar he or she is with the site, the better. Of course, some videographers balk at attending the rehearsal or scoping out the site beforehand, saying their time is valuable. They claim they'll figure out the camera angles when they get there. Whether you want the videographer to wing it or not is up to you.

2 Exactly what will the final product look like? Find out how long the video will be and what type of editing or graphics will be done. Often we've seen demos with music synced to the action, fancy script graphics and even dissolves or other effects. Then we've been informed that all those options are extra, on top of the package price. Watch out for these tactics.

3 Who exactly will be shooting my video? Again, remember that some companies, especially in busy summer months, may send out unskilled amateurs (or stringers) to some of their weddings. Meet the actual videographer and see his or her work before booking. Unfortunately, some studios only assign their best camera people to the highest-priced packages.

4 Are there any photographers in town that you have had difficulty working with? The fit between photographer and videographer is critical—if they don't work together as a team, the scene may get ugly. Unfortunately, it may be difficult to get a truthful answer here since many videographers don't want to offend you or bad-mouth local photographers.

5 Explain your general wedding shooting schedule. This way you can find out what they do before the ceremony, whether they do interviews or not and how they expect the evening to run.

6 Will I get the master tape (or digital file) and how many copies come with the package? The master tape is the original tape or digital file. Some videographers keep this and give you copies just as photographers keep the negatives. If you want the master, shop for a videographer with a different policy. As for additional copies, they are usually extra. Plan ahead for this extra expense. The cost per copy could range from $20 to $100–or more. One note on master tapes: as technology evolves that lets consumers record their own DVD's, we expect more videographers will be building copyright-protection technology into their wedding DVD's . . . or keeping their master tapes to avoid unauthorized duplication of their work. In the past, if you copied a master onto another VHS, there was a noticeable decline in quality. With DVD's, that doesn't happen–and that fear will drive some videographers to drop master tape sales or encrypt DVD's to prevent copying.

7 Do you have back-up equipment? Do you edit your own work? Do you offer a guarantee? Back-up equipment is a critical issue–the best videographers have back-up equipment with them at your wedding, not in a van or office across town. Even if it takes just a few minutes to run out to a vehicle, you can miss important moments. Another point to ask about: what happens if the videographer gets sick? Do they have a substitute cameraperson who can cover the event?

8 Will you take a little time to educate me about video production? This is a trick question suggested to us by a New Jersey videographer. He told us you're not looking for a technical lecture but insights into the videographer's philosophy. The videographer should acknowledge that each wedding is different–and be honest about the shortcomings of his or her work. "Beware of the person who doesn't or can't explain things to you. Or one who thinks he's the greatest on earth. Deep down, he is probably insecure. Picking a down-to-earth 'realist' is often a better bet than a 'braggart.'"

9 Tell me about a wedding where something went wrong. How did you handle it? This is a great question for all wedding merchants, not just the videographer. The wrong answer: "nothing bad has ever happened on a wedding shoot." Come on–weddings are attended by human beings who make mistakes. Professionals roll with the punches and still produce an excellent product. One common area for problems: the photographer. See the box below for more info on this perennial problem.

10 When will my DVD/video be ready for pick-up? Most professional videographers offer some kind of post-editing for their video packages. Even though digital cameras and editing software make this process go quicker, it still takes a LONG time to get your final video. The average is about eight to 12 weeks after your wedding! One videographer we interviewed takes six MONTHS to deliver the final product. Be sure to ask so you are not surprised.

77 Do you shoot in SD or HD? As we discussed earlier in this chapter, there are two types of wedding videos: standard-definition (what you see on a regular TV) and high-definition (HDTV). Some videographers in big metro areas have gone HD . . . but it will cost you. Ask to see samples in both SD and HD; and ask the videographer about what you'll TV equipment to best play back a HD wedding video (hint: an expensive HDTV set and high-end DVD player).

Bridal Bargains Wedding Planner: Videographers

Does the videographer you are considering offer multi-camera coverage? How many copies do you get? Are there time limits on the package? Compare three videographers side-by-side with a special worksheet in our *Bridal Bargains Wedding Planner.* Once you've selected the videographer, track the details on the package you are getting (How much do copies cost? When is the balance due?) with another worksheet in the *Passport.* See the back of this book for details.

Photographers and Videographers: The Balkans of Bridal?

Sometimes videographers and photographers behave like the Hatfields and the McCoys—and it usually is the consumer that suffers.

To understand why these so-called professionals sometimes act like guests on Jerry Springer, it is important to understand the roots of this feud. For years, the only person who documented a wedding was the photographer. This cushy role insured a steady stream of clients and profits. During the 80's, video came on the scene and things haven't been the same since.

Some photographers view video as a major threat to their livelihood. Despite the fact that most weddings today are *both* videotaped and photographed, this feeling still dominates the photography profession. Photographer paranoia kicked into even higher gear in recent years when video went "digital" and videographers began talking about selling "digital stills" as prints to their customers. Most videographers and photographers realize the day is not far away when just one professional takes both digital video and still pictures. And that means "someone" is going to lose out on the lucrative bridal "memories" market.

Top Money-saving Secrets

1 Use a professional to tape the ceremony only. Many professional videographers offer discounted "ceremony-only" packages costing anywhere from 40% to 60% less than complete packages. For the reception, consider asking friends and relatives to bring their cameras to shoot footage. Note: beware that some studios use their least-experienced videographer to shoot the "ceremony-only" packages. Confirm who will be your videographer and view his work before booking. (Other studios may refuse to do ceremony-only bookings unless it is the slow time of the year).

2 Have a friend tape your wedding. Only as a last resort! If you choose to go this route, make sure your friend or relative has a tripod (to avoid those wobbly shots) and plenty of extra batteries. Frankly, this is not our first choice to saving money with wedding video. First, your "friend" will be stuck behind a camera for most of the day, missing out on all the fun. And while digital video cameras have improved the quality of homemade wedding videos in recent years, it still takes skill and effort to shoot a great video. Most amateurs simply don't have the camera skills.

Hence, the bridal vendor version of Celebrity Death Match. Photographers complain that videographers interfere with their ability to capture the event on film—all the lights, boom mics and other video apparatus make photographers cringe. A typical battleground is the formal "posed" pictures that are taken of the bride and groom before the wedding. These are big moneymakers for the photographer and they jealously guard this turf.

Some photographers go as far as banning videographers from taking video of the formal posed picture sessions; they argue (somewhat unconvincingly) that their unique posings of the bridal party are their copyrighted images.

Videographers, for their part, claim that photographers try to sabotage their video by blocking shots and other sleazy tricks.

So, what's a bride and groom to do? First, make sure you tell the photographer you plan to have the wedding videotaped. If they turn red and start spouting obscenities, then it might be time to find a different photographer. And be careful to look through a photographer's contract to make sure there are no restrictions on what can be videotaped. Photographers should learn to co-exist with videographers, for the sake of everyone's sanity.

3 Use iMovie. If you go the do-it-yourself route, see if a friend has a newer Mac. These computers come with Apple's ingenious iMovie software (it's free) that lets you whip up professional-looking videos (with special effects, editing, music and titles). Then you can burn a DVD of your wedding video with iDVD, also included on most Macs. Another idea: ask the videographer to just shoot raw footage (no editing). Then edit the video with iMovie yourself. (Note: the videographer will have to shoot with a digital camera for you to import it into a computer for editing). This requires a significant amount of hard disk space, so you'll have to be a techie in order to accomplish this.

4 Negotiate lower rates for less-popular wedding days/months. It never hurts to ask!

5 Ask the videographer if they will do a scaled-back package for less money. Fewer bells and whistles (post-editing, special effects) mean less time for the videographer. Ask them if they can work out a "special package" that meets your budget.

6 Request a volume-discount for DVD/tape copies. If you need several copies, the video company should be able to offer you a volume discount off their normal prices.

7 Use multi-camera coverage only at the ceremony. While it's a nice luxury to have two or three cameras to cover the wedding ceremony, it may be overkill at the reception.

8 Use your company's video or photo department. Some large corporations have in-house photo or video departments. This can be a good money-saving strategy–some of these same experienced camera people free-lance on the weekends at much lower rates than you'd find in the bridal market.

9 Check the next town over. Not surprisingly, we found the most expensive videographers were the ones in big cities. By contrast, video companies in smaller towns or outlying suburbs often charge 20% to 40% less. And most videographers are willing to travel 50 to 100 miles one way to a wedding without an extra charge. So try to look at the next town over to save. The only trade-off: videographers in smaller towns usually offer fewer perks and choices for fancy video effects. But if that doesn't matter to you, go for the savings.

10 Consider a weekend warrior. About half of all wedding videographers are part-timers, so called "weekend warriors."

Since wedding videos aren't their full-time job, they often charge less than their full-time competitors. Are these videographers any less professional? Nope, weekend warriors can produce just as professional a tape as full-timers. Of course, check their references carefully and view several demos of actual weddings to make sure the part-timer is up to the job.

11 Don't mention what you're spending on still pictures. When negotiating with a videographer for a lower rate, there is one cardinal sin—*never* reveal what you are paying your still photographer. Many video companies have an inferiority complex when it comes to photographers, thinking they always get the short end of the bridal budget stick. And they're jealous of photographer's bigger paychecks. So whatever you are paying for wedding photography, keep it to yourself!

12 Hire a student or professor. A bride emailed us this smart tip—she found a local university had a "media studies" department, which is a great source for videographers. The bride hired a professor who shot her entire wedding and reception, edited the tape and transferred it to DVD all for $400!

13 Skip the HD video. High-definition is currently the rage with TV's . . . and you can get a HD video. BUT it will cost you, as most videographers who shoot in HD are charging a premium for this. Yes, the prices for HD will come down as time goes on. But for now, take a good look at a standard-definition video—it might fit your current TV and budget better.

Destination Wedding Tips

Like photography, booking a wedding video on a tropical island or other destination hot spot will likely be a less-fancy production than what you'd see with a home wedding. You're more likely to find part-time shooters than professional video production companies. With that caveat, make sure all the contract details are spelled out in writing (part-timers can be a bit weak with contracts).

Our advice: see if the videographer has some stock footage of your destination wedding locale. When you get home, you can build a montage of your wedding video, the stock footage, photos from the event and more—mix them together in a program like iMovie and you've got a complete wedding memory!

Biggest Myths About Videography

Myth #1 *"We had a friend videotape our wedding. The video was just OK—there were several parts that are out of focus and shaky. Our friend said we could just get that fixed."*

Don't count on it. You can't just "fix" a bad video that's blurry or missing audio parts. The best you can do is cut out the bad parts and try to piece it together. We've heard quite a few horror stories from couples that had a well-meaning friend or relative tape their wedding, only to end up with a video that needed extensive "fixing."

Myth #2 *"I watched my friend's wedding video and found myself straining to hear the couple say their vows. We're writing our own vows and we really want to be able to hear what we say to one another on our video. Is it true that it's impossible to get clear sound on a video?"*

Sound quality depends heavily on the type of microphone. We recommend the use of a high-band wireless microphone attached to the groom's lapel. This type of microphone will overcome the disadvantages discussed earlier that come with boom microphones and hard-wired mics. If you can't find anyone with a wireless high-band microphone, listen carefully to the sound quality on demos and decide who offers the best sound.

Some videographers today use multiple microphones to capture audio at the ceremony. The best companies even mix the audio "live" at the site, adjusting the volume level during the ceremony to make sure the best possible video is made.

Myth #3 *"I saw one sample demo that had interviews of the guests on it. I thought the interviews were kind of embarrassing and the guests seemed uncomfortable. Do I have to have interviews on my DVD?"*

The answer is an obvious "no." We've seen several videos where a good friend had too much to drink and related a sick joke. In another case, a guest suddenly had a microphone shoved into her face and made a few boring comments that didn't need to be saved for posterity.

Well this doesn't have to happen in your video. First, if you don't want any interviews, be specific with the videographer—especially if he or she has these segments on demos. But if you do want interviews, choose a package that will allow you to edit out any embarrassing comments made by your guests. And don't forget to specify what kind of interviews you want. One couple we talked to asked their videographer to only interview relatives. Another couple specified interviews of guests who really wanted to speak on the video. These precautions should help you avoid the "video from hell."

Helpful Hints

1 Choose a package with enough time to cover the event. A four to six hour package should provide enough time to capture a typical wedding (allow more time for sit-down dinners or receiving lines). If you think your reception will go over, ask about overtime availability and charges. Some packages end when the cake is cut while others run to the reception's end. Ask when overtime kicks in—if the cake is cut an hour late? What if the bride gets to the church 45 minutes late? Confirming the exact conditions that lead to overtime charges is important.

2 Many uncontrollable factors can affect the quality of your video. For example, church P.A. systems can interfere with low-band wireless microphones. Another problem may be caused by your officiant or site coordinator. At one wedding we attended, the priest requested the videographer stand in a certain spot. The videographer thought she would have a good view of the couple's faces. However, the priest then decided to hold the entire ceremony with the couple facing the congregation. This left the videographer taping their backs for the entire wedding!

We feel its best to try to keep a sense of humor about these uncontrollable events. Having the videographer attend the rehearsal should also cut down on surprises.

Pitfalls to Avoid

PITFALL #1 DVD PROBLEMS

"I purchased a DVD copy of my wedding video, only to find it would NOT work in my DVD player! What went wrong?

Yes, you've just experienced the cutting edge of technology—incompatible DVD formats. While the technical discussion of why this happens is beyond the scope of this book, brides and grooms should realize that DVD technology is still evolving. As of yet, there is no one standard for recording DVD's, hence the possibility that the DVD your videographer whips out may not work on your DVD player. A word to the wise: get the videographer's promise in writing that his DVD will be something you can actually view!

PITFALL #2 "DIRECTOR'S DISEASE"

"I was a bridesmaid in a friend's wedding recently and I was very shocked at the behavior of the videographer. He kept ordering everyone around, telling us what to do. Is there a way to avoid this problem at my own wedding?"

Occasionally, we've run into an inexperienced wedding videographer who suffers from that strange malady known as "director's disease." These camera people tend to expect weddings and receptions to conform to some sort of script for an all-star movie production. Instead of simply capturing the day as it happens, they try to direct the actors (bride and groom) in a performance (the wedding).

In many ways, however, a wedding is a videographer's nightmare—unscripted and unrehearsed, things often happen spontaneously. Experienced videographers will have discovered this fact and (hopefully) will adapt to each fun, yet frantic event on your wedding day. If you check references carefully and ask former brides about this aspect, you can avoid a videographer infected with "director's disease."

PITFALL #3 MISSING KEY EVENTS

"One of my friends complained that her wedding video was missing one of the events of the evening she thought was most important: her brother giving the toast. I don't want anything to be missed at my wedding. How can I prevent this?"

The bouquet toss, garter throw, toast and cake cutting among other things, are of paramount importance to most brides and grooms. Your videographer should at least be around for these events at your wedding. Amateurs and unseasoned professionals have been known to miss them—be sure to check with references.

To be fair, we should note a videographer does not typically tape EVERY moment of your wedding and reception. Some videographers even leave before the event is over.

When you hire a professional, you should also meet with him or her prior to the wedding to discuss those things you want in your video. Be specific and have him write your preferences down. Any key events you want covered should be clearly detailed in writing. Also bring him a list of important people you want in your video. Have a copy of this list with you at the wedding.

PITFALL #4 BIG SCREEN TVS.

"My wedding video doesn't look very good on my parent's big-screen TV. It looked fine on our 19" TV—what's the problem?"

The problem: some big screen TV's use a projection process to get the picture onto the screen. Unfortunately, this process causes a video's resolution to suffer. In other words, most videos (including movies) may look fuzzy on a big-screen TV. Don't blame the videographer for this problem! One solution: consider getting your wedding video on DVD instead of tape. This typically solves the resolution problem.

PITFALL #5 DECEPTIVE DEMO TAPES.

"We saw this video company at a bridal show. They were playing a demo tape that looked great. When we asked them where it was shot, however, they sheepishly told us it wasn't really their work. What gives?"

Some franchised video companies will give their new franchisees generic demo tapes to help drum up business (since the fledgling company may not have examples of their own work yet). Confirm the tape you are seeing is actually their work. While every new videographer has to start somewhere, we'd recommend he not learn the ropes at your wedding.

PITFALL #6 NICKEL AND DIME CHARGES

"One video company in my area advertises a super-low price for wedding coverage. When I met with them, however, there were several 'additional charges' that inflated the package price."

We've heard this complaint from several of our readers. In Wisconsin, for example, we discovered a video company that charges extra for each microphone ($50 a pop). And, wouldn't you guess it, the videographer recommends *lots* of microphones. Other additional charges could include exorbitant fees for editing, music, graphics, special effects and copies. The best tip to avoid this is to get "apples to apples" bids from several companies. Don't be fooled by super-low prices that seem too good to be true.

PITFALL #7 OVERTIME SURPRISE

"At our wedding, slow caterers forced our videographer into 'overtime.' Unfortunately, he didn't inform us about this until 30 minutes into overtime—and then he said we couldn't get any of the footage after his time expired unless we coughed up another $100!"

Yes, overtime can be a thorny issue. While that four-hour package seems adequate, unforeseen events (a pokey photographer, a slow caterer) can make you run out of time in a hurry.

Our advice: find out what the overtime charges would be *in advance*. Get in writing that you will be notified 15 minutes BEFORE overtime will begin, so you can make a decision on whether to go forward or not. While we don't expect you to keep a constant eye on your watch during your wedding, it would be smart for a friend or relative to help make sure the photographer or videographer's clock isn't about to expire.

Some sleazy videographers (and photographers) make a bad situation worse by using hardball tactics to sell more overtime. Like in the above example, some will shoot for an extra 30, 40 or 50 minutes beyond the contracted period of time—and then refuse to give you the video (or pictures) for that time UNLESS you cough up the extra cash.

We say overtime issues are a two-way street. If the videographer has a strict policy on overtime, inform them the time they spend eating dinner (a meal you probably will pay for) is NOT on the clock. In fact, any significant time spent not shooting (such as the time it takes to drive from the ceremony to the reception) should not be counted toward your package limit.

A related issue to this scam: videographers (and other vendors) that charge your credit card for payments, overtime and other fees *without your permission.* We've heard an increased number of complaints about this. Couples say they give their credit card to the vendor to pay for a deposit. Then a payment or other fee is charged to the card without their permission. Make sure your agreement with the videographer (or any vendor) does *not* enable them to automatically charge your card when they (the vendor) think they are owed money. That is fraud. Require your signature on any credit card payment.

Trends

♥ **High definition videos.** It's the big debate among videographers now—do brides and grooms want a high-def video? These super-sharp videos are shot in a wider picture ratio (16:9) and feature incredible resolution. But that also means your make-up had better be flawless, as these cameras show EVERY detail. And bring your wallet: most videographers offering HD videos are charging a premium.

♥ **Voice overs.** More videographers are adding "voice overs" (a commentary track from the bride or Mom and Dad) to give videos a new dimension. The narration gives background and emotional impact to certain video scenes. Instead of boring interview scenes (showing a father of the bride at the reception), more videographers are using this audio track over the processional, etc.

♥ **Web casting.** Did your grandmother miss the wedding? Today, some videographers can stream your wedding live on the 'net for distant relatives to enjoy. Yes, grandma needs a high-speed connection to make this work, but she's wired, right?

♥ **VIDEO "PRINTS."** As more videographers use digital video cameras, we are seeing an increase in companies selling video stills. No, they aren't as sharp as the photographer's prints, but the stills may be a good option if the photographer missed a key shot. And technology is improving, so these digital video stills may soon be a reasonable alternative to still photos. Most videographers are selling them for $10 to $20 for a 5x5.

♥ **TIME SHIFTING.** There is no law that says your video must be edited in exactly the same sequence as the events happened. Some videographers are creatively shuffling various scenes to tell the day's story. Of course, this is tricky—a videographer needs skill to interweave wedding day events for maximum impact . . . and not confuse the viewer.

♥ **TV THEME OPENINGS.** One Toronto videographer produces elaborate TV-style openings for his wedding videos. Sample: the bride, groom and bridal party clown around in a park during a pre-wedding shoot that's edited to look like the opening for "Friends." Or the "Brady Bunch." Another videographer uses a GroomCam—a small camera the groom carries around to catch various shots, which are edited into the videographer's footage. And still another videographer uses a "steadi-cam" for fluid movement shots like those in movies. Want to spice up those guest interviews? One video company we met uses "Chroma Key" technology (like TV weathercasts) to project footage of the wedding behind guests as they talk about the bride and groom.

♥ **RETROSPECTIVE PACKAGES.** Here's an interesting twist on wedding video: why not do a post-wedding interview where you reminisce about the wedding? Take that footage and cut-in "flashback" scenes of the wedding and you've got the "retrospective," a new video add-on that some videographers are selling. The price: $850 to $1500—that's *in addition* to the regular wedding video package. The retrospective interview is usually done the morning after the wedding (when memories are fresh) or after the honeymoon.

♥ **BETTER MICS.** New wireless mics have less interference problems and new "plug-on transmitters" can turn any mic into a wireless mic. These can be hidden in podiums to capture the ceremony vows or in the DJ equipment to capture the night's audio.

♥ **BONUS MATERIAL.** Wedding DVD's now rival the latest release from Hollywood—you get menu navigation, buttons, bonus material and more. One videographer even divides up his DVD's into Bride and Groom areas, with specific content relevant to each.

♥ **SPLASHIER GRAPHICS.** These new and constantly improving techniques make videos less like home movies and more like Hollywood productions. Adding still photos of your childhood at the tape's beginning and snapshots of your honeymoon at the end provides a complete video "album" feel. Of course, all these goodies tend to push up the price of wedding videos.

♥ **Combo photo/video studios.** Some photography studios have the attitude "if you can't beat 'em, join 'em" when it comes to video—many are adding "video divisions." Whether this involves sub-contracting out to another video company or actually having a "staff videographer," photographers have seized on the video trend as a lucrative sideline. Of course, just because the studio offers excellent photography doesn't mean they know beans about video. Be skeptical. Shop for each service as if they were separate companies.

♥ **Foiling pirates.** In the last few years, videographers have started using new technology to prevent couples from copying their wedding DVD or tapes at home. How? Video companies can encrypt their videos/DVD's with a signal that scrambles the video when you try to copy it, similar to the technology that's used on rental movies to foil pirates.

We notice quite a bit of hypocrisy on this issue, however. Videographers who jealously guard their copyright are often the same folks who'll use pop songs as background music on their videos. And trust us, they are not paying a royalty to Maroon 5 or any other artist for their copy written compositions. We've even seen videographers who brazenly use snippets of pirated Disney animated movies on their wedding videos.

Now that you've received a doctoral degree in wedding video, let's talk music for your wedding and reception. That's what's up next.

Chapter 12

Entertainment

From harpists to dance bands to DJ's, choosing music for your wedding and reception can be challenging. In this chapter, you'll learn ingenious ways to find your city's best musicians. We'll also take an in-depth look at the controversy between bands and disc jockeys (no, it has nothing to do with stealing music online) as reception entertainment.

What Are You Buying?

♥ **Ceremony Music.** From royal weddings to Vegas nuptials, music has been an integral part of weddings for hundreds of years. However, the role music plays varies from ceremony to ceremony. The main issue for religious wedding ceremonies is the difference between liturgical and secular music. Basically, liturgical music features sacred words from the bible, while secular music does not. Policies about what is and what is not appropriate will vary from site to site.

Nevertheless, most churches have a staff organist or music coordinator who will help you with selections. Organists charge a fee based on the amount of time needed to rehearse, learn new pieces, etc. Other musicians (such as soloists, pianists or harpists) may also be employed for the ceremony. Ceremony music can generally be broken down into three categories:

1 The Prelude. Typically 20 to 40 minutes prior to the ceremony, prelude music sets the mood. Even if you don't have specific pieces in mind for the prelude, you can tell the organist/musicians your preferences for happy, upbeat music or perhaps more somber, quiet pieces. Sometimes an eclectic mix of different tempos and musical styles is a nice compromise.

2 Processional/Recessional. Processional music heralds the arrival of the bridesmaids and, later, the bride to the wedding ceremony. At the end of the ceremony, recessional music is basically the music everyone walks out to. Typically, the slower processional has a more regal and majestic feel than the quicker-paced recessional music. Sometimes, different musical selections are played for the entrances of the bridesmaids and the bride. Or the same piece can be played at a different tempo as the bride enters the ceremony site.

3 Music during the ceremony. Soloists or the congregation's choir are often used during this part of the ceremony.

Average total costs: Most ceremony musicians charge $60 to $175 per musician per hour. Some may have two to three hour minimums. When you hire ceremony musicians, the only thing you may need to supply is sheet music for unfamiliar pieces. If you're having a string quartet, don't forget to provide chairs without arms so they can bow!

♥ **Reception Music.** Ah, now the party starts! Whether you plan to have only soft background music for listening or a raucous rockin' bash, there are several aspects to what you're buying. For listening music, a harpist, string quartet or guitarist may do double duty (playing at both your wedding and reception). If dancing is preferred, you have two basic choices:

1 Bands. When you hire a live band to play at your reception, you are contracting for a particular set of musicians to play a specified period of time. Most bands require periodic breaks throughout the evening and union rules may mandate break times. Bands provide everything (from instruments to the amplification system), but your reception site may need to provide a piano. Sometimes bands throw in a free hour of light, cocktail music while guests dine. A specific repertoire of music is often implied in the contract—the best reception bands play a wide variety of music to please everyone's preferences.

So how much does a band cost? The price for four hours on a Saturday night can range from $500 to $5000. The key variables are the number of musicians and the popularity of the band. The majority of four-piece bands in major metropolitan cities charge $1000 to $3000 for a four-hour reception (the lower figure is for smaller metro areas;

the bigger number for the largest cities). Want a seven-piece orchestra? Or a locally famous club band? Expect to shell out $3000 to $5000 . . . or more. Deposits for a band can range from nothing (which is rare) to one-third down.

2 Disc Jockeys. When you contract with a DJ, you basically get one DJ (plus, perhaps, an assistant), an entire sound system and a wide variety of music. Some DJs will add specialized lighting (colored spots that pulse to the music, for example) for an extra charge. Also extra may be rare or unusual song requests (such as ethnic music). A few pricey DJs may offer karaoke.

DJs are much less expensive than bands since, quite simply, DJs require less manpower. The average price for a professional DJ for four hours on a Saturday night in most cities is $125 per hour—about $500 for a typical four-hour reception (a deposit of $100 is typical). In bigger cities, DJ's might fetch $600 to $800 for a reception . . . and in New York City, a popular club DJ might even command $4000 for a night's performance.

What is the difference between a plain DJ and a "DJ entertainer"? The latter is more of a master of ceremonies, leading guests in special dances, hosting sing-alongs and more. As you can imagine, this costs about twice to three times the amount for a plain DJ—$1400 to $1700 is an approximate range.

Average total costs: Overall, couples spend about $830 on the average for music at the ceremony and reception. If you live in a big metro area like New York or LA, you can double or triple that figure. What inflates entertainment costs in big cities are minimums. One Chicago bride told us bands there often have an eight-person minimum—that is, the bandleader insists on having eight musicians on stage. That inflates the cost. The Chicago bride told us prices range from $3500 to $6500 for popular wedding bands.

Sources to Find a Good Entertainer

Every major metropolitan area has a plethora of good wedding entertainers. The only problem is finding them. Ceremony musicians, reception bands and DJs typically keep a very low profile, choosing to work by word-of-mouth referral. Many of the most successful bands don't advertise their services. So how can you find these people?

♥ **Ceremony/Reception site coordinators.** For ceremony music, the wedding coordinator at your ceremony site may be able to suggest a few names of harpists, soloists, trumpeters, etc. Music directors are also another source since they have worked in close contact with local musicians. For reception music, the catering manager at your site will undoubtedly have heard a wide variety of bands and DJs. Ask who really kept the crowd hopping. See the pitfalls section later in this chapter for a disadvantage to using this source.

♥ **Independent caterers.** If you are having your reception at a site where you are bringing in a caterer, you may ask that caterer for entertainment suggestions. They usually can provide a referral to several entertainers.

♥ **Wedding announcements in the local paper.** Here's a sneaky way of finding good entertainers. Some local newspapers print wedding announcements that often list the names of the musicians that played at the ceremony or reception. Call the ceremony or reception site to find out how to contact the musicians.

♥ **Music schools at local universities/colleges.** Many students who are talented musicians pick up extra bucks by performing at weddings and receptions. A nice plus: most are more affordable than "professional" musicians. Be sure to get a contract from them, however. Also make sure the student will be dressed appropriately.

♥ **Municipal symphony organizations.** Most symphony musicians moonlight by playing at weddings and receptions. Call your local symphony for any leads.

♥ **Associations.** Looking for a DJ? Call the American Disc Jockey Association (301) 705-5150 (web: adja.org) for a local referral.

♥ **The union directory of local musicians.** Most cities have musicians' guilds or unions that publish a directory of members. If you know a musician who is a member, this directory may be a good source. However, in some parts of the country (like California), musicians that specialize in weddings are often not members of the local union.

♥ **Piano stores.** Looking for a great pianist? One reader recommended checking with the staff at local piano stores. Since employees have to be able to play the product to sell it, you can often find a talented pianist working at a piano store. She found a jazz pianist with a degree from the Berklee School of Music for her wedding.

♥ **Our message boards.** Who's the best wedding DJ in Seattle? The best band for receptions in Miami? Check the local talk message boards on our web site (BridalBargainsBook.com) to chat with other readers about the best entertainers in your town. We keep our boards ad-free and spam-free so you can be assured you are getting real advice, not some paid-for plugs you see on other sites.

♥ **Agents.** Last but not least, many bands and some DJs are booked through agents. Larger agents may book a wide variety of entertainers that specialize in weddings and receptions. In some cities dominated by unions, agents may be the only way to book a band. There are several advantages and disadvantages to using agents, which we will discuss later in this chapter in the spotlight "Secret Agent Man: Helping Hand or Scum of the Earth?"

Brides in Cyberspace: What's on the Web?

The Internet is awash in wedding and reception music info—here's a look at some of the best sites to search:

♥ **ProDJ** (prodj.com) has a great search engine to find a local DJ. Find your geographical region, then your state and you can pull up DJ names. We searched for Cincinnati and found an amazing 22 prospects, complete with a paragraph description of each company, contact info and email link. Clearly the larger listings paid more to be first, so don't ignore the smaller listings below.

♥ **Wedding Tips** (weddingtips.com/wtfavori.html) this site tracks the current top 30 "first dance" songs played at weddings and provides other music suggestions as well.

Figure 1: ProDJ.com's web site has extensive DJ listings, as well as good advice articles.

Getting Started: How Far in Advance?

Don't leave the music for your wedding and reception to the last minute. For ceremony music, you must give the musicians time to learn and practice a special request. Meeting with ceremony musicians a month or two in advance will smooth the process.

For reception music, many of the best bands and DJs book up months in advance. In general, three to six months are enough time to book an entertainer in smaller towns and for "off-peak" wedding months. In the largest metropolitan areas, popular dates (the summer months and December) book up anywhere from six to twelve months ahead.

So what if you only have two months left to plan? Don't panic. You may get lucky and find a good band or DJ with an open date. It just may take a little more legwork.

Step-by-step Shopping Strategies

Ceremony Music

♥ **Step 1:** Ask your ceremony site for any policies on wedding music. Realize that houses of worship often have varying policies about what is considered "acceptable" wedding music. For example, music like the "Wedding March" is not allowed at some religious sites because it's deemed too secular.

♥ **Step 2:** Meet with the music director of your ceremony site several weeks before your wedding. If you need to bring in musicians, use our sources to find three good candidates. Interview the musicians and discuss your ideas for the ceremony music.

♥ **Step 3:** Ask to hear samples of various selections. If you're getting married at a church, ask the music director if you can attend a wedding ceremony. Listen to how certain pieces sound on the organ or other instruments.

♥ **Step 4:** If you hire outside musicians, get a written contract specifying the date, time, place and selections of music. Find out if the musicians/organist will come to the rehearsal (and if there is any fee for this).

Reception Music

♥ **Step 1:** As soon as you have your wedding date confirmed, start your search for an entertainer. Decide what type of music fits your reception. Some important considerations include:

A. The e time of day of your reception—For example, in the afternoon, few people feel like putting on their dancing shoes. Perhaps a good choice here would be a guitarist to play soft background music. But, hey, it's your reception so choose the music you want.

B. The ages of the guests—You can't please everyone but selecting a band/DJ that plays a wide variety of music will help keep everyone dancing.

C. The size of the reception—Typically, the "reception music axiom" says the larger the crowd, the bigger the band you need to keep the event hopping. In reality, a four or five-piece band can play a reception of 500 guests as easily as 200 guests. Do what your budget allows and don't get talked into a certain size band because you have X number of guests. For DJs, the size of the crowd may determine whether extra speakers/amplification are needed.

♥ **Step 2:** After deciding on the type of music you want, identify three good bands/DJs using our sources list. Call each of them on the phone and ask the questions we outline below. Ask to see them perform at an upcoming reception. Is it tacky to ask a band/DJ to visit them at someone's else's wedding? We don't think so. See the following box on the next page for more on this topic.

♥ **Step 3:** When you visit the reception, don't go during dinnertime. Instead plan to stop in later in the evening around 10:30 when the dancing gets going full swing (ask the band or DJ for a suggested time to visit). Look for three key factors:

A. Is the band/DJ correctly reading the crowd? In other words, are they playing the right music for the guests at the wedding? Is anyone dancing? Are they ignoring one generation?

B. How much talking does the band leader/DJ do? Is this amount of chatter helping or hurting the reception? Do you like their announcing style?

C. Is the band/DJ professional? Are they dressed appropriately? Is the volume at a good level or a deafening roar? Is the entertainer varying the tempo, mixing fast and slow selections?

♥ **Step 4:** After you preview as many entertainers as time allows, select the band/DJ you want. Get a written contract that includes the specific date, hours and place as well as the price and overtime charges. Also get the names of the exact musicians who will be there and the instruments they will be playing. If necessary, specify what dress you want the band members/DJ to wear. Finally, have specific sets of music written out such as your first song, special requests, etc. You may even want to attach a song list to the contract.

♥ **Step 5:** Remember that the better you specify the music, the more likely you'll get the music you want at your reception. Don't be ambiguous here by saying you want just "rock" or "dance music." Identify specific artists and songs and then star your favorites. For some artists, specifying a certain time period may be helpful. Don't forget to clearly mark the song you want for a first dance.

♥ **Step 6:** Meet with the bandleader or DJ a couple of weeks before the

"The Tackiest Wedding Book I've Read So Far!"

That was a comment from a reader of this book posted in a review on Amazon (fortunately for our fragile egos, most of the rest of the reviews on Amazon are more positive than that). What was this person so upset about? Our suggestion that you ask the band or DJ to see them perform at another wedding before booking. "Think about it," the reader wrote, "How would you feel if a complete stranger showed up at your wedding reception to review the band/DJ you were paying to entertain you? As far as I'm concerned, the band/DJ can do their advertising on their own time!"

Well, let's take a look at this issue. First, we suggest the entertainer get permission of the bride and groom BEFORE a prospective client visits their reception. Second, if you do visit someone else's wedding, use some common sense. Dress appropriately and stand in the back of the hall. No eating or drinking, of course. You are there to just observe the band or DJ for a short time.

And, there is a quid pro quo here. If you visit a reception to check out a band, the same band might ask permission for another couple to do the same at your wedding—and we don't see any problem with that, of course.

Yes, there are some bands and DJ's who refuse to let couples see them perform before booking. We think that is the bigger concern—we wonder what they are trying to hide.

wedding to go over the evening's schedule and any last minute details. Meet them at the site if they're unfamiliar with it to gauge any needs or problems.

Questions to Ask an Entertainer

Ceremony Music

1 What is the ceremony site's policy on wedding music? Does the church/synagogue have staff musicians or soloists? What is the fee? Don't assume anything is free.

2 Does the church have any restrictions on the music I can have at my ceremony? This is a particularly sticky area since some sites may have numerous restrictions on what is deemed "acceptable."

3 Do staff musicians require extra rehearsals if I bring in outside musicians too? Will there be an extra charge for rehearsals?

4 Who exactly will be performing at my ceremony? Especially when you hire outside musicians, confirm the exact performers who will be at your wedding.

5 How familiar are you with my ceremony site? Obviously this question is only for outside musicians. Inform them of any restrictions the site has on music. A pre-wedding meeting at the site might be a good idea in case there are any logistical questions (access to electricity, amplification, etc.)

Reception Entertainment:

1 Who exactly will be performing at my wedding? Be very careful here. The biggest pitfall couples encounter with bands/DJs is hiring one set of entertainers and getting another set at your wedding. See the Pitfalls section later in this chapter for strategies to overcome this problem.

2 For disc jockeys, do you have professional equipment? Novice DJs are most likely to use home stereo equipment from Radio Shack. While that's nice for a living room, it may not work in a large reception site. Experienced DJs have professional equipment (amplifiers, mixers and speakers like you'd see in a club) that produces crisp sound and has enough power to fill up the largest ballroom. Another question: do you have back-up equipment? CD players can break; speakers blow out—make sure the DJ has a plan to fix any problem.

3 How do we choose the music? A simple but critical question. How open is the band leader/DJ to letting you select the evening's music? Do they want you to submit a song/artist list? Some bands/DJs will interview you and your fiancéé to find out your musical preferences. If the entertainer is evasive about this question or replies that they "have a standard set they always play," you may want to look elsewhere.

4 Can we see you perform at a wedding or other event? The best way to gauge whether a band/DJ is worth their asking price is to see them perform live. Most entertainers should let you attend an upcoming reception, with the permission of that bride and groom, of course. We've talked to some couples who feel uncomfortable attending a stranger's party. See the box earlier in this section for tips on this. If you can't see the band/DJ live, you might be able to view a video or listen to a demo tape (see the pitfalls section for drawbacks to this suggestion). Another smart idea is to call a few recently married couples for references. Ask the reference if there was anything they would have changed about the evening's entertainment.

5 How many breaks will you take? Will you provide a CD to play during those times? Instead of having silence during a band's breaks, consider playing a CD of dance music to keep the reception hopping.

6 Does the price include background music during dinner or cocktails? Some bands and DJs throw in a free hour of background music during dinner. One bandleader we met said he always throws in a free hour of cocktail music. Besides being a nice freebie for the bride and groom, this gives the entertainer an opportunity to scope out the crowd. Then, when the dancing begins, the band is better attuned to the music guests want.

Top Money-saving Secrets

1 Go for an iPod wedding. Simply mix together your favorite songs on an iPod playlist and poof! Instant party. A couple of tips here: be sure to find a place to plug the iPod in. Yes, the battery lasts for up to 12 hours, but you don't want to have the battery die in mid-party. And, no, we do not suggest stealing the music for your party by illegally downloading songs. Purchase tracks from Apple's iTunes online store or tap into your own (and family's) music collection.

What about the sound system? Yes, you can now RENT audio equipment (speakers, amplifier, iPod connection) from most rental companies for just $75 to $150 for an evening. Some DJ's are now even renting basic audio equipment for couples to do their own iPod event.

Of course, we realize DJ's are probably having a fit right about now.

Memo to DJ's: relax. iPods are not going to replace DJ's at all weddings. DJ's argue (and we agree) that mixing the music for a wedding does take some effort . . . and sometimes you have to *adjust* the mix of tunes depending on the crowd, evening's events and so on.

That said, we recommend the iPod wedding for couples who want the ultimate control over their reception music. For smaller wedding or for folks on a very tight budget, an iPod wedding may be the alternative to not having any music at all.

2 Get married any other night than Saturday. Okay, we realize that this is not a popular alternative, but few people realize bands/DJs often give a 10% to 20% discount for Friday or Sunday weddings.

3 Get married during the "non-peak" wedding season. This varies from region to region, but generally entertainers offer discounts for particularly slow months like November and January. Entertainers that would normally sit idle during these slow times might be willing to knock 5% to 15% off their regular rates. Ask and ye shall receive.

4 Don't get married in December. This is an absolute no-no. Corporate and private holiday/New Year's Eve parties push up the demand for entertainers and (surprise!) up go the prices. One popular band we interviewed regularly charges $1500 for a typical reception. However, dates in December go for $2750 and (are you sitting down?) New Year's Eve goes for a whopping $5000.

5 Hire a DJ instead of a band. DJs charge an average of 60% less than most live bands. If your parents can't stand the thought of recorded music at your wedding, a possible compromise could involve incorporating live music at the ceremony and then a DJ at the reception. We'll examine the pros and cons of bands and DJs later in this chapter.

6 Select a band with fewer musicians. Prices for bands are often scaled to the number of musicians. Fortunately, today's technology enables a four-piece band to sound like an orchestra (or at least a larger band). That's because synthesizers and drum machines can add a string section to a ballad, a horn section to a swing tune or even Latin percussion to a salsa song. We met one pianist who uses a computer and keyboard to simulate a several piece band for receptions. Another band we interviewed augments a live drummer with a drum machine to add a complex percussion track to current dance songs. Fortunately, couples today don't have to pay for an extra percussionist or horn section to get the same sound.

7 If the DJ doesn't have the ethnic music you want, borrow it from the public library. Many public libraries have an extensive collection of music (from polkas to Santana) all available to the public on loan. This is a cost-effective way of getting the music you want at a price you can afford.

8 Use a band member to play cocktail music. As we mentioned earlier in this chapter, some bands throw this in as a freebie. Or

Real Wedding Tip

The Smart Way to Hire Student Musicians

Recent bride Melissa Martinez had a unique perspective to share on how to hire student musicians—she works for the music department at Rice University in Houston, Texas. Here are her thoughts: *"I get at least eight to 10 calls per month from brides looking for cheap entertainment. It's amazing how abusive some people can be when I say that I can't help them. I am not a booking agent, and I can't make a student take the job offered. I can only pass on information as I receive it. And some people try to take advantage of student labor. One person offered $25 for a six-piece jazz combo to play for a four-hour reception! That's total, not per musician!"*

"Our jazz instructor is a professional musician whose talents are well known in Texas. Occasionally I will pass on names and numbers to him to handle, since he knows better than anyone which students can handle a job. Sometimes he offers his own services. Once again, I will get calls asking why I referred them to him, because he is too expensive, or he doesn't play the right kind of music, or he wanted a contract . . . I don't know if many music administrators have the same problems that I have, but it IS a problem. Is there any way that brides can be told not to harass us innocent working types?"

Here's Melissa's advice for brides-to-be: *"The couples who have had the best results in my experience have been the ones who come in person to the music or band department with a printed notice of what they are looking for, with all pertinent information also listed, and a number to contact or a time/location for auditions. Students see these on bulletin boards or on job postings, take them down and photocopy them, and follow through far more frequently than on phone messages."*

they may offer you a cut-rate since they are already there.

9 Consider hiring student musicians from a local university or college. As we mentioned earlier in this chapter, many students charge 20% to 30% less than so-called professional musicians. If you go this route, be careful to audition the musicians before signing a contract. For more on how to do this, check out the Real Wedding Tip below. Another reader recommended approaching bands you see at clubs. She noted that a new band that she found was willing to play at her wedding for only $400 for four hours.

10 Think about the acoustics. Does the reception site have large expanses of windows? Or hardwood floors? Good news: such sites will let you get away with a SMALLER band, as the acoustics will compensate for fewer musicians.

Biggest Myths About Entertainers

Myth #1 *"I'd never consider having a DJ at my daughter's wedding. All DJ's are unprofessional, dress sloppily and play disco music."*

We often hear this refrain from parents. Yes, it's true that most DJ companies owe their entire existence to John Travolta and his infamous white suit. The good news is that most DJs have moved beyond disco and, with sophisticated equipment and a broad music repertoire, have become a credible threat to live bands. We'll discuss the pros and cons of DJs in "Canned vs. Fresh: Should you have a DJ or a band at your reception?" on the next page.

Myth #2 *"For our reception, we've decided to hire a great band that plays in several local clubs here. Is this a good choice?"*

Be careful. A great club band does not necessarily make a great wedding reception band. The main reason is variety. Playing a wedding reception requires musicians to be "jacks of all trades." Not only must they play John Mayer and Weezer for the bride and groom but they must also satisfy Mom and Dad's request for Stones and Grandma's request for Glenn Miller. Switching between the Rolling Stones and Benny Goodman can be vexing for even the best bands.

While good club bands may feature competent musicians, they often play to a narrow audience. For example at one wedding, we saw one great club band that did excellent covers of 60's standards. While the bride and groom and their friends loved this music, the parents and grandparents stood in the back of the room for most of the evening.

Of course, you can't please everyone all the time. However, bands should play music for all the generations present at a wedding. Before you hire that great club band, make sure they have a wide repertoire encompassing many musical eras.

Helpful Hints

1 For ceremony music, remember that sheet music is often written for instruments other than a church organ. Hence, give the organist plenty of time to transpose and rehearse the piece so it's perfect by the wedding day.

2 Should you feed the band/DJ? Obviously, this is up to you. You may not want to provide a meal to each band member at a $75 per plate sit-down dinner. However, at least try to arrange with the caterer to provide them with some snacks or sandwiches. Remember that bands/DJs have to be at the reception a long time, and a well-fed entertainer performs better than one with an empty stomach (the same goes for the photographer and videographer). Of course, the flip side of this argument is that entertainers can often figure out how to pay for their own meals the other six days of the week, so why do you have to feed them at your wedding? Whatever your decision, inform the band leader/DJ about food arrangements before the wedding.

3 Tracking down obscure ethnic music. Unfortunately, your typical chain store rarely stocks ethnic music today. Hence, DJs may find it challenging to locate certain songs. A better solution may be to let them borrow your family's CD's or albums. Specifically point out the songs you want.

Spotlight: Bands vs DJ's

Canned vs. Fresh: Should you have a DJ or a band at your reception?

DJs are often the Rodney Dangerfield of wedding reception music—they just don't get any respect. For example, we've read many other books on weddings that don't even mention DJs as an entertainment alternative. Instead, *Emily Post's Complete Book of Wedding Etiquette* suggests "a full orchestra" complete with a "string section for soft background music before the dancing starts." We don't know about you, but hiring a 40-piece orchestra with accompanying string section was just a teensy bit out of our wedding budget.

According to Emily Post, if you're having a small, informal wedding, "a record player provides adequate and lovely music." A record player? Nowhere are the words "disc jockey" mentioned. Even more disturbing is the venerable *Bride's Book of Etiquette,* which, after talking at length about the merits of "small orchestras" at wedding receptions, says "taped, pre-recorded music is a good alternative when live music is not available." Of course, instead of mentioning DJs, the book suggests you "ask a music buff friend to pre-mix your selection on one long-playing tape."

Hey! What's going on here? Do the etiquette fanatics who write this drivel just have their collective heads in the sand? Or is there a conspiracy to deny the existence of DJs? If all these wedding experts are convinced that only live orchestras are appropriate for wedding receptions, then explain to us why disc jockeys dominate reception music in most major cities.

Well, let's take a look at why DJs are so popular. According to a recent survey in *Bridal Guide*, 64% of all brides choose a DJ—that's much more than those who hire a band (22%) or have no music at all (14%). Another survey pegged DJ use at weddings at 72% in 2005—up from just 30% in 1992. Of course the number-one reason is cost—DJs cost only about $500 to $700 for an evening, compared to the $2000 to $5000 (or more) bands demand. With the cost of a wedding soaring, couples are obviously opting for the affordable alternative.

Perhaps a more subtle reason may be the state of pop music today. Almost all the dance music you hear on the radio is a complex mix of programmed keyboards and drum machines. For a live band, trying to reproduce this music is perilous at best and embarrassing at worst. Sure, bands can play Glenn Miller and Johnny Mathis rather realistically, but many reception bands we've heard make every modern tune they attempt sound like "New York, New York."

To their credit, DJs have also cleaned up their act in recent years. Many companies are now professionally run businesses with tuxedo-clad DJs and professional sound equipment. This is a far cry from the late 1970's, when less-formal DJs spun mind-numbing disco hits complete with throbbing disco lights. Of course, disco is still with us (under the new label of "dance music") but many DJs diversified their music collection to include rock, country, and rap, as well as the hits from the 50's through the current top 40.

In fact, musical versatility is one of the top reasons couples choose DJs. Since most weddings feature several generations of guests, a good mix of music is a must. While some bands play a variety of music, many are most proficient at one or two musical genres. The lack of variety is one of live bands' biggest disadvantages.

Another plus for DJs: they never take breaks. Most DJs play music continuously, unlike bands that need to take breaks every hour. Just when the crowd gets into a particular groove, the band shuts down for five to ten minutes. Obviously, this can kill the mood. With a DJ, the beat never stops until the party ends.

So what does Emily Post suggest if you want continuous music? Hire *two* orchestras, so one can play while the other is on break! No, we are not making this up.

Of course, we could rattle off a million advantages of DJs over bands, but that wouldn't faze those hard-line etiquette gurus. With their noses firmly planted in the air, they'd say something like "only live music such as a combo or orchestra is appropriate for a proper reception."

Still, bands do dominate in some areas, especially in cities with a thriving live music scene (that is, New Orleans, some East Coast cities, etc.). Also, bands are still the most popular choice for those large "society" weddings.

Sure, we admit that watching a live band crank out "Louie, Louie" is more visually interesting than seeing a DJ play the same song via a CD. All we are saying is don't get bullied by the etiquette police into hiring a band when a professional DJ might fit your musical (and financial) preferences better.

Pitfalls to Avoid

Pitfall #1 Bait and switch with bands and DJ's

"My fiancéé and I saw this great band perform at a friend's wedding so we hired them for ours. At our reception, different musicians showed up and it just didn't sound the same."

This is perhaps the #1 problem brides and grooms have with their reception entertainment. We've known some agents and bandleaders who play "musical chairs" with backing musicians—sometimes known as "pick-up bands." Here a group of musicians are thrown together at the last moment ... and the lack of rehearsal shows. You might hire a certain "name brand" band but then the bandleader substitutes some different (and possibly inferior) musicians at your reception. Hence, you don't get what you paid for, that is quality entertainment. Large DJ companies with several crews are also guilty of this tactic. You can prevent this deceptive practice by specifying in a written contract the exact musicians/DJ you want at your wedding. Stay away from agents, bandleaders or DJ companies who won't guarantee the entertainers who will be at your reception.

PITFALL #2 CHATTERBOX BAND LEADERS AND DJS

"We recently attended a wedding where the band leader incessantly talked to the crowd. No one found this constant chatter amusing and it detracted from the elegance of the reception."

Band leaders and DJs often have their own "schtick"—a certain routine they do at a wedding. How "energetic" you want the band to be is your call since, of course, it's your money. Don't be surprised by a chatty band/DJ. See them perform at another reception or event before you sign that contract. If you have any doubts, ask them about the amount of talking and tell them what you believe is appropriate for your reception.

PITFALL #3 DECEPTIVE DEMO TAPES.

"We heard a demo CD from a band that sounded great. But later we saw the same band live and boy was it disappointing! What happened?"

Some demo CD's are produced in studios where a battery of sophisticated electronic equipment can make the weakest band sound like a stadium headliner. Add a little reverb to the vocals and clean up the guitar with some equalization and poof! Instant superstar band! In the harsh reality of a live performance, however, none of these studio tricks can save a lousy band. Listen to the demo for "style," not production quality. Beware the slick demo and try to see the band perform in person.

We heard about a twist on this scam from a bandleader in Boston. Call it the Ashlee Simpson or (for those who prefer old school cheats) Milli Vanilli syndrome—like those artists, some wedding bands fake their performances on demo tapes. Some bands don't just "clean up" their demo tape in a studio, but use *entirely different* musicians to record the tape! That's right, the band pictured on the videotape is *not* the one that has recorded the soundtrack.

PITFALL #4 KICKBACKS AND "REFERRED" LISTS.

"My wedding site recommend a musician who turned out to be lousy! Meanwhile, several great musicians in my town are nowhere to be found on their 'recommended list.' What's going on here?"

Kickbacks are a problem with some wedding site coordinators (as well as catering managers at reception sites). Believe it or not, some of these coordinators demand fees from entertainers to be placed on the site's "recommended list." A harpist in Northern California told us this unscrupulous practice is rampant there. Ask the coordinator if they take fees from recommended musicians. If you don't get a straight answer, be careful.

PITFALL #5 DISCO MAY BE HAZARDOUS TO YOUR HEALTH

"I went to a wedding last weekend where the DJ had a fog machine. That was cool, except it left a slippery residue on the dance floor–several folks lost their footing!"

Disco effects (fog, strobes, pulsating lights) might be fun in a nightclub, but sometimes they can be hazardous at a wedding reception. Example: fog machines that leave a slick film on the dance floor. Excessive use of strobe lights can cause seizures among elderly guests. And watch out for that bubble machine–the soap solution that's used for bubbles can stain the delicate fabric of your wedding dress. (If you use wedding bubbles as a send-off substitute for rice, make sure the solution is non-staining).

Trends in Wedding & Reception Music

♥ **IPOD WEDDINGS.** See our money saving tip earlier in this chapter for this latest trend.

♥ **NEW TECHNOLOGY.** CD's, mp3's, iPods and digital tapes have enabled DJs to provide crystal clear sound, replacing scratchy vinyl and mediocre cassette tapes. In the live music world, bands now have access to increasingly sophisticated computerized synthesizers and drum machines. With these computers, bands can add a phalanx of horns or a dash of strings to their "basic" sound, enabling them to compete better with a DJ in music reproduction.

♥ **DJS ARE REPLACING BANDS AT MANY RECEPTIONS.** Perhaps it's the cost. Or better technology. Whatever the reason, bands are losing the wedding market to DJs in most towns.

♥ **ETHNIC MUSIC AND BANDS.** Mariachis are chic in the Southwest, while a good Polka band is still in vogue in the Midwest. Couples are not only celebrating their own family heritage but also reflecting a new cultural diversity. One recently married Anglo couple in Miami had a Caribbean-flavored reception complete with a salsa band. When their caterer asked why they selected this theme, the couple responded that this was the music they grew up with.

♥ **AT THE CEREMONY, THE "WEDDING MARCH" IS BEING REPLACED BY A WIDER VARIETY OF CLASSICAL AND MODERN MUSIC.** This is partly due to some churches forbidding this song on religious grounds. To others, the song has become too cliched.

Special Touches to Make Your Wedding/Reception Music Unique

1 Personalize the wedding and reception music with your favorite songs. Incorporating special songs that have personal meaning for you and your fiancéé is a great way to make your celebration unique. Before the wedding, give the band leader/DJ a list of special requests.

2 Instead of standard organ music, consider different musical instruments. The combinations here are endless. Many couples enjoy harp and flute duos, while others attest to the regal splendor of a single trumpeter. Classical guitar as well as violin are beautiful alternatives, too.

3 Use ethnic music to celebrate family heritage. Several weeks before the wedding, talk over the possibilities with your band/DJ. Some songs may take a band time to rehearse or a DJ time to track down.

4 If you're unsure about classical music for your ceremony, consider checking out a local library. Many have extensive music selections (including wedding music) you can borrow to see what might work for your wedding. Looking for a special song to dedicate to parents? Mikki Viereck of New Traditions Music (new-wedding-traditions.com) has crafted "A Song for My Son" from the CD New Wedding Traditions ($9 for the CD single) in response to requests from couples for a "mother-to-groom" song. Mikki has three full CDs ($18 each), which include other weddings songs (including a "Father's Song") as well as instrumental and country versions of her songs. These CDs are available from Amazon.com as well as numerous other online sources.

Spotlight: Agents

Secret Agent Man: Helping Hand or Scum of the Earth?

So, what exactly is an entertainment agent? Agents function as middlemen between bands or DJs and consumers. An agent's primary activity is booking bands and DJs at various engagements—in return they receive a commission. The standard commission is 15% of the band's regular performing fee. Now, the power of agents varies from city to city. In cities with strong musicians' unions, agents tend to proliferate. In general, we've found agents more likely to dominate older cities such as New York and Chicago rather than Sun Belt towns like Atlanta and Dallas.

Agents cite several reasons for their existence. First, they can more effectively market the bands to engaged couples by pooling their resources. Also, many bandleaders (who have other daytime jobs) hate the paperwork associated with deposits, contracts, etc. Agents do all the legwork and remove the administrative hassles.

Fine, you say, but what can an agent do for me as a consumer? Well, agents provide "one-stop shopping," enabling you to make one call and get information on a wide range of bands and DJs. If you are in a hurry or just aren't aware of the entertainment options in your area, an agent can certainly help. Agents don't charge you a fee for their services; instead they collect a commission from the bands.

As you might imagine, some entertainers are less than enthusiastic about giving agents a 15% cut of their salary. Many of the entertainers we interviewed for this book held unanimously negative opinions about agents. And, frankly, we've met some agents who were in desperate need of a personality transplant. Other agents make used car salesmen look like Mother Teresa.

The main gripe we have with agents is their lack of "product knowledge." Too many just book a band or DJ without giving thought to whether their music is appropriate. Other agents deny brides and grooms the right to preview the band/DJ at a wedding before booking—a cardinal sin in our view.

Another major factor in this controversy: many bands say off the record they will give brides and grooms discounts off their regular rates if they book them directly. For example, one band told us they would knock off 15% (which, of course, is equal to the agent's commission) from their $2000 normal reception rate if you book them directly—that's a savings of $300, no small potatoes.

Agents respond to our criticism by claiming they can save brides and grooms money. One agency told us they can "get a lower price because they do a volume of business with a band, whereas a band leader contacted directly can get very greedy." Furthermore, agents claim that legitimate, professional bandleaders will keep their prices the same—whether the booking comes directly from the couple or through an agent.

Well, we've "mystery shopped" dozens of bands and DJs and have yet to find any entertainer quoting a fee over their "regular rates." Agents gave us no special discount deals and we often found many professional bandleaders who offered a quiet discount when approached directly.

So what should you do? Try to book a band/DJ directly if you have found them from one of our sources listed earlier. If you need help, call an agent. Be careful to check out any band/DJ the agent recommends before you sign that contract. You might even call the local Better Business Bureau to check on the agent. Most importantly, meet the band to talk over the music, scheduling, and other reception details.

Now that the music is settled, what about the rest of the details for your wedding? In the next chapter, we'll tackle a host of small details—from the wedding rings to the honeymoon and more.

Chapter 13

Extra

How do you get the best deal on a limo? What the heck is wedding insurance? Do you really need a wedding consultant? This chapter gives advice on these and more bridal topics. Plus, we'll examine online gift registries, wedding rings, and honeymoon bargains.

Limousines: Getting to the Church on Time

What is it about limos? Sure, a limo is a special treat for most folks—but many brides find a limo ride is the road to hell. The complaints? Late limo. No limo. Stinky limo. You name it, we've heard it.

And it's not just limo companies that target the bridal market—we've heard plenty of complaints about all sorts of limos from other consumer advocates. The industry seems rife with sleazy operators and questionable tactics. Here's our advice on how to book a limo without getting taken for ride:

What Are You Buying?

♥ **The Limousine.** A stretch limousine has several basic amenities such as an extra long body, plush carpeting, a stereo, possibly a TV, sunroof and telephone, and a privacy window. More luxurious models have been known to contain even a hot tub or other interesting amenities.

When limo companies give you a quote on a stretch limo, ask how many people the limo will hold. Why? Let's say you choose a limo for six adults. This passenger limit assumes that each person weighs an average of 150 lbs. But if you have two or three big men in your wedding party, you can see that you'll be packed in pretty snugly (and that doesn't include the train of your gown). So if you have a large party, ask for a bigger limo (like an SUV limo) or consider renting more than one.

Of course, there is no law saying brides and grooms must be driven to their reception in a limo. Non-traditional forms of transportation include horse-drawn carriages, antique cars and even buses or trolleys.

♥ **The Driver.** Every type of transportation you hire will include a driver. The driver should be dressed appropriately, either in a dark suit and chauffeur's cap or a black tuxedo.

Average Cost: Limousines will cost approximately $75 to $150 per hour. Usually, they have a three-hour minimum rental time, with the total cost for the car between $225 and $450 per car per evening. The driver is paid with an additional mandatory gratuity of about 15% to 20%. The price you pay for a limo depends on the type of car—basic stretch limousines are less than Rolls Royce or Excalibur packages. For non-traditional transportation, the cost usually starts at $100 an hour and goes up depending on the vehicle you rent.

Sources to Find Transportation

By all means, ask a recently married friend for recommendations and look for information about transportation companies at bridal shows. Another creative idea: Google (or scan the phone book) for classic or antique car clubs. These non-profit groups of car buffs may have members who'll rent out their vehicles by the day.

Brides in Cyberspace: What's on the Web?

♥ Jeff & Nancy Ostroff are a couple that have put together a web page (**BridalTips.com**) of their hard-won consumer knowledge about all things bridal. Their section on hiring a limo is a great example of their clear, concise advice. From there, you can explore other topics, from gowns to gift registries.

♥ The **National Limousine Association** (nlaride.com) has a great site to help brides find a limo. Just input the kind of vehicle you're looking for and your city and state. They'll locate companies in your area. The information will include web site (if available) phone numbers, and types of vehicles available. You can even ask them to submit a price request to the company. No legwork for you!

Getting Started: How Far in Advance?

For most limousine companies, you may not need to start looking until a month or two before your wedding date. If limos are popular in your area and you have a wedding date in the busy summer months, consider planning three months in advance. For carriage companies, you may also have to plan farther in advance because the demand is greater and the supply limited.

Step-by-step Shopping Strategies

♥ **Step 1:** Using the sources mentioned above, identify two or three companies that offer the transportation you need.

♥ **Step 2:** Find out what type of vehicle you will be hiring. See if you can visit the company and see the cars or carriages. Get details on available options, minimum required hours and the cost per hour.

♥ **Step 3:** Visit the company and check out the vehicles. See how clean the cars are and what amenities they have. Find out who will be driving and what they will be wearing. Don't just rely on a phone call to book a limo—seeing is believing.

♥ **Step 4:** Consider contacting the National Limousine Association (800-NLA-7007; web: nlaride.com, to find out if the company you want to hire has adequate insurance and is licensed. These folks can give you that information or at least inform you of how to find it for yourself.

♥ **Step 5:** Choose the company you like the best and get a contract detailing the exact vehicle, date, pick-up times and any special requests. As you get closer to your wedding day (say a week before the event), call to remind them of your date and time. Clearly identify arrival times and other special requests IN WRITING. Another smart tip: get the vehicle license number for the car you are reserving IN WRITING. That helps prevent a last-minute substitution of a substandard vehicle.

Questions to Ask with Limos

1 **Will we be able to bring champagne?** Will you provide us with ice and glasses? Some companies will

allow you to bring alcohol while others will even supply it. However, in some areas, it is illegal for the limo company to provide the alcohol, but they will bring ice and glasses for BYOB. As a side note, don't expect the limo company to provide good champagne—it usually is the cheapest stuff they can find.

2 **Who will be the driver?** How much is the gratuity for the driver? Typically, you aren't given a choice about how much the gratuity will be. Gratuities range from company to company, so check around before you book.

3 **Do you have any discounts available?** As we mentioned above, many companies will discount their service for weeknights. Other discounts may be available if you hire more than one vehicle or if you hire them for longer time periods.

4 **Do you specialize in weddings?** Those companies that do may have special bridal packages or other freebies. Confirm the basic amenities of the car.

5 **How many vehicles do you own?** Small companies may only have a handful of limos. If things get busy, they might contract out cars and drivers from other companies—that's a major problem. If you go with a smaller limo company, make sure you get IN WRITING a promised car the service actually owns and the driver you expect. Even better: get the owner to agree to do the driving.

6 **How much is overtime?** Even the best-laid plans can go awry. Make sure you know what overtime rates will be and get that in writing. That way the driver won't just make up a high overtime charge on the fly.

7 **Do you have a back up in case the car breaks down?** It's always possible that a car will break down or get a flat on your wedding day. Find out what the limo company will do for you so you can make it to your wedding on time.

Top Money-saving Tips

1 **Call a funeral home.** Yes, you read right—call a funeral home for a great deal on a limo rental for your wedding! Now, we should say right off the bat that this sounds nutty, but it does work. And we are not talking about renting a hearse from the funeral home but a limo they normally use to shuttle relatives back and forth. We heard about this bargain from recent bride

Stephanie Kampes in Drexel Hill, PA. She priced regular limo companies at $275 for three hours, plus a 15% gratuity. "Then I called a reputable funeral home and was surprised with the price!" Apparently, this funeral home rents out its standard stretch limos during down times (Saturday night must not be a big time for funerals). The cost? $125 for the evening. "This may sound rather morbid, but it works!" she said. "While they don't have hot tubs or TV's, funeral homes have lovely limos!" While not every funeral home rents out limos for weddings, it's worth a try.

2 Find a transportation company with a short minimum time requirement. Most companies require you to hire them for a minimum of three hours. You may be able to find someone who requires only an hour or two-hour minimum, thus saving 30% to 60%.

3 Rent a trolley! A bride in Trenton, NJ called in this great idea—she found a company that rents a 30-seat trolley for four hours for $715 (which includes a gratuity for the driver). We found trolley companies in other cities that had even lower rates (look online or in the phone book under "Weddings Services," "Limousine Rental" or "Buses-Charter/Rental"). If you're having a large wedding party and don't want to rent a fleet of limos, this might be a smart idea.

4 Consider a "pick-up/drop-off" service. Instead of having the limo driver wait outside the church during the ceremony, simply hire a limo to pick you up after the ceremony and go to the reception. Often this will cost you much less than hiring someone for three hours.

5 Have your wedding on an off night. Some companies offer deals for brides having weddings during the week.

6 Rent a luxury car. Many car rental companies rent Cadillacs and Volvos, even Hummers for as little as $75 to $125 per day. While you'll need to find a driver (perhaps a friend or relative), this is a big savings over a limo. A bride in Turnersville, NJ rented a white Corvette for $179 for her wedding transportation. And that fee was for 24 hours!

7 Consider hiring a "regular limo." These are regular luxury cars—not the stretch variety. Many limo companies offer these cars at reduced rates. Another tip: ask if the limo company has discounts for slightly less fancy limos (like those without window tint).

8 Hire a corporate limo company. Companies that specialize in limos for executives and business travelers sometimes have better deals than limo companies that target the bridal market. Why? Corporate limo companies can get really lonely on the weekend and hence discount their rates. One bride told us she saved 35% by going this route.

9 Don't say the word "wedding." Bridal packages at limo companies always seem to be more than corporate rates. You might want to leave the word "wedding" out of your discussion with a limo company at first just to make sure you see ALL their rates. Negotiate for a better rate if the bridal package is 30% more than the regular rates.

Pitfalls to Avoid

PITFALL #1 COMPANIES THAT DON'T SHOW UP.

This is one of the biggest problems with limousine companies. We recommend you check with the Better Business Bureau in your area to verify the limo company's track record. Checking with the city agency that licenses limousines will also determine whether the company you are considering meets local requirements.

PITFALL #2 WE DON'T OWN THE CAR!

Some limo companies advertise they carry exclusive brands like Rolls Royce. The problem—they don't actually own the car, they just contract for it from another company. As you can imagine, this is a major cause for limo headaches (such as cars not showing up) since the company

Sleazy Limo Driver Award

A bride-to-be in Atlanta Georgia wrote us with this limo scam story—her sister-in-law fell victim to the "early arrival/over-time" surprise rip-off. How does this scam work? First, she wrote, *"the limo showed up at the bride's house over 30 minutes early. The driver was insistent that the bride and her mother finish dressing and ride to the church, which they did. After the wedding and after all the guests left the ceremony site for the reception, the driver boarded the wedding party into the limo. He then informed the couple 'the limo is on overtime' and demanded $60 before he would take them to the reception.*

"Since neither wedding gowns nor bridesmaids dresses have pockets (another bad idea), the groom and best man frantically scraped together the ransom. The limo company reluctantly refunded part of the additional charges only after several unpleasant telephone calls during the next few weeks." How can you prevent this from happening to you? First, if the limo arrives early, don't get in it, no matter how insistent the driver is. Realize that the moment you step inside, the driver's clock is running. Try to pay any overtime fee or deposit by credit card—then you can dispute the charge later if you feel you were mistreated.

doesn't have control over the vehicle. Bottom line: if the company doesn't own the car you want, don't book them.

Pitfall #3 Small limo companies may not have enough cars

If you've decided you'll be needing more than one limo to take you and your bridal party (and others?) to the wedding, you may be in the market for two or more limos. In that case, your limo company will often contract out with another limo operator for additional cars. Ask if this is the case before you sign a contract. And if your limo operator will be contracting out, ask to meet and interview the company who will supply the additional cars.

The problem here: the other company may not be as professional as the original. If you have any doubts, look for another limo operator.

Destination Wedding Tips

Remember the National Limo Association (nlaride.com) we mentioned above? They can even help find you a limo company in locations all over the world . . . such as Barcelona, Spain. Yes, the NLA site lists two sources there and you can get a quote online. (For the curious, a limo in Spain runs about 200 to 300 Euros).

Wedding Rings

The good news about wedding rings is you can buy a beautiful band in just about any budget range. Unlike other goods and services you're purchasing for the wedding, there is a plentiful supply of jewelry stores and other sources to find rings. For example, in our town of 100,000 people, we have just one bridal dress shop, but over 40 jewelry sources (from chain stores in the mall to independent shops and custom jewelry makers). The plentiful supply means you'll probably find something to fit your budget and style. And online sources like BlueNile.com offer even more choice.

What Are You Buying?

What does a set of rings cost? Couples spend on average $1980 for wedding bands. Yes, that's $nearly $1000 per ring. Prices range from as little as $30 for a plain 14K gold ring to $1500 (each) or more for a heavy, solid platinum ring.

What does 14-karat mean? That number refers to the purity of gold in the ring—and that's just one factor that influences a ring's value. Here are the five key aspects to keep in mind when ring shopping:

♥ **Gold purity.** The "karat" is a term that refers to the purity of the gold. 24-karat (24K) gold is pure, 100% gold. Most wedding rings, however, are 18K, 14K and even 10K gold. 18K has 75% gold (25% other metals), 14K is 58.5% gold and 10K has a mere 41.6% gold. Which is best? There are trade-offs to each karat class. While 18K has a higher gold content, it's also softer (and perhaps more susceptible to damage). By contrast, 14K is harder and wears better—and it's less expensive.

♥ **Other metals.** In our last edition, we noted that platinum was a hot metal for wedding rings and bands. But platinum's popularity has been a double-edged sword. Limited supplies and surging demand have pushed prices for platinum wedding rings up 40% or more in the last year. At the same time, designer brands have been heavily advertising their pricey creations in bridal magazines; that has led to a bigger market for so-called "designer" rings.

So what's the solution? Some grooms are opting for titanium, tungsten or steel rings. Even white gold will offer a huge savings over platinum. For example, a $1500 platinum men's band would retail for $300 in white gold. Brides, on the other hand are still matching the metal in their band to the metal used in their engagement ring (gold, white gold or platinum). Hence some couples will have rings of two different metals—platinum for the bride and gold (or another alternative) for the groom.

If you're still set on having platinum rings, consider this consumer tip: ask the jeweler if the platinum ring is pure platinum. Since platinum rings are so pricey (yet so popular), many mall jewelers have begun offering water-downed rings with just 65% to 75% platinum (the balance are other metals) to sell at a lower price point. Rings should be stamped with their purity; 95% pure platinum rings are best.

Can't make up your mind between platinum and gold? Now you don't have to—many stores now carry two-metal weddings bands. These are available in combinations of 18 ct. gold and platinum or 14 ct. yellow and white gold (a 50% savings over the platinum/gold combos).

♥ **Style.** Consider color. While pure gold comes only in one color (yellow, as you might guess), gold can be combined with other metals to form different colors. A 14K white gold ring is a mix of gold (58.5%) plus copper, nickel and zinc. In order to cover over any yellow tint, white gold rings are often coated with rhodium, a metal that's a member of the platinum family. In addition to color, the style of the ring also refers to its shape. Rings can be either flat or half-round—a dome-like or curved appearance.

♥ **Width.** Ring width is measured in millimeters (mm). Most women's wedding bands are 2 to 5mm, while men's are 4 to 7mm. Of course, the wider the ring, the more expensive it is. Other widths are also available.

♥ **Finish.** Just like the icing on a wedding cake, a ring's finish can range from simple to ornate. Like the shiny look? Then choose a high polish ring, instead of a matte finish. Rings can have monograms, diamond cut patterns and other finishes. A milgrain edge is popular today—that's an ornamental border on the edge of the ring that resembles a string of tiny beads. Want diamonds in your wedding ring? You can have stones that encircle the band or just on top.

Top Money-saving Tips

1 Go for a 14-karat ring. Yes, it has less gold in it than 18K or 24K rings, but this is also an advantage. As we mentioned above, 14K gold is harder and wears better than higher-karat rings. And, best of all, it's much less expensive. While a 10-karat ring would be even less expensive, a reader noted that the stronger metal could actually snap when sized. She recommended staying away from the 10-karat option.

2 Check out pawn shops. Divorces and other financial mishaps often lead folks to pawn their wedding rings. As a result, pawnshops have an incredible selection of jewelry at very good prices. One of our readers found an antique engagement ring at a Denver pawnshop for only $400. She had it appraised for $3400. Another good bet: estate sales (usually advertised in newspapers) often feature rings and other jewelry.

3 Comparison shop. Which place has the best deals on wedding rings—mall stores or independent jewelers? Well, there is no one answer. Sales, special deals and other events may make one jeweler temporarily less expensive than another. Make sure you're comparing "apples to apples" with rings (same width, gold purity, etc.).

4 Don't forget about antique stores. One bride called us with this incredible bargain: she found a platinum wedding band from the 1920's at an antique store. The ring, which had a half-carat diamond and sapphires, cost her $700. She had it appraised at $1400.

5 Go mail order or surf the web. See the Spotlight: Best Buy below for a discount mail-order source for wedding rings.

6 Consider the new synthetics. If you have your heart set on a diamond wedding ring but your wallet can't handle diamond prices, consider new synthetic alternatives. One option: Moissanite (moissanite.com), a diamond look-alike that is made by Charles & Covard (a lab that fabricates man-made gemstones). A one and three-quarter carat Moissanite ring runs $1650; a similar-size and quality diamond would run you $5000. The only bummer: Moissanite is only available at certain jewelers (check their web site for a dealer near you); some states only have a small number of Moissanite dealers. New this year, JCPenney is now selling Moissanite jewelry.

Another source for synthetic diamonds (not Moissanite): Diamond Nexus Labs (diamondnexuslabs.com). Their synthetic diamonds are priced at about $80 per carat. Austrian Brilliants (austrianbrilliants.com) and Russian Brilliants (russianbrilliants.com) also sell synthetic diamonds.

7 Check out warehouse clubs like Costco. A reader noted that she saw engagement and wedding rings available from Costco at a huge discount. She noted that quality and selection varies by store, but you can special order a certain size. Another reader also recommended Costco: "The telephone operators are helpful and friendly and will fax GIA certificates of any diamond you are interested in within minutes. Their employees are not on commission and it shows because there is no pressure to buy. They then ship the ring to the closest store to your home and if after seeing it you decide you don't want it there is no obligation. If you do decide to purchase it, they guarantee it will appraise for a retail value of 200% above what you paid or you will get a refund, the cost of the appraisal reimbursed, plus $100 for your inconvenience."

Helpful Hints

1 Independently confirm the ring's quality. If you're buying a ring online or from a self-described "discounter" find an independent appraiser to check out the ring after you buy it. Make sure that the price you paid is what the stone is worth.

2 Confirm return policies. Be certain to check with each retailer for his return policy. Some only give you 30 days or less to return a ring. Have the ring appraised with enough time to return it if the ring's quality and value is questionable.

3 If you're spending a lot of money for a ring, buy a loose stone. The ring's setting may hide flaws in the stone. As one bride noted, her diamond had an inclusion (defect) that was easily seen in the loose stone, but was hidden completely by the setting. She got a great price on it because of the defect, but no one could see it once it was set. While she knew of the problem and was fine with it, you might never know about it with a pre-set diamond until you want to reset it or appraise it. Then you may find out you spent too much and got less than you expected.

4 Before you order or buy a ring, check to see if is a cast band. A cast band is made to a specific size and cannot be sized down to fit. One bride contacted us about just such a problem. In trying to downsize a cast ring, the jewelry store dented the band. Ultimately, the bride put her foot down and they reordered her band in the correct size.

5 Titanium caveats. Yes, titanium wedding bands have increased in popularity in recent years. But consider these tips: first, titanium rings are DARKER than platinum or gold. Although they are marketed as scratch-resistant, a titanium ring WILL show scratches (good news: the rings can be polished to address this). Finally, titanium rings are nearly impossible to re-size. It is very difficult to make a titanium ring larger or smaller.

That said, we should note that titanium rings are very durable while at the same time, very lightweight. That makes a titanium ring perfect for the guy who doesn't like wearing rings—or works in a hands-on job like construction.

Brides in Cyberspace: What's on the Web?

As with every aspect of today's wedding, you can buy your wedding bands (and even engagement ring) online. Web-based jewelers make up about $2 billion of the $45 billion jewelry industry—and that share is increasing at a rapid clip.. Even Amazon.com has joined the many online options with their own fine jewelry store online.

So what's the big attraction? Price. The typical retail jeweler marks up items as much as 60% to 100%. But online retailers limit their markup to about 15%. By bypassing convoluted supply lines and cutting out middlemen, online jewelers can offer consumers deals on diamonds and bands of as much as 40%.

Is there a big risk to buying online? No, nearly all online jewelers offer 30-day money back guarantees—so you can take your items to a gemologist for an appraisal.

Spotlight: Best Buy

Wedding Ring Hotline

(800) 985-7464 or (732) 972-7777; weddingringhotline.com

Tired of the high prices of mall jewelry stores? Like the prices but not the styles of discount, catalog showrooms? Well, we found a great alternative: The Wedding Ring Hotline of Englishtown, New Jersey.

Owner Mitch Slachman has been in the business since 1983 and has developed a loyal clientele in New York and New Jersey. The Wedding Ring Hotline not only carries Mitch's custom designs, but also the styles of leading designers' lines as well. If you see an advertisement for a name-brand ring or have the style number, you can get a price quote.

And talk about good deals—The Wedding Ring Hotline's prices are 25% to 33% below retail on most designs. Or Mitch can custom-design a ring for even bigger savings. Wedding Ring Hotline's retail showroom (under the name Bride & Groom's West) in Englishtown, New Jersey has over 1000+ styles on display. (It's best to call for an appointment).

If you don't live in that part of the country, you can surf their extensive web site. We saw an impressive number of styles, from monogrammed bands to diamond-studded rings. A simple 4mm plain band in 14K white or yellow gold starts at $65. A simple men's style in white gold is about $200 range. Want platinum? For a man's solid platinum ring sells for only $1000.

Another cool part to the Wedding Ring Hotline: they also sell designer brands like Christian Bauer (among others) at attractive prices. So if you see a ring advertised in a bridal magazine, call them first to get a price quote before you pay a hefty mark-up at a retail store.

The Wedding Ring Hotline takes all major credit cards and has a 30-day 100% money-back guarantee if you're not happy. There's also no sales tax if you live outside New Jersey, a big money-savings as well.

FIGURE 1: Why pay retail for your rings? Sites like the WeddingRingHotline offer discounts up to 70% off mall jeweler prices.

More web sites for diamond rings:

♥ **Blue Nile** (bluenile.com) is fast becoming one of the most popular sites online to find affordable wedding and engagement rings. They offer an FAQ on selecting a ring as well as a customizing option if you don't see the design you want. We liked playing with the "Build Your Own Ring" options. We could choose any shape, size, color or clarity we wanted. Being the crazy idiots we are we went for the $32,000. Oh well, we can dream.

♥ **Diamond Cutters** (diamondcutters.com) has an excellent tutorial on buying a diamond. Check out their "Education" section to learn what rip-offs to avoid when diamond shopping. Diamond Cutters offers an option similar to Blue Nile to create your own ring. They offer to show you different shapes of diamonds into different settings—and you can choose settings by price—pretty cool.

♥ **Diamond** (diamond.com) also offers brides an opportunity to customize their own engagement rings along with name brand options. Check out their clearance section for some bargains.

♥ **Ice** (ice.com) Ice's wedding boutique includes everything from the engagement and wedding rings to gifts for the wedding party and even men's cuff links.

♥ **Amazon** (amazon.com) lets you shop by price using their sort feature. You can also choose to browse by setting type, material and brand. Check for sales—they're frequent.

♥ **Trade Shop** (tradeshop.com) offers custom wedding rings you can help design yourself. And they post pictures of your ring as it "takes shape" while they're making it.

♥ **Diamond.ca** (diamond.ca) Yep, you read right, it's a Canadian company (part of Canadian Diamond Exchange). Diamond.ca cells only diamonds from Canada—so you can avoid buying a "conflict diamond" that may be funding some despotic regime or terrorist organization. A side benefit: they also claim their diamonds are 30% to 50% cheaper than comparable diamonds on the market.

Further reading. This section just addresses wedding bands. We assume you already have a diamond engagement ring. Yet, if you're more interested in learning how to purchase diamonds and colored stones, there are three excellent books to read (all are available on Amazon.com or in bookstores):

♥ **The Diamond Ring Buying Guide: How to Spot Value & Avoid Rip-offs** (pictured) by Renee Newman (2002, $17.95, International Jewelry Publications).

♥ **Engagement & Wedding Rings: The Definitive Buying Guide for People in Love** by Matlins, Bonanno, Crystal (1999, $18.95, Gemstone Press 800-962-4544, 802-457-4000).

'Net Tutorials There are several online sources for basic information on buying a diamond or other gemstone. Here are some of the best:

♥ **Diamond Talk** (diamondtalk.com) was recommended by former bride

Royal Prestige: Cookware pitch exposed

Royal Prestige pitches engaged couples to come to their seminars to learn about their cookware and win a free honeymoon. Many of our readers, however, think the cookware is a joke and the sales tactics are heavy handed at best. The following letter, from a reader who has extensive experience in the cookware and china biz, summed it up best:

"After attending a local bridal show at which I registered, I was called by Royal Prestige and invited to a 'marketing presentation' at a local hotel with dinner included. Even though I was skeptical, I didn't have any plans that evening, so I dragged my fiancéé out for what I thought would be a fun presentation.

"When I got there, surprise, surprise, it was a sales pitch! The focus of the sales pitch was their waterless cookware and china. Rather than focusing on exactly what you would be getting for your hard-earned money, the salesperson focused on the substantial savings to be gained by using less energy to cook the food, and using no oil! He also spelled out the benefits of healthy cooking and the easy payment plan. The 'dinner' was a small piece of cooked chicken, and a few carrots and pieces of broccoli, followed by a glass of water! Some dinner—and it was a long presentation, at dinnertime.

"I was amazed at how they distorted the facts. For example, they showed off their four ugly china patterns, and told us that the patterns have never been discontinued, and never will be. Lenox china, however, discontinues 50% of their china patterns every four years, he told the appalled group of brides and grooms to be. All that hard-earned money spent on Lenox china, and after four years, there was a 50% chance that the pattern wouldn't be around! What he failed to accurately mention is that the majority of patterns sold by Lenox are in their Top 25 line, which does not get discontinued. Any bridal consultant can easily obtain that information and educate prospective customers. His other point was that if a piece or two gets broken, then Lenox makes you buy the entire place setting, not just a dinner plate! Helloooo, ever heard of open stock? You have to ASK someone at the store, and it usually requires a special order, but it is not difficult to just buy one piece of china!

"His talk about the cookware was also full of inaccuracies, but

Anita Carmichael. She liked using the site's extensive forums to pick the brains of gemologists, jewelers, appraisers and other experts. She managed to save her fiancéé $1000 on her engagement ring by following the advice of other posters!

one in particular stands out. While talking about their lifetime guarantee, he referred to one of the best cookware brands on the market—Calphalon. At that point, he whipped out a Calphalon box, and showed it to all the amazed attendees. The warranty on the Calphalon box was only for ten years! All that money, and such a small warranty period! The nerve of Calphalon to do such a thing! He neglected to explain to everyone that the box he was holding was part of Calphalon's "Pots & Pans" line, which is its low-end cookware. You don't spend a lot of money to get that set! All their other lines do come with a lifetime warranty, but he never mentioned that.

"By this point, everyone was ready to thank this guy for doing them such a favor. And he was ready for the kill. There were reps available now to discuss the payment plans with you. If you made the purchase today, then you would get a 40% discount, in the form of a gift. Will wonders never cease? For free, you would get a service for four of any china, crystal AND flatware pattern that they carry. Hmmm, don't most people buy a service for 8 or 12? Could this be yet another ploy to con people into spending more money?? I wonder. . . .

"Everybody had to speak to a rep to get his or her "free" voucher at Divi resorts. I had already checked into it, and found out they had timeshares, so I put two and two together. Still, I wanted the voucher, just to check it out. I was not one of the first people called, so I had to wait. Fortunately, another couple who my fiancéé knew happened to be there as well, and they were up first. While she had bought into the scam, she wasn't ready to put up $2,000 for the 17-piece cookware set, which, by the way, contains only five or six pots—another issue they failed to mention. She left the rep, and started talking to me, where I started educating her on the scam that she had just witnessed. Other confused brides started coming up to me, to hear what I had to say. Lo and behold, I was immediately called as being next! It took me about two seconds to inform the rep with really bad breath that I already had everything I needed. He looked scared, handed me a voucher, and I walked out.

"I don't plan on wasting another weekend at Divi Resorts. However, my fiancéé was interested in the benefits of waterless cookware, and wanted to look into it. I bet him I could find it on the Internet for at least half the price they were selling it at. Guess what? I bought a complete set on eBay for about $70!"

♥ **Diamond Grading** (diamondgrading.com) has an extensive FAQ on diamond buying as well as a chat group and other helpful info.

♥ **Price Scope** (pricescope.com) has an excellent tutorial on buying a diamond. You can also use the site to search for the perfect loose diamond for your ring.

♥ **Jim Kokernak's "Frequently Asked Questions (FAQ) about Diamonds."** This 16-page guide includes sections on finding a jeweler, the basics on diamonds, how not to get ripped off and more. You can find this FAQ at the http://www.rpi.edu/~kokerj/diamond/diamond.html.

Dubious Items: Wedding Insurance, Name Change Kits

What's the silliest bridal accessory we've discovered? Would you believe lucky pennies for $5 each? Yes, that's what a company in Texas was selling—a penny wrapped in tulle and tied with a ribbon. If that wasn't enough, we found another catalog selling "lucky six-pence" for $12. Last time we checked exchange rates, a six-pence was worth, say, ten pennies. What a deal, eh? Here are some more dubious items:

♥ **Wedding insurance.** Do you need wedding insurance? Fireman's Fund/R.V. Nuccio (800-ENGAGED, web: rvnuccio.com) offers a policy (Weddingsurance) that protects you in case of cancellation of the wedding, lost photos, damaged bridal attire, lost gifts and personal liability for bodily injury or property damage at your wedding and reception. Premiums start at $200. So, should you buy? Well, *Money Magazine* picked wedding insurance as a great example of insurance you really don't need, pointing out that the skimpy coverage doesn't justify the hefty premiums. We have mixed feelings about this insurance—if your reception site requires you to purchase liability insurance, this might be an affordable alternative. If your spouse is in the military and you worry a surprise overseas deployment may scuttle the wedding plans, this insurance may also help. Of course, read the policy carefully to catch all the fine print. Wedsafe.com is another wedding insurance vendor with premiums starting at $185.

So what's covered by wedding insurance? Accidents that occur at the wedding or while guests are on their way home as well as vendors who don't show up, cancellation by the site, damage or destruction of wedding attire, theft of gifts or jewelry, illness among key members of the wedding party, site fees and loss of rental property among other items. Weather is also covered but only if it is disaster level (Florida hurricanes anyone?) that keep guests from attending. Military deployment is covered as well, but only if it was totally unexpected at the time you bought the policy. Those in the military reserve may not be covered.

♥ **Watch out for name change rip-offs.** Don't fall victim to "name change scams" where companies promise they'll handle your name change for a fee. Authorities have been cracking down on such rip-offs and recently arrested a Las Vegas couple that tricked thousands of women into paying them for services the Social Security Administration offers for free. The couple ran a business that mailed out letters to "help" brides change their names on their Social Security cards for a fee of $15. Yet forms for that purpose are available to the public *free of charge* from local Social Security offices (check the web at ssa.gov or the government listings in your local phone book for locations).

Bridal Shows: Fun Afternoon or Highway to Bridal Hell?

If you need a good laugh, attend a local bridal show in your town. If you aren't convinced that the wedding "industry" is a joke, this is the place to give your cynical side a booster shot.

Basically, most bridal shows attempt to stage a fashion show (we use the word "fashion" here very loosely) and a trade fair. The latter consists of various booths with displays from merchants with names like "Brides 'R' Us" and "Fred's Professional Wedding Photography." Like sharks smelling blood in the water, these merchants crawl out of their subterranean homes and swim circles around brides, passing out little gifts like potpourri balls, which will emit such a pleasant perfume that it will take you three months to get the smell out of your purse.

The fashion show is the alleged bait to get you (the consumer) into their (the merchants') clutches for two hours of unabashed commercial plugs. During this fashion show, you will actually see live and in person many of those hideous bridesmaids gowns that you only thought existed in the bridal magazines and in the backs of closets. After hearing the announcer say for the twentieth time, "Here's a lovely taffeta design with PUFF SLEEVES" you'll probably be able to actually feel your teeth grind.

What's most interesting about these runway shows is the realization of how far removed the bridal apparel industry is from reality. If you look closely, you'll notice the "new design for this year" looks suspiciously like one from a wedding you attended in 2002.

After the show and the non-stop commercial plug-a-thon (yes, Bob, we'd love to thank Burt's Wedding Chair Rental for providing the chairs you're sitting in today! Aren't they just lovely! And they're just $7.95 plus deposit!), you have time to walk around the booths and chat with local merchants. Many of these merchants will lunge at you from their booths and shove a brochure in your hand while simultaneously complimenting you on how LARGE your engagement ring is—all with a look of sincerely feigned sincerity. While visiting a recent bridal show, we were struck by the sheer ingenuity of wedding entrepreneurs who have invented brilliant ways to separate you from your money.

Perhaps the best known bridal show operator is Bridal Expo, based in that state known for bridal bliss, New Jersey (just ask Bruce Springsteen). Bridal Expo mounts this massive multi-media show that admittedly is much more polished than the typical dog-and-pony show put on by locals. Slickly choreographed, Bridal Expos are thick with plugs for the Official Sponsors.

What's most hysterical about the Bridal Expo is that these folks from New Jersey think that the world is simply dying to see what newest horror the New York bridal designers are trying to heap on us consumers. At one show in Denver, we couldn't help but notice the crowd audibly

Real Wedding Tip

Welcome to the jungle!

Heather K. of Southgate, MI discussed her recent experience at a bridal show: *I have read your book. and I just wanted to write to thank you for all the great tips and advice. Unfortunately I didn't get to the part about bridal shows until after I went to one. It was at a local hotel and it was just a zoo. I wanted to go with my mom thinking it would be fun to just get a look at some stuff. My mom wanted to bring some extra money just in case, but I told her only to bring enough for the entry fee ($3) and that I just wanted to get some ideas. We got there, paid our fee and were handed a checklist. We were told that if we got all the vendors to check off the list when we went to their booth, we would get a free "bridal gift".*

For a while we shuffled along behind the other brides to be and got our little lists checked and took information and (oops) filled out the little "drawing slips". After a while I had so much information that my cheap little plastic bag broke and I was just checking the list off myself as I passed booths that didn't interest me. (I did get some really great info for the most part though and MANY of the vendors were really nice.) Only a few of the booths wanted me to book that day and I said, "Thanks, but no," and moved on. My "bridal gift" at the end? A tube of VERY waxy chapstick with the hotel's name on it and they didn't even look at my list! We were so tired by that point that my mom and I decided to skip the "fashion show" and go get some lunch. After I read the bridal show section of your book I am glad we did.

guffawing at several bridal gowns that some designer must have dreamed up in his Manhattan loft during a bad acid trip.

The biggest scam at all these bridal shows is the so-called door prizes. As you enter, most bridal shows will ask you to register for A FREE EXCITING HONEYMOON TRIP TO SLOVENIA. Of course, besides your name and address, the "registration card" will ask for your phone number, fiancé's name, yearly income, birth place, blood type, and so on. As you wander around the booths, the wedding merchants will ask you to fill out entry forms for such tantalizing door prizes as "A FREE NAPKIN (WHEN YOU PURCHASE $1000 WORTH OF PICTURES)!"

As you fill out the forms, you'll notice the merchants and show organizers will barely be able to keep the drool from dripping down their shirts in sheer excitement. That's because this whole door prize thing is a big sham—what these bridal shows really want is your phone number, email and mailing address. Then they can call you frequently at dinnertime to inform you that they have a BIG SPECIAL this month and that if you sign up NOW you won't be killed by their bridal death squad.

Yes, bridal merchants pay hundreds of dollars to do these shows and THE BIG REASON is that list of brides, all neatly alphabetized with their home phone numbers, wedding date, bank account numbers, and more. Many brides are alarmed to find after attending a bridal show that they must buy a six-foot mailbox with forklift to handle the volume of mail that will give new meaning to the word junk.

The lesson? If you've got an afternoon to kill and would like to overdose on sugar from 67 cake samples, then a bridal show may be for you. But, if you value your privacy, be careful out there. Nothing says you have to give these shows or merchants your real address, email or phone number.

Wedding Consultants

Wedding planners have been satirized in movies, lionized by bridal magazines—and generally ignored by brides. Once a fixture of weddings in the 1950's, wedding consultants were hunted to near extinction in the 1970's when weddings were less formal affairs usually held on a beach.

As weddings have become more complex and formal events, professional wedding consultants have made an impressive comeback. We should note, however, that there are several types of wedding consultants. Many people who work at bridal shops or retail florists call themselves "wedding consultants." In addition to helping the bride with their own specialty, these folks pass along referrals of other bridal professionals. While they may be helpful, these are not the wedding consultants we are referring to in this section.

We define a "professional wedding consultant" as an independent businessperson who, for a fee, helps plan and coordinate the entire wedding. They don't actually bake the cake or sew the gown—this is done by outside suppliers. In a sense, a wedding consultant is like a personal shopper. Or as some planners have discovered, like a low-paid waitress.

So How Much Do Wedding Consultants Cost?

Most charge an hourly fee or a percentage of the wedding budget. For example, one consultant we met charges a 15% fee on wedding expenditures. So, if you spend $20,000 on a wedding and reception, you then write out a check for $3000 to the consultant. Other party planners we met charge a flat hourly fee ($75 per hour, for example) no matter what your budget. Many consultants offer different levels of help—coordinating just the rehearsal and wedding ceremony costs a small fee, while planning the whole affair from the ground up will run you much more.

Sources to Find a Consultant

♥ **Call a professional association.** June Wedding (702) 474-9558 (junewedding.com) will give you a referral to a local bridal consultant (their membership is mostly in the Western US). Another group is the Association of Bridal Consultants (860) 355-0464 (bridalassn.com). Unfortunately, they ask you to fill out a form before they'll send you a list of consultants in your area. And, no surprise, they ask you for your wedding budget. Why do they ask this? So consultants can cherry pick those brides with the biggest budgets. Don't enter your budget on the form—wait for the opportunity to speak to the consultants in person.

♥ **Ask your friends.** The best planners work by word-of-mouth referrals.

Questions to Ask a Consultant

1 Exactly how do you work your fees? Do you accept commissions or finder's fees from other bridal merchants? See the Pitfall section below for more information on this practice. Ask the consultant to clearly explain his/her fee schedule.

2 How will you incorporate my tastes into the wedding? If the consultant will be doing the majority of the legwork, ask them how they will personalize your wedding. Will they get your approval at various stages in the planning process?

3 How long have you been a consultant? How many weddings have you planned? This is a key question. Many "consultants" we've met in the course of researching this book were far too inexperienced to entrust with the planning of a $20,000 wedding. Some have been in business for less than a year or so. We recommend you trust your wedding only to a seasoned professional with at least three years minimum experience. Sure, consultants with less experience can still plan and coordinate a beautiful wedding—but be careful. You don't want someone "learning the ropes" on your big day. Other related questions: How many weddings do you do in a year? On a typical weekend?

4 Are you certified? If the bridal consultant belongs to a professional organization, that's nice . . . but it's even better if they've been certified or accredited. Check out the organization that certified the planner to insure they are in good standing—and ask how they certify consultants (education, experience, license requirements).

5 Do you have five vendor referrals? Yes, you want to check with past clients of the consultants. But then go one step further: ask for referrals from five wedding *vendors* they work with all the time (photographers, florists, etc.). You'll get an idea of the caliber of the consultant's contacts by the names they provide.

6 Will you provide regular written updates? Communication is key—you should be updated on the planning at regular intervals via email.

7 Can you work within our budget? Yes, that's the $64,000 question. Sure, you may not have a firm grasp on what the budget should be, but a good consultant should be able to estimate what the wedding you want will cost. If the consultant can't work within that budget, ask if you can hire them on a "per meeting" basis. Many planners offer this "limited service" option, which enables couples to tap the planner's expertise without paying full price.

Special thanks to Robbi Ernst of June Wedding for providing some of the questions to ask listed above.

Pitfalls to Avoid with Wedding Planners

Pitfall #1 Kickbacks and vendor referral fees

"I visited a wedding planner who recommended I buy my wedding gown from a particular bridal shop. Later, I learned the shop paid her a commission for recommending me. Is this legitimate?"

Well, it certainly isn't ethical. This points up a central problem we have with some less-than-professional consultants. In a clear conflict of interest, some consultants collect "finder's fees" or "commissions" (read: kickbacks) from other bridal merchants on the products and services they recommend to brides. So who are they representing—the bride or the merchants? We don't believe a consultant can negotiate effectively for the bride when they receive a kickback from bridal merchants. If you use a consultant, make sure the consultant clearly identifies how they get paid.

PITFALL #2 PERCENTAGE-BASED FEES MAY ENCOURAGE GREED.
"One bridal consultant told me she could save me hundreds of dollars. However, her fee is based on a percentage of the money I spend. Where is her real incentive to save me money?"

Of course, a professional consultant relies on word-of-mouth referral for new clients. If they don't deliver what they promise, word will spread quickly. However, we do agree that a conflict exists here: when their income is based on how much money you spend, less-than-ethical consultants may feel the temptation to encourage lavish spending. Or at least, the incentive to save you money comes in conflict with their bottom line. Realize that all consultants do not charge a percentage-based fee—others charge flat fees or hourly rates. This might be a better alternative.

PITFALL #3 COUNTERFEIT CONSULTANTS.
"I called a so-called 'wedding consultant' from the phone book. Instead of offering a consulting service, she pitched me on her wedding chapel and reception site."

Yes, many "all-in-one" wedding companies deceptively advertise themselves as wedding consultants. Don't be fooled—these businesses aren't interested in consulting on your wedding. They just want you to book their wedding and reception site, photography and so on.

PITFALL #4 LACK OF REGULATION.
"I contacted a wedding consultant to talk about my wedding. Boy was I surprised! This person knew nothing about weddings. Aren't these guys suppose to be licensed?"

Unfortunately, very few laws regulate wedding consultants. When you think about it, wedding consultants are quasi-financial planners—they advise people on how to spend money. Big money. Unlike other financial planners, however, there is very little regulation. Anyone can

call himself or herself a wedding consultant—and sometimes it seems like everyone is. Some cities do require wedding consultants or party planners to be licensed. In most areas, however, the industry is left to police itself. Consider hiring a consultant who is a member of a professional association. Many require their members to subscribe to a basic ethics pledge. Other groups offer on-going training through seminars and workshops.

Advantages of Consultants

♥ **BRIDAL CONSULTANTS CAN SAVE YOU TIME.** If you and your fiancéé are working too many hours to plan your wedding, you may find a wedding consultant to be worth the expense. Frankly, planning a wedding is very time-intensive (it takes about 100 hours to plan a typical wedding). Realistically evaluate your schedules and time commitments to decide if you can handle it alone. Brides planning large and expensive wedding may find consultants a necessity.

♥ **LONG-DISTANCE WEDDINGS MAY REQUIRE SUCH HELP.** Planning a wedding in another city is quite challenging. Having a local bridal consultant to coordinate the details may be prudent.

♥ **SEASONED EXPERTS MAY BE ABLE TO NEGOTIATE MORE EFFECTIVELY, GETTING YOU A BETTER DEAL.** Now we aren't talking about novices here but wedding consultants with years of experience. These people are on a first-name basis with catering managers and other bridal professionals. Some consultants are tough negotiators who can make sure you get the best price. Other consultants claim that other bridal professionals have a vested interest in doing their very best work for their clients—if they don't, they may lose future business. We are not sure to what extent these claims are true but we do believe one thing: a talented, experienced consultant may be worth the extra expense.

Disadvantages of Consultants

♥ **THE "PROFESSIONAL ORGANIZATIONS" FOR BRIDAL CONSULTANTS AREN'T THAT PROFESSIONAL.** Unlike other fields, most bridal consultant associations don't have rigid standards for membership. Printed up business cards that say you're a wedding consultant? Have a pulse? That's enough for some wedding planner associations. Their main business is selling "home study" courses that are of dubious value.

Other groups are better—June Wedding (702) 474-9558 (junewedding.com) is probably the best-run professional organization of the bunch. Director Robbi Ernst teaches on-going training courses for both new and experienced wedding planners. And June Wedding takes a

strong position on the kickback issue; they advise members to NEVER take vendor referral fees.

So what does this mean for you? While it's a good sign if the bridal consultant you've discovered is a member of one of these groups, don't assume they are all-knowing "experts." Check references and ask some tough questions to weed out the amateurs.

Gift Registries

Bridal gift registries have been around in various forms for over 50 years and it's no wonder: they offer convenience for both the guest and bride. Last year, the wedding gift industry racked up $19 billion in sales of china, salt and pepper shakers, toasters and a gazillion other items.

Yet, for all the promise, registries are among the bigger complaint areas for brides and grooms. Just about everything that CAN go wrong has happened with these so-called "convenience" services–items that are out of stock for what seems like a decade, surly clerks, technical snafus and more. We'll discuss all of the sordid details in Pitfalls to Avoid later in this section. Also, *Consumer Reports* offers a periodic *Brides Guide* magazine that rates Internet registries online at consumerreports.org.

For years, the bridal registry biz was dominated by big department stores. These stores offered gift registries for a limited selection of china, crystal, flatware and so on. Fortunately, this all began to change in the 80's and 90's when discount stores and specialty chains added gift registries, giving couples more choices.

Yet, the biggest news of all in recent years is the advent of the online gift registry. The marriage of the gift registry (essentially a database, of course) with the web (open 24/7) promised to give both couples and their guests more convenience. Now, you can register for gifts at 3am in your pajamas, see what items your guests are buying and even change the registry as your wedding draws near. Like everything with the 'net, however, the promise of making bridal registries work better has fallen somewhat short in reality.

On the plus side, there are more competitors than ever in the gift registry biz. Dot-coms like TheKnot.com are battling with established department stores for the online gift registry market and the biggest winner so far is the consumer. We'll review the best sites to register on line next.

Brides in Cyberspace: What's on the Web?

Wedding Channel and The Knot

Web: weddingchannel.com; theknot.com

What it is: The largest online wedding gift registries

Comments: The recent merger between the two large wedding websites now creates the mother of all online wedding registries. It's unclear whether the Knot will keep the Wedding Channel site as a stand-alone brand or eventually fold the site into the Knot's registry. So here's a brief overview of each site as it stood when we went to press:

♥ The Wedding Channel.

The Wedding Channel works with an impressive group of retailers including Neiman Marcus, Crate & Barrel and REI. They even have a honeymoon registry. But that's not all. The site included detailed advice and a guide on how to register. They have suggestion on what items to register for as well. Specific etiquette on alternative registries is interesting to check out. Alternative registries include honeymoon, charity and home improvement registries among other options.

How does the Wedding Channel registry work? In some cases you register directly on the Wedding Channel site, while in other cases, the site transfers you to the stores' individual sites to register (you can still

FIGURE 2: The Wedding Channel's gift registry is the 'net's largest, thanks to several department stores partners.

access these registries from the Wedding Channel).

Finally, the Wedding Channel offers detailed advice and articles on how to register and what to register for. Be careful, however for inconsistent advice. For example: under registry etiquette, site advises you to NOT include registry info in invitations. Yet, on another page, the Wedding Channel enables users to print out "enclosure cards" with registry info for your invitation. Huh?

♥ The Knot

The Knot has a bit of a different take on wedding registries. They offer a couple options. First you can do a search by brand (Noritake, Lenox and Baccarat, for example) or by type of china (fine, everyday, designer, stemware, gifts and flatware). Instead focusing on national retailers like the Wedding Channel, the Knot's emphasis is on their own in-house registry. (The only exception: the Knot does offer a way to register with Target, Michael C. Fina and Linens & Things. For Target, the Knot transfer you directly to Target's registry—but you can still access your Target registry from the Knot).

As with all online registries, the Knot allows couples to add to and delete from their registries 24 hours a day.

Finally, the Knot offers a registry guide. This is a series of cheat sheets including advice on what type of bakeware you prefer (glass or ceramic—what? You didn't know there were different types of bakeware?). Plus you can learn exactly how many crystal champagne flutes one should own.

♥ Other online gift registries. A reader recommended **Felicite** (felicite.com):

"Felicite's concept is not unique but their service is outstanding. It is a gift registry that can arrange any gift from anywhere. This allowed us to setup donations to a non-profit and to register gifts from unique and local stores while still giving people around the world access to our registry to purchase the gifts through Felicite.com. Once people visited he registry and purchased the gifts through Felicite.com, we had the option to pick up the gifts, have them delivered or take the cash directly. They also have a partial purchase feature so people can pitch in together on a single expensive gift. What distinguishes this gift registry from others is their EXCELLENT customer service. They were readily accessible on the phone or via email."

Looking for a simple, free registry? One reader recommended **FindGift** (findgift.com). "It enables you to add gifts manually rather than gifts from certain stores. And it provides guests with a web link to purchase the gift online."

Pitfalls to Avoid with Gift Registries

PITFALL #1: OUT OF STOCK!

"We registered for a china pattern, but when guests made their purchases, we found the items were out of stock! And we'd have to wait three MONTHS for delivery."

Yes, stores are famous for letting you register for items that have long been out of stock. Then when you go to pick up the items, you get the bad news—thanks to a back-order, you can come back in several WEEKS or MONTHS to get the gifts! A word to the wise: BEFORE you register, check the stock status of items you want. If the store doesn't stock many of the items, it could be a recipe for frustration.

PITFALL #2: SEASONS CHANGE.

"We thought we'd be smart if we registered six months in advance of our wedding, only to learn that by the time the wedding rolled around, some of the items we wanted were long gone!"

Sometimes, it DOESN'T pay to plan ahead. Registering too early can be a problem—items change, get discontinued, go on back-order or worse as time rolls by. Our advice: wait until two or three months before your wedding to register for gifts. Sure, you can do shopping before that, but don't actually create the registry until closer to the wedding. Guests don't start buying gifts until right before the bridal shower, so you aren't making anyone's life difficult by waiting. Another tip: don't register for seasonal merchandise. Such items typically go out of stock or are heavily discounted, making returns or exchanges difficult.

PITFALL #3: SIXTEEN SALT AND PEPPER SHAKERS

"Hey! I thought the gift registry was supposed to stop duplicate gifts! We registered and STILL got three toasters, four blenders and other duplicates!"

Theoretically, when your guests buy a gift from a registry, a computer sitting in a climate-controlled room somewhere in Delaware is supposed to SUBTRACT that item from your list. That way, your Aunt Mabel doesn't buy you that sixteenth salt and peppershaker set. Yet, note we used the word "theoretically" in that first sentence. The reality: sometimes clerks still have to hand-enter gift items into a computer . . . and those clerks forget. Or the registry fails to get updated for a myriad of reasons only a computer tech knows. Expect glitches and deal with a store that has good customer service to handle such problems.

PITFALL #4: CHANGES, WHAT CHANGES?

"We registered with a department store that promised we could see our registry online. Yet when we went to the web site, all we could do was SEE it. No changes were allowed!"

That's right. Some department stores have put their gift registries online—but that only means you can VIEW the registry and guests can buy items online. Want to change an item? Update a quantity? You'll still have to go into a store to do that. Yes, it is the 21st century and you do all sorts of amazing things online . . . but don't assume your bridal registry will be that easy!

Money Saving Tips with Gift Registries

1 Price shop BEFORE you register. Don't assume one store has the lowest prices just because they offer a "low price" guarantee. That usually means they will refund you the difference if you find a better price. Before you register, visit at least three different stores to get an idea about prices, policies on returns and other details. Be aware that "sale prices" at one store may be higher than the "everyday low price" at another.

2 Consider lower-price alternatives. No, you don't have to just register at a department store. Off-price retailers have moved into the bridal registry biz in recent years and offer a great alternative. Remember that not ALL of your guests can buy $250 gift items at department stores; giving them a wide option of items at different price points in several stores is smart.

3 Get sale guarantees in writing. Department stores are famous for running numerous sales throughout the year. Unfortunately, some "forget" to give your guests the discounted price when purchasing a gift. Double check the registry's promises regarding sale prices and verify purchases to make sure you get the best price.

4 Go for a discounter to fill in purchases. Get 7 of 8 place settings you wanted? Want to fill in the final items? Consider buying china and tableware from a discounter. Ross Simons (ross-simons.com) offers popular patterns at discounts of up to 30%, with additional coupon deals and clearance items (especially flatware). Ross Simons has been around since 1952 and has excellent customer service.

5 And don't forget to consider registering for your honeymoon! This is a particularly attractive idea for couples that already have all the dishes, coffee pots, etc. they could ever use. You can set up a honeymoon registry with most full service travel agencies. Now you just have to figure out where to go on your honeymoon.

6 How can you turn unwanted wedding gifts into cash? Use a in-store credit card. If you want to return a gift (say you got three salt and pepper shakers but two are plenty), many couples will have the returned gift credited to their in-store charge account. Now what's the big deal with this? Well, federal law requires that the store refund any positive balance to the cardholder if they request it. So you get cash back! Needless to say, retailers are not happy about folks discovering this loophole (particularly those like Target with incredibly strict refund policies). In fact, some stores now will not credit back items to your credit card—they only issue a store credit voucher. Check with the stores you are registering with to see if they will allow returns to be charged back to in-store credit cards. Marshall Field's and Macy's have such lenient return policies as of this writing. And other stores like Crate & Barrel and Williams-Sonoma are willing to refund cash for any exchange. Check with your registry.

Honeymoons

What are the best honeymoon deals? How can you hurricane-proof your honeymoon? Where do you go online to save? We'll explore these and other tips in this section.

What are you buying?

The average honeymoon costs $4086 and lasts eight days, according to a recent bridal magazine survey. Honeymoons can be found in almost any price range. On the dirt-cheap end, close-to-home get-aways can be had for under $1000. Conversely, a week's stay on a posh Caribbean island can be double or triple the "average" honeymoon budget.

Remember the golden rule of honeymoon shopping: NEVER PAY RETAIL. Honeymoons are an $8 billion business. But we'd guess 90% or more of honeymoons are sold at prices that are discounted off the "brochure price," "rack rate" or other stated rate.

What are the most popular sites to honeymoon? Travel agents say Hawaii, Jamaica, Mexico, Tahiti, Bermuda, Italy, Las Vegas, Aruba, St. Lucia and Orlando are the top honeymoon destinations. Cruises are also at the top of the list.

Sources to find honeymoon info

♥ **THE NEWSPAPER.** Yep, even though it is low-tech, the travel section in your Sunday paper is a good starting place for honeymoon planning. You'll see what vacation packages are available in your area, what sales might be on and more.

♥ **TRAVEL AGENTS.** A few do still exist and if you can find a good one, they can be invaluable. Savvy agents know which hotels have the most romantic views and which tour operators are most reliable. Sadly, it is hard to find a decent agent these days, much less one that is a "honeymoon expert." Ask friends and co-workers if they know good agents.

♥ **THE WEB.** If there is one thing the web is great for, it's travel. From discount airfare sites to official tourism bureaus for far-flung locales, the web can't be beat. We'll go over some of our favorite 'net spots for deals later in this chapter.

Money Saving Tips with Honeymoons

1 **Go "off-season."** Discounts of up to 40% can be had on lodging and airfares when you travel in the so-called off-season. But just when is the off-season? It depends on the location. See the chart on the next page for details.

2 **Try the shoulder seasons.** If you don't want to go to a tropical island in the heat of summer, consider the "shoulder seasons." These are times in between the peak and off-peak seasons. For example, in the Caribbean, packages in the weeks after Easter before the summer rush and between Thanksgiving and Christmas can be great deals. Ask an agent if the destination you want has any shoulder season discounts.

3 **One word: Orlando.** There are so many deals to Orlando and so much to do there (it's more than just Disney) that you can't go wrong. Many airlines offer $500 packages (per person) for a week in Orlando—that includes airfare, hotel and a car rental. One airline that offers such great deals is Southwest Airlines. Which brings us to tip number #4:

4 **Two words:** Southwest Airlines. This low-cost airline has expanded in recent years and now serves such honeymoon friendly destinations as Orlando, Salt Lake City (think ski vacation) and Ft. Lauderdale (a great jumping off point for a cruise).

When is the Off Season?

You can save big when you take a honeymoon in the off-season. Here's a list of what's off when:

Destination	Off-Season
California Wine Country	Fall months (September and October)
Rocky Mountains	Summer has great deals at ski resorts; From Easter until Thanksgiving.
Europe	November through March.
Caribbean	mid April to mid December. (But watch out for hurricane season).
Orlando	after Easter to early June. September to before Thanksgiving and the month of December up until Christmas; January after New Year's Day.
Hawaii/South Pacific	prices can be slightly higher in winter (especially the Christmas holiday) but they don't change much year-round. Fall (Labor Day to mid December) usually brings fare sales and hotel deals.

5 Alternative airports. Low-fare airlines like Southwest tend to fly out of smaller airports that enable them to avoid congested hubs. Hence you'll find lower fares out of Midway in Chicago compared to O'Hare. Always consider an alternative (usually smaller) airport when trying to save.

6 Plan in advance. The cheapest seats and hotel rooms tend to go first; booking several months ahead of time will ensure you won't have to pay premium prices for peak season dates.

7 Don't plan in advance. Okay, we know that contradicts #6, but think about it. There are many last-minute honeymoon options that can be steals. For example, later in this chapter we'll review a web site that offers cut-rate deals for cruises booked at the last moment. Tour companies like Sun Trips (suntrips.com) also advertise deals on packages that depart within a month—check their web site or the travel section of your newspaper for details.

8 Take an e-fare honeymoon. Speaking of not planning in advance, many airlines now post super-low airfares for travel the following weekend. You leave on a Saturday and must return on a Monday or Tuesday—and you won't know where you are going until Wednesday before the honeymoon (that's when the airfares are posted).

9 For destination weddings, see if the airline has a "bridal discount." If you plan to take ten of your closet friends and/or relatives on a destination wedding, ask about discounts. American and other airlines offer a 5% to 10% discount on the lowest fare for wedding parties of ten or more. American even provides the bride and groom with a packet of airline "upgrade" coupons, car rental discounts and coupons for free drinks and headsets.

10 Book early for peak times. Be careful if your honeymoon corresponds with any peak travel times, like Europe in the summer, the Caribbean over the holidays, spring break in Orlando and so on. In those cases, booking early to get the best deals is prudent.

11 Travel on off-days. The slowest days for air travel (Saturday, Tuesday, Wednesday) often see the lowest fares. In contrast, fares tend to be higher on busy travel days like Thursday, Friday and Sunday.

12 Follow the disaster. A hurricane just hit a Caribbean island? A heat wave bakes a region in Europe? Such events usually create tremendous bargains, as other travelers cancel their plans. Go against the flow for good deals.

13 Bid on a bargain. Many couples have found deals on Priceline.com and other travel auction sites. But beware: Priceline tickets often require bizarre schedules (6am departure, anyone?) and connections that leave you open for delays. Hint: check web sites like BiddingForTravel.com to see what current winning bids are on Priceline!

14 Consider a consolidator. The cheapest way to fly internationally is to check out travel consolidators, who buy blocks of tickets from airlines to re-sell at good prices. A good example: onetravel.com.

15 Tour companies. Vacation package companies like Apple Vacations (applevacations.com) and Sun Trips (suntrips.com) book affordable vacations with charter airlines and decent hotels. These combined deals can be great steals—$630 per person for a week in Cozumel, including airfare and hotel, for example.

One cautionary note: we have heard occasional complaints about tour companies (Apple seems to be the worst). If the hotel you are expecting to stay in is full, they will move you to another, not necessarily comparable hotel. In fact, one reader noted that this happened to her in Cancun: "When we got there, we were told that there wasn't a room available. We had to stay at another hotel down the road (which ended up being much smaller and not nearly as nice as the original hotel). We were never refunded the difference in price between the hotels, and no apologies were offered,"

Hurricane proof your honeymoon

Most weddings (and therefore, honeymoons) are in the summer. And since many couples opt for a beach getaway, the temptation to hit the Caribbean is high. Unfortunately, so is the risk for hurricanes. While the hurricane season peaks in September, you can encounter a vacation-destroying tempest anytime from June to November.

So, what can you do to hurricane proof your honeymoon? Remember your ABC's. Not all Caribbean islands are in the high-risk zone for hurricanes–the "ABC" islands of the Dutch Antilles are a good example. Aruba, Bonaire and Curacao each have a 2% or less chance of getting whacked by a hurricane in each year. And here's another bonus: the summer "low season" produces some great deals to these tropical getaways.

If you like diving, Bonaire is your island. For a more European feel, try Curacao. Aruba has more of a party atmosphere, with casinos, great beaches and decent restaurants.

Other destinations with very low hurricane risk include Panama, Tobago and Margarita (an island off the coast of Venezuela; to book call Servitorus 305-381-9026).

Finally, consider booking a honeymoon vacation with a company or resort that offers a refund guarantee. For example, Club Med offers guests a Future Travel Certificate if a hurricane impacts the resort at any time during the vacation. Sandal's/Beaches resorts offer a free replacement vacation at any one of their resorts should a hurricane directly hit the resort you're staying on. Many cruise lines also have hurricane guarantees.

Companies that offer low cost hurricane "insurance" include TNT Vacations, FunJet Vacations, Worry-Free Vacations and United Vacations. Some web sites like Expedia.com and CheapCaribbean.com offer to waive cancellation fees and help you rebook or get credit vouchers. Be sure to check with your resort, booking agent or discount web site for their policies.

Pitfall to Avoid

PITFALL #1 THE FREE HONEYMOON SCAM.

"I was contacted recently by a travel agency who offered me a free vacation in the Bahamas. They said all I'd have to pay is the taxes on the package, but I have to put down a deposit immediately to qualify for this package. Is this really a good deal?"

If it sounds too good to be true . . . well, you know. This is a common scam perpetrated by a few unscrupulous travel companies. In the instance above, the "taxes and fees" came to $320. In searching the Internet, we discovered you could get a similar package at the same hotel for $310, including all taxes. The lesson here? If you can't wait a day or two to think about and research the deal, it's no deal.

Another twist to this scam: you are contacted by a company that is offering a free honeymoon . . . all you have to do is buy airfare through the travel agency. Great deal, right? Wrong. The airfare will be grossly inflated (several times what you could book yourself) and often, the "free hotel stay" turns out to be a stay in a cheap time share hotel. And you are required to attend a high-pressure sales presentation as part of your freebie.

Brides in Cyberspace: What's on the Web?

Sure, you know about Expedia and Travelocity. But what are some offbeat sites that can help you save on a honeymoon? Here are our picks:

♥ **FARE COMPARE** (farecompare.com) gives you a snapshot of what the average fare is from your home city to any destination worldwide. The site lists current best deals as well as historical averages for fairs so you know whether the price you're being quoted is a bargain or not. See the next page for a graphic.

♥ **SPUR-OF-THE-MOMENT CRUISES** (800) 343-1991, web: spurof.com has last-minute specials from cruise lines. Samples: $629 for an inside cabin for a seven-night Alaska cruise. Or try a weeklong cruise in the Caribbean for just $499 per person.

♥ **VACATION DIRECT** (vacationdirect.com) lists vacation rentals made available directly by owners. You can rent a guest cottage, villa or condo anywhere in the world. The site enables you to search by location, event or interest/activity. You deal directly with the property owner, saving money by eliminating any agent fees.

FIGURE 3: What are the lowest fares between Chicago and the Caribbean right now? In six months? Farecompare.com gives you the answer, plus historical averages.

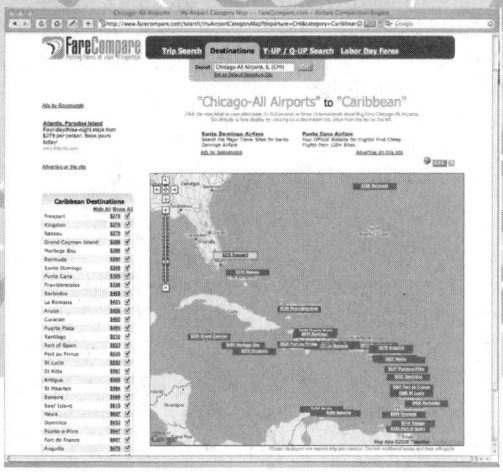

♥ **TRIP ADVISOR** (tripadvisor.com) is a good site that lists travel deals as well as user reviews of hotels, restaurants and more.

Helpful Hints

1 Don't forget the bed! When you book your honeymoon accommodations, be sure to at least book a double if not a queen size bed. This includes cruises.

So many islands, so little time

For tropical getaways, the Caribbean and Hawaii offers plenty of options. But what is best for different interests? Here are some thoughts:

Best Scuba: Cozumel and Bonaire.
Best Snorkel: Cozumel, St. Croix and Virgin Gorda.
Best Shopping: Bermuda.
Best Music: Jamaica.
Best Beaches: Aruba, Antigua and Barbados.
Best for food: Martinique, Guadeloupe, Curacao.
Best for Eco Trips: St. John, US Virgins.
Best Upscale: St. Maarten, St. Bart's, Nevis and Anguilla.
Best Volcanoes: Big Island Hawaii.

2 Go for at least one special treat. On other vacations in your life you can cut corners, but this is your one honeymoon. So go for the room upgrade. Book the helicopter flight around Kauai. Go for the day spa package.

3 Don't be afraid to tell people you're on your honeymoon. When the flight attendants on our British Airways flight to London found out we were honeymooners, we got a free upgrade to business class–a plus on that long flight.

Creating your own wedding web site

Forget the snail-mail wedding newsletter of years past. Instead tap the Internet for the ultimate wedding information source: your own wedding web site. You can post all the details about your spouse-to-be (and you), your wedding party and more. Add maps to your wedding and reception site, include a schedule of the wedding day and even post links to exciting activities in your wedding town the weekend of your wedding. "Great," you think, "but how do I do it?" Here are our five tips to setting up your wedding website:

♥ **Find the right service for you.** Sure you can go to the big guys like the Knot and the Wedding Channel, but don't forget the little guys like eWedding.com and theWeddingTracker.com. They specialize in wedding web sites with lots of extra options the Knot and Wedding Channel don't have.

♥ **Decide whether you want to pay a fee or do it on the cheap.** Free sites often restrict what you can post (the Knot only allows one picture per page) while the options really open up on the paid sites. Prices range from $70 to $120 for a year.

♥ **How secure are the sites?** Password-protected areas protect your privacy.

♥ **Make sure the site is easy to navigate.** Remember, a wedding attracts relatives and friends of all ages and computer experience. An easy-to-navigate site is a must for the less computer literate amongst your guests.

♥ **Details can make the site.** Most sites offer MapQuest links and such, but some like Wedding Channel go a step further and include written directions as well.

Chapter 14

Canada

Canadian brides face some of the same challenges as their US counterparts, with one exception: in a country as vast as Canada, how do you find local resources to plan a wedding if you're in Vancouver and the wedding is in, say, Toronto? Well, we found an excellent Canadian web site that covers just about everything that's bridal in the Great White North. Plus, we review some of Canada's best invitations catalogs and discuss the best ways to save while gown shopping in Canada.

Bridal gowns

The average bridal gown in Canada sells for $800 to $1200 Canadian. When you factor in the exchange rate, this works out to about $715 to $1070 –that's about the same as brides spend in the US, give or take a hundred dollars.

How does that compare to total wedding expenses? In Canada, the average wedding is about C$19,925, so the bridal gown is about 5% of total expenses. The average Canadian couple invites about 125 guests to the wedding–that's much less than the 175 guests invited to US weddings:

Average Wedding Costs in Canada

(all figures in Canadian dollars)

Apparel (includes headpiece and veil)	$1350
Rings	4000
Flowers	850
Cake	525
Reception	9700
Photography	1500
Videography	950
Invitations	200
Music	850
TOTAL	**$19,925**

In other ways, the Canadian bridal market is similar to the US. The average engagement is 10.7 months and over half of the couples are paying for their wedding themselves. The average age of Canadian brides and grooms could have something to do with that statistic: the bride is typically 29, the groom 30.

Of course, there are important differences. The number of weddings in Canada each year is about 151,344 (2005 figures). That contrasts to the US, with 2.3 million weddings annually. As a result, Canada's bridal "industry" is not as developed as the US –and that's both good and bad news. On the upside, the less-lucrative nature of the Canadian market means scam artists are more likely to concentrate their efforts in the US. However, the smaller number of brides translates into a smaller number of wedding merchants. And less competition usually means higher prices and less selection.

Top Money-saving Tips

Yes, the average bridal gown in Canada costs C$700 to C$1000. Is that too much for you? Here are five tips to save money:

1 **Order online.** Many of the gown discounters we review in Chapter 2 will ship to Canada; unfortunately, they usually don't note this on their web sites. So call or email in advance. You can save up to 40% by ordering online.

2 **Watch out for "designer dumps."** What happens when bridal designers have too many gowns and not enough customers? It's sale time! Yet, American designers don't want to sully their fancy, full-price image in the United States. So, they load up the truck and head north. The designers rent a hotel ballroom, take out ads that scream "MONSTER BRIDAL DRESS SALE! ONE DAY ONLY" and let the bargains rip. While there is no schedule to these sales, you might want to keep an eye on the papers to see if one comes to your town.

3 Check out David's. As we mentioned earlier in this book, David's is an off-the-rack operation that has dozens of outlets in the US. One is in Tonawanda (near Buffalo) New York (716) 834-6101, which told us they see quite a few brides who make the short trip from Toronto. David's periodically has $99 gown sales, but even their regular dresses ($500 to $700 US) are pretty good deals. (Since David's is growing rapidly, you may be able to find a store closer to you by calling 800-480-BRIDE; web: www.davidsbridal.com). Of course, cross-border shopping has its own drawbacks—call your local Revenue Canada office for duty information. On the plus side, the recent surge in the Canadian dollar makes that cross-border shopping a better deal.

4 Go for one of our "best buy" designers. Affordable gown makers like Mon Cheri, Eden and Mori Lee are all available in Canada. See the designer's web sites for Canadian stores.

5 Dicker the price. Off the record, Canadian bridal manufacturers tell us it is a buyer's market for wedding dresses in Canada. The plain fact: there are too many gowns chasing too few brides. As a result, shops are hungry for business and may make you a deal. While that doesn't mean they'll knock 40% off that dream dress, you might be able to negotiate a small discount . . . it can't hurt to ask!

Canadian Bridal Designers

As a Canadian bride, you basically have two choices when it comes to selecting a bridal gown: imported or domestic. Many US importers have Canadian distribution (most notably Mori Lee and Demetrios/Sposabella). Therefore, you can use the US designer reviews earlier in this book to gauge various styles and price options/

Of course, you can go domestic. Canada has a dozen or so manufacturers of bridal gowns and their reputation for quality is earning fans on both sides of the border. Unlike their US counterparts, most Canadian bridal designers actually make their gowns domestically. On the upside, the workmanship and construction quality is generally excellent, especially compared to the imports. On the downside, the price is usually higher.

For reviews of Canadian designers, go to our web page BridalBargainsBook.com and click on "Bonus Material."

Invitations

Many of the mail order invitations catalogs we review earlier in this book ship to Canada. A prime example is Dawn, which markets extensively to Canada. Dawn's web site is www.InvitationsbyDawn.ca. Here are other choices:

Classic Canadian Weddings
To order call: (800) 833-6761; web: www.classiccanadianwedding.com
Or write to: PO Box 1761, Winnipeg, Manitoba R3C 2Z9
Canada's largest wedding invitations mail-order outfit, this company offers both traditional and contemporary designs. Orders ship within 48 hours. Besides invites, the catalog also sells a wide variety of accessories, including "Western cake tops," favors, memory albums and more. The site is part of Dawn, mentioned earlier in the book.

Discount Invitations
To order: (888) 969-9394; web: www.discount-invitations.com
This site, in business since 1998, offers professionally printed invitations in two days for Canadian brides. A catalog is available, or you can see their invitations online. The styles we saw ran the gamut from plain cards to fancier floral creations and more. Discount Invitations claims to offer a 20% discount off Canadian invitations books and prints its prices in Canadian dollars. While their web site is a bit confusing and cluttered, owner Lano Tondu does provide personal service.

Brides in Cyberspace: What's on the Web?

Wedding Bells

Web: www.weddingbells.ca
What it is: Canada's coolest wedding web site.
What's cool: Trying to find a photographer in Edmonton? A florist in Winnipeg? Then, you need to check out this massive web site, run by Wedding Bells, a Canadian bridal magazine. Our search for reception sites in Calgary, for example, yielded an amazing 43 possibilities, from historic homes and local parks to four-star hotels. Each listing provides contact info and a descriptive paragraph that provided basic facts (capacity, special features, etc.). There's even a French version of the site for Quebec. Besides local wedding merchant info, other sections of the web site featured fashion news, Canadian bridal trends and traditions, etiquette issues and an email monthly newsletter with "fresh new ideas" that aren't on the web site.
Needs work: Since the site is so huge, it can be daunting to navigate. While the site recently grouped its content into channels, it is still a bit

hard to find your way around. We would also liked to see more links to vendor home pages in the local resources section.

Other web sites to consider: we love the **Frugal Bride** (www.frugalbride.com), which has some great money-saving tips and advice, all with a Canadian focus. The only bummer: the site is rather heavy on ads. And Frugal Bride lets vendors "opt out" of being discussed on their message boards. That's right, you can't discuss a few vendors that have threatened the site with legal action because of negative reviews on the message boards. While we aren't experts on Canadian libel law, we think this policy fails to serve brides and protect consumers.

Another good site: WeddingCanada.com, which has regional vendor listings by province.

Looking for a message board that focuses on Canada weddings? Both the FrugalBride.com and WeddingBells.ca have active boards.

Cakes. The traditional Canadian wedding cake—the fruit cake—is out of favor as brides opt for more gourmet options. A baker in Mississauga told the *Toronto Star* recently that the only exception are Jamaican dark rum cakes, which are sometimes cut up in souvenir pieces for guests to take home. Otherwise, Canadian brides are going for mousse, fresh fruit fillings or cheesecakes. Prices for a two-tier cake in Ontario start at C$275, while three-tier confections are C$550 and up.

Entertainment DJs must have their businesses registered with the Audio Video Licensing Agency, Inc. (www.AVLA.ca) to legally play prerecorded music in Canada. A good question to ask a DJ before you hire him.

Our local message boards for Canadians. Yes, we have special message boards on our web site (BridalBargainsBook.com) that lets local brides swap tips and advice. No, we haven't forgotten about Canada! You will see specific boards for the provinces, plus special boards for Canada's largest cities. Need a florist in Vancouver? A photographer in Montreal? Wonder who is the best wedding cake baker in Toronto? Log in to chat with other Canadian brides. Best of all, the boards are ad-free and spam-free.

Notes

Bridal 911

What can you do to deal with these last-minute wedding crises? Here's our answers to a Bridal 911.

Okay, let's assume you're the perfect consumer. Instead of using cash or a check, you've put all the deposits on a credit card. All the agreements with each service are in writing. You've dotted all your "i's" and crossed all your "t's." But what if your wedding day arrives and, for example, the florist delivers dead flowers? Or the photographer sends a last-minute "stand-in"? Or the wrong wedding cake is delivered? Here are some thoughts on how to deal with such crises.

Meet the Surrogate Bad Cop

No matter how careful you are, things can still happen at your wedding and reception that are not according to plan. That's why you need a Surrogate Bad Cop as an "enforcer" to fix last minute problems and correct wayward merchants.

Who can be a surrogate bad cop? Anyone you believe is trustworthy and reliable. This can be your best friend, your mother or a close relative. Of course, if you were hiring a professional wedding planner, they would play this role typically.

What does the surrogate bad cop actually do? *Their job is to make sure you enjoy your wedding.* While you're greeting guests and having fun, it's the surrogate bad cop's role to tell the florist to fix the flowers. Or track down the photographer. Or find out why the wrong wedding cake was delivered and see if it can be fixed.

In addition to major problems, the surrogate cop also handles any minor situations. One bride told us she was upset with the band she hired when the musicians launched into an unscheduled set of grunge. While she was posing for pictures, the bride had her surrogate bad cop (her sister) talk to the bandleader. She informed him of the band's mistake and said the bride had requested they change the tempo. And the band complied.

The Surrogate Bad Cop's Bag of Tricks

Any good enforcer needs the right tools at their disposal to do their job effectively. Here's a look into their "bag of tricks," a special folder/notebook that you give to them on the wedding day:

1 Phone numbers of every contracted vendor (cell, business, home). Okay, it's Saturday night, the wedding is in one hour and the florist is nowhere to be found. You call the shop and, of course, it's closed. Now what? That's why you also need a home number for the key contact at every service. Even better: get cell and/or pager numbers as well. These numbers will be crucial if your surrogate needs to track down an errant florist, photographer, DJ, etc.

2 Copies of each contract and proposal. Let's say the florist has shown up, but she's missing several arrangements. Or a special orchid corsage for your grandmother. However, the florist claims you never ordered that. What can you do? Well, if you're smart, you'll put copies of every contract and proposal into your surrogate cop's bag of tricks. That way she can whip out the florist's proposal and tactfully point out that, yes, there is suppose to be an orchid corsage. Usually, florists carry a few extra flowers with them (or they can perhaps pop back to their shop and pick up the missing pieces). One hopes that you won't have to resort to producing written contracts to correct problems, but it's a nice back-up just in case. Also, it helps the surrogate bad cop figure out just what you ordered.

3 Authority to act on your behalf. This "invisible" tool is important. You must tell each service (photographer, florist, caterer, DJ, band, etc.) that this special person will be acting on your behalf during the wedding and reception. If your surrogate comes to the merchant with a request, they should know it is your wishes.

4 Cell phone. Communication is key—making sure your surrogate bad cop has a cell phone or pager is critical to correcting problems quickly. Don't assume you'll have access to a phone at the ceremony or reception site. If you arrive at the church and the doors are locked, a cell phone will be a lifesaver.

The Final Check-Up

A week or so before your wedding, you should schedule a "final check-up" with each merchant and service. Whether it is an in-person meeting or by telephone, you should discuss the following:

♥ **Confirm all dates, days, times and locations.** You need arrival or drop-off times from such services as the florist and baker. Be careful if you're not getting married on a Saturday—make sure the merchant knows your wedding is a Friday or Sunday. We've heard stories of "no-show merchants" who assumed all weddings are on Saturday. Don't forget to call the officiant—you can't get married without him or her.

♥ **Get all the phone numbers we mentioned above.**

♥ **Tell them the identity of your "surrogate bad cop."** While you may not use those words exactly, let the companies know that this one special person will be helping you that day. They should treat any request from this person as your direction.

♥ **Confirm the order.** Now is the time to make sure that the florist can do bird of paradise flowers in your bouquet. Or that the wedding cake will be a certain flavor. Go over the menu with the caterer and fix any problems. Make sure they have your special requests in writing in their files.

♥ **Pay the balance.** Many services and merchants will require the payment of the balance due at this time. Try to pay by credit card.

Strategies for Dealing with Wedding Day Crises

Bridal 911 problems fall into one of three categories:

1 **Improper deliveries.** What can you do if the wrong cake is delivered or the caterer serves the wrong main course? While you (or your surrogate cop) may be able to contact the company before the start of the ceremony, there may not be enough time to fix the problem. Solution: ask the company to make an "adjustment" in your final bill. This doesn't mean you get the item for free—but a discount or partial refund may be in order.

2 **No shows/Late arrivals.** If the photographer is late, use the contact numbers to track him/her down. Solution: anyone who charges by the hour should make an adjustment in their bill if they run late. Or they may be able to make up the time by staying later.

3 Inferior quality. You were promised big, beautiful roses, but the florist has delivered half-dead, miniature roses. The DJ said he had an extensive collection of country music, but it turns out that it's just one Garth Brooks CD. Honestly, there isn't much you can do on the day of the wedding if a company has deceived you about the quality of their products or services. However, after the wedding, you may want to dispute the charge on your credit card. If you paid by check or cash, you may have to take the merchant to small claims court to recover your money. Document the problem with pictures or video. Also, complain to the Better Business Bureau and your city/county's consumer affairs office.

Many so-called wedding "disasters" are due to the lack of written agreements or ambiguous contracts. You can stop this problem by simply getting everything in writing.

Another source of problems are "early deliveries." One bride in Texas told us about a wedding cake that was delivered six hours before her reception. As the hotel was setting up the ballroom, someone with a ladder whacked the cake. The lesson: don't have the flowers, cake or other items delivered too early. There's just too much of an opportunity for problems.

Finally, some goofs are due to a lack of organization on the businesses' part. Whether the mix-up is an honest mistake or an intentional fraud, it doesn't matter. As a professional, the vendor should act to correct the mistake or give you a refund. Sadly, not all wedding merchants are professionals and you must take steps to protect yourself as a consumer.

The Bottom Line

While there's no such thing as a perfect wedding, there is such a thing as a consumer-savvy bride and groom. With credit cards, complete written agreements and a well-armed surrogate bad cop, you can get the quality that you're paying the big bucks for at your wedding and reception.

Putting It All Together

After reading through all the tips and advice in this book, your first thought may be "Let's elope!" And, if you didn't question your sanity in this process at least once, we would be worried about you.

Of course, it's easy for us to sit here in our Ivory Tower and tell you that you need to keep your "perspective" while wedding planning. In truth, perhaps many married couples take perverse joy in seeing engaged couples go through the anguish of planning a wedding. It's almost like a boot camp for marriage: if you can survive this, then you are fit to join the rest of us on the other side of the fence of marital bliss.

Even if weddings are some sinister plot to initiate the single into the married world, this doesn't excuse the fact that the entire US wedding industry, your friends and relatives are trying to convince you that YOUR WEDDING DAY IS THE SINGLE MOST IMPORTANT DAY OF YOUR LIFE. And, of course, unless you get everything perfect, the wrath of the WEDDING GODS will be on your head.

We hope this book is useful as you plan your trip down the aisle. We sincerely appreciate your purchase of this book and we want to help you any way we can. If you have any questions about this book or just want to chat, see the "How to reach us" page at the end of this book.

In the face of all this, our message to you is quite simple: have a good time. Don't take this bridal stuff too seriously. Remember that you are planning a party to celebrate you and your fiancé's relationship. And, theoretically, people are supposed to have fun at parties. Even the guests of honor.

Appendix A

The Budget

The first step in setting the budget is to prioritize your needs–and consider your larger financial goals. Next, you will set the overall budget you want to spend. Finally, we will show you how to budget money according to your priorities.

A financial check-up

As you plan your wedding, now is a great time to talk about the one subject most folks like to avoid: money. Planning your finances while you plan your nuptials has one major benefit: it can keep you from getting divorced. Since arguments over money are the number one reason couples split, now is a great time to give yourselves a financial check-up.

Some basic tips: both partners should be involved with family finances (paying bills, etc.). Decide whether you will have joint accounts–and joint goals toward money management and other financial issues. Talk about debts, credit cards and retirement planning. While many of these issues are beyond the scope of this book, it's important to consider all angles.

Prioritizing Your Needs

We suggest that both you and your fiancéé (and your parents if they will be contributing to this event) sit down together with separate sheets of paper and make a list like one on the next page.

Once everyone has drawn up a "priority worksheet," rank each category in order of importance from one (most important) to nine (least important). Be sure not to confer on your choices until everyone is finished.

In order to understand exactly what each

Spending Category	Priority
Apparel	_____
Flowers	_____
Cake	_____
Reception/Catering	_____
Photography	_____
Videography	_____
Invitations	_____
Music	_____
Miscellaneous	_____

category entails, the following is a brief explanation, including average costs.

1 Apparel. This includes the bride's gown, veil, shoes, accessories, undergarments, and alterations. It may also include a separate going-away outfit. The groom's formal wear is also part of this category. The average cost for apparel is $1532 (gown plus all the trimmings). The groom's tux is typically free (when you get four or five additional tux rentals, which most folks do). Yet, as you read earlier in this book, if you get carried away with accessories, the bride's tab alone could top $2000. Or $3000.

Note: For parents who are paying for the wedding, include the price of your gown and/or tux in this section. Also, some couples or their parents may pay for siblings' formal wear. Include such extra apparel expenditures in this category if necessary.

2 Flowers. This category includes "personal" flowers (bouquets, boutonnieres, corsages) as well as flowers for the ceremony and reception sites. Most weddings average about $1103 but elaborate floral decorations can cost $2000 to $3000 or more.

3 Wedding Cake. A groom's cake or a dessert table may also be included. For 175 guests, the average cake costs about $525.

4 Reception/Catering. Basically, this category includes all food (except the cake), beverages, labor and rental items. Charges to rent the reception facility are included here, when applicable. For a basic sit-down dinner or hors d'oeuvre buffet, we've budgeted about $53 per person—that includes beverages and gratuities. That's the national average.

5 Photography. The bride and groom usually only need to budget for their album and possibly a bridal portrait. The average couple spends about $2000 for professional wedding photography—but the photo tab in larger metro areas is more like $3000 to $5000. Parents should include a separate album in their budget as well as any additional photos they will want.

6 Videography. A rough estimate for a professionally-shot video is about $1000. However, prices can range from $800 up to $5000.

7 Invitations. First, you buy the invitations and/or announcements. Add on any extras like reception or response cards and other enclosures. Don't forget napkins, programs, and favors if you want them. You'll need informals (a.k.a. thank you notes) for all those gifts, and you may want to add in calligraphy. Don't forget to account for postage too. When you add in all these extras, the average expenditure here is about $426.

8 Music. Ceremony music may consist of as little as a church organist or as much as a string quartet and a soloist. As for the reception entertainment, choices range from a pianist to a professional DJ or band. Music costs average $830 for entertainment at both the ceremony and reception if you have a DJ; plan for $2000 and up for a band.

9 Miscellaneous. This isn't actually a fair category because it covers many things, but we mention it anyway. Some areas to think about are ceremony fees, blood tests and/or marriage license fees, accessories like guests books, beauty make-overs, transportation, or even lodging for members of the wedding party. A fair average for this category is about $1939—that figure can also cover cost overruns in one of the other categories if necessary. Two other items not included in our calculations are the engagement and wedding rings. For the curious, the average engagement ring costs about $4086 and wedding rings now average $1980 for the pair.

Now compare worksheets. Are everyone's priorities the same? Probably not! In fact, by using the priority worksheet, you may be able to spot possible conflicts before you get started.

For example, Mom may think that flowers are extremely important to make a wedding festive; the bride may be more concerned about her dress, while the groom's priority is the reception music. Now is the time to discuss differing opinions before they cause major problems with your wedding planning.

The Overall Budget

As you read in the introduction, the average wedding in the U.S. today costs about $25,000! And averages are deceiving—brides and grooms in expensive metro areas like New York can easily shell out two or three times that average.

Our message: you can spend HALF as much and still have a wonderful wedding. The cost involved is dependent on several items: how far in advance you can plan, what time of day and day of week you want your wedding, where (in the U.S.) you get married, what time of year you choose, and what your priorities are.

♥ **How far in advance.** When you have little or no time to plan in advance, you may have to accept what is available regardless of quality or price. Bridal gowns are a good example. Many of our bargain sources require more advance planning than buying at retail.

♥ **Time of day and day of the week.** Yes., the most popular day of the week to have a wedding is Saturday. If you choose a Saturday to get married, you will have to compete with many more brides than if you choose a Friday evening or a Sunday. Weekdays will be even more open. Some bridal businesses offer discounts for non-traditional days.

Time of day is also an important factor with your budget. If your budget is very tight, consider having your wedding in the morning or the afternoon instead of the evening. Food is the largest expense for most wedding receptions and dinner is the most expensive meal to serve. A late morning brunch or afternoon tea reception may save considerable money. These options and even a cake and punch reception are perfectly acceptable alternatives to the high expense of evening receptions.

♥ **Time of the year.** If you plan on having a holiday reception (such as Christmas or New Years), you should also plan on higher expenses. For example, flowers are more costly during December because of high demand and limited availability. Caterers are also busy with corporate parties at this time of year, as are bands and DJ's. As a result, prices are higher than at other times of the year. Other holidays such as Memorial Day, Valentine's Day, Labor Day, and Thanksgiving weekend may be similarly more expensive.

♥ **Number of people invited.** Since we noted above that food is your highest expense, it makes sense that cutting down on your guest list will save money. Enough said.

♥ **Your priorities.** When you look at your priority list, remember that you want to spend a larger part of your budget on the highest priorities. For example, if the reception catering is a high priority, this could be as much as two-thirds of your total budget. Even more if you are serious about food.

And that leads us to our next section: allotting money. First, before we do that, you need to come up with a total figure you want to spend on your wedding. We do not recommend that you go into debt to have the kind of wedding you want. In fact, there is no reason you should have to. There is also no magic formula for determining an overall amount. Look at what you *can* afford and determine the total from there.

Allotting Money

Again, take up your illustrious priority worksheet. At the top write in your total budget figure. Begin to allot your money to correspond with your priorities. Spend money where you think it is important. The following is a sample priority worksheet with a budget.

Total Budget: $10,000

	Priority	Your Budget
Apparel	1	$1,000
Flowers	5	600
Cake	6	350
Reception/Catering	3	4,500
Photography	2	1,000
Videography	7	500
Invitations	8	300
Music	4	900
Miscellaneous	9	850
	Total	**$10,000**

With this sample, the reception, the photography and the dress are the highest priorities, therefore we are going to spend $6500 or 65% of our budget on these three items. You may decide you don't want to spend this much on the dress for example, and you will order a gown through a discounter. Instead you may want to spend more money on the flowers because you want a bright garden-like wedding. And so on. The choices are up to you! That's what makes planning a wedding both exciting and challenging.

Here's another good tip: open up a new checking account for wedding expenses. By separating out funds from your personal monies, you'll be able to get a better grip on the budget and expenditures.

Tradition vs. Reality

Traditionally, the bride's family paid for nearly the entire wedding and the groom's family paid for the rehearsal dinner. Of course, that was in 1955. Today, couples are writing their own rules. In some cases, families split the expenses 50/50. Other wedding budgets are split three ways among the families and the couple. Still other couples pay for the *entire* wedding themselves. Obviously, this is a personal decision.

One more thing we'd like to add: We believe that it is too easy to get caught up in the planning and paying for a wedding. Even with our own wedding, we found ourselves having to step back from the event and remember why we were getting married in the first place. In fact, it's good to keep in mind that all you really need to get married is a license, a bride, a groom and an official. All the rest is fluff. If you keep this in mind and remember that the wedding is the beginning of your lives together, instead of a huge social event used to impress your friends and family, it will be easier to keep calm and cool!

Notes

Phone/Web Directory

Wonder where these contact names appear in the book? Check the index for a page number. **Remember that many of these contacts do not sell to the public directly; the phone numbers are so you can find a dealer/store near you.** Refer to the chapter in which they are mentioned to see which companies offer a consumer catalog, sell to the public, etc. For space reasons, we omitted the "www." prefix in front of the web site addresses.

Contact Name	Toll-Free	Phone	Web Site
Introduction			
Alan & Denise Fields (authors)		(303) 442-8792	bridalgown.com
Apparel for the Bride			
The Wedding Channel			weddingchannel.com
The Knot			theknot.com
White House, Black Market			WhiteAndBlack.com
Romantic Headlines			romanticheadlines.com
Veils A La Mode			veilsalamode.com
August Moon Designs			bridalstuff.com
Aloha Originals			custombridalheadpieces.com
Discount Dyeables			discountdyeables.com
Bridal Gloves			bridalgloves.com
Federal Trade Commission		(202) 326-2222	ftc.gov
JCPenney's bridal catalog	(800) 527-8345		jcpenney.com
Barenecessities.com			barenecessities.com
Bridesmart			bridesmart.com
eBay			ebay.com
Fabric sources			
Hyman Hendler		(212) 840-8393	hymanhendler.com
Dulken & Derrick		(212) 929-3614	DulkenAndDerrick.com
Greenburg & Hammer	(800) 955-5135		Greenburg-Hammer.com
David's Textiles	(800) 548-1818		
The Fabric Mart	(800) 242-3695		
Fabric Depot	(800) 392-3376		
McGowen's		(908) 965-2298	
Milliners Supply			milliners.com
Vogue Fabrics		(847) 864-1270	
Sense & Sensibility Patterns		sensibility.com	
RomanticThreads.com			RomanticThreads.com
Consigntment Shop Search			consignmentshopsearch.com
Nearly New Bridal			nearlynewbridal.com
PreownedWeddingDresses.com			PreownedWeddingDresses.com
Bridal Couture (book)	(800) 258-0929		
Academy of Fashion	(888) 493-3261		
Making Memories		(503) 252-3955	makingmemories.org
Just Once (rental)		(212) 465-0960	
An Alternative (rental)	(888) 761-8686	(816) 761-8686	
Filene's Basement sale		(617) 542-2011	filenesbasement.com
Nat'l Assoc. of Resale & Thrift Stores			narts.org

Nearly new Bridal			nearlynewbridal.com
VeilShop			veilshop.com
BridesAndProm.com			BridesAndProm.com
ShoeBuy.com			ShoeBuy.com
Gown manufacturers			
Alex Hanson	(800) 817-0767		alexhanson.com
Aleya Bridal	(888) 797-4023		aleya.com
Alfred Angelo	(800) 531-1125	(561) 241-7755	alfredangelo.com
Alfred Sung	(800) 295-7308		alfredsungbridals.com
Ann Barge		(404) 873-8070	annbarge.com
Alvina Valenta		(212) 354-6798	alvinavalenta.com
Amsale	(800) 765-0170	(212) 971-0170	amsale.com
Barbra Allin		(416) 469-1098	barbraallinbridal.com
Birnbaum & Bullock		(212) 242-2914	birnbaumandbullock.com
Bonny	(800) 528-0030	(714) 961-8884	bonny.com
Casablanca		(714) 758-8888	
Chris Kole		(718) 786-3319	
Christos		(212) 921-0025	christosbridal.com
Cupid		(314) 726-0416	
Demetrios/Ilissa		(212) 967-5222	demetriosbride.com
Diamond Collection		(212) 302-0210	diamondbridal.com
Eden	(800) 828-8831	(626) 358-9281	edenbridals.com
Emme	(888) 745-7560	(281) 634-9225	emmebridal.com
Eve of Milady		(212) 302-0050	
Exlcusives by A.C.E.		(901) 385-1400	
Forever Yours	(800) USA-Bride		foreverbridals.com
Group USA			groupusa.com
Helen Morley		(212) 594-6404	helenmorley.com
Impression	(800) BRIDAL-1	(281)634-9200	impressionbridal.com
Jacquelin		(941) 277-7099	jacquelinbridals.com
Janell Berte		(717) 291-9894	berte.com
Jasmine	(800) 634-0224	(630) 295-5880	jasminebridal.com
Jessica McClintock	(800) 333-5301	(415)495-3030	jessicamcclintock.com
Jim Hjelm	(800) 924-6475	(212) 764-6960	jlmcouture.com
Judd Waddell		(212) 354-5402	
Justine	(800) 866-4696		
L'Amour	(800) 664-5683	lamourbridals.com	
Lady Roi	(888) 802-8588	ladyroibridals.com	
Lazaro		(212) 764-5781	lazarobridal.com
Maggie Sottero		(801) 255-3870	maggiesotterobridal.com
Marisa		(212) 944-0022	marisabridals.com
Mary's		(281) 933-9678	marysbridal.com
Mon Cheri		(609) 530-1900	mcbridals.com
Monique L'Huillier		(310) 659-9888	moniquelhuillier.com
Moonlight	(800) 447-0405	(847)884-7199	moonlightbridal.com
Mori Lee/Regency		(212) 840-5070	morileeinc.com
Paloma Blanca		(416) 235-0585	palomablanca.com
Priscilla of Boston		(617) 242-2677	priscillaofboston.com
Private Label by G/Ginza	(800) 858-3338	(562) 531-1116	privatelabelbyg.com
Pronovias		(516) 371-0877	pronovias.com
Reem Acra		(212) 431-9232	
Robert Legere		(212) 631-0606	
Scaasi/Forsyth		(804) 971-3853	
St. Pucchi		(214) 631-4039	stpucchi.com
Stephen Yearick		(212) 221-8188	
Sweetheart	(800) 223-6061	(212) 947-7171	gowns.com
Tomasina		(412) 563-7788	tomasinabridal.com
US/Little Angels		(213) 624-4477	usangels.com
Venus	(800) 648-3687	(626) 285-5796	
Vera Wang	(800) 839-8372	(212) 575-6400	verawang.com
Vicortia's		(714) 847-2550	victoriascollection.com

Chinese Gown Sellers			
BlueCatalog.com			BlueCatalog.com
China-Ekt			1koo.com
JuliusBridal.com			JuliusBridal.com
Bridal Marketplace			bridalmarketplace.com
Dori Anne Veil			DoriAnneVeils.com
GownsOnline		(408) 985-5594	gownsonline.com
NetBride			netbride.com
Pearl's Place		(504) 885-9213	pearlsplace.com
Priceless Bridal		(818) 340-6514	bargainweddinggowns.com
RK Bridal	(800) 929-9512		rkbridal.com
Wedding Expressions		(319) 753-5217	
weddingexpressions.com			
PlusSizeBridals			plussizebridals.com
Stump's Party			stumpsbridal.com
David's	(800) 399-2743		davidsbridal.com
Bridal Garden			bridalgarden.org
Jessica McClintock Company Stores			jessicamclintock.com
South San Francisco		(415) 553-8390	
Mont Clair, CA		(909) 982-1866	
Huntington Beach, CA		(714) 841-7124	
El Paso, TX		(915) 771-9550	
BridePower			bridepower.com
Bridal World Outlet		(619) 426-2100	
Alfred Angelo Company Store	(954)846-9198		alfredangelostores.com
JcPenney outlets		(800) 222-6161	
Affordable Bridal Warehouse		(602) 279-4933	
Container Store	(800) 733-3532		containerstore.com
I Do Veils book	(800) 295-0586	(440) 333-3143	

Apparel for the Wedding Party

BestBridesmaid.com			bestbridesmaid.com
Formals Etc		(318) 640-3766	formalsetc.com
ShopShop.com			shopshop.com
Jessica London			jessicalondon.com
Dillards			dillards.com
Bloomingdales by Mail	(800) 777-0000		
Spiegel catalog	(800) 345-4500		
Talbot's catalog	(800) 882-5268		talbots.com
Chadwicks of Boston	(800) 525-6650		chadwicks.com
One Hanes Place	(800) 300-2600		onehanesplace.com
Ann Taylor			anntaylor.com
Outlet Bound			outletbound.com
Alexia	(800) 235-0681		
Bridesmaid Manufacturers			
After Six	(800) 444-8304	(212) 354-5808	aftersix.com
Alyce Designs		(847) 966-9200	alycedesigns.com
Bari Jay		(212) 391-1555	
Belsoie	(800) 634-0224	(630) 295-5880	belsoie.com
B'Gezell		(972) 239-8447	bgezell.com
Bill Levkoff	(800) LEV-KOFF		billlevkoff.com
Champagne		(212) 302-9162	champagneformals.com
Dessy Creations	(800) 52-DESSY	(212) 354-5808	dessy.com
Jordan		(212) 921-5560	jordanfashions.com
Loralie		(817) 605-9004	loralie.com
Marlene	(800) 826-2563	(412) 243-7560	marlenesbridal.com

New Image	(800) 421-4624	newimagebridesmaids.com
Watters and Watters	(972) 960-9884	watters.com
Moa Kid's		moakids.com
Britches & Bows		britchesAndBowe.com.
Dandylasses.com		dandylasses.com
Tux Express	(480) 991-6655	
Gingiss		gingiss.com
Etuxedo.com		etuxedo.com
Cheap Tux		cheaptux.com
Men's Wearhouse		menswearhouse.com

Ceremony Sites

USA CityLink		usacitylink.com
Places (book)	(212) 737-7536	

Flowers

Assoc of Spec Cut Flowers	(440) 774-2887	
Flint Hill Flower Farm	(301) 607-4554	
Flowersales.com		flowersales.com
International Floral Picture Database		flowerweb.com
C. O. D. Wholesale		codwholesale.com
Bliss' Floral Chart		www.blissezine.com/weddingfloral/
Romantic Flowers		romanticflowers.com
Obie's Floral		obiesfloral.com
Save-On-Crafts		save-on-crafts.com
Annie * & Co		AnnieAndCompany.Homestead.com
LA Flower District		LAFlowerDistrict.com
Elegant Cheesecakes	(650) 728-2248	
elegantcheesecakes.com		
Iluminations catalog	(800) CANDLES	illuminations.com
Linen & Lace	(800) 332-5223	linen-lace.com
Butterfly Celebration	(800) 548-3284	butterflycelebration.com
Butterfly Chateau		butterflychateau.com
Amazing Butterflies.com		amazingbutterflies.com
WireStore (floral supplies)		wirestore.com
2G Roses	(800) 880-0735	freshroses.com
Fresh Petals		FreshRosePetals.com
Sommer Flowers		sommerflowers.com
TheFlowerExchange.com		TheFlowerExchange.com
BridesNBlooms.com		BridesNBlooms.com
FiftyFlowers.com		FiftyFlowers.com
Oriental Tradiing		orientaltrading.com
Wax Wizard (candle discounter)		waxwizard.net
BridalShopStore.com (candle discounter)		bridalshopstore.com
GenWax (candle discounter)		genwax.com
Get Fresh		getfreshwithme.com
eFlowerWholesale		eflowerwholesale.com
RibbonTrade		ribbontrade.com
Michaels Arts & Crafts	(800) 642-4235	michaels.com
Hobby Lobby	(405) 745-1100	hobbylobby.com
MJDesigns	(817) 329-3196	mjdesigns.com
Candle sources		
Little Cindy Candles		littlecindycandles.com
Candle Comfort Zone		candlecomfortzone.com
Printed Candle		printedcandle.com
Rosewood Candle and Craft		rosewoodcandleandcraft.com

Invitations

WedNet		wednet.com

Einvite			einvite.com
Invitations4Sale			invitations4sale.com
Wedding Invitations 411			weddinginvitations411.com
Custom Shots (photo invites)			customshots.com
Absolute Invitations			absoluteinvitations.com
SandScripts			sandscripts.com
Invitation by Karina			invitationsbykarina.come
Catalog Orders Headquarters			catalog.orders.com
Costco			costco.com
ED-iT Software			ed-it.com
My Party Pal (napkins)			mypartypal.com
Little Cindy Candles			littlecindycandles.com
Candle Comfort Zone			candlecomfortzone.com
Printed Candle			printedcandle.com
Rosewood Candle and Craft			rosewoodcandleandcraft.com
Invitation Printers/Manufacturers			
Carlson Craft	(800) 328-1782		carlsoncraft.com
Chase Paper		(508) 478-9220	chaseprinting.com
Checkerboard Invitations		(508) 835-2475	checkernet.com
Crane	(800) 472-7263		crane.com
Elite	(800) 354-8321		elite.tc
Embossed Graphics	(800) 362-6773	(630) 236-4001	embossed.com
Encore	(800) 526-0497		encorestudios.com
Jenner		(502) 222-0191	jennerco.com
Pacific Thermo.	(800) 423-5071	(818) 998-2000	
NuArt	(800) 653-5361		
Regency		(717) 762-7161	regencythermo.com
William Arthur	(800) 985-6581	(207) 985-6581	williamarthur.com
Mail order catalogs			
American Wedding Album	(800) 428-0379		theamericanwedding.com
Ann's Wedding Stationery	(800) 821-7011		annswedding.com
Creations by Elaine	(800) 452-4593		creationsbyelaine.com
Dawn	(800) 332-3296		invitationsbydawn.com
Heart Thoughts	(800) 648-5781		heart-thoughts.com
Now & Forever	(800) 521-0584		now-and-forever.com
Precious Collection	(800) 537-5222		preciouscollection.com
Reaves Engraving		(910) 610-4499	reavesengraving.com
Rexcraft	(800) 635-3898		rexcraft.com
Willow Tree Lane	(800) 219-1022		willowtreelane.com
Julie Holcomb Printers	(877) 877-8905		julieholcombprinters.com
Clover Creek invitations	(800) 769-9676	(802) 425-5549	
Invitesite			invitesite.com
Fine Paper Co		(626) 584-9804	
Dreamland Designs			dreamland-designs.com
Designer Paper			designerpaper.com
Wedding Invit. CD-ROM	(888) 727-3772		
easytoprintpapers.com			
Invitation Hotline	(800) 800-4355	(732)536-9115	invitationhotline.com
Invitations 4 Sale			invitations4sale.com
YoureTheBride.com			
Elegant Brides Invitations			ElegantBrides.Invitations.com
Paper Direct	(800) 272-7377		paperdirect.com
Paper Showcase	(800) 287-8163		papershowcase.com
Art Paper			artpaper.com
Avery			avery.com
C&J Papers			cjpaper.com
First Base			first-base.com

Geographics		geographics.com
Grafcom		grafcomm-inc.com
LCI Paper		lcipaper.com
Marco's		marcopaper.com
Paper Zone		paperzone.com
Paperstruck		paperstruck.com
Paper & More		paperandmore.com
Southworth		southworth.com
Nashville Wraps		nashivillewraps.com
Fairy Tale Brownies		brownies.com
Hercules Candies	(800) 924-4339(315) 463-4339	herculescandy.com
Tender Seed Co		tenderseedcompany.com
Moosie Wrappers		moosiewrapper.com
Friends & Family Cookbooks		friendsAndFamilyCookBooks.com

Reception Sites

UniqueVenues.com		UniqueVenues.com
Minnesota Zoo	(612) 431-9215	
CitySearch		citysearch.com
FieldTrip		fieldtrip.com
Here Comes the Guide (CA)		herecomestheguide.com
ChairCovers.com		chaircovers.com
DeNormandie linens		

Catering

WeddingChat		weddingchat.com
National Association of Catering Executives		nace.net
About.com		weddings.about.com
Food Network		foodtv.com
Sam's Club		samsclub.com
BJ's Wholesale Club		bjswholesale.com
How to Feed 100 for $100		angelfire.com/bc/hobbyhorse/
Cooking Hospitality Institute (Chicago)	(312) 944-0882	
Wizard Publications		Wizardpub.com

Photography

Waterhouse Albums	(860) 526-1296	waterhousebook.com
Professional Photographers of America		ppa.com
Wedding and Portrait Photographers		eventphotographers.com
Photoworks.com		photoworks.com
Our Album		our-album.net
Collages.net		collages.net
Club Photo		event.clubphoto.com
ShotsOnline		shotsonline.com
PhotoReflect		photoreflect.com
Proshots		proshots.com
The Wedding Photographers Network		theknot.com
Kodak Wedding Party Pak	(800) 242-2424	
Exposures catalog	(800) 222-4947	exposuresonline.com
Art Leather albums	(718) 699-6300	artleather.com
C&G Disposable Cameras		cngdisposablecamera.com
Albums & Frames		albumsandframes.com
Toppers With Glitz		topperswithglitz.com
DesignerdDsplayCakes.com		DesignerdDsplayCakes.com

Cakes

SugarCraft supplies		sugarcraft.com
International Cake Exploration Societe		ices.org
Wilton		wilton.com
Portraits in Clay		portraitsinclay.com

Videos

WEVA	(800) 501-9381	(941) 923-5334	weva.com
Videomasters			videomaters.com
YesDVD			yesdvd.com
Video-On-DVD			video-on-dvd.com
Prof. Videographers Network (So Cal)			pvn.org

Entertainment

ProDJ			prodj.com
Intac song lists			intac.com
The Ceremony Music Resource page			castle.net/~energize/CMRP/
The Ultimate Wedding Song Library			ultimatewedding.com/songs/
Song for my Son CD	(800) 447-6647		new-traditions-music.com

Etcetera

Limo consumer tips			bridaltips.com
National Limo Assoc.	(800) NLA-7007 limo.org		
Moissanite			moissanite.com
Wedding Ring Hotline	(800) 985-7464	(732)972-7777	weddingringhotline.com
Engagement Rings book	(800) 962-4544	(802) 457-4000	
Diamond FAQ			
http://wam.umd.edu/~sek/wedding.html			
Diamond Cutters			diamondcutters.com
Diamond Grading			diamondgrading.com
Wedding insurance	(800) 364-2433		rvnuccio.com
Way Cool Weddings			waycoolwedding.com
June Wedding (assoc.)		(702) 474-9558	junewedding.com
Assoc. of Bridal Consultants		(860) 355-0464	bridalassn.com
Felicite (registry)			felicite.com
Michael Round	(800) 4 MROUND		mround.com

Honeymoons

SunTrips			suntrips.com
1Travel.com			1travel.com
SmarterLiving			smarterliving.com
Site59			site59.com
Carribean Concepts	(800) 423-4433		
Caradonna Tours	(800) 328-2288		
Vacation Travel Mart	(800) 288-1435		vacmart.com
Servitours		(305) 381-9026	
Spur of Moment Cruises	(800) 343-1991		spurof.com
Fare Compare			farecompare.com

Canada

Bridal gown manufacturers			
Amici		(905) 264-1466	
Catherine Regehr		(604) 734-9339	
Gordon		(416) 593-0688	
Guzzo		(416) 585-9820	guzzobridal.com
Ines Di Santo		(905) 856-9115	
Justina McCaffrey	(888) 874-4696	(613) 789-4336	jmhc.com
Madison Collection		(416) 789-9911	
Rivini		(416) 977-1793	
Wedding Canada		weddingcanada.com	
Frugal Bride		frugalbride.com	
Invitations			
Classic Canadian Weddings	(800) 833-6761		
Nicole	(800) 228-0486		
Discount Invitations	(888) 969-9394	discount-invitations.com	
Wedding Bells			weddingbells.com

INDEX

About.com, 266
Academy of Fashion Design, The, 45
Accessories, 79, 107, 114, 162, 178; affordable, 59, 203; album, 299; bridesmaids, 120; cost of, 423, 424; formalwear, 134, 137; invitation, 181, 196, 203, 215; mark-ups for, 100–101; online, 101; saving on, 20; shopping for, 57 (fig.), 137, 166
Addressing, 197, 203
After Hours, tuxedos from, 133, 134, 137
After Six, 128; bridesmaids dresses from, 115; rating for, 130–31; sizing by, 125
Agents, bands/DJs and, 359, 370, 373–74
Agfa, single-use cameras by, 303
Airfares, honeymoon, 406
Albums, 294, 307; buying, 304, 310; creating own, 308; delivery of, 295, 300; described, 281–82; digital, 13, 282-83, 289, 299, 308; leather, 298, 304; mail-order, 296, 304; memory pages in, 318; packages, 284; reviewing, 296, 297-98, 309, 314–15; sample, 306; scrapbook, 304; video, 354; vinyl, 298
Albums and Frames, 304
Alcohol, 245, 269; alternatives to, 263–64; bringing in, 256, 266; budgeting for, 263, 274–75; cost of, 254, 263, 268, 273, 276–77; etiquette and, 255; liability issues and, 255; limiting, 255, 264; in limousines, 377-78; premium/house, 262, 267; saving on, 267–68; scams with, 247, 275, 276, 277
Alex Hanson, rating for, 80–81
Alexia, bridesmaids dresses from, 128
Alfred Angelo, 60, 97, 102, 129; bridesmaids dresses from, 115; marketing statement by, 129; rating for, 80-81, 130–31; saving on, 37
Alfred Sung: bridesmaids dresses from, 113; rating for, 80-81, 130–31
Allure, rating for, 80–81
Aloni, Nicole, 271
Alstroemeria lilies, 163
Alterations, 40, 59, 62, 93, 107, 114; arranging for, 44, 85, 87; botched, 32, 72-73, 104, 105, 106; bridesmaids dress, 111, 115–16, 123; charges for, 19, 20, 32, 58, 68, 123; described, 24; estimates for, 28, 30, 32; extensive, 74; free, 32, 71, 106; overpriced, 25, 106; quality, 32; seamstresses and, 30, 73; size charts and, 122
Alvina Valenta, rating for, 80–81
Alyce Designs, rating for, 130–31
Amalia Cabrara, 76
Amazing Butterflies, 173
Amazon.com, 64, 362; music from, 373; rings from, 385, 387
Ambiance, 223, 224, 246
American Airlines, honeymoons and, 406
American Disc Jockey Association, 358
American Stationery, Wedding Invitations by, 196–97
American Wedding Album, 183; invitations from, 196, 210–11
Amsale, 41; rating for, 80-81, 130–31
Amy Michelson, rating for, 80–81
Andaluzia Couture, rating for,

80–81
Angel & Tradition, 76
Angelfire.com, 271
Angeri.com, review of, 90
Anjolique, rating for, 80–81
Ann Barge, rating for, 80–81
Annie and Company, silk flowers from, 157
Ann Taylor, 46; bridesmaids dresses from, 119–20; Celebrations by, 119–20; rating for, 80-81, 130–31
Announcements, 212, 358; designing, 195
Anthuriums, 180
Antique stores, rings at, 383
antzinternational, 92
AOL, 287
Apparel: budgeting for, 423; priority for, 424
Apparel industry, 17, 63
Apple: iMovie software by, 346; iTunes by, 364
Apple Vacations, 406
Appointments, 27, 28, 104, 324-25; making, 55
Art Leather, 281, 282, 291, 298; accessories by, 299; albums by, 298, 310; gift folios and, 299
Art Paper, invitation paper from, 216
Association of Bridal Consultants, 394
Association of Specialty Cut Flower Growers (ASCFG), 151
Audio, 338, 340, 341, 348; equipment, renting, 364
Audio Visual Licensing Agency (AVLA), 415
Austrian Brilliants, synthetic diamonds from, 384
Avery, 218
Avine Perruci, 76

Baccarat, 400
Bait and switch, 65-66, 67, 124, 370
Bakeries/bakers, 294; advice on, 243; appointments with, 324-25; deposits with, 330; extra charges by, 325-26; finding, 13, 322- 23, 324-25; home, 327, 331; off-site, 257; online, 323; overhead of, 327; questions for, 325–26; small/large, 331
Balloons, 159
Bands, 270, 358, 425; agents and, 370, 373–74; bait and switch with, 370; breaks for, 364, 370; club, 367–68; described, 356–57; DJs and, 365, 367, 368-70, 372; ethnic, 372; feeding, 309, 368; finding, 355, 361; hiring, 357, 359, 374, 424; marketing, 374; meeting with, 362; pitfalls with, 370–72, 417-18; previewing, 364, 374; professionalism of, 361, 362; reception, 366-67, 369; versatility of, 368, 369, 373
Bankruptcy, 33-34, 64, 66, 67
Barbara Allin, rating for, 80–81
Barenecessities.com, 57
Bari Jay: bridesmaids dresses from, 115; rating for, 130–31; sizing by, 125
Barry, Dave: on wedding industry, 4
Bartenders, freelance, 267
Baseball receptions, 236
BBJ Linen, chair covers from, 247
Bead Shop, The, 49
Belly bands, 213
Belsoie/B2, rating for, 130–31
Berklee School of Music, 358
Be–Seat.com, 247
BestBridesmaid.com, 113
Best Buy, 300, 338
Better Business Bureau (BBB), 90, 107; agents and, 374; bridal shops and, 21; cleaners and, 109; contacting, 39, 60, 420; invitations and, 184; limousine companies and, 380
Beverages: cost of, 230, 254–55, 262, 275, 277; flat charges for,

index

255–56; local, 270–71; packages for, 268
Bianchi, 90, 92, 102
BiddingForTravel.com, 406
Bill Levkoff: bridesmaids dresses from, 113, 115, 116, 118–19, 128; rating for, 130–31
Birchcraft, 215; review of, 204
Birnbaum & Bullock, rating for, 80–81
BJs, 268; alcohol from, 266
Black tie invited/black tie optional, 137, 138
Bloomingdales, 68; bridesmaids dresses from, 116, 117, 118–19
Bloomlife Plastic Wax, 169
BlueCatalog.com, 92
Blue Nile, rings from, 381, 387
Bonny, rating for, 80–81
Bouquets, 175; bling on, 170; bridesmaids, 170; color of, 170; foregoing, 157; hand ties/wrap with, 168; holders for, 168; ideas for, 153 (fig.); large-bloom, 162; reusing, 160; silk, 178; smaller/compact, 171
Boutonnieres, 166, 171
Bras, shopping for, 57 (fig.)
BridalBargainsBook.com, 2, 13, 50, 79, 90, 94, 129, 134, 225, 413; bakers and, 324; Canadians and, 415; caterers and, 258; entertainers and, 358; florists and, 151; message boards at, 20; photographers and, 286, 305-6; videographers and, 335
Bridal Bargains Local Talk, 13, 141
Bridal Bargains Wedding Planner, 10, 12–13; caterers and, 263; ceremony sites and, 146–47; flowers and, 156; gowns and, 32; groom's attire and, 134; invitations and, 191–92; photography and, 301; reception sites and, 230; videos and, 344
Bridal Building, 95, 96
Bridal clock, 11–12
Bridal Co. Outlet, 97
Bridal Couture: Fine Sewing Technique for Wedding Gowns & Evening Wear (Khalje), 40
Bridal Expo, 392–93
Bridal Garden, 96
BridalGloves.com, 57
BridalGown.com, 58
Bridal Guide, survey in, 369
Bridal magazines, 21, 391, 393
Bridal Mart Factory Outlet, 98–99
Bridal Originals, 77; bridesmaids dresses from, 115
Bridal packages, 234, 242, 244; cost of, 264, 266
Bridal Pink roses, 172
BridalQuote, 58
Bridal shops: avoiding, 13; bankrupt, 33-34, 55, 64-65, 66-67; bridesmaids dresses at, 127, 128; competent and, 35–36; dishonest, 17; finding, 20–21; games by, 48–61; as gown auctioneers, 39; photographers and, 286; questions for, 31–32; sample gowns from, 40; service at, 61; shipping dates and, 30; trunk shows and, 54; tuxedos from, 133; wedding consultants and, 393
Bridal Shop Store, 166
Bridal shows, 389; bakers and, 323; photographers and, 286; reception sites and, 226; scams at, 393; stationers and, 185; thoughts on, 391–93; transportation and, 376
BridalTips.com, 376
BridalVeilCreations.com, 47
Bride & Groom's West, 386
Bride Power, 98
Bride's, on wedding industry, 4
BridesandProm.com, 68; bridesmaids dresses from, 114
Bride's Book of Etiquette, on music, 369
Brides by Demetrios, 97

Brides Guide, 398
Bridesmaids: deadbeat, 121–22; flowers for, 157, 158, 170; measuring, 114–15; tough-to-fit, 121
Bridesmaids dresses: as wedding dresses, 41; alterations for, 115–16, 123; alternatives to, 112; buying, 111–12; color of, 115, 125, 126–27; compared, 118–19; consignment of, 114; cost of, 8, 129; couture, 111; delivery of, 123; disposable, 129; flowers and, 153; hints with, 121; knock-off, 121, 128; mail-order, 119–20, 126; online, 36, 111, 112–14, 117; ordering, 53; package discounts with, 115; pitfalls with, 111, 122–28; quality, 116; renting, 129; return policies on, 117; rush cuts with, 117; saving on, 13, 84-85, 115-16, 128; sewing own, 115; shopping for, 111, 114-15, 121, 125; silk, 112, 117; size problems with, 122, 123, 125; special order, 116, 124, 125, 127
BridesNRibbons.com, flowers from, 178
British Airways, honeymooners and, 410
Bronica, 290
Brown-Parish, Shelley: gown preservation scam and, 107
Brunches, 233, 264
Budgets, 425, 426 setting, 6, 9, 422, 427
Buffets, 227, 267, 271-72
Business clubs, receptions at, 245
Business hotels, receptions at, 234
Bustle, practicing, 64
Butterflies in Bloom, 173
Butterfly Celebration, 173
Butterick, headpieces from, 48
Cache albums, 299
Cake-cutting fees, 239, 275-76, 326-27
Cake-design books, 325
Cake factories, 322, 331
Cake knives, 164, 178
Cakes, 13, 264, 266, 268, 419; bringing in, 257; budgeting for, 423; buying, 11, 319-20, 324, 327; Canadian, 415; cheese, 332; colors of, 321; cost of, 239, 320-21; deconstruction of, 321, 328; decorating, 326, 327; delivery of, 320, 325, 326, 332, 420; deposit for, 34, 321; Dr. Suess, 321; elements of, 319-20; ethnic, 332; flavor of, 322; flowers and, 326; fondant, 329-30, 331; friends/relatives and, 331-32; mini, 321; offbeat places for, 327-28; pitfalls with, 319, 329-32, 417; preparing, 326, 332; pricing of, 320-21; rolling in nuts, 327, 328; saving on, 10, 319, 326-27, 328, 329; set-up of, 320, 326; slices of, 325; taste testing, 324, 325, 329; torte-style, 320; trends in, 321-22, 332
Cake stands, 328
Cake toppers, 321, 324
Cake tops, 327, 330
California roses, 172
Calla lilies, 157, 180
Calligraphy, 189, 197, 213, 215, 424
Calphalan, 389
Camera hogs, 299
Cameras, 71; 35 millimeter, 291, 292; angles with, 339-40; backup, 297; digital, 283, 284, 289, 290, 291, 292, 300, 316-17, 345, 346, 353; editing equipment and, 339; HD, 338-39, 344; medium format, 289-90, 292, 315; Panasonic, 338; SD, 338, 344; single-use, 302-3, 315
CameraWorld.com, 302
Canadian Diamond Exchange, rings from, 387

Candia roses, 172
Candids, 281, 297; portraits and, 306
C&J Papers, invitation paper from, 216
Candle Comfort Zone, candles from, 201
Candles, 166, 201; affordable, 203; online, 162; rules regarding, 143
CandlesJustOnline.com, 162
Canopies, 232
Capri Album, 281, 282
Carlson Craft, 183, 208, 214; review of, 204; samples from, 215
Carmela Sutera, rating for, 80-81
Carmi Couture, 90
Carmichael, Anita, 389
Carnations, 163
Carolina Herrera, 96
Casablanca, rating for, 80-81
Cash bars, open bars and, 255
Cast bands, 385
Catalogs, 99, 411
Caterers, 260; advertising by, 258; affordable, 258, 263; alcohol and, 277; booking, 11, 258-59; cakes and, 322, 326-27; commissions for, 244, 247, 262; communication with, 238; contracts with, 257, 260, 261, 262; costs for, 271, 273, 275; entertainers and, 358; in-house, 223, 224, 228, 229, 246, 257, 258, 273; kickbacks for, 238; licenses for, 261; meeting with, 228; minimums and, 259; negotiating with, 265; off-premise, 223, 224, 231, 239, 246, 248, 252, 257, 262, 263, 273, 274; online, 258; on-premise, 257, 273; photographers and, 258; price increases and, 278-79; problem handling by, 261; problems with, 238, 418; proposals from, 254, 259, 260; questions for, 253, 260-63; scams by, 238, 242, 277; service by, 256, 259; shopping for, 259-60; types of, 257; wedding consultants and, 397
Catering, 13, 233, 243; approved, 229, 248; budgeting for, 259, 423; civic sites and, 249; cost of, 224, 239, 253, 257, 268, 276; described, 224; do-it-yourself, 266, 279; hints about, 274-75; myths about, 271, 274; pitfalls with, 253, 275-79; planning for, 263; priority for, 426; reception sites and, 224, 231, 258; saving on, 252, 253, 263-69, 271, 279; surcharges for, 230, 239; religious restrictions and, 143
Catering halls, 142, 223, 254, 270; alcohol and, 266, 276; beverage service and, 268; ceremonies at, 243; cost of, 243-44, 245, 247
CD Favors, favors from, 218
Celebration, 183
Centerpieces, 160, 175, 179, 244, 257; edible, 159; height of, 159; reasonable, 158
Ceremony sites: bridesmaids dresses and, 125; calling, 147; decorating, 146; entertainers and, 358; fees at, 139, 143; finding, 141, 142-43; florists and, 146, 154, 155, 156; flowers at, 158, 160, 423; invitations and, 188; music policies of, 363; online, 141, 142; overlooked, 139; photographers and, 286, 294; questions for, 143-46; receptions at, 231; religious restrictions at, 143; renting, 140-41; reserving, 11; saving on, 147; selecting, 139; tax deductions with, 147; videographers and, 341, 342
C'estpapier, 214
Chadwick's: bridesmaids dresses from, 112-13, 113 (fig.), 117,

118-19; rating for, 130-31
Chair covers, saving on, 247
Chairs, renting, 231
Chambers of commerce, ceremony sites and, 141
Champagne, 269, 276; limousines and, 377-78
Champagne (dressmaker), bridesmaids dresses from, 115
Champagne roses, 172
Charity sales, wedding gowns at, 45, 108
Charles & Covard, synthetic diamonds from, 383
Chase Paper, 183; review of, 204-5
CheapCaribbean.com, cancellation fees and, 407
cheapribbons.com, 152
CheapTux.com, tuxedos from, 136
Checkerboard Invitations, 215; review of, 205
Cheesecakes, 332
China-Ekt, 92
Chris Kole, rating for, 80-81
Christian Bauer, 386
Christian Dior, saving on, 38
Christina, 76
Christmas sales, checking out, 162
Christos: rating for, 80-81; wedding gowns from, 36
Chrysanthemums, 163
Churches: ceremonies at, 140; invitations from, 183; non-denominational, 141-42; receptions at, 231, 251
CitySearch.com, reception sites and, 226
Civic sites: cost of, 248; popularity of, 248-49; receptions at, 230, 241, 248-49
Civil ceremonies, 140, 148; planning, 141; religious ceremonies versus, 140; sites for, 139-40
Civil clubs, receptions at, 246
Clark, Beverly: on accessories, 100-101
Classic Canadian Weddings, invitations from, 414
Classifieds, wedding gowns in, 37
Classique, 76
Cleaners: bridesmaids dresses and, 128; competent, 35-36; gown cleaning/preservation by, 109; inexperienced, 74
Cleanings, 107-9; extensive, 74; multiple, 129
Clubhouses, 248; receptions at, 230
Club Med, Future Travel Certificates from, 407
Clubs: receptions at, 246, 252; service at, 246; types of, 245-46
C.O.D. Wholesale, 152, 174
Collages.Net, 287
Colleges, receptions at, 235, 248
Colored ink, 182, 189, 192, 196
Consolidators, honeymoons and, 406
Consultants. *See* Wedding consultants
Consumer Reports, 398
Consumption bar, 255
Container Stores, 109
Continental Gown Cleaning, 107
Contracts, 279, 367, 377, 420; with caterers, 257, 260, 261, 262; with entertainers, 362, 370, 374; organizing, 10, 11; with photographers, 295, 312, 315; reading, 260, 295, 312, 315; surrogate bad cops and, 418
Convention and Visitor Bureaus (CVB), 225; reception sites and, 241
Cookbooks, 218-19
Cooking Hospitality Institute, 268
CookingSchools.com, 268
Cookware, high-pressure pitch for, 389-90
Coors Brewery, receptions at, 235
Copyright protection, 121, 343, 354; thoughts on, 218
Corking fees, 256, 269, 276-77, 278
Corsages, 166, 170, 175

Costco: alcohol from, 266; bouquets from, 161; deals at, 268; flowers from, 176; invitations from, 186-87, 197; rings from, 384; single-use cameras from, 302
Costs, 5-9, 6 (fig.), 7 (fig.); family income and, 9
Country clubs, 231; alcohol at, 266; caterers at, 223, 257; cost of, 247; receptions at, 241, 245-47
Country Elegance by Susan Lane, 90
Couture, 25
Couture Bridal, rating for, 80-81
Couture gowns, alterations with, 106
CraigsList.org, 44, 287, 326; ceremony sites and, 141; wedding gowns and, 37, 108
Crane: alternatives to, 193-94; colored invitations by, 322; review of, 205; scams by, 202; thermography and, 198
Crane's Wedding Blue Book (Feinberg), 138, 194, 195, 195 (fig.), 199
Crate & Barrel, 399; in-store credit with, 403
Credit cards, 132, 422; deposits with, 31, 32-34, 65, 67, 78, 165, 167, 380, 417; disputing charges with, 420; eBay and, 38-39; fees with, 380; in-store, 403; paying with, 79, 352, 419; refunds with, 33, 34; surcharges with, 53
Crises, dealing with, 417-20
Crowning Glory, 169
Crystal, 76
Culinary students, hiring, 268
Custom fitting. *See* Alterations
Custom Shots, 187
CyberGown.com, bridesmaids dresses from, 113-14
CybernetPlaza.com, bridesmaids dresses from, 127
Cymbidium, 180

Dandylasses.com, flower girl dresses from, 124
Darling roses, 172
David's Bridal, 46, 58, 90, 97; advertising by, 105; alterations by, 105; bridesmaids dresses from, 114; in Canada, 413; closing of, 64; criticism of, 55, 102-3, 105; knock-offs from, 59; outlet by, 98; plus sizes at, 103; rating for, 80-81, 130-31; service at, 104; special orders at, 103, 105; tuxedos from, 133, 137; wedding gowns from, 18, 24, 37, 45
David's Textiles, fabric from, 40
DaVinci Bridal, 45-46, 105; rating for, 80-81, 130-31
Dawn, 414; invitations from, 210-11
Day, Samantha: on alcohol, 273
DBS. *See* Discount Bridal Service
Debit cards, 33
Decorations: pew, 160; reception site, 165
Deliveries: cake, 320, 325, 326, 332, 420; dates for, 30, 72; delays in, 30; early, 420; fees for, 156, 160; flower, 156, 420; free, 32; improper, 419; photo/video, 290-91, 295, 300, 343; rush, 30
Delores roses, 172
Demetrios/Ilissa, 52, 76, 77, 97; rating for, 80-81; sizing by, 69
Demetrios/Sposabella, 413
Dendrobium orchids, 162, 180
DeNormandie, linens from, 272
Department stores: bridesmaids dresses from, 116; flower girl dresses from, 124; gift registries and, 398, 402; invitations from, 182, 184; sizing charts at, 68; trunk shows and, 54; wedding gowns from, 18, 19, 41
Deposits, 30, 44, 52, 295; credit

cards and, 31, 32-34, 65, 67, 78, 165, 167, 380, 417; disappearing, 330; florists and, 150, 154, 167; making, 20, 29; non-refundable, 51, 57, 61, 167; reception site, 223; refundable, 57, 167; security/damage/cleaning, 262; special order, 65; special sale price, 76; stealing, 66
Deputy Marriage Commissioner for a Day, 147
DesignedDisplayCakes.com, 326
Designer dumps, avoiding, 412-13
Designers, 95; bait and switch by, 65-66; bankrupt, 90; bridesmaid dress, 111; calling, 67; discounters and, 85, 87; ratings for, 80-81, 128-31; rental dresses and, 129; tags and, 51; unadvertised, 66, 75
Designs by Dorain, cake toppers by, 324
Desserts, 253, 254, 319; cake and, 267
Dessert tables, 10
Dessy, 128; rating for, 130-31; sizing by, 125
Destination weddings: bridesmaids dresses and, 128; catering and, 270, 271; ceremony sites for, 148; flowers and, 171; honeymoons and, 406; invitations and, 212; limousines and, 381; photographers and, 308; receptions and, 236-37; tips for, 13, 35-36; videographers and, 347; vows at, 148
Dewberry Engraving, invitations from, 210-11
Diamond (diamond.com), rings from, 387
Diamond.ca, rings from, 387
Diamond Cutters, rings from, 387
Diamond Grading, 390
Diamond Nexus Lab, synthetic diamonds from, 384
Diamond Ring Buying Guide: How to Spot Value & Avoid Rip-Offs, The (Newman), 387
Diamonds: loose, 384; pre-set, 384; synthetic, 383-84
Diamond Talk, 388-89
Dienno, Adele: cake toppers by, 324
Dietary restrictions, 242-43, 259
DigitalCity.com, reception sites and, 226
Digital files, receiving, 342-43
Digital tapes, music from, 372
Digital technology, 283, 285, 290
Dina's, gloves from, 116
Director's disease, 293, 350
Disco, health hazards with, 372
Discount Bridal Service (DBS), closing of, 23
DiscountBridalShoes.com, 101, 118
Discount buying services, invitations from, 182, 184-85
Discounters, 58, 96, 426; accessories from, 20, 101, 162; bridesmaids dresses from, 115; business addresses and, 109; checking out, 12; designers and, 85, 87; gift registries and, 402; invitations from, 214-15; ordering from, 63; pros and cons with, 91; rings from, 384; shopping with, 84; wedding gowns from, 20, 27, 28, 29, 36-37
Discount Invitations, invitations from, 414
Discounts: discretion with, 87; guaranteed, 402; planning and, 425; problems with, 58, 59; special-order, 58
Discount web sites, best, 84-85
Diva, 76
DJs, 239, 257, 270, 353, 358, 425; agents and, 370, 373-74; bait and switch with, 370; bands and, 365, 367, 368-70, 372; booking, 360, 374; breaks and, 364, 370; described, 357; equipment of, 363; ethnic

music and, 366, 368; feeding, 309, 368; finding, 355, 359, 361; hiring, 357, 361, 424; iPod weddings and, 365; meeting with, 362; music collections of, 369; pitfalls of, 367, 370-72, 418, 420; previewing, 362, 364, 374; problem handling by, 363; professionalism of, 361, 362; request lists for, 373; technology and, 372; versatility of, 369-70
Door prizes, thoughts on, 393
Dori Anne Veils, review of, 86-87
Drafting Deals, vellum from, 216
Dreamland Designs, 213
Dried Flowers Direct, flowers from, 157
Dried Flowers R Us, flowers from, 157
Dulken & Derrick, fabric from, 40
DVDs, 333, 338, 339, 341, 347, 351; copies of, 334; copyright protection for, 343; cost of, 334-35; creating, 334, 346; delivery of, 343; embarrassing moments on, 348; problems with, 349; volume discount on, 346
Dye lots, problems with, 126
DyeableShoesOnline.com, 57, 101, 118

Easy Share Gallery (Kodak), 287
EasytoPrintPapers.com, 214
eBay, 47, 75; bargains on, 38; cake stands on, 328; Chinese gowns on, 91, 92-93, 93 (fig.), 94; credit cards and, 38-39; favors on, 219; flower girl dresses on, 124; language of, 38, 92-93; wedding gowns on, 10, 25, 36, 38-39, 108
Eden, 77, 413; rating for, 80-81, 130-31; saving on, 38
Elegant Brides Invitations, invitations from, 215
Elegant Cheesecakes of Half Moon Bay, 159
Elite, 183, 215; review of, 206
Elite/Infolio, 214
eInvite, invitations from, 185-86, 186 (fig.)
Emanuelle, 76
Embossed Graphics, 214; review of, 206
Emily Post's Complete Book of Wedding Etiquette (Post), 368-69
Enchantment, 76
Encore, 214, 215; review of, 206-7
Engagement & Wedding Rings: The Definitive Buying Guide for People in Love (Matlins, Bonanno, Crystal), 387
Engagements, chronicling, 318
Engraving, 189, 193-94; described, 192; myths about, 198; saving on, 194; thermography and, 192, 197
Entertainers: advice on, 243; contracts with, 362; hiring, 357, 363; interviewing, 364; non-peak seasons and, 365; online, 359; pitfalls with, 370-72; previewing, 362; questions for, 363-64; reception sites and, 257; saving on, 364-65, 366; searching for, 360-61; sources for, 357-59. *See also* Bands; DJs
Entertainment, 257; in Canada, 415; myths about, 367-68; reception, 363-64
Envelope liners, 182, 193
Envelopes: designing, 195; extra, 189, 199; switcheroo with, 202
Episcopal Church, fees by, 143
Epson, printers from, 317
Ernst, Robbi: June Wedding and, 395, 397
Espresso bars, 263
Essence of Australia, rating for, 80-81
Eternity, rating for, 80-81
Etiquette, 1, 2, 208; alcohol and,

255; formal wear, 132-34; invitation, 194, 213; music and, 369; printers and, 202; registries and, 198, 399, 400
ETuxedo, tuxedos from, 136
Eva Forsyth, 76
Evangel Christian Invitations, invitations from, 210-11
Eve of Milady, 76; rating for, 80-81
EventPix.com, 284, 287
eWedding.com, 410
Excalibur package, 376
Exclusives by A.C.E., rating for, 80-81
Expedia, 407, 408
Exposures (company), albums from, 304
Extra Fancy roses, 172
Extreme, 196
EZ Bowmaker, 160

fabiancouture.com, tuxedos from, 134
Fabric: combo, 127; costs with, 75; extra, 85; fraud with, 51; ordering, 126; sources of, 40; substituting, 71; swapping, 44; tuxedo, 135; white, 41
Fabric Depot, fabric from, 40
Fabric Mart, The: fabric from, 40
Fairy Tale Brownies, favors from, 217
Family functions, ruse with, 234, 264, 265-66
Fancy roses, 172
Fantasy, 76
Fare Compare, honeymoons and, 408, 409 (fig.)
Farmers markets, flowers at, 160, 162
Fashion shows, 391, 392
"Father's Song" (Viereck), 373
Favors, 216-19, 266; avoiding, 10; charitable giving in lieu of, 218; ecological, 217; origins of, 216-17; saving on, 216; sources of, 217-18; spending on, 8
FCGI, tuxedos from, 134
Fed Ex, gown shipping by, 35
Federal Regulation C, 33, 34
Federal Trade Commission (FTC): gown preservation scam and, 108; registered numbers by, 50; tags and, 50, 52; WEVA and, 336
Federated Department Stores, 103
Federation of Women's clubs, 246
Fees: alterations, 58, 68; bogus, 32, 52-53, 55, 56, 75, 244, 263, 312; cake-cutting, 239, 275-76, 326-27; ceremony, 424; consultation, 156, 167; corking, 256, 269, 276-77, 278; credit cards and, 380; delivery, 156, 160; food and beverage, 244; marriage license, 424; negotiating away, 276; no show, 54, 96; penalty, 53, 75; percentage-based, 396; rental, 224, 228, 233, 278; rush, 75; set-up, 155, 278; shipping, 53, 56, 201; storage, 54; as tax deductions, 147; try-on, 52-53; vendor referral, 395-96, 398
Feinberg, Steven, 194
Felicite, gift registry at, 400
FieldTrip.com, 235
FiftyFlowers.com, flowers from, 178
Filene's Basement Bridal Sale, 38-39, 42; MOB dresses at, 126
Final check-ups, 419
Financial check-ups, 422
FindGift, gift registry at, 400
FineStationery.com, invitations from, 187
Fink, 90
Fireman's Fund/R.V. Nuccio, wedding insurance from, 390
Fireworks, 174, 250
First Base, invitation paper from, 216
Flinthill Flower Farm, 161
Floral bill, 149, 165, 167; total, 150

Floral wreaths, head measurements for, 166
Florists, 294; advice on, 243; affordable, 150-51; bakers and, 322; bids from, 153, 167-68; booking, 152; cash and carry, 150, 168; ceremony sites and, 146, 154, 155, 156; deposits with, 150, 154, 167; fees by, 156, 167; full service, 150; holiday dates and, 157; interviewing, 167-68; online, 151-52; payment policies of, 156; photographers and, 151; problems with, 418; questions for, 154-56; reception sites and, 154, 155, 156, 257; refund/cancellation policies with, 154, 167; rental items from, 155; set-up and, 154, 155-56; specialist, 150, 151; types of, 150; wedding consultants and, 393, 395; wedding coordinators and, 151
Flower arrangements, 155, 158, 166, 169-70; adequate, 175; churches and, 161; creating, 160; gift table, 164; horticultural schools and, 161; making own, 151; recycling, 160
Flower Council of Holland, 151, 152 (fig.)
Flower girl dresses, 124, 126
Flower girl's baskets, 164-65
Flower girl wreaths, 166
Flowers: best buy, 149, 163-64; bridesmaids dresses and, 153; budgeting for, 423; buying, 149-50; categories of, 149-50; ceremony site, 150; decorating with, 170-71, 326, 327; delivery of, 156, 420; deposits on, 34; donating, 147; dried, 155, 157; European ideas on, 165; exotic, 10, 157, 165; hairpiece, 164; labeling, 166; myths about, 164-65; online, 157, 159, 160, 161; personal, 150, 156, 166, 175; pitfalls with, 166-70; planning for, 174; priority for, 424; proposal for, 154; reception site, 10, 150; regional, 157; rehearsal dinner, 150; rules regarding, 143, 165; saving on, 156-62; seasonal, 157; shopping for, 149, 153-54, 168; silk, 47, 155, 157, 160, 178, 326; single, 157, 170; spending on, 8, 165; wholesale, 13, 174-75, 177 (fig.)
Fondant, 329-30, 331
Food, 251, 252; ambience versus, 224; budgeting for, 274-75; cost of, 230, 253, 254, 425; frozen, 275; handmade, 275; labor- intensive, 265; local, 270-71; preparing, 261; presentation of, 259; quality of, 224, 228, 244, 247; serving, 266; specialized, 261; substituting, 279
Food Attitude, cakes and, 329
Food Network, The, 266
Forever Yours, 76, 77; rating for, 80-81
Formality, degree of, 26, 132, 189
Formalwear: etiquette for, 132-34; online, 134; profits on, 101; spending on, 8. *See also* Tuxedos
Four Seasons, 239, 336
Free services, asking for, 32
Freesia, 163
Fresh Petals, flowers from, 152, 176-77
freshroses.com, 159
Friends and Family Cookbooks, 218-19
Frugal Bride, 415
FTC. *See* Federal Trade Commission
FTD design books, 153, 155
Fuji, single-use cameras by, 302, 303
"Fun Saver" (Kodak), 302
Funeral homes, limos from, 378-79

FunJet Vacations, hurricane insurance from, 407
Futura albums, 298
Future Travel Certificates, 407

Galina, 90, 102
Garden ceremonies, 248; wedding gowns for, 26
Garden Clubs, 246
Gardenias, 169
Gartner's "Do-It-Yourself Printables," 214
Gen Wax, 166, 201
Genuine Fractals, 291
Geographics, invitation paper from, 216
Gerbera daisies, 163-64
Gift folios, 281, 299, 302
Gift registries, 375; honeymoons and, 403; invitations and, 198; online, 198, 398, 399-400, 402; pitfalls with, 198, 398, 401-2; savings on, 402-3
Ginza Collection, 76
Gladiolus, 164
GlamourCloset.com, bridesmaids dresses from, 114
Glamour Magazine: on accessories, 100; on shoes, 101
Glausha, David: cleaning/preservation and, 109
Gloves, 116; shopping for, 57 (fig.)
Going-away packages, 274
Gold, 9, 382
Gown auctioneers, bridal shops as, 39
Gown bags, 28, 37
Gown preservation, problems with, 107-9
Gradschools.com, 161
Grafcom, invitation paper from, 216
Graphics, 334, 353-54
Gratuities, 378; gratuitous, 277-78; mandatory, 256, 275, 278, 376, 379; percentage, 256
Greenberg & Hammer, fabric from, 40
Greenery, 159, 160
Gresl, Nancy: on ordering invitations, 200
GroomCam, 353
Groom's cake, 10, 325, 327, 328
Groomsmen: deadbeat, 121-22; out-of-town, 134; procrastinating, 137
Group USA, rating for, 80-81
Guest books, 196
Guest List Inflation, 3, 425
Guide books, receptions and, 237
Gussets, making, 85

Haggling, 36-37, 43
Half-full glasses, scam with, 277
Hangar hazards, 36
hartco.com, tuxedos from, 134
Hartz, tuxedos from, 134
Hasselblad, 290, 292
HDTV, videos and, 338, 339, 344
Headpieces: cost of, 19; finding, 95-96; making, 48-49, 95; mark-ups for, 58, 95; saving on, 46-47; shopping for, 57 (fig.); spoilage of, 95
Heart Thoughts, invitations from, 210-11
Heather, 164
Helen Morley, 98; rating for, 80-81
Henry Roth, rating for, 80-81
Hercules Candies, favors from, 217
HereComesTheGuide.com, 235
Historical societies, ceremony sites and, 141
Historic sites, receptions at, 227, 233, 236
Hobby Lobby: albums from, 304; craft supplies from, 174, 179; flowers from, 160
Holzer, Robin, 250
Home: receptions at, 231, 249, 251-52; weddings at, 148, 232, 241, 249, 251-52
Home Depot: accessories from, 162; greenery from, 160; pot-

ted plants from, 158
Honeymoon suites, 242
Honeymoons, 374, 375, 403-10; booking, 407; e-fare, 406; gift registries and, 403; hints about, 409-10; hurricane-proofing, 403, 407; last-minute, 405; off-day travel on, 406; online, 404, 408-9; peak season, 405, 406; pitfalls with, 408; planning for, 404, 405; popular sites for, 403; saving on, 404-5; special treats on, 410; spending on, 8
Hors d'oeuvres, 260, 266, 272; cakes and, 325; charges for, 274; passing, 267
Horticultural schools, help from, 161
Hotel Pennsylvania, Vera Wang sale at, 39
Hotels, 224, 231; alcohol and, 276; beverage service and, 268; bureaucracy at, 238; business, 234; caterers at, 223, 257, 254; ceremonies at, 243; consumer abuse at, 242; cost of, 243-44, 245, 247; destination weddings at, 271; dietary restrictions and, 242-43; receptions at, 233, 241-45, 252
Hotel sales, 39, 74
Houston Marriott, group rate at, 243
HP, printers from, 317
Hurricane season, honeymoons during, 403, 407
Hydrangeas, 164
Hyman Hendler & Sons, fabric from, 40

Ice, rings from, 387
Icing: butter cream, 320, 330, 331; meringue, 320, 331; off-white, 320; royal, 329; whipped cream, 320; white, 319, 320, 330-31
iDVD, 346
Image boxes, 299
iMovie, 346, 347
Imperial Gown Restoration, cleaning/preservation by, 109
Impression, 76; rating for, 80-81, 130-31
Informals, 182
Inner Circle, 76
Insurance, 232, 273; homeowners, 230, 251; hurricane, 407; liability, 230, 250, 251, 261, 390; reception site, 230, 390; wedding, 375, 390; wedding gown, 53
International Cake Exploration Societe, 323
International Cake Exploration Societe, 323 (fig.)
Internet, 20, 21-22
Interviews, 341, 349; embarrassing, 348
Intrigue, 77
Invitation Hotline, invitations from, 194, 214-15
Invitations: accessories for, 181, 196, 203, 215; addressing, 188; after-wedding party, 212; budget for, 189, 424; cakes and, 322; Canadian, 414; changes in, 201-2; colored, 322; color/ink for, 212; cost of, 182, 193; custom, 213; designing, 194, 195; do-it-yourself, 13; engraved, 10; etiquette and, 194, 213; extras with, 192-93; mailing, 188, 203, 212; mail-order, 196-97, 200, 203, 208-9, 210-11, 215; mistakes in, 188, 191, 200; motifs with, 212; myths about, 198-99; online, 182, 184, 185, 187, 214-15; ordering, 11, 181, 182-83, 188, 189, 199, 200; papers for, 209, 215-216; proofs of, 191; quality, 198; reception sites and, 189, 190; registries and, 198; reviews of, 204-8; sample, 191, 193; saving on, 147, 192, 199, 200; shop-

ping for, 181, 184, 187-88, 188-89; as sideline, 200-201; size of, 182, 193; spending on, 8; styles of, 184; trends in, 198, 212-13; writing, 199, 209. *See also* Stationery
Invitations by Karina, 187
Invitations 4 Sale, invitations from, 215
Invitesite, invitations from, 212-13
Involuntary lay-away, 78
iPod weddings, 364, 372
ISPs. *See* Internet service providers
It Stays, 64
iTunes, 364

Jacaranda roses, 173
Jacquelin, 76, 77; rating for, 82-83
Jacqueline Kennedy roses, 173
James Clifford, rating for, 82-83
Jamie Lee, invitations from, 210-11
Janell Berte, rating for, 82-83
Japhet, 180
Jasmine, rating for, 82-83
Jaust, Elizabeth, 218
JCPenney: bridesmaids dresses from, 117; Moissanite jewelry from, 384; outlet by, 98; rating for, 130-31
J. Crew: bridesmaids dresses from, 112, 117, 123; rating for, 82-83, 130-31; shopping at, 46; wedding collection by, 63
jeffliu8000, 92
Jenner, 197; review of, 207
Jenny You, rating for, 82-83
Jessica London, bridesmaids dresses from, 114
Jessica McClintock, 41, 97; bridesmaids dresses from, 115; outlet by, 96, 98; rating for, 82-83, 130-31
Jewelers, 383, 385
J Hjelm Occasions, rating for, 130-31
Jim Hjelm, 37, 76, 77; rating for, 82-83
Jim Kokernak's "Frequently Asked Questions (FAQ) about Diamonds," 390
JimsFormalwear.com, tuxedos from, 133
Joann Fabric, 115
Joelle, 90
Jordan, 128; bridesmaids dresses from, 116; rating for, 130-31
Judd Waddell, rating for, 82-83
June Wedding, 394, 395, 397-98
Junior Forums, 246
Junior Leagues, 246
Justin Alexander, rating for, 82-83
Justina McCaffrey, rating for, 82-83

Kampes, Stephanie, 379
Kaufman's, bankruptcy for, 33-34
Kickbacks, 238, 262, 371, 395-96, 398
Kids' buckets, 240
Kinkos, 215, 287
Kleinfeld, 54, 96
K-Mart, 316
Knock-offs, 23, 45, 59, 121, 128
Knot, The, 20, 22-23, 52, 90; ceremony sites and, 141, 142, 142 (fig.); gift registry at, 398, 399, 400; pressure from, 34; sales for, 23-24; service and, 60; wedding web sites at, 410
Knot's Bridal Search, The, 22
Kodak, 287; single-use cameras by, 302, 303

Labor: cost of, 256, 262, 265; double-charging for, 278; gratuities for, 256
Lace, substituting, 71
Ladew Gardens, receptions at, 235
Lady Diana roses, 173
Lady Roi, rating for, 82-83
Lane Bryant: rating for, 82-83; shopping at, 46
Las Vegas weddings, 140
Laundry, rating for, 130-31
Layaway scams, 78-79

index

Lazaro, rating for, 82-83, 130-31
LCI Paper, invitation paper from, 216
Leather Craftsman, 281, 282
LeFevre, Kathy: cookbook and, 218-19
Leica RangeFinder, 292
Lenox, 389, 400
Let's Party by Jake 418, 187
Libraries, music from, 373
Lili, 90
Lilies, 180
Lily of the Valley, 180
Limousine companies: bridal packages by, 378, 380; corporate, 379-80; discounts from, 378; finding, 377; problems with, 380; short minimums with, 379; small, 378, 381
Limousine drivers: gratuities for, 376, 378, 379; sleazy, 380
Limousines: alcohol in, 377-78; cost of, 376; large, 376; off-night weddings and, 379; online, 376-77; overtime with, 378; pick-up/ drop-off service with, 379; pitfalls with, 375, 377, 380-81; questions about, 377-78; regular, 379; renting, 375-76, 377; saving on, 375, 378-79; shopping for, 377
Linens, renting, 272
Linens & Things, 400
Liquidators, 74
Liquor. *See* Alcohol
Liquor licenses, 262
Little Cindy Candles, candles from, 201
Livingvictorian.com, embossers from, 193
Loehmann's, MOB dresses at, 126
Long-distance weddings, wedding consultants and, 397
Lord West, tuxedos from, 134
Los Angeles Flower District, 162
Lucky pennies, 390
Luncheons, considering, 233, 264
Luxury cars, renting, 379
Macheel, Joely, 219
Macy's, in-store credit with, 403
Madame Delbard roses, 173
Madeline Gardner, 77
Maggie Sottero, 39, 46, 59, 69; couture gowns by, 63; dresses by, 63; rating for, 82-83
Mail order: accessories by, 166; business addresses and, 109; discounts with, 84-85; retail and, 84; shipping time and, 85; invitations by, 184, 192, 200, 203, 208-9, 210-11, 215; stationery by, 198
Makaella, rating for, 82-83
Making Memories, 45, 108
Manufacturers, 31, 62; no-name, 58; ratings for, 79-83; sizing and, 69, 70
MapQuest, links to, 410
Maps, 182, 189, 203; designing, 195; printing, 196
Marco's, invitation paper from, 216
Marisa, rating for, 82-83
MarketWatch.com, on photographers, 285
Mark-ups, 65, 75; formalwear, 137; killer, 58, 100-101; mark-downs and, 127; marriage, 169-70, 234, 254
Marniya RB67, 290
Marriage licenses, 7, 148, 424
Marshall Field's, in-store credit with, 403
Marshall's, MOB dresses at, 126
Martha Stewart, 266; cakes by, 329
Martha Stewart Weddings, 169
Martinez, Melissa: on student musicians, 366
Mary's, 97; rating for, 82-83
Masterpiece, Wedding Invitation Kit by, 213
Matthew Christopher, rating for, 82-83
McCalls, headpieces from, 48
McGowen's, fabric from, 40

Measurements, 70; head, 166; problems with, 68, 69
Melissa Sweet, rating for, 82-83
Memorex, 218
Memory pages, 296, 318
Men's Wearhouse: coupons from, 137; tuxedos from, 133, 136-37, 136 (fig.)
Menu: budget busters for, 265; changes with, 261, 279; goofs in, 238; mediocre, 275; regular, 266; sample, 259; specialized, 227, 261
Mercedes syndrome, 166-67
Message boards, 20, 52; in Canada, 415; caterers and, 258; entertainers and, 358-59; florists and, 151; photographers and, 286; reception sites on, 225; tuxedos and, 134, 137; WEVA, 336
Mezzo Album, 298
Michael C. Fina, 400
Michaels Arts and Crafts Stores, 47, 95, 160; albums from, 304; craft supplies from, 47, 174; wedding supplies from, 178-79, 179 (fig.)
Microphones, 353; charges for, 351; sound quality and, 338; types of, 337, 338, 348
Military bases, receptions on, 233, 245
Minimums, 271; confirming, 259
Minnesota Zoo, reception at, 235
Mitchell, tuxedos from, 137
MOB. *See* Mother of the bride
Moissanite, synthetic diamonds from, 383-84
Mom syndrome, florists and, 168
Mon Cheri, 60, 413; rating for, 82-83
Money Magazine, on wedding insurance, 390
Money management, 422, 426
Monique, 90
Monique L'Huillier, rating for, 82-83
Monique Luo, 102
Montage Art Books, 291, 299
Moonlight, 77; rating for, 82-83
Moore's, tuxedos from, 137
Moosie Wrappers, 217-18
Morex Swiss Double Face Satin Ribbon, 219
Mori Lee, 76, 77, 97, 102, 105, 413; bridesmaids dresses from, 112, 115, 116; rating for, 82-83, 130-31; sizing by, 125
Morris, Tracie, 215
Mother of the bride (MOB) dresses, saving on, 126
Mount Deluxe albums, 299
Mountain Cow, Printing Press and, 195
Museums, receptions at, 235, 248
Music, 354; background, 361, 364; budgeting for, 424; ceremony, 355, 356, 357, 360, 363, 368, 372-73; choosing, 355, 360-61, 362, 363-64, 368; cost of, 356; dance, 359, 362; ethnic, 357, 366, 368, 372, 373; hints with, 368; online, 355, 359, 364, 373; organ, 373; personalizing, 373; priority for, 424; reception, 356, 357, 358, 360-61, 364, 365, 366-67, 372-73; restrictions on, 230, 360, 363, 372; saving on, 364-65; trends in, 356, 372-73
Music departments/schools, 358, 366
Musicians, 257, 356; ceremony, 360; contracts with, 370, 374; hiring, 355, 357, 360, 365, 366; meetings with, 360, 363; overtime charges by, 362; previewing, 362; professional, 358, 367; recommended, 371; rehearsals by, 363; student, 366, 367
MyPublisher.com, 308

Name change kits, 390, 391
Napkins, 189, 196
Nashville Wraps, favors from, 217
National Association of Catering

Executives (NACE), 258
National Association of Resale and Thrift Stores, 44, 108
National Association of Wedding Officiants, 141
National Limousine Association (NLA), 376-77, 381
Nationwide Gown Cleaning Service, 107, 108
Nearly New Bridal, 44
Needs, prioritizing, 422-23
Negatives/digital files, 301, 315; buying, 299, 300, 305
Neiman Marcus, 399
NetBride, review of, 87-88
'Net Tutorials, 388
New Image: bridesmaids dresses from, 115; rating for, 130-31
Newman, Renee, 387
New Traditions Music, 373
New Wedding Traditions (CD), 373
NLA. *See* National Limousine Association
Non-denominational churches, ceremony sites and, 141-42
Nordstrom Rack: bridesmaids dresses from, 120-21; MOB dresses at, 126
No refund, no cancellation policies, 78
Noritake, 400
No shows, dealing with, 419
Now & Forever, 77; invitations from, 201, 210-11
Nu Art, review of, 207
Nu Art/Pacific Thermographers, 183

Obies Floral Design, 152, 176
Oceans of Roses, napkins from, 196
Office Depot, 193, 214, 218
Office Max, 214
Officer's Clubs, receptions at, 233
Officiants: finding, 141; friend, 147; honorariums/donations/fees for, 146; licenses for, 146; photographers and, 146; problems with, 419; questions for, 146; rehearsals and, 146
Oleg Cassini, 102
Omni Hotels, group rate at, 243
One Hanes Place, hosiery from, 117
Onetravel.com, 406
Open bars, 254-55, 267; cash bars and, 255
Orchestras, 357, 370; hiring, 368-69
Orchids, 157, 165, 180
Orders: confirming, 419; holding back, 77-78
Organists, 356; charges by, 355; hints with, 368
Organization, importance of, 10-13
Oriental Trading Company: accessories from, 166; candles from, 201; favors from, 219
Orlando, honeymoons to, 404, 405, 406
O'Rourke, Mary, 196
Oscar De La Renta, rating for, 82-83
Ostrich Leather albums, 299
Ostroff, Nancy and Jeff, 376
Outlet Bound, 120
Outlets, 94-95; bridesmaids dresses from, 120; wedding gowns from, 27

Package game, 310, 313
Pallas Athena, 77
Paloma Blanca, 76; rating for, 82-83
Paper & More, invitation paper from, 216
Paper Direct, paper from, 215-16
Papers: laser-compatible, 215; unique, 212-13
Paper Zone, invitation paper from, 216
Parks, receptions at, 248
Parks departments: ceremony sites and, 141; reception sites and, 225-26

Pastry chefs, cakes and, 322
Paula Varsalona, rating for, 82-83
Pawn shops, rings at, 383
PayPal Buyer Protection, 39
Pearls, 23
Pearl's Place, review of, 88-89
Penney's Bridal Party, bridesmaids dresses from, 112
Perma-Bound albums, 298
Petersons.com, 268
Petites, charges for, 75
Pew cards, 182, 195
Pew decorations, scaling down, 160
Phalaenopsis, 180
Phone numbers, list of, 418, 419
Photographers: advertising by, 286, 309; affordable, 284, 287, 295; amateur, 315; awards for, 308-9; bakers and, 322; in Canada, 415; caterers and, 258; celebrity, 311-12; ceremony-only, 302, 315; commercial, 284; communication with, 293, 294; contracts with, 295, 312, 315; deposits with, 34; digital, 283, 291; equipment of, 288-89, 297; feeding, 309-10, 368; florists and, 151; free- lance, 311-12; grandparents and, 317; hints with, 310-11; hiring, 13, 281, 284, 286, 287, 291, 294, 301, 303, 307; home-based, 301; meeting with, 295, 296; newspaper, 307; officiants and, 146; online, 286-89; overpaying, 285, 302; overtime by, 314, 352; packages by, 310, 313, 352; personality of, 293, 295, 310; philosophy of, 296; pitfalls with, 281, 312, 313, 316, 317, 418; portrait, 284; problem handling by, 298-99; questions for, 292, 296-301; receptions and, 227, 303, 314; saving on, 301-8; service from, 300; shopping for, 294-296; student, 305-6; understanding, 288-90; videographers and, 293, 310-11, 336-37, 342, 344-45, 347, 354; wedding consultants and, 395; women, 311
Photographs: after-ceremony, 306-7, 314; archival quality, 289, 300, 317; before-ceremony, 306-7; black-and-white, 300, 318; buying, 305; color, 11; delivery of, 290-91, 300; digital, 289, 290, 297, 316-17; inferior, 289, 292, 294; online, 287, 288, 291; ordering, 294, 305l professional, 287-88l requested, 295, 296; service fees for, 305
Photography, 200, 396; budgeting for, 424; cost of, 283, 309, 315, 424; customs/traditions with, 283; friends/relatives and, 315; low-light, 295; myths about, 308-10; pitfalls with, 311-17; priority for, 426; restrictions on, 306; saving on, 315; style of, 292; trends in, 317-18
Photography labs, dealing with, 316
Photography studios, 286, 289
Photojournalism, 291, 292, 297, 307-8
PhotoReflect.com, 287, 288 (fig.)
PhotoShop, 289, 291, 308
Photoworks.com, 287
Pianos, 229
Piccione, Vincent: on holding order, 77-78
Pictage.com, 284, 287
PictureTrail, 287
Pier One, baskets from, 158
PK Bridal, 23
Place cards, 189, 195
Planning, 9-10, 42, 67, 427; bargains and, 12; discounts and, 425; perspective and, 421; problems with, 424; starting, 425; time for, 12
Plants, renting, 159
Platinum, 9, 381, 382, 383

PlusSizeBridals.com, review of, 89-90
Plus sizes, looking for, 103
Pocket square, 171
Portraits, 283, 284, 291, 292; candids and, 306; canvas-mounted, 309-10; choosing, 310; newspaper photographers and, 307; skipping, 302; specials with, 309; wedding gowns and, 25
Portraits in Clay, cake toppers by, 324
Post, Emily, 132, 368-69, 370
Postage, 182, 424; cost of, 203; saving on, 193, 194
Postcards, response, 194
Potpourri, 217
Precious Collection, invitations from, 210-11
Preludes, 356
Premarital counseling, 139, 146
PreownedWeddingDresses.com, 44
Pressing, 28, 30-31, 35, 128; free, 37
Pressure, 34, 54-55, 76, 104; avoiding, 57
Prestige Gown Cleaning, 107, 108
Price comparisons, 57 (fig.)
Price gouging, 50-51
Price guarantees, 260, 262-63, 279
Priceless Bridals, review of, 89
Priceline.com, bidding on, 406
Price Scope, 390
Price shopping, 49, 127, 128
Princess Collection, 77
Printed Candle, candles from, 201
Printers, 196; changes by, 202; etiquette and, 202; ink-jet, 316-17; mistakes and, 189
Printing Press, 195
Printing, 192, 197, 200; saving on, 181
Prints, 284; choosing, 310; video, 353
Priority worksheets, 422-23, 424-26; sample, 423 (fig.)
Priscilla, 90, 92
Private clubs, receptions at, 241, 245-47
Private Collection, 77
Private Label by G, 76; rating for, 82-83
Processional, 356
ProDJ, 359, 359 (fig.)
Professional Cleaners, cleaning/preservation and, 109
Professional Photographers of America, The, 286
Programs, 182; designing, 195
Pronomas, 77
Pronovias/St. Patrick, rating for, 82-83
Proof books, 291, 294; reviewing, 296, 315
Proofless studios, 290-93
Proofs, 283-84; buying, 305; delivery of, 295; digital, 284; magazine, 284; ordering, 294
Proposals: surrogate bad cops and, 418; writing, 279
ProShots, 291
Punch, cost of, 276
Purvey roses, 173

Quality: Chinese, 93; issues with, 62, 420; savings and, 7
QuickSnap Wedding pack, 302

Ramona Keveza, rating for, 82-83
Ranunculus roses, 173
Ravissant, 77
Raw footage, 334, 341, 347
Raylia, rating for, 82-83, 130-31
Reaves Engraving, invitations from, 194, 210-11
Receipts, organizing, 11
Reception cards, 181, 192, 193, 212; designing, 195
Receptions, 306, 425; affordable, 224, 249; budgeting for, 423; buffet, 253, 254, 256, 261, 262, 266, 272; cake and punch, 191, 253, 425; cocktail, 261, 262, 274; coordination of, 256-57;

cost of, 224, 272, 273; creativity with, 252; dessert, 264; ethnic, 263-64; expensive, 247, 254; holiday, 425; hors d'oeuvre, 253, 254, 266; invitations and, 189; low-cost, 251; mid-afternoon, 263; off-peak times for, 231; photographers and, 303, 314; priority for, 426; style of, 262; tea, 425; videographers and, 349
Reception sites, 396, 410; acoustics at, 367; availability of, 227; bakers and, 322; candles at, 162; capacity of, 228; caterers and, 231, 258; communication with, 228, 240; confirming, 258-59; cookie cutter, 239; decorations at, 165; deposits at, 223, 228; entertainers and, 358; fees for, 275; finding, 141, 224-26, 226-27; fireworks at, 174; florists and, 154, 155, 156; flowers at, 158, 165, 423; hints for, 240-41; insurance and, 230, 390; invitations and, 188, 190; liability issues for, 255; minimums at, 229; multiple bookings at, 229; negotiating at, 240-41; non-traditional, 235, 241, 252; off-peak times at, 265; online, 142, 225, 226; overtime charges at, 228-29; photographers and, 286; pitfalls with, 223, 237-40; planning for, 227; problems with, 238-40; questions for, 228-30; rentals at, 256; renting, 11, 223; saving on, 230-31, 233-34; shopping for, 223, 227-28; tax deductions at, 236; trade-offs with, 224; types of, 241; union rules at, 229; unwritten promises at, 237; videographers and, 341, 342
Recessional, 356
Recommended services, 243, 371; commissions on, 262; scam with, 238
Reem Acra, rating for, 82-83
Refunds, 72, 74; asking for, 420; credit cards and, 33, 34; florists and, 154; partial, 71; policies for, 30, 31, 154; postponements and, 78; promises about, 76
Regency, 183, 193, 208; review of, 207-8; samples from, 215
Registration cards, 53, 393
Registries. *See* Gift registries
Rehearsal dinners, 8, 427
Rehearsals: coordinating, 394; officiants and, 146; photographers at, 297; videographers at, 342, 349
REI, 399
Religious ceremonies: civil ceremonies versus, 140; local customs and, 148; number of, 140; sites for, 139
Remer, Heather, 216
Renaissance Library Bound album, 304
Renaissance Removable album, 304
Rentals, 260, 263, 279, 320; equipment, 249; home weddings and, 251; reception site, 256
Reprints, 300, 307; revenue from, 288
Response cards, 181, 190-91, 192, 193, 194, 203, 213, 424; designing, 195
Response rates, estimating, 190
Retail, mail order and, 84
Retailers, 74; bankruptcy for, 66; pros and cons with, 91; service at, 61; wedding gowns from, 18, 63-64, 65
Retirement parties, ruse with, 233, 234, 274
Returns, policies on, 39, 403
Revenue Canada, 413
Rexcraft, 183, 198; invitations from, 210-11
Ribbons, 152; accenting with, 213, 322; saving on, 174, 219

RibbonTrade, ribbon from, 174
Riccio, 77
Richard Glasgow, 77; rating for, 82-83
Ring pillows, 178
Rings, 374, 375, 424; 10-karat, 383; 14-karat, 383; 24-karat, 383; appraisal of, 384; buying, 381, 385; cast band, 385; designer, 382; finish of, 383; gold purity of, 382; hints with, 384-85; mail-order, 383; metals in, 382; online, 381, 383, 385-87; platinum, 381, 382, 383; quality of, 384; reading on, 387-90; return policies on, 384; saving on, 383-84; shopping for, 383; spending on, 9; steel, 382; style of, 382; titanium, 382, 385; tungsten, 382; width of, 382-83
Rivini, rating for, 82-83
RK Bridal, 96; review of, 89
Romantic Flowers, 152, 174
Romantic Headlines, 47, 57
Room rates, discounted, 242, 243
Roses, 157; bridal, 149; buying, 171; California, 172; color options with, 172-73; Extra Fancy, 172; Fancy, 172; problems with, 420; Select, 172; types of, 171-73; Vega, 172; Visa, 172; white, 172
Rosewood Candle and Craft, candles from, 201
Ross Simons, discounts by, 402
Royal Masterpiece, 183
Royal Prestige, story about, 389-90
Rubrum lilies, 180
Running of the Brides, The, 39, 42-43
Rush charges, 20, 32, 75
Rush cuts, 70, 117
Rush services, 114
Russian Brilliants, synthetic diamonds from, 384

St. Patrick, 77
St. Pucchi, 76; rating for, 82-83
Saison Blanche, 77
Sample gown shell game, 71, 72
Sam's Club: alcohol from, 266, 269; deals at, 268; single-use cameras at, 302
Sandal's/Beaches, 407
Sand Scripts, 187
San Martin, 90
SantanaApparel.com, accessories from, 134
Save-on-Crafts: craft supplies from, 175; silk flowers from, 157
Scaasi, 107
Scaasi Bride, 76
Scaasi/Forsyth, rating for, 82-83
Scams, 5, 18, 50, 79, 388-89; avoiding, 1, 48, 71; in Canada, 412; knock-off, 128
Schwartz, Garry: on service, 104
Seamstresses, 31, 38, 43, 95; alterations by, 30, 73; bridesmaids dresses and, 121; copying by, 61; expert, 72; free-lance, 73, 106; replications by, 37; restorations by, 41; skilled, 61, 85; unskilled, 32, 73
Secrets From a Caterer's Kitchen (Aloni), 271
Segal, Arlene, 214
Select roses, 172
Selesky, Gina: invitations by, 213
Sempliner's, tuxedos from, 137
Sense and Sensibility Patterns, 41
sensibility.com, 41
Service, 63, 104, 300; catering, 256, 259, 268; customer, 84, 93, 101; improvements in, 246; mandatory charges for, 278; paying for, 256; problems with, 60-61, 104
Servitorus, 407
Set-ups, 143, 279; checking, 227; fees for, 278; florists and, 154, 155-56; visiting, 260
Shea Stadium, wedding reception at, 236

Shipping: from China, 92; dates, confirming, 30; fees for, 32, 53, 56; special order, 67; web sites and, 84, 85
Shoebuy.com, 101
Shoes: dyeable, 118, 120 (fig.); online, 101, 117-18, 120 (fig.); problems with, 101, 118; renting, 133, 136; shopping for, 57 (fig.)
Shop Recommends Size, 69
ShopShop.com, bridesmaids dresses from, 113-14, 127
Shot lists, 295, 296, 299, 303, 311
Shutterfly, 287
Silk Reflections, 117
Sincerity, rating for, 82-83
Siri, rating for, 130-31
Sit-down dinners, 189, 234, 253, 254, 267, 368, 423; buffets and, 271-72; cake and, 325, 327; cost of, 245; taste tests for, 260
Size charts, 29, 70, 105; alterations and, 122; checking out, 69; manufacturers and, 69, 70; problems with, 122, 123, 125; wedding gown, 43, 68
Sketchbook Search, 21 (fig.)
Slachman, Marcy, 214
Slachman, Mitch, 386
Slips, shopping for, 57 (fig.)
SL Signature, 77
Small's, tuxedos from, 137
Social Security Administration, name changes and, 391
Sommer Flowers, flowers from, 177-78
Sonia roses, 173
"Song for My Son, A" (Viereck), 373
Southwest Airlines, honeymoons and, 404
Southworth, invitation paper from, 216
Special orders, 20, 24, 25, 29, 31, 53, 75, 105; deposits on, 65; discounts with, 58; fees for, 32; involuntary lay-away on, 78; problems with, 33; shipping, 67
Spiegel, bridesmaids dresses from, 117, 118-19
Sposabella, 77
Spur-of-the-Moment Cruises, honeymoons and, 408
Stampco.com, embossers from, 193
Statice, 164
Stationers: advice from, 191; discounts from, 192; finding, 185, 189; mistakes and, 188, 189, 191; online, 185-86; out of home, 183-84; questions for, 190-91; sample books from, 190
Stationery shops: invitations from, 182, 183, 184; paper from, 209
Stationery, 192; mail-order, 198; ordering, 193; pitfalls with, 199-203; quality, 209; sales on, 192. *See also* Invitations
Steadi-cam, 353
Steaming, 30-31, 35; arranging for, 85; free, 32
Stephanotis, 169, 180
Stephen Yearick, rating for, 82-83
Sterling Silver roses, 173
Store credits, 78
Stringers, problems with, 311-12
Stump's Prom, review of, 90
Stylart, 183
Sugarcraft.com, supplies from, 323
Sun Trips, honeymoons and, 405, 406
Surrogate bad cops: authority for, 418; crises and, 417-18, 420; identifying, 419; photographers and, 295-96
Susan G. Komen Breast Cancer Foundation, 218
Sweetheart: rating for, 82-83; sizing by, 69
Sweets tables, 325, 327
Symphony organizations, entertainers and, 358

Tags, 52; removing, 49-50, 51, 52, 96
Talbot's: bridesmaids dresses from, 112, 117, 120, 123; rating for, 130-31
Tango, 77
Target, 214, 315, 400; accessories from, 162; in-store credit with, 403
Taste tests, 228, 260, 324, 325, 329
Tatex, 183
Tax deductions, 147, 162, 236
Taxes, problems with, 277-78
Taylor Corporation, 183, 208
Taylor's Celebrations, 46
Television stations, videographers and, 336
Tender Seed Company, 217
Tents, 231, 232
Textile Fiber Products Identification Act (1963), 50
TheFlowerExchange.com, flowers from, 178
Thermography, 189, 198; engraving and, 192, 197
theWeddingTracker.com, 410
1385 Broadway, 94-95
Tiaras, 46-47, 95
Tiffany, 77
Tipping, tips on, 270
Titanium, 382; caveats with, 385
TNT Vacations, hurricane insurance from, 407
To the Moon and Back, favors from, 218
Toll, Bernard: on Alfred Angelo dresses, 129
Tomasina, rating for, 82-83
Toppers. *See* Cake toppers
Toppers with Glitz, cake toppers by, 321
Toronto Star, on cakes, 415
Tour companies, honeymoons and, 406-7
Tourism bureaus, reception sites and, 225-26
Touye, Lisa: wedding reception by, 236
Trade Shop, rings from, 387
Transportation: alternative, 379-80; non-traditional forms of, 376; online, 376-77; shopping for, 377. *See also* Limousines
Transshipping, problems with, 59
Travel agents, honeymoons and, 404
Travelocity, 408
Trip Advisor, 237, 409
Trolleys, renting, 379
Trousseau.com, 57
Trunk shows, 54-55, 56
Tulips, 157
Tuxedo shirts, 137, 138
Tuxedo shops, invitations from, 201
Tuxedos: alternatives to, 136; buying, 133; cost of, 423; coupons for, 137; etiquette for, 132-34; Euro-style, 135; hints with, 137-38; measuring for, 137; online, 134; renting, 132-33; saving on, 136; shopping for, 134-35
Tuxedos.com, 134
Tux-Xpress, 133
2G Roses, 159, 175-76

Ultimate Online Wedding mall, 302
Unions, 358, 359, 373
Unitarian churches, ceremony sites and, 141-42
United Vacations, hurricane insurance from, 407
Universities, receptions at, 248
Uprint.com, 214
UPS: risks with, 53, 109; shipping with, 35, 92, 116
Urbans, 299
USA City Link, ceremony sites and, 141
US Post Office, 197-98, 203; invitations and, 188

Vacation Direct, honeymoons and, 408
Vega roses, 172
Veils: cost of, 19; finding, 95-96; making, 49, 95; mark-ups for, 58; overpriced, 95; professional, 49; saving on, 46-47; spoilage of, 95
Veils A La Mode, 47
VeilShop.com, 47
Vellum, 216
Vendor referral fees, 395-96, 398
Vendors: confirmations with, 419; phone numbers for, 418, 419; problems with, 419; tipping, 270
Venus, 76, 77; rating for, 82-83
Vera Wang, 41, 96, 98; rating for, 82-83, 130-31; sales by, 39
Veterans of Foreign Wars (VFW) Posts, 246
VHS, 333, 338, 339, 343
Victoria's, 77; rating for, 82-83
Videographers: ceremony-only, 345; deposits for, 335; equipment for, 338, 343, 345; feeding, 309, 368; hiring, 333, 335-36, 337, 340-41; meeting with, 341, 347, 350; multi-camera shoots by, 333, 335, 346; overtime by, 349, 351-52; packages by, 333, 334, 342, 346, 349, 352; part-time, 346-47; personality of, 310, 341; philosophy of, 343; photographers and, 293, 310-11, 336-37, 342, 344-45, 347, 354; pitfalls with, 349-52; problem solving by, 343; professional association of, 335, 336; professionalism of, 341, 347; questions for, 342; saving on, 345-47; shooting schedules of, 342; sound and, 337-38; style of, 341; understanding, 337-40
Videography: budgeting for, 424; myths about, 348; trends in, 352-54
Videomasters, 336
Videos: big screen TVs and, 350-51; cost of, 8, 334-35, 346; delivery of, 343; demo, 341, 351; edited, 341, 351; friends/family and, 345, 348; future-proofing, 339; good/bad/ugly, 340, 348; HD, 339, 344, 347, 352; hints with, 349; missed events and, 350; post-wedding, 335; production of, 343; quality of, 349, 351; SD, 339, 344, 347; stills, 353; technology for, 339
Viereck, Mikki, 373
Vintage clothing shops, checking out, 41
Visa roses, 172
Visions, 77
Visitors bureaus, reception sites and, 141, 225-26, 241
Vow & Vogue, 90
Vows, writing, 146
Vows Bridal Outlet, 98
Vows: The Bridal Business Journal: on accessories, 100; on alterations, 106

Wait staff, 262; dress of, 261; half-full glasses and, 277
Wall Street Journal, 267
Wal-Mart: accessories from, 162; cake from, 327-28
Warehouse clubs/stores, 75; invitations from, 197; rings from, 384; wedding gowns from, 27, 29
Washingtonian magazine, on catering charges, 254
Watson, Gail, 321
Watters & Watters: bridesmaids dresses from, 113; rating for, 82- 83, 130-31
Wax Wizard, 166; candles from, 201
Web sites, 20; bridal, 22-24; checking out, 13; discounts with, 84-85; price matches

index

with, 85; problems with, 84; sampling of, 88
(fig.); wedding, 410; wedding gowns on, 84-85
Wedding and Event Videographers Association International (WEVA), 335, 336
Wedding and Portrait Photographers, 286-87
Wedding Bells, 414-15
Weddingcakeonline.com, 329
WeddingCanada.com, 415
Wedding Channel, 90; gift registry at, 399-400, 399 (fig.); Sketchbook Search of, 21 (fig.); wedding web sites at, 410
WeddingChannel.com, 21, 23; ceremony sites and, 141; reception sites and, 226; tuxedos from, 134; using, 20
Wedding Channel's Gown Search, The, 21-22
Wedding clock, 11 (fig.)
Wedding companies, all-in-one, 396
Wedding consultants, 375, 393-98; advantages of, 397; budget for, 395; caterers and, 257; communication with, 395; cost of, 394; counterfeit, 396; disadvantages of, 397-98; experienced, 395, 397; fees for, 394, 395, 396; kickbacks for, 395-96; long-distance weddings and, 397; pitfalls with, 395-97; professional associations for, 394, 397; questions for, 394-95; regulation and, 396-97; vendor referral fees for, 395-96
Wedding coordinators, 225, 229; contact with, 145; destination wedding, 148; entertainers and, 357-58; florists and, 151; meeting with, 228; photographers and, 286; questions for, 139; reception sites and, 224; scams and, 238; videographers and, 337; wedding gown restrictions and, 26
Wedding Expressions, review of, 89
Wedding factories, 224, 246
"Wedding Gown Labels: Unveiling the Requirements" (FTC), 50
Wedding gowns: borrowing, 41; buying, 18, 41; in Canada, 411-12; from China, 36, 62, 91-94, 93 (fig.); cleaning, 74, 107-9, 129; consignment, 44, 67, 108; counterfeit, 29, 74; descriptions of, 29-30; designer, 17, 18, 25, 28, 36, 37-38, 61-62, 107; destination wedding, 35; discount, 23, 59; domestic/imported, 62; donating, 108; finding, 17-18, 48; hand-sewing, 62; hidden costs of, 19, 19 (fig.); hints with, 63-64; imported, 413; inspecting, 30; knock-off, 23, 45; mail-order, 30; measuring for, 29, 30; mystery, 48-49; myths about, 61-63; negotiating on, 413; no-name, 58; off-the-rack, 37, 72, 102, 103; off season purchases of, 45; online, 36, 84-85, 412; ordering, 24, 25, 30, 72; planning for, 425; portraits and, 25; preserving, 108-9; priority for, 426; quality with, 27; restrictions with, 26; sample, 40, 68, 73-74; saving on, 36, 84-85, 412-13; second-hand, 44; sewing own, 40; shopping for, 24, 26-31, 63; silk, 31; special-order, 20, 31, 103; spending on, 9, 20, 28; styles of, 28; transporting, 35; transshipping, 29; trying on, 27-28; unadvertised, 66; washing, 107
Wedding industry, 421; secrets of, 107-9; thoughts on, 4-5, 391-93
Wedding Invitation Kit, 213-14
Wedding Invitations, 187, 196-197

Wedding Maps, maps from, 196
"Wedding March," 360, 372
Wedding months, most/least popular, 143, 144-45 (fig.)
Wedding Pack (Kodak), warning about, 303
Wedding Ring Hotline, 385-86, 386 (fig.)
Weddings: cost of, 5-9, 6 (fig.), 7 (fig.), 411-12, 425; customizing/personalizing, 9; daylight, 9; paying for, 8-9, 8 (fig.); size of, 3; truths about, 2-5, 420
Wedding Tips, 359
Wedding Traditions, invitations from, 210-11
Wedding-veil.com, 47
Wedsafe.com, 390
"Weekend Journal" (*Wall Street Journal*), 267
Weinstock, Sylvia, 321
WEVA. *See* Wedding and Event Videographers Association International
WhiteAndBlack.com, 35
White House, Black Market, checking out, 35
Wholesale clubs, alcohol from, 266, 268
William Arthur, 212; review of, 208
Williams-Sonoma, in-store credit with, 403
Willow Tree Lane, invitations from, 210-11
Wilton, supplies from, 323
Winnie Couture, rating for, 82-83
Wizard Publications, guides by, 237
Worry-Free Vacations, hurricane insurance from, 407
Wranglers, hiring, 311
Wyndham hotels, receptions at, 234

"You get the film" packages, 305, 315-16
Young Sophisticates, 77
You're the Bride, 187, 215
"You've Got Pictures" (AOL), 287

Zippers, invisible, 124-25
Zoos, receptions at, 235

index

The Bridal Bargains Planner

By Denise & Alan Fields

The Dollars & Sense Guide to Planning Your Wedding!

Spiral Bound! Pockets!

Finally a wedding planner that tackles the biggest question facing brides and grooms: how are we going to pay for all this? A companion to the best-selling Bridal Bargains book, the Bridal Bargains Wedding Planner is your guide to planning an affordable wedding. Inside, you'll find:

- ♥ *Detailed worksheets to compare vendors side by side so you get the best deal.*
- ♥ *In depth budget advice—including secrets on how to stretch your bridal dollars.*
- ♥ *Count-down checklists and to do lists for everything from the gown to the cake.*
- ♥ *Savvy questions to ask to all your wedding vendors.*
- ♥ *Tricks of the trade on saving on flowers, catering, videos and more.*

Order online at BridalBargainsBook.com

Just $14.95

Shipping to any U.S. address is $3
Order both Bridal Bargains AND the Bridal Bargains Wedding Planner in a special gift set box—see the next page for details!

Available in bookstores nationwide or call 800.888.0385

THE PERFECT ENGAGEMENT GIFT

The Bridal Bargains Gift Set

Get BOTH of our best-selling wedding books in a beautiful gift box!

Give your engaged friends the ultimate gift: a box set of both Bridal Bargains AND the new, spiral-bound Bridal Bargains Wedding Planner!

Order online at BridalBargainsBook.com

Just $29.90

Shipping to any U.S. address is $4

Available in bookstores nationwide or call 800.888.0385

How to Reach us

We want to hear from you! Tell us what you think about this book . . . or give us a suggestion for the next edition.

- ♥ *Email: authors@BridalBargainsBook.com*
- ♥ *Phone: 303.442.8792*
- ♥ *Fax: 303.442.3744*
- ♥ *Address: Bridal Bargains, 436 Pine St, Boulder, CO 80302*

Give Bridal Bargains as a gift for all your engaged friends—go on our web page (www.BridalBargainsBook.com) and click on Order Online. There you'll find all our books, including special pricing when you order both our wedding books.

Did you get this book from a library? Are you reading the latest version? Go to our web page at www.BridalBargainsBook.com and click on "Which version?" You'll find out the latest version of the book, so you can make sure you are up to date!

Our Web Page

If you like the book, you'll love the web site . . .

www.BridalBargainsBook.com

- ♥ *Message boards—chat with other readers about great local sources!*
- ♥ *Free e-newsletter with updates, advice and new bargains!*
- ♥ *Corrections/updates to the book!*
- ♥ *Check out our new wedding planner, the Bridal Passport. See page 462 of this book for more details.*
- ♥ *And more! Read about our other books, order copies of our books as gifts and more!*

www.BridalBargainsBook.com

Our Other Books

By Denise & Alan Fields

Baby Bargains

Secrets to saving 20% to 50% on baby furniture, equipment, clothes, toys, maternity wear and much, much, more!
$17.95 (7th Edition)

- ♥ *Reviews & ratings for baby gear, from cribs to car seats, strollers to high chairs.*
- ♥ *Detailed charts compare brand names and features.*
- ♥ *Dozens of safety tips to affordably baby proof your home.*
- ♥ *The best discount web sites for deals and freebies.*

As seen on Oprah and NBC's Today Show!

Toddler Bargains

Secrets to saving 20% to 50% on toddler furniture, clothing, shoes, travel gear toys and more!
$14.95 (2nd Edition)

- ♥ *The scoop on booster car seats, double strollers and more!*
- ♥ *The complete scoop on gear for toddlers age 2 to 5.*

Order online or call toll free!

800.888.0385 or www.windsorpeak.com

Additional information on all our books is available on our home page **www.WindsorPeak.com**

Shipping to any U.S. address is $3

Our Other Books

By Denise Fields & Ari Brown, M.D.

Baby 411

Clear Answers & Smart Advice for Baby's First Year.
$12.95 (2nd Edition)

- ♥ *The ultimate FAQ for new parents!*
- ♥ *How to pick a pediatrician with detailed questions to ask.*
- ♥ *The truth about "old wives tales" and 'net rumors—how to separate medical fact from fiction!*
- ♥ *Sleep. The best way to get your baby to sleep through the night!*

As seen on CNN, NBC's Today Show and TLC's Surviving Motherhood

Toddler 411

Surviving Picky Eaters, Temper Tantrums, Toilet Training and More!
$12.95 (1st Edition)

- ♥ *The truth about the Terrible Twos!*
- ♥ *Toilet train your child in one day!*
- ♥ *What's normal—and what's not.*

Order online or call toll free!
800.888.0385 or www.windsorpeak.com
Additional information on all our books is available on our home page **www.WindsorPeak.com**
Shipping to any U.S. address is $3

Money BACK GUARANTEE

If this book doesn't save you at least

$500

off your wedding expenses, we'll give you a complete refund on the cost of this book!
No questions asked!

Just send the book and your mailing address to

Windsor Peak Press
436-R Pine Street
Boulder, CO, 80302.

If you have any questions, please call

(800) 888-0385.

Look at all those other wedding books in the bookstore—no other author or publisher is willing to put their money where their mouth is! We are so confident that ***Bridal Bargains*** will save you money on your wedding that we guarantee it in writing!

Remove this card for **QUESTIONS TO ASK** to help plan your wedding and reception.

Is this card missing? Is this book on loan from a friend?

Well, you need your very own copy!

Bridal Bargains is available in bookstores nationwide!

Windsor Peak Press

Questions or comments?

Call (800) 888-0385

QUESTIONS TO ASK

Reprinted from
The *Bridal Bargains* book • Fields

APPAREL FOR THE BRIDE AND BRIDAL PARTY

- ❑ Who is the manufacturer of this dress?
- ❑ How long will it take to get the dress in?
- ❑ What are your payment policies?
- ❑ Can I have a written estimate for alterations?
- ❑ What free services are available?
- ❑ Are there any extra fees for special orders?

CEREMONY SITES

- ❑ Do you have my wedding date available?
- ❑ What are the restrictions, set-up times and clean-up requirements?
- ❑ Who will be my contact at the site?
- ❑ What is the expected honorarium, donation or fee paid to the church/ officiant? When is this normally paid?
- ❑ What kind of equipment must be rented for my wedding?
- ❑ Is any pre-wedding counseling required?
- ❑ For officiants, are there any travel charges, rehearsal fees, or other costs? Do you offer different ceremony options?

WEDDING FLOWERS

- ❑ Is my date available? Is there a deposit needed to hold the date?
- ❑ Do you have actual photographs or samples of your past work?
- ❑ Do you offer any silk or dried flower arrangements?
- ❑ Is there a delivery or set-up fee?
- ❑ How many weddings do you do in a day?
- ❑ Are you familiar with my site location?
- ❑ What rental items do you have? How are they priced?
- ❑ Can I attend one of your weddings during set-up for a look at your designs?
- ❑ What time will you be at my ceremony/ reception sites to set up my wedding?
- ❑ Will you merely drop off my flowers or stay through the ceremony?
- ❑ What happens if flowers I pick aren't available?

INVITATIONS

- ❑ How many different lines do you carry?
- ❑ Given my wedding and reception, what is your opinion of having response cards?
- ❑ Can I see some invitation samples?
- ❑ Who is responsible for any errors that occur?
- ❑ Can I see a proof of the invitation?

Reception Sites

- ❑ How many guests can the space accommodate?
- ❑ How many hours does the rental fee cover?
- ❑ Is there an in-house caterer or a list of approved caterers? Or can you bring in any caterer?
- ❑ Are there any cooking restrictions?
- ❑ Is there a piano available? What about other items like dance floors?
- ❑ What else is happening at the site the day of my wedding?
- ❑ Are there any union rules we must follow?
- ❑ How late can we play music?
- ❑ Are there any insurance requirements?
- ❑ Are there any "surcharges" on outside caterers?
- ❑ Is this your best price? Can you do better?

Catering

- ❑ May I speak with the manager/owner?
- ❑ Can we have a taste test of the foods on our menu?
- ❑ Can we see one of your weddings during set-up?
- ❑ Do you provide a written estimate and contract?
- ❑ Are you licensed?
- ❑ Tell me about a wedding you did where something went wrong—how did you handle it?
- ❑ Do you specialize in certain cuisines or types of menus?
- ❑ Where is the food prepared?
- ❑ When is the menu "set in stone?"
- ❑ How is your wait staff dressed?
- ❑ For cocktail or buffet receptions, how often will the food be replenished?
- ❑ Given the style of my reception, how many waiters do we need?
- ❑ How is the charge for labor figured? Is the clean-up extra?
- ❑ How much does a dessert table cost? Is the wedding cake price included in the package?
- ❑ What are your cancellation/postponement policies?
- ❑ Do you have a liquor license?
- ❑ Are you familiar with my reception site?
- ❑ Do you receive any commissions from services you recommend?
- ❑ Will you guarantee these price estimates?

Remove this card for **Questions to Ask** to help plan your wedding and reception.

Is this card missing? Is this book on loan from a friend?

Well, you need your very own copy!

Bridal Bargains is available in bookstores nationwide!

Windsor Peak Press

Questions or comments?

Call (800) 888-0385